STUDIES OF THE AMERICAS

edited by

James Dunkerley

Institute for the Study of the Americas
University of London
School of Advanced Study

Titles in this series are multi-disciplinary studies of aspects of the societies of the hemisphere, particularly in the areas of politics, economics, history, anthropology, sociology, and the environment. The series covers a comparative perspective across the Americas, including Canada and the Caribbean as well as the USA and Latin America.

Titles in this series published by Palgrave Macmillan:

Cuba's Military 1990-2005: Revolutionary Soldiers during Counter-Revolutionary Times
By Hal Klepak

The Judicialization of Politics in Latin America
Edited by Rachel Sieder, Line Schjolden, and Alan Angell

Latin America: A New Interpretation
By Laurence Whitehead

Appropriation as Practice: Art and Identity in Argentina
By Arnd Schneider

America and Enlightenment Constitutionalism
Edited by Gary L. McDowell and Johnathan O'Neill

Vargas and Brazil: New Perspectives
Edited by Jens R. Hentschke

When Was Latin America Modern?
Edited by Nicola Miller and Stephen Hart

Debating Cuban Exceptionalism
Edited by Bert Hoffmann and Laurence Whitehead

Caribbean Land and Development Revisited
Edited by Jean Besson and Janet Momsen

Cultures of the Lusophone Black Atlantic
Edited by Nancy Naro, Roger Sansi-Roca, and David H. Treece

Democratization, Development, and Legality: Chile, 1831-1973
By Julio Faundez

The Hispanic World and American Intellectual Life, 1820-1880
By Iván Jaksić

The Role of Mexico's Plural *in Latin American Literary and Political Culture: From Tlatelolco to the "Philanthropic Ogre"*
By John King

Faith and Impiety in Revolutionary Mexico
Edited by Matthew Butler

Faith and Impiety in Revolutionary Mexico

Edited by

Matthew Butler

palgrave
macmillan

First published in 2007 by
PALGRAVE MACMILLAN™
175 Fifth Avenue, New York, N.Y. 10010 and
Houndmills, Basingstoke, Hampshire, England RG21 6XS
Companies and representatives throughout the world.

PALGRAVE MACMILLAN is the global academic imprint of the Palgrave Macmillan division of St. Martin's Press, LLC and of Palgrave Macmillan Ltd. Macmillan® is a registered trademark in the United States, United Kingdom and other countries. Palgrave is a registered trademark in the European Union and other countries.

ISBN-13: 978–1–4039–8381–7
ISBN-10: 1–4039–8381–X

Library of Congress Cataloging-in-Publication Data

Faith and impiety in revolutionary Mexico / edited by Matthew Butler.
    p. cm.—(Studies of the Americas series)
Includes bibliographical references and index.
ISBN 1–4039–8381–X
    1. Mexico—Religion—20th century. 2. Mexico—History—Revolution, 1910–1920—Religious aspects. 3. Christianity and politics—Mexico—History—20th century. 4. Christianity and politics—Catholic Church—History—20th century. 5. Mexico—History—Revolution, 1910–1920—Religious aspects—Catholic Church. 6. Catholic Church—Mexico—History—20th century. 7. Mexico—Church history—20th century. I. Butler, Matthew.

BL2530.M4F35 2007
200.973′09041—dc22   2007009481

A catalogue record for this book is available from the British Library.

Design by Newgen Imaging Systems (P) Ltd., Chennai, India.

First edition: December 2007

10 9 8 7 6 5 4 3 2 1

Printed in the United States of America.

Contents

Acknowledgments

Thanks are due to various people and institutions for their help in seeing this book through to completion: first and foremost, I would like to thank both Ella Pearce and Joanna Mericle at Palgrave Macmillan in New York—as editor and editorial assistant, respectively—for all their help, professionalism, and encouragement. In his capacity as series editor, I would also like to express my thanks to Professor James Dunkerley of the Institute for the Study of the Americas in London. In addition, I thank the anonymous referees who reported on the proposal and manuscript for their constructive comments. Finally, I owe a debt of thanks to all the contributors to this volume whose collective endeavors made this project so enjoyable. This book originated in an idea for a conference—"God's Revolution: Faith and Impiety in Revolutionary Mexico, 1910–1940"—which was held at Queen's University Belfast in October 2005. This is a good place, then, to thank all those who took part in this event; I am also indebted to those whose support and logistical help made the symposium possible, the British Academy and Society for Latin American Studies (SLAS), which generously provided conference grants—and both the School of Languages (SLLA) and Department of Spanish at Queen's University Belfast. My individual thanks to people within, or connected to, those institutions go to: Professors David Brading, Tony Kapcia, and, Peter Wade; Isabel Torres, Peter Crowley, Diana Vázquez Maqueda, Professor David Johnston (as Head of SLLA), and Paul Rankin (who first translated the chapter by Jean-Pierre Bastian). The directors and archivists of the excellent Archivo Histórico del Arzobispado de México in Mexico City—Father Gustavo Watson, Marco Antonio Pérez Iturbe, and Berenise Bravo Rubio—also supported the project from the outset and kindly granted permission to use the jacket image (source: Fondo Pascual Díaz Barreto).

My final thanks go to Desmond and Jenny Butler, the Torres Meza family in Mexico City, and, of course, my wife Patricia.

Introduction

A Revolution in Spirit?
Mexico, 1910–40

Matthew Butler

In Mexico, as in France, religion and revolution have long been considered antithetical. "When the Revolution of 1910 broke out," John Mecham wrote in 1934, "the clergy in all the pulpits of the land combated it," while revolutionaries steeled themselves for "the inevitable clerical reaction."[1] This view of the Revolution's sacred history as an institutional clash lives long in the literature. Likewise, the idea that Catholicism was incompatible with the Revolution's secular, patriotic ethos: Eyler Simpson praised the road that reached Ocotlán in 1934, transforming the Otomí into "Ford-conscious" citizens and ending centuries of parochial piety in a dazzling epiphany.[2] "Roads and schools, Fords and books," Simpson praised, invoking Jericho, "these are the trumpet blasts which fell the walls of ignorance and isolation."[3] Here, then, was an enduring cultural characterization: the Revolution as the triumph of "modern" over "traditional," religious values.

Others saw a variety of ontological struggles. For Ernest Gruening, the religious conflict was a "psychological fourth dimension," a contest for Mexico's soul that transcended mere politics;[4] President Calles, Mexico's arch clerophobe, reportedly approached the religious question in a "mystical, apocalyptic spirit," as a Manichean struggle between "light and the shadows."[5] Revolutionaries were thus actors in a grand drama in which Reason and equality would crush privilege and fanaticism: peasants needed radios, not Ripalda, *ejidos* not exegesis, and revolutionaries would see that they got them. As the scattered theological motifs suggest, however, enlightened unbelief could itself be worn into battle with paradoxical fervor.

Revolutionaries were not alone in adopting ahistorical or metaphysical perspectives: for the Catholic historian, Francis Kelley, 1910 was a case of "old political explosives in new shells," as true religion and godlessness did battle once more.[6] For Trinidad Sánchez Santos, editor of *El País*, even Madero—who welcomed the National Catholic Party in 1911—was taboo: no Catholic could be liberal, Sánchez wrote, for Protestantism begot liberalism, which begot socialism. Popular democracy was thus dismissed as a folly

connecting Luther and Rousseau's heresies to those of Marx.[7] Mexico's episcopate, finally, theologized the Constitutionalist (1913–20) and Sonoran
(1920–34) revolutions as providential scourges, red Terrors to punish an
ungrateful nation for turning from God: in this vision, revolutionary anticlericals were virtual antichrists, demons sent to prod errant Catholics heavenward.

Such rhetorical antagonisms were violently reenacted from 1914–38. As
Adrian Bantjes shows, this period was characterized by multiple conflicts;
moreover, this was a *national* phenomenon, albeit one that occurred in localized patterns of aggression and resistance. From 1914, religious conflict was
one of *the* features of Revolution, such that by 1940 millions of Mexicans had
grown up in a sectarian atmosphere. The main spikes in this trend are well
known. The Church's association with the Huerta regime (1913–14), which
revived a liberal clerophobia; the 1917 Constitution, which institutionalized
conflict by proscribing—amongst other things—the Church's legal character;
and the *Cristiada* of 1926–29, which united thousands of peasants in a pitch-
fork crusade against state anticlericalism. The Catholic guerrilla known as *La
Segunda*, finally, scarred the 1930s—a decade that also saw *sinarquista* legions
welling in the Bajío, the mutilation of "socialist" teachers, and, from 1936, a
retreat from anticlericalism under President Lázaro Cárdenas (1934–40).

Daily life was affected, too, as people learned to look at and practise their
religion in new ways, and to experiment with new religious, indeed political,
identities. Religion was not simply politicized; rather, the spiritual landscape
itself was changed during, and by, Mexico's revolutionary drama. Churches
were burned and religion relocated to primitive rural spaces. Religious mobility also increased: the Michoacán schoolteacher and *agrarista*, Salvador
Sotelo—who turned Catholic, Baptist, mason, socialist, and, finally, atheist[8]—
was a classic revolutionary changeling. The sacred was also experienced in
radically new ways and by new actors: lay Catholics had a taste of sacerdotal
power, improvising "white" masses or performing riverside baptisms; others
died ecstatically for priests or rejected them in favor of folk healers, messiahs,
dissidents, and worldly prophets; many "Catholic" villages were torn apart by
sectarian antagonisms, erupting in parish tumults or anticlerical outrages.

The chapters here seek to capture some of the complexity lurking behind
such deceptively stark confrontations. Studies of religion in the Revolution
are not, of course, new;[9] yet the Revolution is not often viewed as a period of
genuine religious ferment as well as social upheaval. Rather, religion is very
often seen as an *object* of the Revolution, while connections between revolutionary and religious change are ignored.[10] Such a focus has given rise to a
literature in which Revolution and religion are seen as monolithic and irreconcilable. The hermeticism, until recently, of many Church archives has
probably reinforced this trend, the documents themselves suggesting that
there was somehow "less" religion after 1910 than before. And revolution-
ary-period religious history was not likely to prosper under Mexico's PRI,
which until the 1990s airbrushed even the *cristeros* from official school texts.

Traditional accounts also proved selective and simplistic, in that they
focused mainly on the *Cristiada* in 1920s western Mexico, and evidenced

one-dimensional approaches to religion. Many early historians, for example, dismissed religion as a structural fig leaf or imputed immaculate degrees of religiosity.[11] A vulgar materialism—Collinson's "crass Marxism"—was often evident;[12] thus the *Cristiada* was a class struggle between revolutionaries and "landed-clerical" interests who duped Catholic cannon fodder into doing their fighting.[13] Jean Meyer's classic work, by contrast, explained the *Cristiada* as a clash of credos and mentalities—*campesinos'* old-time religion against revolutionary modernizers' secular "religion of incredulity."[14]

Mexican revolutionary studies are now moving beyond such dichotomous characterizations; yet the literature has been slower to integrate religious questions than those, say, of revolutionary France, Russia, or Spain.[15] Consequently, the studies that now enrich the colonial Mexican historiography,[16] find few equivalents for 1910. The most recent bibliographical essay devotes a meager four pages to religion, and some "revolutionary" entries in fact cover Porfirian Mexico.[17] There is also a tendency to view religion in rather *causal* terms—what else can it explain? —and thus to argue it away as intangible or commonplace in comparison to more tangible factors. The religious clashes of the 1930s—which pitted revolutionary church-burners against Catholic lynch mobs—were wars of words, says Reich;[18] Jennie Purnell, in an otherwise admirable study of the *cristeros*, argues that religion tells us little about peasants' political allegiances since most Mexicans were "Catholic."[19]

For all their merits, such accounts fall flat in their insistence that religion had little to do with Mexico's *conflicto religioso*. In short, the meaning and practice of religion vanish, rather than becoming the focus for research in their own right.[20] More rounded analyses that incorporate both the affective and sociopolitical dimensions of religion are now appearing. Eric Van Young places indigenous messianism in a vector of factors driving the 1810 Insurgency;[21] and religion was seemingly a prime concern at Porfirian Tomóchic (indeed, debate now focuses more on the *quality*—millenarian? folk?—than basic import of *tomochiteco* religion).[22] For the Revolution, as Jean-Pierre Bastian argues, Protestant ideas shaped *carrancismo*'s northern recruitment patterns and political objectives; and in Michoacán, variations in local religious practice clearly shaped peasant participation in the *Cristiada*.[23]

Nonetheless, a search for the Revolution's "religious origins" will not, I suspect, take us to the promised land.[24] Was religion's place in the postrevolutionary order therefore somehow "negotiated" between revolutionary and religious actors?[25] This postrevisionist model has, occasionally, been transposed to the religious crisis; Marjorie Becker's *danzantes*, who "educated" Cárdenas by dancing before the altars, are the obvious case.[26] Yet the idea of negotiation seems wrong, given the violence of the crisis years. And, if negotiations occurred, this was usually in opposition to the Revolution: the parameters of *fidencismo*, which peaked during the *Cristiada,* were constructed by the child healer, Fidencio, and his sickly throng on the basis of shared miraculous expectations; and lay and clerical roles were radically redefined in the *Cristiada* as laypeople celebrated emergency sacraments. The

conjunctural moment for such negotiations in Catholicism's internal religious field, however, derived from the Revolution's disarticulation of the
Church.

More plausibly, then, religion and Revolution were linked in a dialectic in
which the radicalization of society was accompanied by innovative, often
improvised, responses in the religious sphere. On the one hand, religious
cultures were central to the Revolution's reception; on the other, religion was
energized and transformed as part of the revolutionary process. This did not
just occur at the level of institutional clienteles, but of practice and ideas. The
spiritual economy opened after decades of Porfirian centralization; and there
was a periodic sense of fervor that was not limited, temporally, to the
Cristiada, nor, geographically, to the west/Bajío. Rather, as the chapters
here show, religious change characterized all three revolutionary decades and
touched not only rural but urban Catholicisms in locales ranging from highland Oaxaca to tropical Tabasco and Mexico City; the Revolution also saw
the growth of religious dissidences in parts of northern, central, and southern Mexico.

In sum, while the Revolution's sacred history is often essentialized as an
institutional power struggle, the chapters reveal a complicated set of interactions between the Revolution and the sacred. The Revolution's origins were
not religious; but religion was not simply passed by, acted *upon*. Nor was it
merely the Revolution's reactionary *alter ego*: on the contrary, Mexican religiosities were creatively remade in conjunction with other elements of the
social world after 1910; interacted with—even assimilated—key revolutionary
innovations; and both shaped, and were shaped by, the Revolution's course.[27]
Above all, the chapters suggest that we should view religious change as an
important, if neglected, part of the story, and see Mexico's 1910–40
Revolution as a period of spiritual, as well as sociopolitical, turbulence.

Revolutionary Religions?

Did the Revolution have a religious dimension? Such a hypothesis might
seem far-fetched. After all, the 1917 Constitution suppressed many aspects
of Catholicism on political, cultural, and even theological, grounds. Like
Reformation Protestants, revolutionaries objected not only to priests but to
sacraments such as confession: *agraristas* in 1920s Jalisco denounced
penance as an "obscene" tribunal in which *curas* traded sexual favors for
absolution;[28] "*si eres tú la fiel esposa/de hombre Revolucionario, nunca dejes tus
secretos/en ningún confesionario* [If you are the faithful wife/Of a man of the
Revolution/Never leave your secrets/With a priest in confession]," warned
an anticlerical song in 1930s Yucatán.[29] Fears of revolutionary cuckoldry
added spice to an ideological dislike of Catholic sacramentalism, prompting
fierce exposés and bizarre autos de fe: in 1914, the confessionals in Querétaro
were publicly burned; in Guadalajara, revolutionaries delighted in publicizing
the clerical sexual peccadilloes, which they found recorded in secret
Cathedral archives.[30]

Prophylactic religion was also suspect on grounds of irrationality, antihygiene, and waste: Tabasco's icons were burned in a theatrical attempt to exorcize enchanted belief; fonts of still water and the kissing of *santos* were banned in Mérida to prevent the spread of infection amongst pilgrims.[31] Revolutionaries thus viewed Catholicism as an intellectual relic and disease. And how could villagers buy tractors if they wasted their money gilding tiny plaster saints? Thus Jalisco's revolutionary puritans banned the Christmas feast in 1914;[32] Corpus Thursdays—those canopied fêtings of priestly magic—were also banned, prompting murderous clashes in Levitical cities such as Hidalgo (Michoacán).[33] Conversely, irreligion was associated with bronze-limbed vigor and economic accumulation: church annexes were turned into ejidal savings banks and basketball courts; in public schools—the example is from 1930s Sonora—children were drilled to cries of "*uno, dos, no hay Dios* [One, two, there is no God]."[34]

Such indoctrination might suggest that the Revolution was atheistic. Yet this was the extreme point of a longer continuum; elsewhere, the Revolution's approach to religion was considerably less emphatic. For one thing, until the 1930s the regime was officially committed only to the idea that the state should regulate churches, not eradicate religion—and even this constitutional requirement was implemented patchily under Presidents Carranza (1917–20) and Obregón (1920–24). Such agnosticism and occasional tolerance allowed religion to reemerge in some unexpected places, like the Ministry of Public Education (SEP). Revolutionary invocations of religion also went beyond the ironic deployment of liturgical forms—the printing of "agrarian catechisms" or anticlerical sermons by bogus ecclesiastics such as "Friar Woodworm."[35] Rather, state interventions in the religious field could evidence a rather sectarian bias that derived, seemingly, from particular *views* of religion, not mere indifference.

Revolutionary state-builders deliberately appropriated religious ideas, for example, as they sought to repair and remodel the ideational worlds of Catholic Mexico. Education, particularly in the 1920s, assumed an explicitly apostolic, quasi-religious, redemptive character: literacy was "Eucharistic bread" and rural teachers lionized as the heirs to sixteenth-century Franciscans such as Motolinia; there were revolutionary rituals, sacraments, and liturgies (hymns, Decalogues, and ceremonies), and sacralizations (the building of civic altars and iconography), all of which were designed to build popular faith in the Revolution and interiorize the "gospels"—work, patriotism, unity, cleanliness—on which national "salvation" depended.

Revolutionary campaigns thus obeyed contradictory motives. If some profaned, others had a Durkheimian goal—to expropriate the Church's sacred capital and reinvest it in the Revolution. As Young argues for the Soviet campaigns against Orthodoxy, however, a reforming vision was also at work.[36] Indeed, different *concepts* of religion implicitly informed much revolutionary anticlericalism. We see this, as noted, in the way that revolutionaries targeted Catholicism's extra-liturgical aspects: its material props and "irrational" practices, the clergy's financial exactions and worldly powers.

Smashing Catholicism's temporal extensions—dubbed the products of "*fanatismo*"—presupposed not merely a materialist view of religion but the making of space for purer forms of religion. The implied object of much anticlericalism was not root and branch disenchantment, but a simple Christianity compatible with the regime's projects and patriotic ethos. The trope of religious pristinization was sometimes spurious or tactical, but not always.[37]

For example, revolutionaries distinguished between "true" and "false" religion, underpinning the distinction with an egalitarian vision of clerical-lay relations. Like nineteenth-century liberals—recall Altamirano's *La Navidad en las Montañas* or Pizarro's *El Monedero*[38]—later anticlericals invoked the Rousseauian model of the "citizen priest," that simple preacher of inner piety and social usefulness; and did so with a frequency that contradicts the notion of a uniformly secularist Revolution. The agrarian Antonio Díaz Soto y Gama dreamed of a "revolutionary piety" in which priests would be moral pastors. The Revolution must fight for all liberties, *including* those of the Mexican Church: here echoing the episcopalist-Jansenist rhetoric of the Catholic Enlightenment, Soto y Gama argued that revolutionaries must liberate Mexico's bishops and clergy from Rome, and the country's soul from dogma.[39] Luis León, Calles's agriculture minister, believed in a "revolutionary Christ," persecuted and penniless: after visiting Rome's catacombs in 1921, León was delighted when a Mexican seminarian in the Latin American College—a bastion of intransigent clericalism—agreed that the Revolution was Gospel made flesh.[40] Vicente Lombardo Toledano, too, argued in a 1923 pamphlet—which cited Ambrose, Aquinus, and Leon XIII—that *agrarismo* was nothing less than the realization of the Gospel.[41]

Thus revolutionaries could abide a "just" God whose cult was privately celebrated: as José Guadalupe Zuno, Jalisco's anticlerical governor (and former *monaguillo* in Guadalajara's San José de Gracia parish) put it—"*a los curas, oírles su misa y dejarlos* [Listen to priests at Mass, then leave well alone]."[42] Conversely, they were intolerant of a God who condemned the Revolution as immoral and milked popular credulity with steep religious taxes. And, as some Russian revolutionaries saw Soviet anticlericalism as a form of ascetic purification—a "Bolshevik Reformation"[43]—some Mexican revolutionaries believed the Revolution was fundamentally Christian, and hoped Christian morals would support an emerging revolutionary identity.[44] Their anger that often this was *not* so, in some measure explains their dogmatic anticlericalism.

Still, some revolutionaries aimed not to obliterate but liberate Mexico's spiritual economy. The Archivo General de la Nación's *cultos religiosos* files give some sense of the quickening, if incipient, religious flux of the Revolution as the religious field was opened and the Catholic clergy incapacitated.[45] As part of this increased religious agency, the Revolution saw the arrival or spread of theosophy, Spiritism, Orthodoxy, Mormonism, "Old" Catholicism, Protestantisms, and other denominations; a growth in *curanderismo*, schism, and apparitionism; and a rise in popular dissidence and anticlericalism. Mexico may not have been revolutionary England—that "nation of prophets," in which Diggers, Ranters, and Quakers all trod different paths to heaven[46]— but it was no flat picture of Catholic orthodoxy.

An early sign of aperture was that dissidents joined the Revolution in significant numbers. Indeed, the profusion of non-Catholics among Mexico's political elite after 1910 was something new. While Reform-era liberals were often crypto-Catholics, revolutionaries, especially Constitutionalists, often professed minoritarian religions. Jean-Pierre Bastian argues that *maderismo* and *carrancismo* were driven by a modernizing political ethos forged, in part, in northern Protestant religion. On the one hand, a Protestant rejection of the Porfiriato's Catholic-corporate sacred canopy drove revolutionary militancy; on the other, Protestant pastors were effective organic intellectuals, deploying repertoires of evangelical techniques to spread new ideas. Finally, Protestant religious networks shaped postrevolutionary institutions, such as the *carrancista* education ministry (1917–20) and various state regimes.

Other revolutionaries were freethinkers or inspired by Spiritualism and freemasonry. Madero famously—and Calles belatedly[47]—consulted the spirits; masons also became a significant force under *callismo* (1924–28), when at least three cabinet members (Montes de Oca, Sáenz—also a Protestant[48]— and Tejeda) came from the lodges. Calles himself was appointed Grade 33 mason by the Mexican Rite in 1927, in recognition of his "eminent services" to the *Patria* in fighting Catholicism.[49] And freemasonry remained a major factor, alongside Marxism, in the anticlericalism of the 1930s, when the SEP attracted networks of political masons as it formerly attracted Protestants.[50]

This admixture of religion/irreligion suggests that revolutionary anti-Catholicism was both heterodox and fundamentally ideological. Anticlericalism could, perhaps, obscure other ideological contradictions, lending the regime a façade of unity. Yet, as Alan Knight shows, revolutionary clerophobes were not strategic rationalists but a "people of the book"—an eclectic tribe of dissidents, secular utopians, scientific materialists, and freemasons, drawn largely from the petty bourgeoisie. Such figures, Knight shows, were believers not opportunists, upholders of doctrines with deep intellectual roots in the *Reforma* and Enlightenment.

In some cases, popular or peasant revolutionaries also practised folk dissidences; as the chapter by Keith and Claire Brewster shows, the *delahuertista* revolt in Hidalgo was led by the peasant spiritist, Marcial Cavazos, a "phantom general" who took his orders from the dead. Here the cross-fertilization between elite and popular religious ideas helped to create an otherworldly military charisma which colored even primary revolutionary mobilization. Cavazos's case points us toward another change to the religious landscape: the growth of the social bases of Mexican anti-Catholicism, and of popular anticlericalism in particular.

This growth occurred, firstly, in a downward sense, as anticlericalism penetrated new social sectors. Even in the *cristero* zone, for instance, there were anticlerical—agrarianized, historically liberal, or Protestantized—*pueblos*, such as Zitácuaro (Michoacán), La Cañada (Jalisco), or Jaral (Guanajuato): in the latter, "almost all the men" were anti-Catholic, one *ultra* raged in 1926.[51] But there is growing evidence that this trend also began to spread outward—beyond, that is, the popularization of "rational" Protestantisms or classic liberal anticlericalism.

Indeed, the Revolution gave birth to a small plethora of cults fusing folk/evangelical devotional styles with nationalistic, revolutionary, or *indigenista* doctrines. The schismatic "Mexican" Church of Joaquín Pérez won thousands of indigenous devotees in México, Puebla, Veracruz, and Chiapas during the *Cristiada*. A Constitutionalist *cura*, Pérez added an anti-Romanist, primitive rhetoric to his support for *agrarismo* and festive Catholicism; his "Mexicanist" *curas* also ministered for free, in Spanish, to Indian villagers in *México profundo*.[52] Eusebio González, a Jaliscan Constitutionalist who moved to Monterrey, had visions in 1926 in which God baptized him "Aaron" and told him to found the Church of the Light of the World in Guadalajara. The first Aaronites—poor rural migrants—blended an "Israelite," chosen-people theology with exalted nationalism and Pentecostal fervor.[53] And an evangelical founded a chapel in 1930s Ixmiquilpan, on Hidalgo's arid Mezquital plain. Working with the army and *indigenistas* who supplied bibles translated into Otomí, this pastor formed indigenous migrants into a novel revolutionary-religious colony.[54]

Such cases reveal that studies of northern and southern religiosities are needed, as Adrian Bantjes argues, if we are to have a fuller understanding of the Revolution's sacred history. Such scattered experiments also show how revolutionary institutions could serve as laboratories of religious radicalism, promoting vernacular liturgies, the abolition of religious taxes, freeform devotionalism, and unfettered exegesis. Clearly, then, efforts *were* made to create proto-revolutionary spiritual identities by enfranchizing the laity, abolishing priestly hierarchy, and sacralizing revolutionary reforms. Finally, we see how autonomous religions developed in response to sociodemographic changes, such as rural out-migration.

This last tendency was only the beginning of a still ongoing, nationwide process—but it is worth noting that it began, in some places, in the 1920s. More commonly, as Alan Knight argues, popular dissidence and anticlericalism in the Revolution were associated with popular—labor and agrarian—mobilization. In 1920s Zitácuaro (Michoacán), for instance, *agraristas* converted to the Presbyterianism that was promoted by revolutionary pastors and schoolteachers. Formal theological differences here served as an identity marker for indigenous peasants who sought entry into the revolutionary political nation as *ejidatarios*, and, on the other hand, a religio-moral escape route from a broadly Catholicized village structure.[55]

Even where the Revolution did not lead to pluralism—the great majority of cases—it threatened Catholicism by giving *agraristas* an anticlerical language of despoilment through which to critique socioreligious arrangements. As *campesinos* also had access to a bureaucracy that could transform their economic lives, religious conflicts were therefore likely to the extent that *curas* meddled in *agrarismo*. The geographical mobility associated with the Revolution was significant, too. Ex-combatants brought home anticlerical doctrines—Salvador Sotelo returned from the United States a Baptist, Primo Tapia a Communist—and disdain for the old ways. They also offered alternatives, compounding the religious evasion and clerical flight caused by the Revolution.

To dismiss this as old-fashioned, ad hoc clerophobia is too simple, because there was something new: the identification of a reactionary, depersonalized second estate (*Don Clero, el fraile*) as the enemy. Villagers thus absorbed and applied revolutionaries' Voltairean dichotomy between *fanatismo* and true piety. This rhetorical weapon was useful, in part, precisely *because* it was premised on an incomplete rupture with Catholicism, and hence facilitated a selective, "weapons of the weak," approach to religion, not outright apostasy.[56] Clergy who charged steep fees and spoke against *agrarismo*, for example, were attacked as parasitical drones whose unchristian selfishness prevented the creation of a worldly paradise.

The Revolution thus generated, or voiced, a welter of anticlerical critiques, suggesting that a willingness to contest the bases of Church authority became more common. Peasants in Texcoco (México), for example, complained bitterly about greedy *curas*: Amanalco suffered "priests who, shielded by religion, wickedly exploit all peasants," including their *cura*, who charged ten pesos for Mass;[57] Ocopulco's *agraristas* welcomed the 1926 suspension of public cult and demanded that their churchless *curas* now toil the fields, "so that they learn how we earn our money." "No longer disposed to continue being exploited," these *agraristas* rejoiced that their alms and emoluments "would not now go to Rome, but all would stay in the *patria*."[58]

We may speculate about the local specifics behind such us-and-them encounters: a desire for an *ejido*? peasant nationalism? schismatic influence? echoes of Pedro de Gante's selfless evangelism? Either way, the real point is that villages began to discuss a wider range of religious questions than before, and to review the clergy's role.[59] Ejidal and school committees were key institutions in fomenting such dialogue and demanding that aspects of religion be curbed. Postrevolutionary *curas* complained that their agrarianized flocks skipped church, refused to doff caps, ridiculed, and even spat on the cloth. In agrarian villages in Michoacán, Catholic priests were burned out of their homes, harassed physically, or fled in fear for their lives.[60]

Hence the Church was subjected to new, even violent, popular scrutiny. Attempts to assign religion a new place in the village order were part of a wider cultural revolution that involved symbolic, territorial, and functional conflicts over village space and property. Some anticlericals also delighted in giving sacrilegious, scatological offense: in Querétaro, revolutionaries raised stolen cassocks and defecated over church altars; in 1920s Jalisco, *agraristas* waltzed around with naked images of Mary or booted *santos'* heads about in soccer matches.[61]

Profanation created political difference; for all that, it often seemed haunted by a Catholic culture that exercised a powerful hold over even its profaners' minds. Carlos Fuentes's wry exchange between the moribund Artemio Cruz and his Father confessor ("*Me cago en Dios . . . Porque crees en él . . .*" [I shit on God . . . Because you believe in Him . . .]) rings true for the *agraristas* who begged for confession, the reneging schismatics, and the soldiers who asked clergy for absolution before shooting them.[62] Even the Revolution's inverted, black rituals—its fake consecrations and orgiastic masses—smacked of inside-out religiosity or fist-shaking at God. Anticlericalism was a revolt that opened a rift wide enough to permit freer revolutionary participation and, occasionally, heterodoxy: but, as Alan Knight observes, doing without God entirely—metaphysically—was something else.

We see this, too, in cases where anticlericalism came a full circle and a priestless cult emerged. In the *Cristiada*, revolutionary women celebrated baptisms in Michoacán; there was also an "agrarian baptism" in Texmelucan (Puebla), when *agraristas* immersed a baby in a river; and a "collective baptism" was performed in a Veracruz river by a crowd of peasants crying "*no se necesitan ya los curas* [priests are no longer required]."[63] Thus revolutionary baptists waded into provincial Jordans, dispensing with fonts, fees, and priestcraft. These primitive christenings differed significantly from later "socialist baptisms," which were self-consciously anti-*Christian:* in the 1930s, Salvador Sotelo anointed infant revolutionaries with red sashes and honey while sermonizing on nature.[64]

The "primitive" character of such rites was partly designed to legitimize innovation via appeals to Christian antiquity; in the context of the *Cristiada*, it was also intended to habituate rural Catholics to a new, unmediated, relationship, both with the sacred and the postrevolutionary state. As with the ritual inventions of some French revolutionaries, this was to be a going back to a new beginning.[65]

Clearly, however, the Mexican Revolution professed multiple anti-Catholicisms, some of which meant enabling ordinary people to fulfill their religious obligations by themselves. As Ben Fallaw shows, for example, some Campeche revolutionaries were inspired by ancient or early colonial Christianity and attempted to combine agrarian socialism with a minimalist, anticlerical religion. Catholic *campechanos*, conversely, infiltrated revolutionary state structures in order to deflect such initiatives. Rather than a simple clash between traditional and modern values, here we see a combination of cultural *mestizaje* and localist subterfuge.

Kristina Boylan gives a further insight into changing religious attitudes by showing how some *capitalinos* demanded autonomy in the religious sphere on the basis of revolutionary entitlements—here, by using the revolutionary divorce code to press for ecclesiastical separations. Some Catholics, women especially, clearly found in revolutionary ideas a means to achieve greater control over their personal and religious lives. For them, the Revolution signified religious liberty—a realignment *within*, but not a complete break with, Mexico's Catholic culture.

Catholicism Revolutionized?

If the Revolution incorporated various religious impulses, multiple elements of Catholicism were radicalized after 1910. Catholics, for example, espoused an orderly agrarian reform that, furthermore, chimed in some respects with the official variant: in 1924, Catholic *campesinos* in Jalisco demanded the sale of fractioned hacienda lands through community chests as a first step toward a dynamic, smallholding economy.[66] This charitable yeomanism—ultimately intended to save souls by preventing class war—was not so different, in practice, to Sonoran *agrarismo*, which exalted small farmers as models of efficiency, patriotism, and virtuous self-interest.

Just as revolutionaries used a quasi-sacred idiom, Catholics appropriated secular political culture and defended sacred "rights" on the basis of constitutional articles enshrining freedom of worship; revolutionary techniques of protest and persuasion—mass demonstrations, national petitions, print/radio propaganda—were also developed. In Jalisco, Anacleto González Flores conceived passive resistance as a mystical blood democracy, or "martyrs' plebiscite."[67] The massified asceticism of 1930s *sinarquismo*, finally, clearly paralleled the regime's new corporatism.

In this context, Fernando Cervantes stresses Catholicism's extraordinary adaptability to modern political culture as seen in the correspondences between ritual practice and autonomist politics from colony to Revolution. Robert Curley charts the development of a radical politics among Guadalajara Catholics in 1918, and shows how revolutionary demands for wider sociopolitical participation fused with spiritual intransigence. Ben Smith, finally, shows how religion in Huajuapam fed into the opposition politics of Oaxacan *panismo* from the 1930s. Clearly, Mexican Catholics were *assimilators* of revolutionary political culture, not just the assimilated.[68]

Jean Meyer finds that boycotts and violence were central Catholic resistance strategies in 1930s Oaxaca. Yet his analysis takes us in a new direction by uncovering ritual, properly religious, resistance modes. These involved a reconfiguration of local Catholicism: the holding of secret masses, tolerated by officials; lay-leadership of religious processions; catechesis by women. Catholicism here developed a kind of immunological resistance to persecution, as the faithful defended their religion by endorsing petitionary campaigns, changing its ritual forms and contexts, and giving new roles to lay actors. Oaxaca's passive resistance to persecution, Meyer shows, proved remarkably effective in sustaining the vitality of the religious life.

This suggests that innovations in Catholic practice and identity were also important parts of postrevolutionary history. In places, for example, the Revolution created states of anxiety that sometimes reached an eschatological pitch: in San José de Gracia (Michoacán) in 1910, people feared that Halley's comet's tail would strike them;[69] biblical rains preceded the *Cristiada* in Zacatecas;[70] and the calamities that hit Querétaro in 1917—droughts, crop failures, famine, typhus, Spanish flu, banditry—caused *the bishop* to prophesy that the world's end was nigh.[71]

Popular theologies of revolution were advanced. *Queretanos* saw Satan limping about on one cow's hoof and a cock's foot, ordering people to murder, rob, and fornicate.[72] During the *Cristiada*, cassock-wearing spies were thought to "confess" unsuspecting Catholics, rifling their souls like some *callista* Faust;[73] and a "monstrous *auto de fé*" occurred in Almoloya (Hidalgo) when an old woman—"a witch"—was burned alive by villagers who accused the poor crone of poisoning them with her aphrodisiacs.[74] As evil was believed to stalk the land, extreme reparations were made: in 1920, Lázaro Cárdenas remembered, a man in Tequixquitlán was nailed to a cross;[75] in the 1930s, devotees of Michoacán's *Cruz del Palo* waded into the Pacific, some drowning, as a prophet named Moses tried to part the waves with his staff.[76] Then there were utopian attempts to perfect the Christian life—the *Cristiada*'s village theocracies and ecstatic, cruciform immolations; the desert colony founded by Salvador Abascal's sun-crazed *sinarquistas* in Baja California (1941).[77]

If nothing else, these colorful outpourings should make us wary about claims that class-based or other secular identities had supplanted a religious world view by 1910.[78] Equally, we must be careful not to imply that Catholic Mexico went into a kind of religious freefall after 1910. The breakdown of clerical authority in the Revolution created new spaces for lay religious participation: but to what extent did this result, in Desan's phrase, in a popular "reclaiming" of the sacred?[79] Or, more precisely, *on what terms* was the sacred reclaimed and laicized during the Revolution?

This is a difficult question to answer. As Jean Meyer observes, a dialectic between clerical and lay authority was opened by the Revolution;[80] yet this, I would suggest, is irreducible to a simple, "official" versus "popular" religion, model. The eschatological tinges above, for example, reflect not only a sense that the Revolution was a time of spiritual crisis but the existence of a dialogue between lay Catholics and a Church that responded to Revolution by outlining a providential economy of transgression, repentance, and atonement. The terms of the dialogue may have changed, reflecting the laity's increasing freedom. Yet the flock did not simply bolt from the fold now that the shepherd was gone: rather, people made *localized* responses to the Revolution that incorporated elements of both official and popular religious thinking, and also reflected local circumstances and expectations.[81]

Revolutionary state formation and anticlericalism, too, were very localized and contingent phenomena, and consequently were apprehended and interpreted from many different religious perspectives. Contemporary patterns of religious observance were, therefore, equally diverse. As Adrian Bantjes observes, the key to understanding Mexico's religious conflict is to trace the intersection of cultures with contexts—to overlay specific forms of revolutionary radicalism with specific configurations of local religion, whether these be more clericalized or "popular" in character. Thus varying political conditions elicited manifold religious responses, refracted through many regional or parochial pieties.

Outright appropriations of the sacred after 1910—whether through messianic cults or folk canonizations—tended to be a distinctively *northern* phenomenon: Cruz Chávez's rebellion at Porfirian Tomóchic set the scene. But the cult of Jesús Malverde—the (apocryphal?) bandit saint believed martyred by the *acordada* in Culiacán (Sinaloa) in 1909—also began to develop in the postrevolutionary decades.[82] And an androgynous Bajío *curandero* known as *el niño* Fidencio was also blown north by the Revolution, this time to Espinazo (Nuevo León). From 1926–38, thousands of pilgrims—lepers, lunatics, and cripples—inhabited his desert camp, hoping to receive miracle cures and sacraments.[83] Finally, in 1938, a soldier was executed in a kind of firing-squad Passion in Tijuana's cemetery after confessing to raping and murdering a little girl. Incredibly, Paul Vanderwood writes, the killer was soon absolved by locals and venerated as "Juan Soldado," a sacrificial lamb and victim of revolutionary tyranny.[84] In the relatively unchurched north, then, revolutionary man-gods were the conduits of popular spiritual anxiety.

In the Mexican south, the laicization of everyday religion occurred through rather different modes. As noted, pro-revolutionary schismatic *curas* set up in parts of central-southern Mexico after 1925, tapping into the local festive cycles or agrarian aspirations of Indian Catholics that Roman *curas* either neglected (during the *Cristiada*) or disdained. This happened in Texcoco (México) and Puebla's Sierra Norte, as well as frontier Chiapas (Tapachula), parts of coastal Oaxaca, southern Veracruz, and Tlaxcala. Here indigenous Catholics flocked to schismatic priests because their illicit services were still efficacious in local terms, as a way of honoring village saints and preserving the spiritual order. Perhaps most famously, in Tuxtla (Chiapas) the image of San Pascual Bailón—associated with a morbid death cult—escaped from ecclesiastical control during the 1930s, later reemerging as an icon of Pérez's schism.[85]

Mariophanies were reported, too, as official sanctuaries were profaned. In response, the sacred went alfresco, devolving to forests, mountain tops, caves, and grottos. In Jonotla (Puebla), a boy heard celestial music emanating from a mountain in 1922. As he approached, a stone fell, revealing a carved image of Mary ("La Virgen del Peñón"). Soon indigenous Christians began arriving with offerings of corn, and a rough chapel was built. This assertion of indigenous religiosity was at least threefold, however, being both a reaction to persecution; a rejection of priestly hegemony (the rock—called "Tlaloctepetl" in Nahuatl—was venerated as the home of Tlaloc, the Nahua god of rain and corn); and, finally, an expression of ethnic defiance against *mestizo* interlopers associated with Puebla's coffee economy.[86]

Indigenous variance was not new; but the Revolution hindered effective Church discipline and prised open space in which distinctive religious forms could develop. As Eddie Wright-Rios shows, the *Cristiada* in Juquila (Oaxaca) was associated with village syncretisms and devotional struggles by means of which Catholics kept Church and state at arm's length. Here the visions of a Chatina seer inspired a rustic, anticlerical Marianism that pitted local actors—led by the *maestra*, Matilde Narváez—against the parish clergy.

Such radical pieties—premised here on a revalorization of indigenous spirituality, and the laicization, indeed feminization, of religious authority—amounted to a "revolution in local Catholicism." In Porfirian Oaxaca, such devotions were suppressed or given an ecclesiastical imprimatur, but this centralizing trend was now reversed as religion was *re*-localized.[87]

Massimo De Giuseppe analyzes the case of the Chontal catechist and *rezandero*, Gabriel García—"*el indio* Gabriel"—in 1920s Tabasco, and shows how an original model of indigenous Catholicism emerged during the cultural revolution engineered by Governor Garrido Canabal. Following the clergy's expulsion, De Giuseppe argues, religion was decentralized and passed into the hands of literate lay intermediaries like *el indio*. In Macuspana, Gabriel pioneered a rural syncretism blending the Chontal language and communitarian principles with modern universal devotions (the Sacred Heart, the Apostleship of Prayer) and techniques of diffusion (gramophone recordings of the Mass). Though murdered by *garridistas* in 1930, Gabriel achieved a genuine fusion of modern—here modern *Catholic*—culture and indigenous folkways that evaded both the Tabascan Church and the regime. And in Tantima (Veracruz) *circa* 1923, a *ranchero* calling himself Domingo Guzmán in honor of the Dominicans' founder was driven from church by the *cura* when he refused to stop chanting unscripted praises in Latin. Undeterred, Guzmán built a farm church of *otate* wood and palm leaves: for the next 60 years, crowds of villagers, bandsmen, and *danzantes* gathered to receive illicit sacraments, participate in free prayers, and watch fireworks.[88]

North and south thus went through strange, if spiritually liberating, times during the Revolution, as a result of which prevailing patterns of religious practice assumed innovative forms in line with local preference or tradition. But what of the rest of Mexico? In many places, a third religious method obtained in which public rituals passed temporarily into lay control while priests officiated underground. Such a measured retreat, of course, required a discipline that was not found everywhere—hence this model was particularly strong in the cities, central highlands, and the west, which were, not surprisingly, already the bastions of clerical religion.

This conservatism should not obscure the fact that even orthodox piety changed significantly, with laicization again the leitmotif. We catch a glimpse of this dynamism in the lay-led cults of the *Cristiada*. For Easter Friday, for instance—the citations refer to Mexico City in 1928—morning prayers were sung and the via crucis led "by various seculars," due to the "lack of priests." The "prayers corresponding to the Mass" were read first; then, for the "adoration of the Holy Cross," the laity filed past a nave crucifix, kissing the image. Devotees then prayed the Rosary and at noon there was a "reading of the Gospel of the day by one of the faithful." Sermons by "eminent Mexican sacred orators" were also read. In the evening, "*damas* intoned religious canticles" and led holy hours.[89] Likewise in rural parishes: in Querétaro, people celebrated Easter in the atrium at Amealco in 1927; a "creeping to the cross" took place in Colón, where the faithful also paraded religious images.[90]

In such "white masses," the laity played a greater role than before, assuming liturgical functions previously denied them and doing so regardless of gender. Moreover, lay priests were not "exceptional" Catholics, but ordinary, if literate, faithful—peasants such as Cecilio Valtierra (Jalpa, Guanajuato) or *capitalinos* like Refugio Padilla (in the Islas Marías prison, Nayarit). There were other innovations: the laity now took control *in* church, for example, and, albeit conditionally, performed sacraments including baptism, marriage, and the Eucharist (self-administered only), as well as transporting the Viaticum.[91] Previous manifestations of lay religiosity, home altar cult for instance, were more private;[92] in the 1920s and 1930s, however, public religion was laicized while priestly religion, conversely, was privatized.

Priests nonetheless shaped this lay cult by choosing which rites could be performed and by whom, in line with episcopal declarations. In general, the fit between the elite template and its popular rendition was surprisingly close, especially as conditions conducive to autonomous religiosity—bishopless dioceses, persecution, spiritual hunger, visionary traditions—were in place. Comparable bouts of *kulturkampf* in Catholic Europe had resulted in notorious cases of apparitionism, as in Ezkioga (Spain) and Marpingen (Germany). In southern Mexico, but apparently nowhere else, seers whose relationship to official Catholicism was ambiguous also emerged.[93]

Decentralization was not without tensions. But, compared to northern or southern sees, friction tended in an opposite direction—toward intransigence, not deviance, as lay *ultras* pressed the clergy to resist persecution to the bitter end. The hardcore faithful of León (Guanajuato) held that *curas* who gave their addresses to the authorities in early 1929—even though the bishop himself commanded it—were "schismatics."[94] And in Mexico City, the *Cristo Rey* cult was gradually appropriated by radicals in the 1920s and its universal meanings altered in line with a local, counter-revolutionary piety.[95] Some *cristeros* kept on fighting after the 1929 *arreglos* that ended the *Cristiada*, convinced that duplicitous Mexican hierarchs had betrayed the Church: such village ultramontanes carried a holy flame that nothing—neither certain defeat, nor even, paradoxically, excommunication and papal encyclicals—could douse.[96]

The chapters that follow reveal the great diversity of Mexico's Catholic and other religious cultures, and also show that the broad clamor of revolutionary social change echoed in the religious life. As in other fields, previously under-represented or subordinate groups—peasants, women, *indígenas*—came more to the fore, and began to experiment with diverse forms of spirituality or act out new cultic roles. Rather than just religion's denial, the Revolution generated "plastic religious identities"[97] and saw the creation of new forms of belief and practice as people accommodated or resisted state efforts to revolutionize popular culture. Religiosity was reshaped by the Revolution, and vice versa, as revolutionary notions of popular participation and social justice challenged and fused with religious concerns. The Revolution was not so much God's funeral, then, as a period of religious change and effervescence.

This is not to deny the Revolution's other—agrarian, political—dimensions. Equally, it is not enough to discard religious factors on the basis of *faute de mieux*, "default" theories of religion. The Revolution inspired thoughts of existential dread and celestial longing as well as dreams of social justice: religion therefore remained central, despite the presence of mass organizations that beguiled Mexicans with promises of earthly salvation by the 1920s and 1930s. As in the village of Júpare (Sonora), however—where new Mayo *santos* emerged phoenix-like from the ashes of icons "murdered" on revolutionary bonfires in the 1930s[98]—the search for religious consolation remained an important, and even irreducible, element of Mexico's Revolution.

Notes

1. John Lloyd Mecham, *Church and State in Latin America: A History of Politico-Ecclesiastical Relations* (1934, Chapel Hill: University of North Carolina Press, 1966), 380–1.
2. Eyler Simpson, *The Ejido: Mexico's Way Out* (1934, Chapel Hill: University of North Carolina Press, 1967), 245–6.
3. Ibid., 306–15.
4. Ernest Gruening, *Mexico and its Heritage* (New York: Century, 1928), 217–25.
5. Jean Meyer, *La Cristiada* (3 vols. Mexico City: Siglo XXI, 1973–74), 2:273.
6. Francis Clement Kelley, *Blood-Drenched Altars: Mexican Study and Comment* (London: Geo Coldwell, 1935), 317.
7. Gastón García Cantú, *El Pensamiento de la Reacción Mexicana (1860–1926)* (Mexico City: UNAM, 1987), 245–67.
8. Salvador Sotelo Arévalo, *Historia de Mi Vida: Autobiografía y Memorias de un Maestro Rural en México, 1904–1965* (Mexico City: INEHRM, 1996).
9. *Religious Culture in Modern Mexico*, ed. Martin Austin Nesvig (Lanham: Rowman and Littlefield, 2007), appeared just as this volume was in press. Unfortunately, therefore, its findings for the Revolution could not be integrated here.
10. Cf. Glennys Young, *Power and the Sacred in Revolutionary Russia: Religious Activists in the Village* (Pennsylvania: Pennsylvania State University Press, 1997), 3.
11. Adrian Bantjes, "Iglesia, Estado, y Religión en el México Revolucionario: Una Visión Historiográfica de Conjunto," *Prohistoria* 6 (2002): 203–24.
12. Patrick Collinson, "Religion, Society, and the Historian," *Journal of Religious History* 23, no. 2 (1999): 151–67.
13. José Antonio Martínez Alvarez, *Los Padres de la Guerra Cristera: Estudio Historiográfico* (Guanajuato: Universidad de Guanajuato, 2001), 135, 158–9.
14. Meyer, *La Cristiada*, 2:211.
15. Timothy Tackett, *Religion, Revolution, and Regional Culture in Eighteenth-Century France: The Ecclesiastical Oath of 1791* (Princeton: Princeton University Press, 1985); William Christian Jr., *Visionaries: The Spanish Republic and the Reign of Christ* (Berkeley: University of California, 1996).
16. E.g., William Taylor, *Magistrates of the Sacred: Priests and Parishioners in Eighteenth-Century Mexico* (Stanford: Stanford University Press, 1996); *Local*

Religion in Colonial Mexico, ed. Martin Austin Nesvig (Albuquerque: University of New Mexico Press, 2006).

17. Luis Barrón, *Historias de la Revolución Mexicana* (Mexico City: FCE, 2004), 127–31.

18. Peter Reich, *Mexico's Hidden Revolution: The Catholic Church in Law and Politics since 1929* (Notre Dame: University of Notre Dame, 1995).

19. Jennie Purnell, *Popular Movements and State Formation in Revolutionary Mexico: The Cristeros and Agraristas of Michoacán* (Durham: Duke University Press, 1999).

20. For a critique of overly secular readings of modern Church history in Mexico, see Roberto Blancarte, *Historia de la Iglesia Católica en México* (Mexico City: FCE, 1992), esp. 11–15.

21. Eric Van Young, *The Other Rebellion: Popular Violence and Ideology in Mexico, 1800–1821* (Stanford: Stanford University Press, 2001).

22. Paul Vanderwood, *The Power of God against the Guns of Government: Religious Upheaval in Mexico at the Turn of the Nineteenth Century* (Stanford: Stanford University Press, 1998); Rubén Osorio, *Tomochic en Llamas* (Mexico City: Conaculta, 1995).

23. Matthew Butler, *Popular Piety and Political Identity in Mexico's Cristero Rebellion: Michoacán, 1927–29* (Oxford: OUP, 2004).

24. Cf. Dale Van Kley, *The Religious Origins of the French Revolution: From Calvin to the Civil Constitution, 1560–1791* (New Haven: Yale University Press, 1996).

25. *Everyday Forms of State Formation: Revolution and the Negotiation of Rule in Modern Mexico*, ed. Gilbert Joseph and Daniel Nugent (Durham: Duke University Press, 1994).

26. Marjorie Becker, *Setting the Virgin on Fire: Lázaro Cárdenas, Michoacán Peasants, and the Redemption of the Mexican Revolution* (Berkeley: Unversity of California Press, 1995).

27. Collinson, "Religion," 162–7. Young, *Power and the Sacred*, chs. 5–7.

28. "La Confesión Auricular," *El Fuego*, 2 Mar. 1927. Meyer, *La Cristiada*, 2:87–8.

29. Olcott, *Revolutionary Women*, 210–11.

30. Ramón Del Llano, *Lucha por el Cielo: Religión y Política en el Estado de Querétaro, 1910–1929* (Mexico City: Porrúa, 2006), 117–18. Moisés González Navarro, *Cristeros y Agrarias en Jalisco* (5 vols. Mexico City: Colmex, 2000–3), 1:188.

31. Meyer, *La Cristiada*, 2:248.

32. González Navarro, *Cristeros y Agraristas*, 1:251–60.

33. Butler, *Popular Piety*, 117–20.

34. Wilfrid Parsons, *Mexican Martyrdom* (New York: Macmillan, 1936), 8.

35. Julio Cuadros Caldas, *Catecismo Agrario* (Mexico City, 1929). "Fray Polilla," *Desde Mi Púlpito* (Mexico City, 1933).

36. Young, *Power and the Sacred*, 101–2.

37. Calles swore that he intended to "defanaticize," not "decatholicize," Mexico, but privately hoped to extirpate priests "once and for all." Meyer, *La Cristiada*, 1:8.

38. David Brading, *The First America: The Spanish Monarchy, Creole Patriots, and the Liberal State, 1492–1867* (Cambridge: CUP, 1991), 668–74.

39. Meyer, *La Cristiada*, 2:277.

40. Luis L. León, *Crónica del Poder en los Recuerdos de un Político en el México Revolucionario* (Mexico: FCE, 1987), 142–3, 256.

41. Vicente Lombardo Toledano, *El Reparto de Tierras a los Pobres No Se Opone a las Enseñanzas de Nuestro Señor Jesucristo y de la Santa Madre Iglesia* (Mexico City: Grupo Solidario del Movimiento Obrero, 1923).

42. Moisés González Navarro, *Masones y Cristeros en Jalisco* (Mexico City: Colmex, 2000), 21.

43. Cf., Young, *Power and the Sacred*, 92.

44. "The revolutionary movement is Christian," Obregón claimed. Meyer, *La Cristiada*, 2:126.

45. Guillermo de la Peña, "El Campo Religioso, la Diversidad Regional, y la Identidad Nacional en México," *Relaciones* 100 (2004): 22–71.

46. Christopher Hill, *The World Turned Upside Down: Radical Ideas during the English Revolution* (London: Penguin, 1991). See also *Religion in Revolutionary England*, ed. Christopher Durston and Judith Maltby (Manchester: Manchester University Press, 2005).

47. Jürgen Buchenau, *Plutarco Elías Calles and the Mexican Revolution* (Lanham: Rowman and Littlefield, 2007), 196–7.

48. Pedro Salmerón Sanginés, *Aarón Sáenz Garza: Militar, Diplomático, Político, Empresario* (Mexico City: Porrúa, 2001). Education subsecretary Moisés Sáenz was also a Protestant.

49. Plutarco Elías Calles, *Correspondencia Personal (1919–1945)* (Mexico City: FCE, 1996), 420–1.

50. Cecilia Adriana Bautista García, "Maestros y Masones: La Contienda por la Reforma Educativa en México, 1930–1940," *Relaciones* 104 (2005): 219–76.

51. Archivo de la Liga Defensora de la Libertad Religiosa ALNDLR, Mexico City (henceforth ALNDLR), 1531.2090, Clemencia Vargas, Jaral, 3 Nov. 1926.

52. Mario Ramírez Rancaño, *El Patriarca Pérez: La Iglesia Católica Apostólica Mexicana* (Mexico City: UNAM, 2006); Matthew Butler, *Fathers of Revolution: Mexico's Schismatic Catholic Church, 1925–1940*, ms. in progress.

53. Renée de la Torre, *Los Hijos de la Luz: Discurso, Identidad, y Poder en la Luz del Mundo* (Guadalajara: CIESAS, 2000), 69–81.

54. De la Peña, "Campo Religioso," 46–7; Jean-Pierre Bastian, *Protestantismos y Modernidad Latinoamericana: Historia de unas Minorías Religiosas Activas en América Latina* (Mexico City: FCE, 1994), 201.

55. Butler, *Popular Piety*, chs. 2–3.

56. James Scott, *Weapons of the Weak: Everyday Forms of Peasant Resistance* (New Haven: Yale University Press, 1985).

57. Archivo General de la Nación (henceforth AGN), 2.340.51.3, Amanalco, 21 May 1931.

58. AGN, 2.340.50.26, Ocopulco, 22 Nov. 1929.

59. Cf. Young, *Power and the Sacred*, 33, 51.

60. Butler, *Popular Piety*, 128–38.

61. Del Llano, *Lucha por el Cielo*, 119. Meyer, *La Cristiada*, 3:256. González Navarro, *Cristeros y Agraristas*, 2:181–335.

62. Butler, *Popular Piety*, 59. Ramírez Rancaño, *El Patriarca Pérez*, 225–60. Meyer, *La Cristiada*, 3:250, 255.

63. "El Primer Bautismo al Estilo de los Agraristas Fue Celebrado en San Martín Texmelucan, Pue.," *Excélsior*, 2 Sep. 1926; Olcott, *Revolutionary Women*,

75; "En Soledad Doblado, Ver., No Se Necesitan Ya los Curas," *El Fuego*, 22 Jan. 1927.

64. Sotelo, *Historia de Mi Vida*, 78.

65. Mona Ozouf, *Festivals and the French Revolution* (Cambridge, Mass.: Harvard University Press, 1988), 34.

66. "Los Campesinos Católicos Organizados Piden a los Terratenientes una Reforma Radical," *El Universal*, 7 Oct. 1924.

67. Jean Meyer, *Anacleto González Flores: El Hombre que Quiso Ser el Gandhi Mexicano* (Mexico City: IMDSC, 2004), 56.

68. Cf. Young, *Power and the Sacred*, 276.

69. Luis González y González, *Pueblo en Vilo: Microhistoria de San José de Gracia* (Mexico City: Clío, 1999), 152.

70. Meyer, *La Cristiada*, 3:287–8, 310.

71. Del Llano, *Lucha por el Cielo*, 153–5.

72. Ibid., 163.

73. Condumex, c. 4/f. 362, "Católicos; Alerta," 1926.

74. "Anciana Quemada Viva con Leña Verde: Monstruoso Auto de Fe en Pleno Siglo Veinte en el Pueblo de Almoloya, Hgo.," *El Universal*, 21 Feb. 1928.

75. González Navarro, *Masones y Cristeros*, 90.

76. Meyer, *La Cristiada*, 1:349–51.

77. Jean Meyer, *El Sinarquismo ¿Un Fascismo Mexicano* (Mexico City: Joaquín Mortiz, 1978), 76–96; Meyer, *La Cristiada*, 3:134–201.

78. Adrian Bantjes, "Religion and the Mexican Revolution: Toward a New Historiography," in Nesvig, *Religious Culture*, ch. 10. I am grateful to the author for providing me with a manuscript version of this chapter.

79. Suzanne Desan, *Reclaiming the Sacred: Lay Religion and Popular Politics in Revolutionary France* (Ithaca: Cornell University Press, 1990).

80. Meyer this volume.

81. Carlos Eire, "The Concept of Popular Religion," in Nesvig, *Local Religion*, 1–35.

82. Manuel Lozcana Ochoa, *Una Vida en la Vida Sinaloense* (Culiacán: Universidad de Occidente, 1992).

83. Anita Brenner, *Idols behind Altars* (New York: Payson and Clark, 1929), ch. 1.

84. Paul Vanderwood, *Juan Soldado: Soldier, Rapist, Martyr, Saint* (Durham: Duke University Press, 2004), ch. 1.

85. Carlos Navarrete, *San Pascualito Rey y el Culto a la Muerte en Chiapas* (Mexico City: UNAM, 1982). Butler, *Fathers of Revolution*.

86. Gregory Reck, "Goodbye Ixoxolotl: Acculturation in a Mestizo-Indio Village in Mexico" (PhD diss., Catholic University of America, 1972), 71–7.

87. Eddie Wright-Rios, "Piety and Progress: Vision, Shrine, and Society in Oaxaca, 1887–1934" (PhD diss., University of California at San Diego, 2004).

88. Enrique Hugo García Valencia, "Sistemas Normativos y Nuevas Tendencias Religiosas en Veracruz," ms., 44–51.

89. Archivo Miguel Palomar y Vizcarra (henceforth AMPV), 81.618.573–4, "Méjico: La Semana Santa de los Mejicanos," 27 Apr. 1928.

90. Del Llano, *Lucha por el Cielo*, 212, 219, 264–5.

91. Matthew Butler, "¿Del Fiel Sacerdocio al Sacerdocio de los Fieles? Religión Local y Guerra Cristera en Jalpa de Cánovas," paper given at symposium "A 80 Años de la Cristiada," CIESAS, Guadalajara, Nov. 2006. *No Eramos*

Bandidos . . . Tan Sólo Cristianos, Islas Marías, 1929. Narración Testimonial del Profesor José Refugio Padilla Galindo, ed. Ma. Alicia Puente Lutteroth (Mexico City: UAEM, 2006).

92. William H. Beezley, "Home Altars: Private Reflections of Public Life," in *Home Altars of Mexico*, ed. Dana Salvo (London: Thames and Hudson, 1997), 91–107.

93. Christian, *Visionaries*, 8–16. David Blackbourn, *Marpingen: Apparitions of the Virgin Mary in Nineteenth-Century Germany* (New York: Alfred Knopf, 1994).

94. Butler, *Fathers of Revolution*, ch. 2.

95. Butler this volume.

96. Enrique Guerra Manzo, "El Fuego Sagrado: La Segunda Cristiada y el Caso de Michoacán (1931–1938)," *Historia Mexicana* 55, no. 2 (2005): 513–75.

97. Young, *Power and the Sacred*, 134–5.

98. Adrian Bantjes, *As If Jesus Walked on Earth: Cardenismo, Sonora, and the Mexican Revolution* (Wilmington: SR, 1988), 7.

Chapter 1

The Mentality and Modus Operandi of Revolutionary Anticlericalism

Alan Knight

In a brief but suggestive passage of *La Cristiada*, Jean Meyer presents a thumbnail portrait of the revolutionary anticlerical of the 1920s: an urban northerner, white-collar professional, supporter of the Sonoran regime, admirer of the United States, Protestant sympathizer (if not an actual Protestant), and quite likely a freemason.[1] These "men of the north" (Roberto Pesqueira) looked with disdain on "old Mexico"—the Indian, peasant, priest-ridden Mexico of the colonial heartland.[2] With the Constitutionalist triumph and establishment of the Sonoran regime, northern men and values were imposed on the center; the result, Meyer eloquently recounts, was the *Cristiada*, the resistance of "old" Mexico to abrupt cultural and political imposition.

The *Cristiada* was Meyer's chief concern, hence his analysis of anticlericalism is necessarily limited and, arguably, skewed.[3] However, it remains one of the best we have, and has proved influential. To the extent that historians have rehabilitated the *cristeros*—arguing that they were not the pawns of reactionary landlords but popular actors possessed of autonomous goals and ideas—they have simultaneously denigrated their anticlerical opponents. Thus, the image of an authoritarian anticlerical state, trampling on popular beliefs and practices, has been extended from Calles to Cárdenas, from the 1920s to the 1930s.[4] The ensuing debate has stirred the once turgid waters of Mexican politico-religious history. The old revolutionary orthodoxy—of an enlightened state combating a reactionary Church on behalf of an oppressed people—has been overthrown;[5] revisionist history stresses the state's totalitarian tendencies, its overweening corruption and arrogance, and the resistance it faced from a stout, God-fearing peasantry. The pawns are not benighted Catholic *campesinos*, but luckless *agraristas*, victims of the revolutionary state's new *leva*. Revisionism has spun the wheel in another respect: if the Catholic leaders of revolutionary legend were devious string pullers, who used religion as a device to resist land reform, anticlerical postrevolutionary *caudillos* attacked the Church for similarly instrumental reasons: their policy distracted people from the parlous state of the economy and directed popular resentment up an anticlerical cul-de-sac.[6] Anticlericalism was a tactic as much as a belief: either way, the *cristero* or revolutionary rank-and-file succumbed to top-down manipulation as *campesinos'* genuine (often material) grievances were cynically exploited by Machiavellian elites. The Catholic hierarchy encouraged *campesinos* to puff on the "opium of the people"; the revolutionary state befuddled their wits with the marijuana of anticlericalism.

In this chapter, I reevaluate revolutionary anticlericalism, building on Meyer's foundations. I hope to credit it with the same diversity and autonomy as Catholicism: that is, to distinguish what is contrived and instrumental from what is "organic" and an-end-in-itself; thus, to differentiate between "ideology" and "interests," and/or between "culture" and "economics"/ "power."[7] In doing so, I will necessarily say something about the anticlericals' opponents—political Catholics[8]—since these collective antagonists were jointly responsible for ratcheting up the conflict from the 1910s through the 1930s and the story is necessarily dialectical. Yet, these foes also displayed a strange kinship: their views of the uncommitted masses for whose hearts and souls they struggled were oddly similar; their motivations revealed an uneasy combination of ideological conviction and self-interest; and they shared a concern for austere moral values that were at odds with Mexico's often rowdy and Rabelaisian popular culture.

Mexican Anticlericalism from Colony to Revolution

The diversity of anticlericalism is obvious. One useful way of looking at the phenomenon is diachronically, since a narrative over time suggests a distinct evolution as new—usually more radical—anticlericalisms are born and overlay older, more moderate forms. As Meyer rightly observes, and as recent research by Taylor confirms,[9] the origins of liberal and revolutionary anticlericalism are to be found in the colony, notably with the Bourbon reformers. The latter were not atheistic freethinkers; usually Catholics, they believed that the Church had a role to play as the ally of enlightened absolutism. But they subscribed to Enlightenment values and, in addition, to Gallican and even Jansenist notions of state supremacy. For them, the Church should be the secular power's dependent ally, not equal partner; and aspects of Catholicism that offended enlightened sensibility and, more importantly, royal Realpolitik should be combated: rowdy and drunken fiestas, retrograde monasticism, bloody penitential rituals.[10] Like their liberal and revolutionary successors— also, in their own way, children of the Enlightenment—Bourbon reformers sought to clean and sober up the Mexican people and hence believed in bringing the Church to heel. Not surprisingly, Bourbon anticlericalism provoked resistance (for example, at Guanajuato in 1767),[11] a loss of political legitimacy, and internal Church divisions, which surfaced with the 1810 insurgency.[12]

Perhaps less significant—certainly less well-known—was a strain of popular anticlericalism that ran through the colony and whose links to liberal-revolutionary forms have been neglected.[13] Like the popular anticlericalism of Medieval Europe, this variant focused on corrupt and avaricious priests—those who demanded excessive fees, expropriated Indian land and labor, or repressed popular religiosity ("Catholic," "pagan," or "syncretic").[14] Colonial history is replete with examples of priests being denounced, attacked, run out of town, very occasionally killed.[15] The most extreme cases occurred during major rebellions, like those of the Tepehuanes, the Pueblos, or the Tzeltales.[16] It may be objected that such rebels were not properly converted and their protest was a species of "primary," anticolonial resistance, not genuine anticlericalism.[17] Yet even here, resistance was partly premised on heterodox Catholic notions.[18] The rebels did not repudiate Christianity in its entirety, but rather the perverse form it adopted when controlled by grasping priests. Many lesser village protests displayed even greater discrimination.[19] The capacity to be Catholic while denouncing the *cura* is, of course, common enough; in colonial Mexico, it reflected the structural reality of religious life, whereby priests were thin on the ground and a great deal of religious activity was conducted autonomously by lay people in scattered villages. Not surprisingly, priests who abused their authority or spurned local beliefs were regarded as passing parasites.

In addition, there existed a measure of popular unbelief—evident in scatological blasphemy rather than cerebral skepticism—which went beyond specific attacks on egregious priests. Of course, Indian backsliding and "paganism" were common charges. But, as Taylor convincingly argues, much of eighteenth-century Mexico was effectively "Christianized"; and outright paganism had been pushed into New Spain's distant northern and southeastern reaches, or remote mountain recesses.[20] Popular unbelief therefore assumed forms that were not recognizably pagan, but which—like the heterodoxy of Ginzburg's miller Menocchio[21]—reflected an earthy, autodidact materialism, hostile to transcendent religion. We find it, then, among Spaniards, blacks, and *mestizos*.[22] By the late colony, expressions of Rabelaisian unbelief crop up quite regularly, notwithstanding the tight control of clerical and secular authorities.[23]

Such phenomena cannot be quantified; I do not claim that they were extensive; nor can I establish linear connections between late colonial unbelief and revolutionary anticlericalism. I simply suggest that Mexico was more ideologically diverse than is sometimes thought, and that anticlerical traditions ran deep, especially in certain groups and communities. Analytically, three kinds of anticlerical tradition can be discerned: 1) Bourbon reformism: an elitist, rationalist current of opinion, fed by Enlightenment sources and rightly seen as the direct ancestor of liberal and revolutionary anticlericalism; 2) popular, often Indian, anticlericalism, which targeted specific, oppressive priests (increasingly, within an orthodox Catholic framework); and 3) a subcurrent of dissent—*pace* Febvre, we might call it Rabelaisian skepticism—which combined anticlericalism with a deeper, commonsensical dissent, and was manifested in scatological jokes, curses, and blasphemy.[24] How these traditions fed into the developed—even official—nineteenth- and twentieth-centuries' anticlericalisms remains unclear. But it might be mistaken to see post-Independence anticlericalism as something that, like Pallas Athene springing fully formed from the head of Zeus, leaped out of nowhere in the nineteenth century.

The Bourbon reform project was riddled with contradictions. In politico-economic terms, it suffered the contradictions of Barrington Moore's "revolution from above" in trying to "modernize" aspects of New Spain (trade, taxation, popular mores) while retaining "traditional" features (the caste system, colonial dependency).[25] In more philosophical terms, Bourbon reformers sought to shine Reason's bright light into those murky corners of colonial society they disliked (tax farming, popular piety), while sheltering others (monarchical absolutism, colonial domination) from its rays. With independence, however, light filtered into the whole building. By *circa* 1830, republic had replaced monarch, the caste system had been nominally abolished, and Mexicans, including plebeians, had begun to think and act like citizens, as bearers of individual rights and collective carriers of popular sovereignty.[26] The post-Independence Church, weaker in terms of wealth and personnel but strengthened by virtue of escaping from the royal patronage (*real patronato*), was bound to come under scrutiny. Two generations of liberals now set out to curtail church privileges (*fueros*) and material assets. Their goal—the goal, we might say, of *liberal* anticlericalism—was to separate Church and state, confining religion to the private sphere, and enabling public, political, and economic activities to proceed in a neutral arena where corporate privilege had no place. Liberal anticlericalism, as in Italy, sought a "free church in a free state."[27] Most anticlerical liberals were Catholics, even devout Catholics; parish priests sometimes figured as liberal leaders and Juan Alvarez swore allegiance to the 1857 Constitution prostrate before an altar.[28] As Pamela Voekel argues—a little too strenuously?—religious values underpinned nineteenth-century liberalism: Lizardi, Mier, and Mora were the children not of French-revolutionary secularism but "enlightened Catholicism."[29] And, thanks partly to clerical conservatives' knuckle-headed politics, the liberals eventually triumphed and imposed their generally moderate anticlerical project on an overwhelmingly Catholic Mexico. Church and state were separated, Church lands disentailed.

Díaz of course, conciliated the Church, turning a blind eye to infractions of the Constitution; and the benign Porfirian climate enabled the Church to experience a marked sociocultural revival, paralleling trends in the universal Church.[30] Catholic education and lay associations expanded and prospered. For some provincial towns, particularly in the center-west, the Porfiriato was a time when social stability, economic progress, and clerical authority prevailed;[31] all of which would be brought to a traumatic conclusion with the Revolution. Not surprisingly, some Catholics yearned for the good old days, before the serpent of revolutionary anticlericalism entered Eden.

Díaz's conciliation of the Church was a balancing act, which offended both political extremes. Militant Catholics, never reconciled to the Constitution, began to flex their political muscles; in 1900, the bishop of San Luis impolitically declared the Reform Laws a dead letter.[32] Liberals too protested the resurgent clerical threat—evident in violations of the Reform Laws and grow-ing Vatican influence. Protestants, spiritualists, and freemasons swelled the anticlerical choir.[33] Militant liberals formed the Mexican Liberal Party (PLM), whose 1906 program evinced radical anticlericalism. Several minor spats—as at Velardeña, 1909—showed that Porfirian conciliation was a holding opera-tion rather than a definitive solution.[34] Indeed, given the Church's organiza-tional advance—the Porfiriato's "second spiritual conquest"—the potential for renewed conflict was even greater.

The 1910 Revolution began with a moderate program posing no immedi-ate threat to the Church. Though some revolutionary leaders harbored anti-clerical sentiments, these did not substantially color the Plan of San Luis or the sundry proposals that accompanied the rise of *maderismo*. A few priests—not, I suspect, a great number—were sympathetic to *maderismo*; Madero himself, though hardly a conventional Catholic, eschewed anticlericalism and welcomed Catholics' political mobilization in the National Catholic Party (PCN).[35] The popular rebels who rallied to Madero in 1910–11 were rarely overtly anticlerical. Their concerns were local, political, and agrarian. They sought local autonomy and, in some cases, land reform. Zapata's iconic Plan of Ayala was banged out by a parish priest on his battered typewriter.[36]

Within a few years, however, anticlericalism emerged as a central plank of the revolutionary platform, enshrined in the 1917 Constitution and numer-ous state laws. From 1913–17, priests were exiled, ransomed, imprisoned, and subjected to a host of restrictions. Churches became barracks and stables; Obregón rounded up and ransomed the clergy of Guadalajara and Mexico City.[37] In the United States, Catholic activists collected, embellished, and publicized the atrocities committed south of the border.[38] Though they exag-gerated, such propagandists captured an essential feature of the Revolution: a widespread, decentralized, sometimes violent anticlericalism.

In this respect, anticlericalism resembled agrarianism: it began during the armed revolution as a chaotic, often localized, set of responses; after 1917 it gelled as official policy expressed in the Constitution, state laws, and officially sanctioned media—newspapers, murals, and later radio.[39] Between 1917 and (roughly) 1940, anticlericalism was a staple of the regime and an object of repeated foreign censure. The implementation of anticlericalism, like agrari-anism, varied over time and place (Calles was more committed than Obregón or Cárdenas); and in accordance with cacical power and opinion (Tabasco, Veracruz, and Sonora witnessed more strenuous policies than, say, Puebla or San Luis Potosí). The states and the federation did not march in lockstep; there were marked discontinuities and contrasts.[40] Nevertheless, anticlerical-ism's advance was striking and often radical.

For revolutionary anticlericalism went appreciably beyond its mid-nineteenth-century liberal predecessor. Liberals sought Church-state separa-tion; the revolutionaries of the 1920s wanted to control the Church, to implement, under modern revolutionary auspices, an updated *real patronato*, even to eliminate Catholicism as a set of beliefs and practices. Thus, priests had to register with the state and their numbers were tightly controlled.

Catholic primary education was prohibited and Catholic secondary schools had to conform to state curricula (by 1934, a "socialist" curriculum). Old prohibitions on public religiosity were maintained, and often enforced, but Calles clearly sought to outdo Juárez. When, in response to his legislation, the hierarchy declared a cessation of all church services, Calles applauded: for every week the church doors remained closed, he believed, the Church would lose 2 percent of its flock (Calles was fond of statistics).[41]

The immediate result was the bloody *cristero* rebellion, which, fiercely repressed, resulted in the center-west's devastation. After a 1929 truce, conflict was renewed two years later as revolutionary authorities implemented fresh anticlerical measures. Now, resistance was (somewhat) less violent and the battle between Church and state was fought out in schools, streets, the press, and the new medium of radio. As Catholicism's mass organizations—the rump National League for the Defence of Religious Liberty (LNDLR), the Catholic Association of Mexican Youth (ACJM), Damas Católicas, Unión Nacional de Padres de Familia (UNPF), *Base*, Unión Nacional Sinarquista (UNS), and Partido Acción Nacional (PAN)—confronted the newly "massified" state and its allies (the National Revolutionary Party [PNR], the Party of the Mexican Revolution [PRM], the Regional Confederation of Mexican Labor [CROM], the Confederation of Mexican Workers [CTM], the National Peasant Confederation [CNC]), so the state undertook a sustained effort to win hearts and minds. Repression was therefore complemented by more "constructive" anticlericalism: federal schooling, mass propaganda, new secular fiestas, and orchestrated displays of iconoclasm. From Sonora in the northwest, where Governor (Rodolfo) Calles stripped the altars and destroyed the little saints of the Mayo, to Tabasco on the Gulf, where Garrido promoted a slew of secular fiestas and organized the didactic destruction of crucifixes, the tide of anticlericalism ran high, provoking shrill protests in Mexico and beyond.[42] Not until the later 1930s, as Cárdenas triumphed over Calles and the 1938 oil expropriation prompted a national ralliment, did the tide turn. The candidacy of Avila Camacho—a self-proclaimed "believer"—illustrated that anticlericalism was in decline; and his presidency promoted a new Church-state modus vivendi that, though far from complete or mutually congenial, at least prevented a recrudescence of conflict, especially now that the Cold War served to bring these two old antagonists closer together.[43]

A Causality of Revolutionary Anticlericalism

If the above story is fairly well known—though hardly a matter of historical consensus—the question of causality remains. Which invisible sun or moon determined the ebb and flow of this great anticlerical tide? Why, after a generation of détente, did the Revolution witness renewed—and unusually severe—Church-state conflict? What induced an assorted company—including bearded village patriarchs and embarrassed-looking flappers in bobbed hair—to chop hefty crucifixes to bits for the cameras in Tabasco?[44] Clearly, the conflict involved two sides who were locked in a kind of dialectical relationship; thus, it would be partial to focus solely on one. My chief focus is the anticlerical camp; however, just as Meyer needed to include anticlericalism in his study of the *Cristiada*, so I shall briefly allude to Catholic activism, as it confronted the unprecedented threat of revolutionary anticlericalism. In what follows, I address revolutionary anticlericalism under two broad—and conventional—headings: contingent causes and structural causes. I further divide the latter into two subheadings—"ideational proclivities" and "mass politics"—the first of which concerns ideology, while the second is mostly about power.

Contingent Causes

During the *maderista* period, anticlericalism was notably absent. True, in states where the PCN prospered, alarming its liberal opponents, sporadic clashes occurred.[45] But in most places this incipient liberal-Christian democrat confrontation was weak or nonexistent and electoral politics assumed different guises—personalist, clientelist, and class-based.[46] In some states, social upheaval and rebellion continued, to the detriment of electoral politics, and with scant signs of popular anticlericalism. However, Huerta's February 1913 coup changed the picture abruptly: in 1913–14, as the Constitutionalist coalition coalesced and battered Huerta's *federales* into submission, anticlerical acts came thick and fast. With regard to anticlericalism, therefore, 1913–14 was a watershed.[47] While there were deep-lying "structural" factors at work, we cannot ignore the conjunctural causes of this sudden, striking development. *Post hoc ergo propter hoc* is a perennial trap;[48] but it is hard to escape the conclusion that Huerta's coup and government played a part in generating anticlericalism, thus in triggering deeper structural causes. Maybe the Huerta factor merely determined the timing; maybe a spate of anticlericalism was inevitable, long overdue, on the cards. But even causes which determine timing are significant; and, in my view, the Huerta factor was responsible for more than just timing.[49]

It was, I think, responsible for two developments: one general, one specific. In general, Huerta's coup and its aftermath—the killing of Madero and Pino Suárez, the purge of *maderista* officials, the militarization of government—polarized Mexican politics. Madero's benign view of politics—indeed, of human nature—gave way to more ruthless Realpolitik. *Maderista* "hawks" (not least Carranza) triumphed over the "doves."[50] Thus, while Constitutionalist leaders pledged to restore democracy and avenge Madero's murder, they pursued this "Constitutionalist" mission with severe efficiency, notably in Sonora. To this end, they taxed, administered, confiscated, exported, and built sizeable conventional armies.[51] They did not hold elections and, in the end, did not restore the 1857 Constitution. Enemies of the cause could no longer expect the kid-gloved treatment of Madero. Lands were expropriated, *huertistas* persecuted, prisoners shot. The Church therefore suffered, along with other perceived reactionaries, from the polarization and coarsening of politics that Huerta's coup provoked.

Specifically, the Church did not simply suffer unfair guilt by association but to some extent brought retribution upon itself. There is very good evidence that the Church—bishops, parish priests, the PCN—welcomed Huerta's coup: in Chihuahua, a priest danced for joy and in Oaxaca a service of thanksgiving was held in La Soledad.[52] Subsequently the Church supported Huerta's administration, both the hierarchy and PCN collaborating to a degree. The PCN supported the administration in Congress, even after the October coup d'état.[53] Locally, too, prominent Catholics supported the regime against the Revolution. It is important to stress that this evidence does not derive from ex post facto revolutionary rationalization; the evidence is reasonably reliable contemporary reportage antedating the aggravation of Church-state conflict in 1913–14, when both sides participated in mutual mudslinging and reprisals. Later Catholic denials of such complicity therefore ring hollow.[54]

Why, then, did the Church—relatively unaffected by anticlerical assaults, in some measure a beneficiary of *maderista* liberal democracy—welcome Huerta's coup and even the authoritarian Huerta government? Here we enter the solid but still contentious terrain of structural causality. What predisposed Catholics to support Huerta? And why did revolutionary anticlericals so enthusiastically take up the gauntlet and embark on an anticlerical crusade unprecedented in Mexican history?

The Mexican Church was, of course, a large and heterogeneous organization that, despite its undoubted authoritarianism, did not speak with one voice. Meyer rightly points to the diverse ideological currents that agitated the Church during and after the 1890s, in particular the "social Catholicism" that, in Mexico as elsewhere, represented a Catholic engagement with liberal politics and the so-called "social question."[55] Hence, in 1911, Catholics were well-placed to take advantage of the *apertura* created by Madero. Indeed, Catholic forms of mass mobilization—parties, unions, peasant leagues, lay associations—would remain a crucial feature of Mexican politics throughout the revolutionary period. But the Mexican Church was by no means wholly or even primarily liberal and "social." There is abundant evidence of Catholic engagement with conservative causes too, which is hardly surprising given the tenor of Catholic politics in Europe or elsewhere in Latin America.

In part, Catholic conservatism represented an ideological inclination toward order, hierarchy, property, and stability; a preferential option for the well-to-do, one might say.[56] With this went a profound suspicion of radical movements and a lingering suspicion of liberal democracy, which *Rerum Novarum* failed to dissipate. These general dispositions were realized and accentuated in particular circumstances: in communities where the *cura* formed part of a local oligarchy whose power, status and, perhaps, property seemed threatened by revolution.[57] Of course, Madero's revolution proved short-lived and his regime generally cautious and moderate. Thus, Catholic disenchantment was not premised on Madero's relatively few sins of

commission, but his more numerous and egregious sins of omission: his failure to restore order, repress rebellion and banditry, protect property, and
shore up the Porfiriato's threatened social hierarchies. Not surprisingly, many
Catholics took heart from Huerta's coup, which promised an "iron hand"
and to achieve peace *"cueste lo que cueste."*[58] Thus, the logic drawing
Catholics into *huertismo* was basically sociopolitical, a reflection of the
Church's imbrication with Porfirian society; it was not an *anti*-anticlerical
response.

That sociopolitical logic continued long after 1913. But the events of
1913–14 introduced a specifically anticlerical dimension to revolutionary
discourse and practice—a dimension largely absent under Madero. Now the
Church was stigmatized not just as one supporter among many of the Huerta
regime, but targeted specifically as a carrier of reactionary, antinational
values. This ratcheted up the conflict: the Church felt victimized and
denounced the Godless Revolution (not least in the United States);[59] and in
doing so, confirmed its reactionary, antinational reputation, thus encouraging further anticlerical measures. For this confrontational dialectic to proceed, anticlericals had to add a specific critique of the Church to the general
indictment of *huertismo* and Reaction. And to accomplish this, they mined
the deep strata of anticlericalism that had been laid down over generations.
Huerta's coup determined the timing—and provided some of the fuel, sustaining energy, and moral outrage—but the anticlerical campaign also
derived from deeper "structural" causes, which I loosely disaggregate, first as
"ideological" and, second, as "sociopolitical."

Structural Causes

Ideational Proclivities

First, revolutionary anticlericals bought into an old but evolving tradition
of rationalist Enlightenment thinking. They harked back to Voltaire, the
philosophes, and the French Revolution, and saw themselves as emancipating
Mexico from obscurantism, superstition, and false belief.[60] Catholicism was
foremost among these retrograde ideational systems. It encouraged a cower-
ing, irrational, and fatalistic attitude toward "the universe and social life,"
against which 1930s anticlericals—now calling themselves socialists—
proposed a "rational and exact concept," based on Reason and Science.[61]
Socialism was "scientific," part of "the historic struggle between Religion
and Science."[62] Anticlericals may not have been alone in valuing technology
and productivity (many Catholic activists did, too);[63] but their belief in the
scope of science and its emancipatory function was unusual.[64] Hence, they
lauded scientists and inventors like James Watt, conceived of the world in—
sometimes crudely—evolutionary terms, and railed against popular irra-
tionalism (religious and superstitious).[65] In denouncing Catholic rituals and
miracles, they were at pains to ridicule and to unmask. If some festive anticlericalism harked back to Rabelaisian colonial carousing (decking out oxen
and donkeys as popes and bishops; serenading the bishop of Tepic with

obscene songs into the night), the strident iconoclasm of Veracruz, Tabasco, or Sonora was designed to reveal to the masses that "miraculous" saints were mere chunks of wood or bundles of straw.[66]

Anticlericals believed that such mental emancipation had valuable practical effects. Peasants needed to know, Calles stressed, that drought must be countered by prudent public works, not parading saints around parched fields.[67] They also needed to know that fonts, like coughs and sneezes, spread diseases.[68] Here a strong commitment to this-wordly improvement was galvanized by the experience of Revolution and Depression, which encouraged an almost obsessive commitment to work, reconstruction, hygiene, temperance, and public investment (roads, irrigation, electrification, sanitation, and urban renewal).[69] It is not that Catholics were against such material improvements, of course; but they—logically—placed less emphasis on this material, mundane social redemption, which for the revolutionaries was the be-all and end-all.

We should recognize, therefore, that one powerful engine of anticlericalism was a genuine ideological commitment to a set of (loosely) Enlightenment values, which were broadly progressive, rationalist, scientific, and materialist.[70] Just as the *cristeros* were motivated by beliefs "relatively autonomous" of material interests, so their anticlerical opponents shared a set of "enlightened" ideas, irreducible to mere self-interest. Both sides were "people of the book," who deferred to a "Great Tradition" of their choosing, be it the Church and the Bible or the Enlightenment and *Encyclopédie*. These traditions, of course, needed their expositors and sites of exposition: *curas* and pulpits, on the one hand; schoolteachers and their liberal-patriotic classrooms on the other.[71]

The implementation of these ideas—thus, the creation of a "new" Mexican who would be secular, scientific, and progressive—was extremely difficult and only very partially successful. If some of the grand revolutionary project— nationalism, agrarianism—endured, the aggressively anticlerical, secularizing thrust of the 1920s–1930s was parried. The "new" man, woman, and child did not emerge, and in the process, the state incurred sustained opposition— from *cristeros, sinarquistas, padres de familia*, and a host of informal groups (women in particular), who successfully resisted official efforts to subvert their religious culture.[72] Resistance was so strenuous and the efforts at times so futile that it becomes very hard to sustain the "instrumental" thesis, whereby anticlericalism is seen as a ploy to win support or distract attention from pressing problems such as economic recession. Anticlericalism did not, on balance, win mass support: it was a minority policy or discourse that provoked widespread opposition, hence, in part, Cárdenas' pragmatic retreat after 1935.[73] For nearly 20 years, however, the state—and especially Calles's coterie—took anticlericalism very seriously and rammed it through, "*cueste lo que cueste*," as Huerta would have said.[74] Unless we regard Calles and his cronies as extraordinarily obtuse (which Calles was not), we must conclude that anticlericalism was often a sincerely held belief, a genuine conviction whose implementation would, in the anticlericals' eyes, result in a better Mexico.

But this was a minority conviction. Anticlerical ideas and policies were not only repudiated by the Church, but spurned by many Mexicans who fell into neither of the two antagonistic camps. Popular religion and superstition still flourished in defiance of both enlightened anticlericalism and official Catholicism. So did popular "vices" that anticlericals and Catholics alike condemned: drink, gambling, blood sports, idleness, and casual interpersonal violence. Furthermore, quite a few revolutionaries were leery of anticlericalism, which they saw (often correctly) as politically costly or personally troubling; since, lurking in officially anticlerical ranks were a good many clandestine Catholics, Catholic fellow travelers, or members of families that divided over the Church issue.[75] There were also anticlericals who had broken with Catholicism but not made the bold leap into materialism and atheism. The Revolution seemingly attracted a good many such religious dissidents: Protestants like Pascual Orozco, Aaron Saénz, and José Trinidad Ruiz; spiritualists like Madero and, it is said, several other revolutionary leaders; and credulous believers in folk saints and messiahs.[76] Even Calles, as I note in conclusion, visited the "miraculous" child healer *el niño* Fidencio in 1928.

Of course, this was not entirely new. Folk saviors had a long history in Mexico.[77] But Porfirian socioeconomic and political changes seem to have amplified religious and intellectual heterodoxy's appeal. This was particularly true of the north, where the established Church was weak; and where a more porous, mobile society was open to heterodox ideas, such as Protestantism and spiritualism.[78] Jean Meyer therefore floats the Weberian thesis linking Protestantism and capitalism.[79] In modern Mexico—as in early modern Britain or Germany—this is suggestive; but also notoriously hard to pin down regarding the causal links at work.[80] After all, the bastion of northern capitalism—Monterrey—produced a dynamic Catholic bourgeoisie that was co-responsible for the PAN's foundation in 1939.[81] Guadalajara and Puebla, so-called "*mocho*" cities, also had powerful business interests that set their stamp on local politics and society.[82] Thus, in Mexico as (again) in Western Europe, capitalism and Catholicism were not so antithetical.

However, it does seem probable that Porfirian and revolutionary Mexico experienced a growth of religious heterodoxy and dissent. Moreover, viewed dialectically, such a thesis is quite compatible with the notion of the second "spiritual conquest": as heterodoxy provoked Catholic concern and renewal, the reassertion of Catholic ideas and associations provoked further dissent, including outright anticlericalism. It also seems probable—although I know of no quantitative data, so the argument must remain impressionistic—that the north was disproportionately affected: hence the plethora of heterodox movements that it witnessed, compared to orthodox Catholic regions like Jalisco, the Bajío, and Puebla. Since the Revolution was itself disproportionately northern, it is unsurprising that it carried some of the genetic imprint of heterodoxy: Protestantism, spiritualism, freemasonry, and radical anticlericalism.

It may also be that these tendencies (anticlericalism especially) were accentuated by northerners' contact with the center and south. In other words, it is not just a question of inherited attributes, but of acquired, experiential, "dialectical" characteristics. Confronted by societies in which clerical authority was paramount—where, for example, Indians bowed and scraped to priests—the northern carpet-baggers gave free rein to their anticlerical proclivities.[83] And if northerners inclined more to religious dissent, this was less because of their more developed capitalistic instincts than because in northern Mexico the Church was historically weaker and, in a mobile frontier zone, heterodox ideas could circulate more freely. Indeed, it may be that in the maelstrom of northern society, churned by rapid change, immigration, and boom-and-bust business cycles, heterodox cults offered solace, meaning, and social shelter (compare the Brazilian *sertao*).[84] Anticlericalism and related ideas of work, discipline, and progress were, if I am right, part of a broader spectrum of heterodox (non-, sometimes anti-Catholic) beliefs that exerted particular appeal in the more "anomic" north. In central, especially center-west, Mexico, by contrast, the Church was historically stronger and further strengthened by Porfirian spiritual reconquest; while in the deep "Indian" south, older ("syncretic") beliefs and practices survived lustily, defying Catholic and revolutionary reformers.

Such arguments are necessarily tentative, since establishing links between "objective" social change (here, the development of northern Mexico in the Porfiriato) and "subjective" beliefs (about God, morality, and the afterlife) is notoriously difficult and runs the risk of crude reductionism. However, it is worth making further efforts. Even if the north occupies a special place in the gestation and transmission of revolutionary anticlericalism, the latter was clearly a pervasive phenomenon. Key individuals can be found throughout Mexico: Diéguez from Jalisco; Amaro from Zacatecas/Durango; Múgica and many lesser anticlericals from Michoacán; Tejeda and his cronies in Veracruz; Garrido Canabal in Tabasco; Carrillo Puerto in Yucatán. Anticlerical communities can also be readily identified, even in Catholic heartlands (for example, Zitácuaro).[85] If the pattern seems scattershot—deriving from "random" factors such as prior historical loyalties or the performance of clerical and anticlerical functionaries[86]—there may be some underlying rationale. We might crudely maintain that while the north was more heterodox and anticlerical, the center (especially the center-west) was broadly clerical-Catholic, and the south—in some measure—"folk-Catholic" rather than clerical-Catholic.[87]

Within these broad-brush regions there were discernible variations. First, highland zones were seemingly more Catholic and clerical, while the lowland hot country was more prone to dissent and anticlericalism: such a pattern can be seen in Sonora, Veracruz, Michoacán, and Colima. The young Cosío Villegas, moving from (lowland) Colima to (highland) Toluca, left a fluid, open, and easy-going society ("an egalitarian and democratic environment") for one that was stricter, straight-laced, and censorious: one where "anyone who proclaimed themself an atheist or freethinker would have incurred complete ostracism."[88] The chief cause of these differences, one must assume, was the Church's historic role since colonial times (when *tierra caliente* parishes were often disliked and disregarded).[89] Porfirian proselytization may have aggravated this bias, helping to create a "highly clericalized, sacramental, and parish-based form of Catholicism" in highland regions, stretching in a broad arc from Zacatecas through Jalisco, Michoacán, and the Bajío, to Puebla.[90]

If this was an ancient pattern, it was overlaid by a more recent revolutionary patina, the product, in particular, of agrarianism and federal education. It is clear that communities that benefited from revolutionary policies were more disposed to accept anticlericalism, even if not initially keen. Anticlericalism was the price paid for land and schools: conversely, communities—of *rancheros*, smallholders, or peons—who repudiated agrarianism were more likely to look favorably on the Church and its strident defense of property rights. This we might call the "coattails" (or "two-on-a-tandem") argument.[91] This can be further refined. "Revolutionary" communities—those generally well-disposed toward the revolution and the postrevolutionary regime—fell into two rough categories. The first, which might be called "primary" communities, had pioneered the armed revolution, and, as a result, received early benefits in the form of land and a measure of political empowerment. Morelos's *zapatista pueblos* would be the classic case. They were not usually anticlerical, but neither were they "clericalized"; and they adopted a realistic, reciprocal view of the Revolution—it was not perfect, but it brought benefits. They could tolerate a measure of anticlericalism; and local empowerment—the political promotion of *hijos del pueblo*—meant that these communities could filter and adjust the policy initiatives of the "center." In Morelos, anticlericalism did not become a major issue.[92] Keith Brewster's analysis of the Sierra Norte de Puebla suggests a similar pattern: the Barrios *cacicazgo* had a genuine regional base, the new regime brought benefits (including public order), and anticlericalism could be discreetly finessed.[93]

In contrast, we find communities of "secondary" mobilization: these had not distinguished themselves during the armed rebellion, but rallied to *callismo* or (more likely) *cardenismo*, drawn by the promise of land, schools, and political alliances. Examples would include the Laguna, the left bank of the Yaqui Valley, or Chan Kom (Yucatán), where the schoolteacher "pretty much controls the town."[94] Such communities did not necessarily possess an ancient liberal tradition (which might facilitate revolutionary conversion); some were recent *hacienda* communities; some were new settlements—"communities under construction."[95] In such communities, where clerical authority was weak or absent, the school "did not crash against a wall of established custom and interest" and the regime encountered relatively favorable virgin territory.[96] Here, a younger generation of revolutionary activists—fresh-faced civilian schoolteachers rather than hard-bitten veterans—could successfully propagate a radical *callista* or *cardenista* gospel. Here, therefore, the seeds of anticlericalism could sprout; or, changing the metaphor, the "anticlerical + agrarian" tandem could comfortably pedal downhill.

These collective/structural arguments should perhaps be complemented by an individual and cultural approach. After all, anticlericalism and its ideological enemies fought over ideational as well as material—or power-political—resources. Is it, then, possible to tease out common characteristics, to paint a thumbnail portrait of the Mexican anticlerical? The most obvious feature is that they were men. Of course, most known and named political activists (and all Catholic priests) were also men. But, in the main, anticlericals tended to be men, while women were more prominent in the Catholic cause: in Patience Schell's words, "put crudely, anticlericalism was a program developed by men and aimed at women and children."[97] A few female anticlericals have been identified and studied.[98] But they seem greatly outnumbered by the Catholic women of all classes who joined religious associations, signed petitions, demonstrated, and even rioted. Women regularly petitioned in favor of their priests and, of course, contributed mightily to Catholic boycotts of federal schools. Spine-tingling stories about children being taught by prostitutes or turned into soap and shipped to the Soviet Union were no doubt spread via market, church, or local water pump gossip.[99] In more militant mode, Catholic women volunteered to defend the Basilica of Guadalupe, stoned anticlerical municipal presidents, ripped down anticlerical flyers, and obscenely insulted "socialist" teachers.[100]

We can see glimpses of the sex imbalance in the bosom of the family. In several cases, anticlerical sons or husbands reckoned with Catholic mothers or wives. Cárdenas, who married into a conservative Catholic family, compared his mother—sincere devotee (*"devota sincera"*)—to his father, indifferent to the Church (*"indiferente a la iglesia"*).[101] Cosío Villegas had similar parentage.[102] Abelardo Rodríguez—no rabid *comecuras*, it is true—was devoted to his mother, a trusting believer (*"creyente y confiada"*).[103] And, while Manuel Avila Camacho was—as he famously proclaimed in 1940—a "believer," his wife went further in her stern Catholicism.[104] The list could easily be lengthened.[105]

Of course, this imbalance may partly reflect men's need to conform to the Revolution's prevailing public ethos: some "revolutionaries" were (borrowing a French tag) like radishes—"red" on the outside and "white" on the inside. But the examples are sufficiently numerous to suggest that the gendered bias of anticlericalism is no mere façade. Even if it was, it remains significant that men involved in official politics were debarred from overt displays of Catholicism, while their female relatives enjoyed greater latitude. The causes of the divide are hard to fathom and remain beyond the scope of this chapter: perhaps the most persuasive argument suggests that the Church provided women a public role denied them by the patriarchal state; links to the *cura* offered "prestige and a time-honoured social identity."[106] Whatever the causes, anticlericalism was a strongly male cause, inflected by macho sentiments. The image of the gullible woman, conned (maybe molested) by devious priests, was a commonplace, which even surfaced in the pornographic silent films of the 1920s.[107] Macho revolutionaries like Calles and Gabriel Gavira inveighed against addled-brained *beatas* (pious women), such as those who inhabited Jalisco, the "henhouse of the Republic."[108] Such rhetoric no doubt limited anticlericalism's appeal; and the assumptions behind it helped defer female suffrage for some 15 years.[109]

If the sex imbalance is a clear cut—even undeniable—feature of the religious conflict, it does not exhaust anticlericalism's psycho-cultural bases.

Enrique Krauze suggests, for example, that Calles's strident anticlericalism stemmed from his illegitimate birth, which left him aggrieved against the elites who—in the shape of his natural father—had spurned him and the Church that marked him with the stigma of bastardy.[110] Again, the argument is merely suggestive (though a little better than some psycho-historical speculations). There may be other individual and familial hypotheses worth scouting (such as Sulloway's birth-order thesis),[111] while some experts tell us that characteristics as profound as religiosity are, in some measure, "hard-wired" (taking them beyond the purview of historians).[112] These suggestions may seem unconvincing (I am not wholly convinced myself), but they at least proffer individual psycho-cultural explanations for what are, in many respects, individual psycho-cultural phenomena: namely, commitments to contrasting world views—Catholic, Protestant, liberal, atheistic—which cannot be read off from socioeconomic or geographical origins without severe risk of reductionism.

That said, collective cultural categories may also have explanatory power. Recalling Cobb's portrait of the "*bon sans-culotte révolutionnaire*," we can try to sketch the typical Mexican anticlerical;[113] or, less ambitiously, we can detect some loosely cultural characteristics, which can be combined with the historical and geographical attributes discussed. While ad hoc popular anticlericalism has a long history, the more systematic, doctrinaire anticlericalism of the modern period, which targeted the Church as an institution and Catholicism as an ideational system, tended to be a big-city or small-town affair and its chief protagonists were often professionals, white-collar workers, shopkeepers, artisans, and the like. Thus, in Zitácuaro, we find "schoolteachers, army officers, artisans, and religious ministers"; in Lagos de Moreno, "laborers or skilled craftsmen . . . bakers, cobblers, butchers, carpenters, blanket-weavers, small merchants, and mechanics."[114] Such men were disproportionately literate, read newspapers (particularly the Porfirian penny press), and belonged to mutualist societies, masonic lodges, and incipient political parties; they were classic practitioners of the new political sociability analyzed by Guerra and Forment.[115] In contrast, peasants and workers were probably under-represented. Of course, Catholic associations recruited similar sorts of men (and women) under a different banner. The argument is therefore two-fold: first, this group—loosely, an urban petty-bourgeoisie—was prone to ideological commitment and political association; second, commitment could take either a Catholic or self-consciously progressive, secular, anticlerical form.

Anticlericals formed part of a literate, enlightened "great tradition"; hence the allusions to Voltaire, Rousseau, Victor Hugo, and Henry George (but not, as far as I can see, Marx or Engels). Their kinship to Spanish Anarchism was occasionally reinforced by Spanish migrants;[116] but Mexico was not a major magnet of Spanish or Italian migration, hence kinship was less the product of direct diffusion than unwitting emulation. Why should this emulation occur? Mexico, as we all know, had a vigorous liberal tradition, which embodied a (usually moderate) anticlerical strain. But late-nineteenth-century popular liberalism easily mutated into radical forms that resembled—or even became—anarchism or anarcho-syndicalism (*magonismo* is the classic case. We could also posit a parallel evolution of elite liberalism into Porfirian and revolutionary positivism).[117] It is easy to see why libertarian variants of liberalism—which stressed individual rights and resistance to centralizing authority—should acquire anarchist traits. In a sense, the liberal-anarchist frontier was open and porous. And it is not difficult to see how the "order and progress" Díaz dictatorship should encourage this trend.[118] Regimes have a lot to do with the kind of opposition they provoke.

However, this does not explain why Catholicism was also targeted, especially since Porfirian Church-state détente never remotely threatened a confessional state. The parallel with Catholic Europe is again suggestive: anarchism flourished where the state was authoritarian (to a degree) and the Church—whether allied to the state or not—powerful. Liberal, jacobin, and anarchist assertions of individual rights of expression and association necessarily challenged the Church as well as the state. So it was in Mexico, especially, we might hypothesize, in communities where the Church was powerful and intrusive: in provincial towns and (some) cities, notably "*mocho*" cities where, it is worth noting, radicals and anticlericals had sometimes been educated in the seminary.[119] The phenomenon was less marked in many villages, where the *cura* was a transient visitor and where, perhaps, anticlericalism's socioeconomic bases—the professionals, white-collar workers, shopkeepers, and artisans—were less numerous and influential. Thus, it was in urban communities with (at least) a moderate division of labor, a degree of urban sociability, and a powerful Church presence that radical liberalism and anticlericalism could acquire critical mass. This may help explain why village based peasant movements—like *zapatismo*—were not notably anticlerical (still less were they clerical, of course). Yet new industrial communities were not noticeably anticlerical, either: the miners, railway men, and oil-workers in the vanguard of real proletarian organization did not, by and large, target the Church as a primary antagonist: sometimes because they were devout Catholics;[120] or because the Church had a feeble presence, as in Cananea, Santa Rosita, and El Ebano;[121] and finally, because mass industrial trade unionism was associated with ideological leanings different to those fostered by the small-group sociability of mutualism.

In the grander scheme of things, it is obvious that anticlericalism was a distinctive feature of *Catholic* countries (even those with nonconfessional states, such as Italy or France). Anticlericalism throve where a powerful clergy exerted political, social, and cultural power; it had much less appeal in Protestant societies where churches proliferated and competed (such as the United States), or where, as in England, the established Church had limited powers and ambitions (Wales would be rather different). We need to evoke some sense of the Mexican Church's pervasive, stultifying power (as anticlericals saw it): the constraints on free expression; the endless, lugubrious tolling of bells;[122] and the—often illegal—public displays of religiosity (processions, pilgrimages, shrines, roadside crosses, and rowdy fiestas).[123] Such phenomena offended liberal and anticlerical sentiments irrespective of the Church's overt political role—its alleged connivance with presidents, governors, *caciques*, municipal presidents, landlords, or factory owners. In other words, before and apart from the political stimuli that prompted renewed Church-state conflict after 1913, there were underlying causes—latent tensions, "ideational proclivities"—which made such a conflict possible. A concentrated, vocal minority had come to consider the Church and Catholicism as noxious influences holding back the development of country and community. Some sought a modest reaffirmation of *juarista* liberal anticlericalism; some flirted with religious heterodoxy; a good many opted for a full-blown radical anticlericalism. Such dissent did not fuel the 1910 Revolution, which obeyed different—political, agrarian—causes. But Huerta's coup helped turn powerful underlying sentiments into effective action.

Mass Politics

But there was a second set of structural circumstances, which I term those of "mass politics." Again, there are obvious parallels with Europe and the rest of Latin America, especially the southern cone. While it would be wrong to regard the "entry of the masses on to the political stage" as a choreographed procedure, following a clear linear script, nevertheless the later nineteenth and early twentieth century did witness the growth of mass electorates and mass organizations. Hence, in part, the "social question" and the Church's belated engagement with mass politics after *Rerum Novarum*.[124] The entry—better, the reentry—of Mexico's masses on to the stage was delayed by the *Pax Porfiriana*, when parties scarcely existed, unions were incipient, and politics was the preserve of elite camarillas. The Revolution therefore signaled a sudden, violent, and chaotic breakthrough to mass politics (we could compare Chile and Argentina's more gradual and peaceful transitions). It posed the "social question" in its starkest form: how would newly mobilized workers, peasants, and the (expanding) middle class be accommodated within a new political system and, more broadly, a new set of social relationships? The infant revolutionary state faced both a challenge and an opportunity: it needed to cultivate mass support (which presidents and regional *caudillos* did with unprecedented effort) and to confront rival institutions that competed for mass support. Calles yearned to be "master in his own house"; and Morones was determined to break working-class organizations that rivaled the CROM.[125] In any Catholic country, such a battle for hearts and minds necessarily involved the Church, whose commitment to mass politics had burgeoned since the 1890s. Hence, the formation of Catholic parties, trade unions, and other lay associations; and the ensuing clashes between Church and state, each now possessed of politically mobilized masses. Usually the Church was at pains to avoid outright confrontation with the state: Rome flirted with Italian fascism in the 1920s and German National Socialism in the 1930s. Occasionally, the Church threw in its lot with fascist counterrevolution: with Franco and Salazar in the 1930s. Contemporaries rightly drew parallels between the Spanish Civil War and the sociopolitical conflicts—including Church-state conflict—which affected the Cárdenas presidency and which seemed to threaten renewed civil war in Mexico, too.

In the most basic sense, therefore, the "massification" of politics, in a predominantly Catholic country like Mexico, was bound to generate conflict. But that conflict was aggravated by the Revolution's social tensions. As noted, the Church was bound up with the Porfirian social order: and, though the Church contained progressives who called for reform, there were probably more conservatives who admired the stability of the Porfiriato and lamented its fall (hence the warm reception for Huerta). Thereafter, the Church's conservative inclinations tended to prevail, not least because the regime was strongly anticlerical and its reforms—educational reform particularly—were infused with anticlericalism. In theory, progressive Catholics could have endorsed reforms that did not threaten the Church: the *ejido*, for example, was hardly inherently irreligious and could even claim colonial origins, which might have appealed to Catholic corporatist predilections. But, besides challenging private property, the *ejido* carried on its coattails the federal (and, after 1934, *socialist*) school. It was a package deal and most political Catholics condemned the whole package, even if tens of thousands of Catholics accepted ejidal grants, joined official trade unions, and sent their children to federal schools.[126]

Catholic condemnation and resistance therefore spanned the whole period of revolutionary reform. The nature of resistance was conditioned by state policy. The Church was not purely reactive: lay militants, from the LNDLR to the UNS, entertained a radical, alternative vision of a hierarchical, corporatist, God-fearing Mexico—hence their sympathy for Franco after 1936. Like later Latin American authoritarians, they went beyond a negative antipathy to leftism to espouse a radical "foundational" vision.[127] But in pursuing these goals—or reacting to state initiatives, like the Calles law or "socialist" education—the Church had to adjust to the state's evolving project. This meant that there could be no Christian-Democratic party, as there was in Chile; and, by ruling out this option, the state made Catholic rebellion more likely and Catholic "movementism" virtually inevitable.[128] In addition, by defeating the *Cristiada*, the state showed that—almost certainly—it could not be overthrown by force. Thus, after 1930, when the anticlerical push resumed during the *Maximato*, Catholics had to rely primarily on the *via media* of social protest. That is, they could not mount a Falangist-style insurrection (unlike Franco, they had no army and the "second *Cristiada*" was a very limited phenomenon); nor were they allowed to organize as a democratic opposition (even when the PAN was founded in 1939, it was scarcely allowed democratic breathing space; though, we might add, the early PAN was by no means wholly democratic itself).[129] So, in confronting the "socialist" state, Catholics relied on "movements" (*sinarquismo*); on legal mass organizations of the laity (the UNPDF, ACJM, and Damas Católicas); on informal support and clientelist networks; and on sporadic violence conducted by highly decentralized local vigilantes and "bandits" (as the authorities usually called them).[130]

While the latter caused violence and mayhem, broadly peaceful protest had most success. The Catholic lay organizations of the 1930s were numerous, vocal, and effective. They could mount impressive demonstrations—in which women were prominent—and influence both opinion and action. The revolutionary regime spanned a spectrum from die-hard *comecuras* through liberal anticlericals to covert Catholics. We might surmise that this spectrum very roughly ran from top to bottom of the political hierarchy: thus, anticlerical militancy was probably strongest at the top, especially under Calles, while crypto-Catholicism prospered at the base and in the localities, especially in the center and center-west.[131] Plenty of local officials therefore declined to implement policy, or implemented it halfheartedly. Some were in the pockets of local Catholic elites, who ensured that the federal school was spurned and ejidal grants proceeded slowly if at all; some ensured that Catholics staffed federal schools.[132] Anticlerical schoolteachers complained incessantly of the authorities' indifference—or downright hostility—and of the clerical intimidation that obstructed their efforts.[133] *Agraristas*, too, faced clerical opposition. This was a familiar story in the 1920s, when *agrarismo* was relatively novel and faced an uphill struggle (for example, at Naranja).[134] Land reform was theft and *ejidatarios* little better than robbers; the *cristeros* strung up *agraristas* with bags of earth around their necks: "you want land, here it is."[135] But even after the tide turned and Cárdenas threw his weight behind agrarian reform, with decisive results, clerical and Catholic opposition continued.[136] As the figures show, the *reparto* forged ahead. But resistance was not entirely futile. It delayed reform in some cases, helped ensure a cosmetic reform in others, and most importantly contributed powerfully to a climate of opinion in which *ejidos*—especially "Communist" collective *ejidos*—were seen as failures and *ejidatarios* as parasites. Conversely, "smallholding" (*pequeña propiedad*) was placed on a pedestal, where it exemplified efficiency, social stability, and respect for the sacred rights of property.[137] After 1940, the pace of reform slackened; agrarian *amparos* flowed thick and fast; and the thrust of "socialist" education was blunted. Though Catholic mobilization had failed to overthrow the godless state, it resisted state reforms with some success, and helped ensure a kind of Thermidorian reaction after 1940.

If, in conclusion, we review the outcome of the Church-state conflict of the revolutionary period (1910–40), the honors are roughly divided. The state maintained its ban on confessional parties, thus ensuring that no formal Christian Democrat party could contest PNR/PRM/PRI hegemony. (It is valid to ask the counterfactual question whether the PAN would have won a free election before 2000. My view is that it would not; but the Revolutionary Party of National Unity [PRUN], which was a broader coalition, might well have won in 1940). The state also killed off Catholic trade unions, bolstering the dominant "PNR+CROM" and "PRM/PRI+CTM" axes. Thus, the state could enforce anticlerical vetoes. But the outcome of more positive measures—implementing reform, changing hearts and minds— is much more ambiguous. The state could affect property rights and labor relations, despite clerical opposition. The alliance of clergy and landlords—not uniform, certainly common—could resist but not prevent agrarian reform. It could, however, help ensure that the reform proceeded with a good deal of violence and that—for many—the *ejido* was tarnished by its painful and illegitimate birth. The state enjoyed least success when it sought to create the progressive, secular, scientific "new" Mexican envisioned in the 1930s socialist blueprints. Mass education expanded, but did not bring about a cultural revolution; and mass education continued to expand—under different political auspices—after 1940. The contentious 1940 election revealed deep fissures in the country, with the left on the defensive and the right, including the clerical right, seizing the initiative.

Thus, in the 1930s, as in the 1910s, popular anticlericalism remained patchy. There were a few instances of seemingly "bottom-up" anticlerical, antireligious displays: campaigns against Catholic fiestas, counter-demonstrations of secular jollity, popular songs and street theater that lampooned priests. But it is usually impossible to distinguish such phenomena from agrarian and labor activism. Anticlericalism was usually found where ejidal mobilization and labor militancy set the local tone, often coming in on the coattails of class and socioeconomic concerns. Hence Morelos was more tolerant of anticlericalism than Jalisco. *Ejidatarios* were more likely to welcome the federal *maestro* and to heed the "socialist" message, especially in those nascent "open" communities where school and *ejido* provided the bases of sociopolitical organization.[138] Some labor unions, too, retained something of the old anarchist anticlerical tradition long after socialism and communism supplanted anarchism; but their chief concerns, by the 1930s, were collective contracts, job security, pay and conditions, and, in some cases, workers' control of the shop floor. Communists and big industrial unions had little time for doctrinaire anticlericalism.[139] Meanwhile, anticlericalism itself had very short coattails: it is difficult to find grassroots examples of anticlericalism flourishing without the prior advantages of labor or agrarian mobilization. Unions and *ejidos* fostered and legitimized anticlericalism (as in Naranja), but anticlericalism rarely fostered or legitimized labor and agrarian reform.

There is a pattern to be discerned in this outcome. Interventionist states—by the 1930s meaning most European and several Latin American states—could readily meddle with property rights and labor relations. There were plenty of models to choose from—Soviet, socialist, fascist, corporate-capitalist—and, indeed, Mexican policymakers took a close interest in what was on offer. The character and success of such meddling had much to do with a country's political economy, class structure, and the state's relationship to civil society. Having experienced a genuine social revolution, Mexico possessed an ebullient, mobilized society, which the state strove to control and which often provided the momentum for social reform. Thus, agrarian reform was placed on the political agenda during the decade of armed revolution (the *zapatistas* may claim particular credit, but were not alone); and peasants struggled to make a reality of reform after 1917, even when state elites—like the *callistas* of the *Maximato*—had turned cool. Thus, agrarian reform depended a good deal on pressure from below. Though the urban working class was much smaller, its strategic position enabled it, too, to press for policies that would protect unions, improve workers' benefits, and give organized labor a real voice in the Mexican political system. Thus, both the agrarian and labor movements—crucial factors in postrevolutionary Mexico's development—responded a good deal to "bottom-up" pressure. The same is true of education, up to a point; but the specific commitment to "socialist" and anticlerical education, and to the broader goal of a progressive, secular, scientific society, was much more a minority interest. For a time, those minority groups enjoyed unusual prominence: they had access to the media and they could speak to mass audiences in unions (*sindicatos*) and schools. But their prominence lasted only a generation or so. By the 1940s, new elites with different ideas were coming to the fore: relatively conservative technocrats, more tolerant of the Church, more closely linked to business, friendlier to the United States, and fearful of international Communism. They saw no point in stirring up conflict with a Church whose views, on many issues, were not poles apart from their own (although they rarely said so in public).[140]

Thus, of the policies that made up the grand revolutionary "project," anticlericalism was one of the least successful. Putting it the other way round, of the Revolution's various victims, the Church eventually emerged relatively unscathed, at least compared to the Federal army (annihilated), the Porfirian political oligarchy (removed), the landlord class (transformed), and foreign oil interests (expropriated). Indeed, when we enter the postwar terrain of polling data, we find the Church high on the list of respected institutions (much higher than the agents of the revolutionary state: *políticos*, union leaders, and the execrated police).[141] Anticlericalism's comparative failure, in broad societal terms, and the Church's comparative success, paid tribute to the latter's deep roots and formidable powers. When it came to winning hearts and minds, the Church had a 300 year start on the Mexican state and a 400 year start on the Revolution. It possessed deep wells of support, especially in certain regions; and, compared to the patriarchal Revolution, could command the particular allegiance of women and, through them, the household. The Church also successfully combined traditional means of communication—schools, seminaries, sermons, pastorals, and encyclicals—with more modern media like newspapers, both provincial and national. Even the burgeoning film industry gave the Church pretty favorable coverage.

Underlying all this was an additional factor that, though obvious, is easily neglected. The state could pitch a material, this-worldly appeal: it could offer land to the peasant, wages to the worker, and literacy to the child. Needless to say, the state could also dangle incentives to those hankering after political power. That, however, could carry a social cost: ambitious *políticos* were not usually held in high esteem, while an apolitical Church, debarred from politics and dedicated to spiritual and pastoral tasks, appeared clean and disinterested in comparison. Hence the Church's high poll ratings. Finally, the Church had a competitive edge—at least vis-à-vis the state—in providing both otherworldly solace and supernatural assistance in this mundane vale of tears. When it came to the afterlife and other transcendental truths, the Church enjoyed a dominant position: its competition came, not from the secular state, but from an incipient Protestantism (not a serious and extensive challenge until the 1970s);[142] from a shapeless minority spiritualism; and, most important, from a range of popular magical and superstitious beliefs/ practices that lacked institutional bases and that, additionally, were heavily colored by Catholicism.[143] Thus, the Church enjoyed a near monopoly of institutional mediation between the natural and supernatural. In a time when the vicissitudes of life were severe—the upheaval of Revolution, the Spanish flu epidemic, the *Cristiada*, the Depression, the regular cycle of earthquakes, floods, and harvest failures[144]—and when the state had scant ability to cushion the shocks of war, disease, disaster, and recession, the Church and its saints offered both respite and hope: respite in this life (consider the *ex-votos* and *milagros* adorning Mexican churches) and hope of the life hereafter. It is not surprising that at Easter time the crestfallen *agraristas* of San Lucas Pío (Michoacán) slunk back to the parish church, begging forgiveness (which they were denied); or that an "iconoclast" who allegedly stole a crown from the patron saint of Tamazulapam (Oaxaca) should entreat the parish priest to baptize his newborn child.[145] The secular state could offer no such solace; at best, anticlericals tried to convince credulous Mexicans that religion's promises were false. Yet, confronted by crises, even radical anticlericals wavered in their secular and scientific beliefs: Calles might represent a "dour and utilitarian nationalism," but he still sought the assistance of the child-healer *el niño* Fidencio.[146] If the Revolution's great rationalist and *comecura*—with access to the best doctors in Mexico and the United States—flirted with the supernatural, it was hardly surprising that millions of Mexicans remained durably faithful. They might look to the state for land or labor reform or basic literacy, but those who sought transcendent goals or otherworldly solace had to look to the Church, or to its lesser spiritual rivals. Revolutionary ideology is sometimes termed a "secular religion"; and there is no doubt that the state sometimes plagiarized religious terms, imagery, and rituals.[147] But the analogy breaks down at a crucial point, since something that is secular cannot embody religion's transcendent and otherworldly quality.[148] That quality may be a myth, a hoax, or an intellectual narcotic, but so long as it exerts strong appeal—as it did and still does in Mexico—it guarantees the Church a comparative advantage over the state that the latter, for all its earthly powers, cannot overcome.

Notes

1. Jean Meyer, *La Cristiada* (3 vols. Mexico City: Siglo XXI, 1973–74), 2:193–4.
2. Ibid., 194, citing Vasconcelos.
3. Ramon Jrade, "Inquiries into the Cristero Insurrection against the Mexican Revolution," *Latin American Research Review* 20, no. 2 (1985): 53–69; Robert D. Shadow and María J. Rodríguez Shadow, "Religión, Economía y Política en la Rebelión Cristera: El Caso de los Gobiernistas de Villa Guerrero, Jalisco," *Historia Mexicana* 43, no. 4 (1994): 657–99. In reviewing

Matthew Butler, *Popular Piety and Political Identity in Mexico's Cristero Rebellion: Michoacán, 1927–29* (Oxford: OUP, 2004), Meyer has penned a reasoned and useful reevaluation of his position: *Historia Mexicana* 54, no. 4 (2005): 1242–9.

4. Marjorie Becker, *Setting the Virgin On Fire: Lázaro Cárdenas, Michoacán Campesinos, and the Redemption of the Mexican Revolution* (Berkeley: University of California Press, 1995).

5. Indeed, the whole "myth of the Revolution" (proclaiming a popular, progressive, democratic, majoritarian, nation-wide revolution) has been systematically dismantled. However, since revisionists have failed to establish a convincing, positive alternative (there may not be one), we now inhabit a "postrevisionist" historiographical universe that is more "nuanced," diverse, and subject to debate: see Ben Fallaw, *Cárdenas Compromised. The Failure of Reform in Postrevolutionary Yucatán* (Durham: Duke University Press, 2001), 1–2.

6. As early as 1932, Carleton Beals argued that anticlericalism reflected the government's "desire to throw dust in the eyes of its supporters, to blind them so that they could not see the failure of its most legitimate promises"; in Chihuahua, we read, "like Calles, [Governor] Quevedo substituted rabid anticlericalism for other reforms": Beals, quoted by Hugh G. Campbell, *La Derecha Radical en México, 1929–49* (Mexico City: SepSetentas, 1976), 27; Mark Wasserman, *Persistent Oligarchs. Elites and Politics in Chihuahua, Mexico, 1910–1940* (Durham: Duke University Press, 1993), 58.

7. This sentence conflates at least two mega-questions. First, I assume that it is theoretically—occasionally practically—possible to distinguish a genuine belief from an expedient rationalization; second, I follow what is quite common practice in slicing up the great maremagnum of human activity into, roughly, the economic, the power-political, and the cultural (or ideational). I make no great explanatory claims for this tripartite categorization: it is simply a way of ordering history's huge complexity (cf. W. G. Runciman, *The Social Animal* [London: HarperCollins, 1998], 114, which defines "three forms of power," corresponding to the "modes of production, persuasion, and coercion"). Thus, an anticlerical might attack the Church 1) in pursuit of an ejidal grant; 2) in order to advance a political faction; and/or 3) out of a genuine belief in the evils of Catholicism. Jennie Purnell, in her excellent study of the *Cristiada*, takes me to task for differentiating "economic" and "cultural": "nor does it make much sense to talk about cultural versus economic grievances . . . because these were so thoroughly interwoven in the symbolic and institutional life of many rural communities": Jennie Purnell, *Popular Movements and State Formation in Revolutionary Mexico: The Agraristas and Cristeros of Michoacán* (Durham: Duke University Press, 1999), 220n45. The practical fact of "interweaving" is true; but cannot stand in the way of analytical disaggregation, without which explanation becomes almost impossible (note that Purnell distinguishes "symbolic and institutional," which, though clearly interwoven in practice, here receive different analytical labels). The key question is whether the labels are useful, whether the disaggregation works. Purnell's lucid resumé of community allegiances (70–1) blends what I call economic, political, and cultural factors: in Zacapu, *agraristas* "embraced revolutionary anticlericalism . . . with enthusiasm," recovering land and "defeat[ing] personal and political enemies"; Zacán, in partial contrast, lobbied for land, "while keeping the state at arm's length"; and San José de Gracia, in complete contrast, rejected agrarianism, anticlericalism, and

"the consolidation of the new state," while defending the status quo in respect of "property rights, religious practice, and political authority" (note the familiar triad—which also appears in the title of Shadow and Rodríguez Shadow's article).

8. That is, Catholics whose political stance was strongly determined and colored by religion; plenty of politically active Mexicans were Catholics, but not necessarily *political* Catholics. The distinction is, of course, one of degree and, in some cases, may be difficult to draw; but it remains important.

9. Meyer, *La Cristiada*, 2:9–16; William B. Taylor, *Magistrates of the Sacred. Priests and Parishioners in Eighteenth-Century Mexico* (Stanford: Stanford University Press, 1996), 13–26.

10. Taylor, *Magistrates*, 48–51; Butler, *Popular Piety*, 23–6.

11. Following the Crown's expulsion of the Jesuits.

12. Taylor, *Magistrates*, 449–73, 491–501.

13. On the grounds 1) that the phenomenon of popular colonial anticlericalism was insignificant (which seems unconvincing); 2) that the documentary record is inadequate (likewise); and 3) that, even if arguments 1) and 2) are rejected or qualified, it is impossible to establish links across the dark abyss of the early nineteenth century (more plausible). For stimulating evidence that all three claims are exaggerated, see Terry Rugely, *Of Wonders and Wise Men. Religion and Popular Cultures in Southeast Mexico, 1800–1876* (Austin: University of Texas Press, 2001), which finds plenty of examples of popular religious dissidence: "some men hated priests," "ostensible impiety," "unorthodox ideological adaptations," and "a stubborn streak of anticlericalism" (83, 138, 169, 170). Yucatán is not Mexico; but Butler, *Popular Piety*, 20, also discerns a "precocious anticlericalism" in colonial lowland Michoacán.

14. Abundant examples in Taylor, *Magistrates*, especially chs. 14 and 17; see also Eric Van Young, *The Other Rebellion. Popular Violence, Ideology, and the Mexican Struggle for Independence, 1810–1821* (Stanford: Stanford University Press, 2001), 213–18, 227–8.

15. Taylor, *Magistrates*, 367; also 247, 331, 337, 352, 447, 506–7; Van Young, *Other Rebellion*, 206–7, 228–30; Rugely, *Of Wonders and Wise Men*, 42–7.

16. Charlote M. Gradie, *The Tepehuan Revolt of 1616* (Salt Lake City: University of Utah Press, 2000), 148–72; Andrew L. Knauth, *The Pueblo Revolt of 1680* (Norman: University of Oklahoma Press, 1995); Kevin Gosner, *Soldiers of the Virgin. The Moral Economy of a Colonial Maya Rebellion* (Tucson: University of Arizona Press, 1992) chs. 5 and 6.

17. The primary/secondary distinction derives (I believe) from African studies and differentiates between initial, "outright," root-and-branch resistance to colonial rule and subsequent resistance, which followed "initial acceptance" and involved some engagement with European ideas and institutions: Basil Davidson, *Africa in Modern History* (Harmondsworth: Penguin, 1978), 150–1.

18. Gradie, *Tepehuan Revolt*, 150; Gosner, *Soldiers of the Virgin*, 116–46.

19. William B. Taylor, *Drinking, Homicide, and Rebellion in Colonial Mexican Villages* (Stanford: Stanford University Press, 1979), ch. 4.

20. Taylor, *Magistrates*, 7, 19, 68; also Fernando Cervantes, *The Devil in the New World. The Impact of Diabolism in New Spain* (New Haven: Yale University Press, 1994), 50.

21. Carlo Ginzburg, *The Cheese and the Worms. The Cosmos of a Sixteenth-Century Miller* (Harmondsworth: Penguin, 1982).

22. Cervantes, *Devil in the New World*, 79 (a mulatto slave, 1650, explicitly "deny[ing] God and his saints"), 83–4 (another mulatto, 1614, declaring: "I do not believe there is a God in heaven"); see also 88. These examples derive from cases of alleged diabolism; but, as the author states, 89, "as a rule self-assertive diabolism was markedly irreligious," being concerned with mundane affairs: wealth, power, sex, and good times. Thus, in a pre-Enlightenment society, where the natural/supernatural distinction was lacking, irreligion (or "unbelief") assumed ostensibly diabolistic—rather than explicitly secular—forms (see note 24). The relative absence of Indians reflects the limitations of the (Inquisition) sources; but, Cervantes plausibly suggests, diabolistic irreligion may have appealed chiefly to mobile, "self-centred," *macho* individuals who had no place in the corporate, "community-oriented" religious structures of Indian villages. Here, we find a distant parallel with—or precursor of—modern anticlericalism (see below). On the association of *machismo* and "ostensible impiety," see Rugely, *Of Wonders and Wise Men*, 83, and John M. Ingham, *Mary, Michael and Lucifer. Folk Catholicism in Central Mexico* (Austin: University of Texas Press, 1986) 139–40ff.

23. Taylor, *Magistrates*, 413–14, gives eighteenth-century examples, including the mayor of Autlán (Jalisco), denying transubstantiation and declaring that "there was no God other than money"; Bernardo de Gálvez, gaoled in Oaxaca during the insurgency, was scatologically explicit: "God and the Virgin Mary and all the saints were pricks": Van Young, *The Other Rebellion*, 315.

24. The risk of using the "Rabelaisian" tag—to denote an earthy, mundane, popular skepticism—is that Lucien Febvre took Rabelais to exemplify the argument that early-modern Europeans were conceptually incapable of atheism (an argument that clearly has relevance for colonial and perhaps also postcolonial Mexico): Lucien Febvre, *The Problem of Unbelief in the Sixteenth Century: The Religion of Rabelais* (Cambridge: Harvard University Press, 1982). As David Wootton, "Lucien Febvre and the Problem of Unbelief in the Early Modern Period," *Journal of Modern History* 69, no. 4 (1988): 695–730, lucidly explains, Febvre's work and terminology raise complex questions, the subject of continued debate; the conclusion that I—as an interested bystander—draw from this lively exchange is that forms of disbelief clearly existed in Rabelais's time (therefore simple denials of disbelief are unconvincing: note Ginzburg, *The Cheese and the Worms*, xxiii); but disbelief could not assume a thorough-going secularist form until science, rationalism, and Enlightenment values made such a distinction possible. And, if we pursue the European analogy, we can see that later Mexican generations could likewise draw on science, rationalism, and Enlightenment values in order to bolster a root-and-branch secularist anticlericalism that was conceptually denied their colonial ancestors, just as it had been denied Rabelais.

25. Alan Knight, *Mexico: The Colonial Era* (Cambridge: Cambridge University Press, 2002), 241–2.

26. Peter Guardino, *Peasants, Politics and the Formation of Mexico's National State: Guerrero, 1800–1857* (Stanford: Stanford University Press, 1996); Peter Guardino, *The Time of Liberty. Popular Political Culture in Oaxaca, 1750–1850* (Durham: Duke University Press, 2005).

27. David I. Kertzer, "Religion and Society, 1789–1892," in *Italy in the Nineteenth Century*, ed. John A. Davis (Oxford: Oxford University Press, 2000), 192.

28. Richard N. Sinkin, *The Mexican Reform, 1856–76. A Study in Liberal Nation-Building* (Austin: University of Texas Press, 1979), 73.

29. Pamela Voekel, *Alone Before God. The Religious Origins of Modernity in Mexico* (Durham: Duke University Press, 2002), 169; and, more boldly, Pamela Voekel, "Liberal Religion: The Schism of 1861," paper presented at the American Historical Association Congress, Seattle, Jan. 2004.

30. Meyer, *La Cristiada*, 2:43–53; Purnell, *Popular Movements*, 92–5; Manuel Ceballos Ramírez, *El Catolicismo Social: Un Tercero en Discordia. Rerum Novarum, la "Cuestión Social," y la Movilización de los Católicos Mexicanos (1891–1911)* (Mexico City: El Colegio de México, 1991); for comparative purposes, *The Politics of Religion in an Age of Revival. Studies in Nineteenth-Century Europe and Latin America*, ed. Austen Ivereigh (London: ILAS, 2000).

31. Luis González y González, *Pueblo en Vilo. Microhistoria de San José de Gracia* (Mexico City: El Colegio de México, 1972), part 1; also Butler, *Popular Piety*, 92.

32. Daniel Cosío Villegas, *Historia Moderna de México. El Porfiriato. La Vida Política Interior* (Mexico City: Hermes, 1972), 2:688.

33. Jean-Pierre Bastian, "El Paradigma de 1789. Sociedades de Ideas y Revolución Mexicana," *Historia Mexicana* 38, no. 1 (1988): 99–100.

34. On the Velardeña (Durango) incident—when an official banned a religious procession, provoking a riot that led to 15 deaths—see Rodney D. Anderson, *Outcasts in Their Own Land. Mexican Industrial Workers, 1906–1911* (DeKalb: Northern Illinois Universty Press, 1976), 227.

35. Alan Knight, *The Mexican Revolution* (2 vols. Cambridge: Cambridge University Press, 1986), 1:398–404.

36. J. Womack Jr., *Zapata and the Mexican Revolution* (New York: Vintage, 1970), 396.

37. Knight, *Mexican Revolution*, 2:206–8; Purnell, *Popular Movements*, 57–8.

38. Matthew A. Redinger, *American Catholics and the Mexican Revolution, 1924–36* (Notre Dame: University of Notre Dame Press, 2005), 36–8, 48–52.

39. While neither anticlericalism nor agrarianism were planks of the *maderista* platform and began as scattered, decentralized phenomena, which only later became officialized and centralized, they differed in important respects, particularly the contrasting balance between "top-down" and "bottom-up" inputs. In crudely schematic terms, anticlericalism was (initially) decentralized but "elitist" (a minority concern), while agrarianism was decentralized but popular.

40. For example, following the 1929 *arreglos* there was a two-year diminution of Church-state conflict; but after 1931 anticlericalism revived, both federally and in several states. Within states gubernatorial changes also produced marked swings in policy: see, for example, Ben Fallaw, "Accommodation or Acrimony? Church and State in Revolutionary and Postrevolutionary Yucatán, 1926–40," paper given at the Congreso Internacional Iglesia y Estado en América Latina, Mérida, Mexico, Apr. 2000.

41. Jean Meyer, *The Cristero Rebellion: The Mexican Pople Between Church and State, 1926–29* (Cambridge: Cambridge University Press, 1976), 44, quoting

Calles to the French diplomat Ernest Lagarde; on Calles's positivistic fondness for statistics, see Luis Javier Garrido, *El Partido de la Revolución Institucionalizada. La Formación del Nuevo Estado en México (1928–1945)* (Mexico City: SEP, 1986), 193.

42. Adrian Bantjes, *As If Jesus Walked on Earth. Cardenismo, Sonora and the Mexican Revolution* (Wilmington: SR, 1998), 6–15; Carlos Martínez Assad, *El Laboratorio de la Revolución. El Tabasco Garridista* (Mexico City: Siglo XXI, 1979), 36–48.

43. Roberto Blancarte, *Historia de la Iglesia en México* (Mexico City: El Colegio de México, 1992), 63ff.

44. The scene was captured in jerky film footage shown at the Museo Nacional de Arte exhibition, Los Pinceles de la Historia, III, Sep. 2003–Feb. 2004. Two frames can be seen in *Los Pinceles de la Historia: La Arqueología del Régimen, 1910–1955*, ed. Jaime Soler Frost (Mexico City: Munart, 2003), 40–1.

45. Knight, *Mexican Revolution*, 1:402–4.

46. Ibid., 405–16.

47. Purnell, *Popular Movements*, 55; Butler, *Popular Piety*, 48.

48. David Hackett Fischer, *Historians' Fallacies. Towards a Logic of Historical Thought* (New York: Harper and Row, 1970), 166–7.

49. I have elsewhere discussed *huertismo*'s "counter-factual" significance: Alan Knight, "The Mexican Revolution: Five Counterfactuals," in *El Siglo de la Revolución Mexicana*, ed. Jaime Bailón Corres, Carlos Martínez Assad, and Pablo Serrano Alvarez (2 vols. Mexico City: INEHRM, 2000), 1:46–9.

50. Knight, *Mexican Revolution*, 1:391–2, 451–4; 2:102, 104.

51. Héctor Aguilar Camín, *La Frontera Nómada. Sonora y la Revolución Mexicana* (Mexico City: Siglo XXI, 1985), chs. 7, 8.

52. Knight, *Mexican Revolution*, 2:1–2; on the Catholic press's endorsement of Huerta, see Robert E. Quirk, *The Mexican Revolution and the Catholic Church, 1910–29* (Bloomington: Indiana University Press, 1973), 37; and, regarding the quasi-official dedication of Mexico to the Sacred Heart of Jesus in Jan. 1914, Alicia Olivera Sedano, *Aspectos del Conflicto Religioso de 1926 a 1929* (Mexico City: INAH, 1966), 53–5. Michael C. Meyer, *Huerta: A Political Portrait* (Lincoln: University of Nebraska Press, 1972), 167–9, reviews the relationship, seeking to exonerate Huerta.

53. Knight, *Mexican Revolution*, 2:77, 203, 543n500, dates the end of the PCN's dalliance with Huerta to late 1913 (and it was Huerta who broke off the relationship). Also see Jorge Adame Goddard, *El Pensamiento Político y Social de los Católicos Mexicanos, 1867–1914* (Mexico City: UNAM, 1981), 180–2.

54. Notably those of Joseph Ledit, *Le Front des Pauvres* (Montréal: Fides, 1954) which, on the basis of Catholic interviews conducted in Mexico in the 1940s–1950s, asserts, 25–6, that the "revolutionary orgy" merely used allegations of Catholic support for Huerta as an excuse; that Huerta was innocent of Madero's murder; and that, at the very least, Huerta was "not as bad as Venustiano Carranza, who overcame him, thanks to an American intervention." Worthless as history, this viewpoint captures what some (probably well-to-do) Catholics thought 35 years later.

55. Meyer, *La Cristiada*, 2:48–53; Ceballos Ramírez, *Catolicismo Social*; Adame Goddard, *Pensamiento Político*, 125ff.

56. Thus, Butler, *Popular Piety*, 76–7, notes a crucial "historical association between the Church and the local elites" in "highly clericalized" Maravatío

and Zinapécuaro in Michoacán; for the same state, see Becker, *Setting the Virgin On Fire*, 24, 38; and John Gledhill, *Casi Nada. A Study of Agrarian Reform in the Homeland of Cardenismo* (Albany: Institute for Mesoamerican Studies, SUNY, 1991), 80–1, 91–2, which discerns an increasingly "organic link between the Church and the landed oligarchy" in the Porfirian Ciénega de Chapala, such that "the Church succeeded in serving agrarian capitalism while conserving much of its social power among the lower classes." Clearly, Michoacán is not typical of Mexico; but as a *Cristiada* heartland it is a crucial case; and similar arguments could be advanced, *mutatis mutandis*, for other Mexican regions.

57. On the revolutionary threat and clerical/landlord collusion: Butler, *Popular Piety*, 58, 62; Purnell, *Popular Movements*, 70–1, 128; and more broadly, Ernest Gruening, *Mexico and its Heritage* (London: Stanley Paul, 1928), 217–19.

58. Knight, *Mexican Revolution*, 2:1–2, 59, 65, 77.

59. Redinger, *American Catholics*, 23, 35–6, 50–1, 203n33; David C. Bailey, *¡Viva Cristo Rey! The Cristero Rebellion and the Church-State Conflict in Mexico* (Austin: University of Texas Press, 1974).

60. Bastian, "El Paradigma"; François-Xavier Guerra, *Le Mexique: de l'Ancien Régime à la Révolution* (2 vols. Paris: L'Harmattan, 1985), vol. 1, chap. 7.

61. Victoria Lerner, *La Educación Socialista* (Mexico City: El Colegio de México, 1979), 82.

62. Alan Knight, "Popular Culture and the Revolutionary State in Mexico, 1910–40," *Hispanic American Historical Review* 74, no. 3 (1994): 419.

63. Catholic activists readily took advantage of new mass media: see Patience A. Schell, *Church and State Education in Revolutionary Mexico City* (Tucson: University of Arizona Press, 2003), 156–7 (film); Christopher R. Boyer, *Becoming Campesinos. Poltics, Identity and Agrarian Struggle in Postrevolutionary Michoacán, 1920–35* (Stanford: Stanford University Press, 2003), 160 (newspapers, flyers); Edward Wright-Rios, "Re-Visions of Oaxacan Catholicism: Indian Women, Revelation, and the Negotiation of Belief and Practice, 1911–34," paper given at the American Historical Association Congress, Seattle, Jan. 2004, 26 ("pilgrimage advertising").

64. The argument involves a distinction between technology (practical means that Catholics were as prepared to use as anticlericals) and science (a distinctive world-view, potentially hostile to revealed religion). See Lewis Wolpert, *The Unnatural Nature of Science* (Cambridge: Harvard University Press, 1998), ch. 2.

65. Knight, "Popular Culture," 419. For a good example of the rhetorical concatenation of evolution, science, and revolution, note the speech made by the one-eyed radical firebrand Herón Proal, apropos of an eclipse of the sun, during the Veracruz tenants' strike of 1923: Andrew Grant Wood, *Revolution in the Street. Women, Workers and Urban Protest in Veracrtuz, 1870–1927* (Wilmington: SR, 2001), 169.

66. Martínez Assad, *El Laboratorio*, 47–8; Bantjes, *As If Jesus Walked on Earth*, 12–15; Knight, "Popular Culture," 408–9.

67. Daniels to State Department, Mexico City, 5 Nov. 1934, State Dept. Records (series M1370), 812.42/303.

68. Becker, *Setting the Virgin On Fire*, 139–40, raises the interesting case of Jarácuaro, an island community in Lake Pátzcuaro, where, in 1937, the

doctor temporarily closed the church in order—he said—to prevent the spread of contagious disease. Becker interprets this as aggressive official anticlericalism, part of a *cardenista* "assault" on local "material and spiritual life." While this may be true of officials such as Erongaricuaro's municipal president, here the doctor's action was a seemingly legitimate public health measure. In other words (no historiographical revelation) different constructions can be put upon events, as the documents describe them. The correspondence is in Archivo General de la Nación, Ramo Presidentes, Lázaro Cárdenas, 547.4/133 (Becker found the same material in a different *legajo*, 547.4/257, and dates the affair to 1936, whereas the correspondence I have seen relates to 1937).

69. Knight, *Mexican Revolution*, 2:524–6.
70. I derive this checklist from Jonathan I. Israel, *Radical Enlightenment. Philosophy and the Making of Modernity 1650–1750* (Oxford: Oxford University Press, 2001), 4, 6, 12, 14.
71. E.g., Cárdenas's liberal-patriotic schoolmaster, Jesús Fajardo: Lázaro Cárdenas, *Obras. I—Apuntes 1913–1940* (Mexico City: UNAM, 1986), 5.
72. Meyer, *La Cristiada*; Pablo Serrano Alvarez, *La Batalla del Espíritu: El Movimiento Sinarquista en el Bajío* (2 vols. Mexico City: Conaculta, 1992); Kristina Boylan, "Mexican Catholic Women's Activism, 1929–40" (D. Phil. diss., Oxford University, 2000).
73. Mary Kay Vaughan, *Cultural Politics in Revolution. Teachers, Peasants and Schools in Mexico, 1930–40* (Tucson: University of Arizona Press, 1997), 35, 67; Salvador Camacho Sandoval, *Controversia Educativa entre la Ideología y la Fe. La Educación Socialista en Aguascalientes* (Mexico City: Conaculta, 1991), 186. Some local *políticos* espoused anticlericalism partly to ingratiate themselves with Calles, hence political expedience sometimes played a role: e.g., Butler, *Popular Piety*, 73–4, and Benjamin Thomas Smith, "Anticlericalism and Resistance: The Diocese of Huajuapam de León, 1930–1940," *Journal of Latin American Studies* 37, no. 3 (2005): 484, regarding Oaxaca's *callista* governor, Francisco López Cortés. However, this could be a risky tactic, since the sympathies of "the centre" were mutable, whereas local (Catholic) opinion tended to be enduring. In short, the political expedience argument has rather limited application.
74. Knight, *Mexican Revolution*, 2:9 (Huerta's catchphrase). A strong historiographical consensus stresses Calles's personal obduracy: Meyer, *The Cristero Rebellion*, 43–4 ("profound hostility towards religious practices"); Redinger, *American Catholics*, 32, on Calles's continued "visceral hatred" of the Church while in exile.
75. Butler, *Popular Piety*, 72, 87; Knight, "Popular Culture," 420–1; Vaughan, *Cultural Politics*, 73, 123; Shadow and Rodríguez Shadow, "Religión, Economía y Política," 676. Meyer also notes the case of Joaquín Amaro, a onetime jacobin who, as his political fortunes fell, returned to the Church: compare Purnell, *Popular Movements*, 58, and Meyer, *La Cristiada*, 2:200.
76. Bastian, "El Paradigma," 81, 104–5; Butler, *Popular Piety*, 68, 98–9; Bastian and Brewster in this volume.
77. Serge Gruzinski, *Man-Gods in the Mexican Highlands: Indian Power and Colonial Society, 1520–1800* (Stanford: Stanford University Press, 1989); Van Young, *The Other Rebellion*, 453–94.

78. Paul Vanderwood, *The Power of God Against the Guns of Government. Religious Upheaval in Mexico at the Turn of the Nineteenth Century* (Stanford: Stanford University Press, 1998); Alan Knight, "Rethinking the Tomóchic Rebellion," *Mexican Studies/Estudios Mexicanos* 15, no. 2 (1999), 373–93.

79. Meyer, *Cristero Rebellion*, 24. Butler, *Popular Piety*, 71–2, 99.

80. Gordon Marshall, *In Search of the Spirit of Capitalism. An Essay on Max Weber's Protestant Ethic Thesis* (London: Hutchinson, 1982), for theoretical problems.

81. Alex Saragoza, *The Monterrey Elite and the Mexican State, 1880–1940* (Austin: University of Texas Press, 1988); Soledad Loaeza, *El Partido Acción Nacional: La Larga Marcha, 1939–1994* (Mexico City: FCE, 1999), 98–9, 152–3; Donald J. Mabry, *Mexico's Acción Nacional. A Catholic Alternative to Revolution* (Syracuse: Syracuse University Press, 1973), 31, 36.

82. Alicia Gómez, "Una Burguesía en Ciernes," in *Jalisco desde la Revolución: Movimientos Sociales, 1929–40*, ed. Laura Patricia Romero (Guadalajara: Gobierno del Estado de Jalisco, 1988), 27–72; Wil Pansters, *Politics and Power in Puebla: The Political History of a Mexican State, 1937–87* (Amsterdam: CEDLA, 1990).

83. Knight, *Mexican Revolution*, 2:239, 241, 244, 246.

84. Knight, "Rethinking the Tomóchic Rebelion," 388–91.

85. Butler, *Popular Piety*, 66–75, 95–103; likewise Purnell, *Popular Movements*, ch. 5. Such contrasts were often associated with dyadic rivalries between neighboring communities, such as San José de Gracia/Mazamitla, or Totatiche/Villa Guerrero: González, *Pueblo en Vilo*, 44, 73, 109; Shadow and Rodríguez Shadow, "Religión, Economía y Política."

86. Purnell, *Popular Movements*, stresses the historical traditions of communities. Butler, *Popular Piety*, 68–9, 138–42; González, *Pueblo en Vilo*, 87, and Rugely, *Of Wonders and Wise Men*, 42, 236, highlight the role of key individuals (*curas* and *maestros* in particular).

87. For the south, see Rugely, *Of Wonders and Wise Men*.

88. Daniel Cosío Villegas, *Memorias* (Mexico City: Joaquín Mortiz, 1976), 13, 21. For a literary invocation of a yet more closed, conservative Catholic community (presumably based on the author's home town of Yahualica), Agustín Yáñez, *Al Filo del Agua* (1947, Mexico City: Porrúa, 1986).

89. E.g., Taylor, *Magistrates*, 107–9.

90. Butler, *Popular Piety*, 107.

91. The tandem metaphor appears in Knight, "Revolutionary Project," 427 and is creatively developed by Smith, "Anticlericalism and Resistance," 501.

92. This may be a risky *ex silentio* argument. More cautiously: my understanding of Morelos and *zapatismo*, derived from Womack, *Zapata*, Samuel Brunk, *Emiliano Zapata! Revolution and Betrayal in Mexico* (Albuquerque: University of New Mexico Press, 1995), 68–9, and other trustworthy sources, strongly suggests that anticlericalism was not a major issue during the Revolution, or even during the 1920s (admittedly, less thoroughly researched). Robert Redfield, conducting fieldwork in Tepoztlán as the *cristero* rebellion broke out, talks about folk religion (*Tepoztlan. A Mexican Village* [Chicago: University of Chicago Press, 1930], ch. 11), but makes virtually no mention of anticlericalism or Church-state conflict (215 contains a passing reference).

93. Keith Brewster, *Militarism, Ethnicity and Politics in the Sierra Norte de Puebla, 1917–1930* (Tucson: University of Arizona Press, 2003).

94. Barry Carr, *Marxism and Communism in Twentieth-Century Mexico* (Lincoln: University of Nebraska Press, 1992), 82–105; Vaughan, *Cultural Politics*, ch. 7; Robert Redfield to Margaret Park Redfield, 24 Jan. 1930, Redfield Papers, University of Chicago Library, Box 1, f. 10. The teacher was anthropologist-to-be Alfonso Villa Rojas.

95. Vaughan, *Cultural Politics*, 177.

96. Ibid., 177; also Butler, *Popular Piety*, 97. Shadow and Rodríguez Shadow, "Religión, Economía y Política," 662, note that the more liberal, revolutionary, and anticlerical communities of Villa Guerrero and Cañadas were "relatively young," while Villa Guerrero's *cristero* enemy, Totatiche, was an ancient settlement (here, questions of landownership and political hierarchy also contributed to the outcome). Of course, this is only a rule-of-thumb: recently established communities could, given successful clerical involvement, become "*mocho*," just as older *pueblos* might espouse liberal/revolutionary causes: e.g., San José de Gracia/Mazamitla: González, *Pueblo en Vilo*, 4, 73, 109.

97. Schell, *Church and State Education*, 181.

98. Jocelyn Olcott, *Revolutionary Women in Postrevolutionary Mexico* (Durham: Duke University Press, 2005); Stephanie Bryant Mitchell, "'La Noble Mujer Organizada': The Women's Movement in Mexico, 1930–40" (D. Phil. diss., Oxford University, 2002).

99. Camacho Sandoval, *Controversia Educativa*, 151.

100. Meyer, *Cristero Rebellion*, 36; Purnell, *Popular Movements*, 75–7; Knight, "Revolutionary Project," 422; also Stephen E. Lewis, *The Ambivalent Revolution. Forging State and Nation in Chiapas, 1910–1945* (Albuquerque: University of New Mexico Press, 2005), 72, and Moisés Sáenz, *Carapán. Bosquejo de una Experiencia* (Lima: Librería Gil, 1936), 48–9. I have come across many similar cases in my current research into the politics of *cardenismo*.

101. Cárdenas, *Obras. I—Apuntes*, 5.

102. Cosío Villegas, *Memorias*, 21.

103. Francisco Javier Gaxiola, *El Presidente Rodríguez (1932–34)* (Mexico City: Editorial Cultura, 1938), 58; also Miguel Alemán Valdés, *Remembranzas y Testimonios* (Mexico City: Grijalbo, 1987), 20, 31–2.

104. Sara Sefchovich, *La Suerte de la Consorte* (Mexico City: Oceano, 2002), 288, 294.

105. The wife of Joaquín Amaro—a virulent anticlerical, at least in his younger days—not only attended clandestine services (which was common enough) but, it was said, "intrigued against the Government and cared for the orphans of the *cristeros*": Meyer, *Cristero Rebellion*, 96–7 and Meyer, *La Cristiada*, 2:208n158. Marta Beatriz Loyo Camacho, *Joaquín Amaro y el Proceso de Institucionalización del Ejército Mexicano, 1917–31* (Mexico City: FCE, 2003), 101, notes that Amaro, like many revolutionary leaders, married (socially) above himself, but she limits her analysis to Amaro's public rather than personal life. Variants on this theme—*políticos* whose personal relationships were vexed by religion—could be suggested: Eva Puig Casauranc refused her husband (a *callista* minister of education) a divorce; as a student, Francisco Múgica was enamored of a girl whose family vetoed

their relationship and, in consequence, the girl "went straight to the Catholic myth, limiting her love to the Christ child . . . and her whole life to the shadow of the cloister": *Un México a través de los Prieto. Cien Años de Opinión y Participación Política*, ed. Luis Prieto R., Guillermo Ramos, and Salvador Rueda (Jiquilpan: Centro de Estudios de la Revolución Mexicana "Lázaro Cárdenas," 1987), 469, and Múgica, diary entry for 26 Jan. 1930, in *Nuevos Ensayos sobre Francisco J. Múgica* (Mexico City: INEHRM, 2004), 739–40.

106. Wright-Rios, "Re-Visions of Oaxacan Catholicism," 32. Also Butler, *Popular Piety*, 122–4, and Rugely, *Of Wonders and Wise Men*, 82–5.

107. Carlos Monsiváis and I once appeared—as token talking heads—in a British TV documentary devoted to this genre. I regret that no more precise citation can be given. For literary versions of sex-in-the-confessional, see Meyer, *La Cristiada*, 2:203.

108. Knight, *Mexican Revolution*, 2:208; Calles to Governor Sebastián Allende, Guadalajara, 17 Nov. 1933, in *Plutarco Elías Calles. Correspondencia personal (1919–1945)*, ed. Carlos Macías (Mexico City: FCE, 1993), 320. Meyer, *La Cristiada*, 1:9.

109. Olcott, *Revolutionary Women*, 180–5.

110. Enrique Krauze, *Reformar desde el Origen. Plutarco E. Calles* (Mexico City: FCE, 1987), 14, 81.

111. If we take the view (as most would) that clerical as against anticlerical allegiances—or, more profoundly, belief versus unbelief—cannot be neatly inferred from socioeconomic categories, and may be related to individual and psychological characteristics, which diverge within families, birth-order inquiries are, at least, worth considering: see Frank J. Sulloway, *Born to Rebel. Birth Order, Family Dynamics and Creative Lives* (New York: Vintage, 1997). Cárdenas, for example, was the oldest of 7 siblings, Amaro of 10; Calles, too, was the oldest of a smaller "sibset" of adopted brothers, while his son Rodolfo, the radical anticlerical governor of Sonora, was the oldest of 9 siblings who survived beyond infancy. Unfortunately, the Sulloway thesis proposes, 70, 74, 284, that younger siblings turn out to be dissidents and rebels; so no simple explanation of antireligious attitudes is yielded. On the other hand, Sulloway argues, 75–6, 79, 298, that firstborns tend to be ambitious, domineering, warlike, and even authoritarian, hence they figure, 288, 297, 303, among the "founding fathers" of revolutionary regimes: Mao, Stalin, Che Guevara. It is not, perhaps, surprising, to find Calles—known for the "dominant role" he exercised among his siblings—in this company: Carlos Macías Richard, *Vida y Temperamento. Plutarco Elías Calles, 1877–1920* (Mexico City: FCE, 1995), 49.

112. There is now an extensive and serious literature on the supposed genetic bases of religiosity: see Pascal Boyer, *Religion Explained: The Human Instincts That Fashion Gods, Spirits and Ancestors* (New York: Basic, 2001); Scott Atran, *In Gods We Trust. The Evolutionary Landscape of Religion* (Oxford: Oxford University Press, 2002). Leaving aside simplistic notions of the "God-gene," there is good evidence of physiological explanations of some religious experiences. However, even if true, this does not help historians much; since, if we conclude that genetic make-up (mediated through environment), helps explain why, for example, Madre Conchita thought and behaved differently from Múgica, the explanation remains, in respect of

individuals, beyond the usual range of historical inquiry (which is limited to the environment, broadly defined). Hardwired predispositions may be presumed, but they cannot be proven. In aggregate terms, however, such a conclusion carries historical significance, since it suggests that attempts to extirpate religion (or superstition) and to create a thoroughly secular/scientific society were bound to fail, given the innate propensities of a great many humans (Atran, *In Gods We Trust*, 274–80). Critics may say that this is reductionist (true), but reductionism per se is not necessarily wrong: demographic historians, after all, recognize "reductionist" biological constraints on human fecundity and longevity.

113. Knight, "Revolutionary Project," 418.

114. Butler, *Popular Piety*, 54, 67–9, 117–18; Ann Craig, *The First Agraristas. An Oral History of a Mexican Agrarian Reform Movement* (Berkeley: University of California Press, 1983), 89–90.

115. Guerra, *Le Mèxique*, 1:142–63; Carlos A. Forment, *Democracy in Latin America, 1760–1900, 1, Civic Selfhood and Public Life in Mexico and Peru* (Chicago: University of Chicago Press, 2003).

116. Wood, *Revolution in the Street*, 70; on the libertarian and anarchist tendencies of the early twentieth-century Mexican left, see Carr, *Marxism and Communism*, 15, 21, 38–40.

117. Alan Knight, "El Liberalismo Mexicano desde la Reforma hasta la Revolución (Una Interpretación)," *Historia Mexicana* 35, no. 1 (1985): 59–92.

118. The phrase comes from Eric R. Wolf and Edward C. Hansen, "Caudillo Politics: A Structural Analysis," *Comparative Studies in Society and History* 9 (1966–7): 168–79.

119. Ex-seminarians include Múgica, a pupil with Generals Rafael Sánchez Tapia and José Alvarez y Alvarez in devout Zamora; and José Guadalupe Zuno, Basilio Vadillo, and Silvano Barba González (all revolutionary governors of Jalisco): Meyer, *La Cristiada*, 2:144, 205; Luis González, *Zamora* (Zamora: El Colegio de Michoacán, 1994), 136; William Cameron Townsend, *Lázaro Cárdenas. Mexican Democrat* (Ann Arbor: George Wahr, 1952), 14–15; Gabriel de la Mora, *José Guadalupe Zuno* (Mexico City: Porrúa, 1973), 74, 101; and Pablo Serrano Alvarez, *Basilio Vadillo Ortega. Itinerario y Desencuento con la Revolución Mexicana, 1885–1935* (Mexico City: INEHRM, 2000), 38–9, where Vadillo's break with his Catholic education is mentioned (aged 16, he grew "increasingly put off by the rigidity of seminary studies"; "his conscience and intellect were more developed, which enabled him to connect social realities with Catholic doctrinal teaching which . . . led him to contradictions and doubts"). Of course, the seminary offered an option for bright sons of relatively poor families (like Cárdenas); as a result, some went with little or no vocation and the experience was, not surprisingly, negative, like Vadillo's. Negative experience left its mark: at the very least, ex-seminarians-turned-anticlericals knew their enemy. As French anticlerical Emile Combes put it, quoting Racine, "brought up in the seraglio, I knew all its ins and outs": D.W. Brogan, *The French Nation. From Napoleon to Pétain, 1814–1940* (London: Arrow, 1961), 203. Zuno, too, was fond of displaying his knowledge of scripture: De la Mora, *José Guadalupe Zuno*, 109.

120. For example, the miners of Tlalpujahua or Guanajuato: Butler, *Popular Piety*, 65, 125; Elizabeth Emma Ferry, *Not Ours Alone. Patrimony, Value, and*

Collectivity in Contemporary Mexico (New York: Columbia University Press, 2005), 110–12.

121. Bantjes, *As If Jesus Walked On Earth*, ch. 9, discusses Sonoran miners in terms of political economy, not religion. Monterrey's steelworkers tended to anticlericalism, but even when bosses played the Catholic card in the 1930s, "secular appeals remained the order of the day": Michael Snodgrass, *Deference and Defiance in Monterrey. Workers, Paternalism and Revolution in Mexico, 1890–1950* (Cambridge: Cambridge University Press, 2003), 86, 212.

122. Knight, "Revolutionary Project," 417; Yáñez, *Al Filo del Agua*, 5–6; Butler, *Popular Piety*, 118 (which describes how Ciudad Hidalgo's church bells were used first to mobilize Catholic demonstrators, then to celebrate the anticlerical authorities' violent defeat).

123. Butler, *Popular Piety*, 105; Rugely, *Of Wonders and Wise Men*, 86–96.

124. Purnell, *Popular Movements*, 55–6.

125. Meyer, *Cristero Rebellion*, 19, 34–5; Barry Carr, *El Movimiento Obrero y la Política en México, 1910–1929* (Mexico City: Era, 1981), 213–23. In light of my previous argument suggesting that artisans were more prone to anticlericalism than factory workers or miners, it is worth recalling that many active *cromistas* fell into the former category: as Zuno (an enemy of the CROM), observed: "that piglet (Morones) says I betrayed the workers. Yes, working-class workers like him. He knew nothing of workshops or factories, only barbershops, tailors, and low-level offices": De la Mora, *José Guadalupe Zuno*, 96. On CROM's make-up, Carr, *Movimiento Obrero*, ch. 5.

126. On the nature of the "package," Butler, *Popular Piety*, 52, and Craig, *The First Agraristas*, 88–9.

127. Jeffrey A. Frieden, *Debt, Development and Democracy. Modern Political Economy and Latin America* (Princeton: Princeton University Press, 1991), 151, citing Manuel Antonio Garretón.

128. Regime dictates conspired, in some measure, with some Catholic activists' tendency to prefer vigorous and organic militancy to dessicated electoral politicking: Héctor Hernández, *The Sinarquista Movement, With Special Reference to the Period 1934–1944* (London: Minerva, 1999), 261–6.

129. Mabry, *Mexico's Acción Nacional*, 36–40, notes the early PAN's corporatist, Thomist, and Falangist leanings.

130. The so-called "Second *Cristiada*" of the 1930s was of very limited scope and impact compared to the first; but the 1930s saw continued low-level, local violence perpetrated (in part) by Catholic activists and vigilantes, particularly against "socialist" schools and schoolteachers: e.g., David L. Raby, *Educación y Revolución Social en México (1921–1940)* (Mexico City: SepSetentas, 1974), 181–93.

131. As suggested (n.73), some local activists and *políticos* (like Cejudo of Michoacán and López Cortés of Oaxaca) depended heavily on federal patronage and therefore toed the official (*callista*, anticlerical) line; we also find cabinet ministers dissimulating their own or their families' Catholic leanings. Out in the sticks, the federal government's writ did not run, or ran haltingly, hence local opinion counted for more and dissent and evasion were greater. No doubt a similar pattern could be discerned in other areas of Federal policy, both then and since.

132. Butler, *Popular Piety*, 141, 162–4; Smith, "Anticlericalism and Resistance," 490, 493; Lewis, *Ambivalent Revolution*, 89. My own research on *cardenismo* has also thrown up numerous examples.

133. For example, Vaughan, *Cultural Politics in Revolution*, 67, 118–19, 122–3; Raby, *Educación y Revolución*, ch. 5.

134. Paul Friedrich, *Agrarian Revolt in a Mexican Village* (Chicago: University of Chicago Press, 1977).

135. Craig, *The First Agraristas*, 73. See also Boyer, *Becoming Campesinos*, 163; Butler, *Popular Piety*, 54–5, 188, 191; Meyer, *Cristero Rebellion*, 110.

136. Smith, "Anticlericalism and Resistance," 494; Lewis, *Ambivalent Revolution*, 156–65; Camacho Sandoval, *Controversia Educativa*, 104, 140–1.

137. Hernández, *The Sinarquista Movement*, 407, 415–18, illustrates conservative Catholic thinking on the agrarian question; Luis Medina, *Historia de la Revolución Mexicana. Periodo 1940–1952. Del Cardenismo al Avilacamachismo* (Mexico City: El Colegio de México, 1978), 231–81 charts the "agrarian rectification" of the early 1940s which, according to the Archbishop of Mexico—cited by Stephen R. Niblo, *Mexico in the 1940s. Modernity, Politics and Corruption* (Wilmington: SR Books, 1999), 106—reflected Avila Camacho's commendable "repression of Communism."

138. Vaughan, *Cultural Politics in Revolution*.

139. This is partly another argument *ex silentio*: in the northeastern industrial heartland of Monterrey, for example, the *Cristiada* "barely caused a ripple" and labor relations do not appear to have been much affected by *Catholic* paternalism (entrepreneurial paternalism was another matter); even when the bosses, at odds with Cárdenas, imported some Catholic sloganeering, city politics remained resolutely secular: Snodgrass, *Deference and Defiance*, 131, 212. Carr, *Marxism and Communism*, says very little about the Church question, likewise the memoirs of Communst activists like José Valadés and Valentín Campa.

140. Alemán Valdés, *Remembranzas y Testimonios*, 43–4, 85, 116, 135, recalls boyish horror provoked by iconoclasm (in Orizaba, 1915), seems to put in a good word for the martyred brothers Pro, and describes his impressive church wedding in 1931 (to Beatriz, quoted to the effect that "family unity is one of God's greatest blessings"); as Governor of Veracruz, Alemán rapidly reversed Tejeda's anticlerical measures and promoted detente with the Catholic hierarchy (161–2).

141. Gabriel A. Almond and Sidney Verba, *The Civic Culture* (Boston: Brown Co., 1965), 68–71; Ulíses Beltrán, Fernando Castaños, Julia Isabel Flores, Yolanda Meyerberg, and Blanca Helena del Pozo, *Los Mexicanos de los Noventa* (Mexico City: UNAM, 1996), 132; Roderic Ai Camp, *Crossing Swords. Politics and Religion in Mexico* (New York: OUP, 1997), 112–13.

142. Davd Martin, *Tongues of Fire. The Explosion of Protestantism in Latin America* (Oxford: Blackwell, 1990), 95–8, 211–14.

143. Alan Knight, "Superstition in Mexico: From Colonial Church to Secular State," paper given at the *Past and Present* conference on superstition, Essex University, May 2005; publication forthcoming in volume, ed. S.A. Smith.

144. We sometimes overlook the natural disasters which, on top of man-made upheavals, afflicted Mexicans, usually in the absence of effective relief measures: e.g., the "destructive Oaxacan earthquakes of the late 1920s and early 1930s," plausibly seen as contributors to religious cultism: Wright-Rios, "Re-Visions of Oaxacan Catholicism," 10.

145. Butler, *Popular Piety*, 58–9; Smith, "Anticlericalism and Resistance," 490.

146. Butler, *Popular Piety*, 84; Paul J. Vanderwood, *Juan Soldado. Rapist, Murderer, Martyr, Saint* (Durham: Duke University Press, 2004), 216.

147. Bantjes, *As If Jesus Walked On Earth*, 15–18; Knight, "Popular Culture,"
     406–8. Plagiarizing religious forms does not make a secular ideology a reli-
     gion (any more that it makes, say, football a religion, except in a loose
     metaphorical sense). The (mistaken) idea of a proper secular religion, deriv-
     ing from the *philosophes*, the French Revolution, and "the religion of the
     Enlightenment," owes a good deal to Carl L. Becker, *The Heavenly City of
     the Eighteenth-Century Philosophers* (1932, New Haven: Yale University
     Press, 1959), 102 and passim: a distinctly slim, shaky, and assertive founda-
     tion on which to build such a big thesis.

148. Atran, *In Gods We Trust*, 267–70, 274–80, lists some of religion's distinctive
     features, which set it apart from science or secular rationalism. In particular,
     "because religious beliefs are counterintuitive, their truth cannot be vali-
     dated by logical inference or empirical observations" (270); hence appeals
     to evidence (including iconoclasm) or self-interest (what has God done for
     me lately?) easily fall on deaf ears, whereas similar tests of secular beliefs
     (scientific, social, or political) can prove fatal. Indeed, disasters may actually
     fortify belief, yet—as the events of 1985 in Mexico City showed—they can
     delegitimize governments.

Chapter 2

Mexico's "Ritual Constant": Religion and Liberty from Colony to Post-Revolution

Fernando Cervantes

Few areas of study awaken more suspicion among historians than religion, not least when it is brought into topics traditionally considered as emblematic of advancing secularism. For a long time the Mexican Revolution, like the French and the Russian, was such a topic. If religion was referred to, it was invariably in a negative light, for it was seen as the bête noire of revolutionary historiography, an intractable hurdle delaying the otherwise inevitable triumph of reason over superstition, universality over particularity, progress over backwardness. In the case of Mexico, this was especially evident in the historiography of the popular religious uprising that erupted in central Mexico in the 1920s, whose participants came to be known as *cristeros*—a curious epithet first used by the regime to mock the rebels' battle cry: "*¡Viva Cristo Rey!*" ("Long live Christ the King"). Denigrated by revolutionary ideologues as pawns of reactionary clericalism, and hailed by Catholic apologists as heroes in a sacred war against Leviathan, the *cristeros* were not apt to attract the interest of dispassionate scholars who, by and large, preferred to sidestep the issue of religion and to focus on the revolt's institutional history.[1]

The situation began to change after the events of 1968 made it possible for revisionist historians to recast the Mexican Revolution as the unwelcome advance of a secular and capitalist form of authoritarian statism upon hapless traditional communities. Notably, Jean Meyer took advantage of this new climate of opinion in a monumental study of the revolt that has dominated the field since publication in 1973–74.[2] Meyer's study was the first serious attempt to get inside the minds of the *cristeros*. Yet, as Matthew Butler observes, despite "vividly bringing the *cristeros* to life and dignifying them with a coherent world view," Meyer nonetheless relied on a number of "rigid dichotomies . . . which both exaggerate the ideological transparency of the *cristeros* and oversimplify the relationship between the peasantry, the Church, and the state."[3]

But such emphases on ideological factors leave some obvious questions unanswered. How, for example, did an allegedly "traditional," clerical, and ostensibly Catholic rebellion happen to erupt in roughly the same geographical area that 70 years before provided the liberals—allegedly progressive, anticlerical, and secular—with their most faithful adherents. This coincidence only becomes more puzzling when put in the context of studies that reveal liberalism's clear, programmatic logic.[4] Yet a merely sociological explanation will not work, either: for the liberal constituency was "a broad, shifting coalition," as David Brading once called it, "a peculiar union of rural *caciques* and progressive state governors, of old insurgents and new radicals, of ideologues and the mob," united against a common enemy—the Church, the army, and the Spaniards.[5] Fortunately, recent investigations seem to confirm Brading's hypothesis that the political struggle in nineteenth-century Mexico was not primarily between the Church and the army, on the one hand, and liberals on the other, but between center and periphery: between Mexico City and Puebla—the conservative heartland of the Aztec Empire and New Spain—and the "arc" that stretched from Guerrero to Veracruz, cutting across Michoacán, Jalisco, Zacatecas, and Guanajuato.

Brading, of course, had good evidence for this hypothesis. Juárez excepted, all the leading liberals came from this area: Juan Álvarez (Guerrero), Melchor Ocampo (Michoacán), Pedro Ogazón (Jalisco), Santos Degollado (Guanajuato), Jesús González Ortega (Zacatecas), Sebastián Lerdo de Tejada and Manuel Gutiérrez Zamora (Veracruz).[6] Moreover, this arc was largely settled during the colony, giving rise to a more dynamic process of miscegenation than in central Mexico. Indeed, Brading discovered complex structures of social stratification and production throughout this region in the eighteenth and nineteenth centuries. Beneath the "middle segment" of small proprietors and tenant farmers lay an amorphous stratum of yearly tenants, laborers, squatters, and sharecroppers; the scattered urban centers housed artisans, workers, and miners; and surviving Indian villages were experiencing acculturation.[7] It comes as no surprise, then, that as early as the late sixteenth century this area was home to some of the most ostensibly irreligious forms of social expressions: pacts with the devil, and a dismissal of religion as effeminate and unworthy of herdsmen and muleteers.[8] This was the ideal setting for individualist radicalism, one where many would find in liberalism an ideal vehicle to voice grievances or promote their ambitions.

From this perspective, the historical coincidence that concerns us clearly needs to be explained from multiple perspectives, necessarily avoiding the tendency to give undue emphasis to the impact of ideological preoccupations on political allegiance. Another obvious approach would be to highlight the fact that both nineteenth-century liberals and twentieth-century *cristeros* opposed governments that were centralizing and broadly insensitive to local traditions and customs. This suggests that political allegiances in both cases depended, to a much larger degree than formerly assumed, on the circumstances of local factionalisms. Guy Thomson's reconstructions of the political geography of mid-nineteenth-century Tetela (in the Sierra de Puebla), for instance, reveal the existence of active Jacobin, anticlerical, freemason, Methodist, and proto-indigenist movements; but Thomson also reveals genuinely conservative and traditional Catholic elements that might have become more prominent had *serranos* needed to confront a *centralist* liberal state.[9] As Alan Knight suggestively points out, "any map of the 'geography of revolution' seeking to capture popular allegiances and identities is likely to resemble a Seurat more than a Mondrian . . . If we stand back the picture assumes a rough pattern: the north and parts of the gulf coast are redder; the center—whose politics are as convoluted as its landscape—appears pink; the center-west is white. But close up the pattern dissolves into a host of local particularities." Consequently, it seems, "in Mexico, as in France . . . popular political culture is something of a myth; we should talk instead of numerous popular political cultures, many of them specific to individual communities."[10]

Now, the regional studies needed to define this picture accurately are still being written. Nevertheless, for some areas of the *cristero* revolt we now count on studies that shed light on our puzzle. Jennie Purnell, for instance, argues that the Michoacán highlands resisted the advances of the postrevolutionary state and its *agrarista* allies in areas where villages retained effective control over their landed base and politico-religious institutions. In areas where villagers failed to do this, by contrast, the population was willing to embrace revolutionary *agrarismo*. Thus, the former supported the *cristeros* and the latter did not, but the motives of both groups were fundamentally similar: the first group saw *agrarismo* as an unwelcome encroachment on its agrarian and politico-religious organization, the latter saw it as a welcome opportunity to contest the dominance of local elites by using the state's power to their own advantage.[11] In both cases the primary motive was fundamentally the same: the defense of local, traditional forms of land tenure and politico-religious organization against external threats.

All this suggests a previously unacknowledged set of historical interactions between religious—especially ritual—and modern, even revolutionary, political forms. My contention in this chapter is that, in all these cases, religion played a central and fundamental role. In what follows, I want to track back from the Revolution and trace the colonial origins of such a cosmovision, setting such revolutionary cases—and those described in other chapters in this book—in their long-term historical context. In so doing, I hope to suggest that the extraordinary adaptability of local ritual and religious culture to a changing sociohistorical milieu forms, *mutatis mutandis*, something of a *constant*, albeit one that was subject to significant, even revolutionary, innovations.

This may seem rather a bold claim, so some caveats are in order. To stress religion's importance is not to claim that religiosity was more (or less) important in the past than today, or that people were more (or less) pious. In fact, these issues are impossible for historians to measure with any degree of accuracy. As Butler argues for the 1920s, religion was a "multiple variable." The spiritual landscape of west-central Mexico, for example, encompassed a rich variety of religious cultures ranging from "the ultraclericalized catholicity of the Jalisco highlands and the Zamoran Bajío to the syncretic and relatively declericalized religions of the Tarascan and Otomí sierras; from the Methodist and Presbyterian belts of Southern Jalisco and East Michoacán to the Church of the Light of the World founded in Guadalajara in 1926." Add to this "the host of local devotions" and the "different models of ecclesiastical government at parochial and diocesan levels," and we can only expect varied and unexpected responses to state encroachments on traditional local customs.[12]

Nevertheless, it would be grossly misleading to ignore an undeniable constant, which even skeptical critics acknowledge. For instance, in a recent article (reviewing Paul Vanderwood's *The Power of God against the Guns of Government*), Alan Knight writes that one point is broadly agreed in the debates over the *cristeros:* "in meddling with religious *practice* (not so much *belief*), the state touched a sensitive nerve and guaranteed stiff resistance." It was "when the secular state started to mess with religious ritual," that "matters came to a head."[13] Why was ritual so important? Knight suggests that its importance lay in its economic utility, in the fact that "it was geared to material necessity: the alleviation of drought."[14] But it is possible to go much further than that; not just because all ritual, no matter how outlandish it might look, is inherently geared to the material necessities of those who engage in it, but because rituals express fundamental and surprisingly long-lasting cultural expressions that demand a special imaginative effort for modern minds to understand them. A retrospective look at some examples in Mexican history will allow us to establish some links and to determine some continuities that will, I hope, make this imaginative effort a little easier when considering the history of revolutionary and postrevolutionary Mexico.

Religion and Liberty from Postrevolutionary to Colonial Mexico

My first "stop" is the *Cristiada*, when—as Purnell shows—interlocking religious and agrarian grievances proved crucial in filling *cristero* ranks with peasant fighters. Even amidst the state's anticlerical educational reforms it is possible to detect, among those implementing them in the localities, the persistence of traditional forms of religious culture. Indeed, in order to maximize their efficiency, revolutionary reformers sought to replace Catholicism through conscious imitation of its ritual forms. They did this, Butler demonstrates, on four levels: ideologically, through the "sacralization" of revolutionary doctrines with quasi-religious programs; institutionally, through attempts to replace churches with schools (*casas del pueblo*); socially and ethically, through an attempt to replace Catholic devotions, pilgrimages, and catechesis with revolutionary marches and morality codes; and physically, through attempts to replace the blood sports held on holy days with team sports, and to demystify natural phenomena through the promotion of agronomy and pediatrics.[15] Religion's presence as a massive, objective, unquestionable power that impressed its mark on the external as well as the internal world, a power that was in everything and explained everything, was implicit even in the minds of revolutionaries who opposed it and sought to replace it.

My second "stop" is the mid-nineteenth century, commonly seen as the golden age of "popular liberalism." On close analysis, however, it is striking that the movement does not reveal any conscious secularization program. Quite the opposite: even the popular anticlericalism of the 1850s–60s emerges more as a "mere dislike of priestly meddling in corporate affairs," as Butler aptly puts it.[16] Indeed, more often than not peasants embraced liberalism for reasons "diametrically opposed" to those of liberal ideologues, often depending on the ease with which liberal solutions could be adapted to address existing local problems—typically, the defense of communal holdings or local festive religious rituals.[17] As Brian Hamnett has argued, from such a perspective popular liberalism becomes a shifting notion, one that is "superimposed on existing identities which reflect more traditional preoccupations and habits of behaviour," and beneath which "village or locality, corporate or peer group, region or profession, clearly predominate as factors of mobilization," even in a period of political parties.[18]

My third, more complex, "stop" is the early-nineteenth-century insurgency, specifically the years between the Napoleonic invasion of Spain (1808) and Mexican Independence (1821). For good reasons, this period is often seen as marking a clear rupture with the past. It has even been argued that whereas 1808 was still "traditionalist," 1810 was "modern" and willing to accept republican ideas. And indeed, a widespread newspaper circulation that responded to "new forms of sociability" and the emergence of a new "public opinion," with characteristics that were, as Guerra insisted, recognizably modern, is discernible at this time.[19] So, too, is the disappearance of censorship and the sudden emergence (and widespread use) of the word "colonies" to describe the kingdoms that, until 1808, regarded themselves as integral parts of the Spanish monarchy. These departures contributed to the formation of a rhetoric that sought to interpret the previous 300 years as a dark period of tyranny and exploitation from which the insurgent movement would rescue the budding Spanish American nation-states.

This vision allowed historians to claim that 1810 marked a radical rupture with the past. But it would be misleading to ignore that the same modern rhetoric can be found concurrently in Spain, complete with references to 300 years of alleged tyranny and exploitation. This suggests that the Napoleonic invasion triggered a dilution of power away from the center to the periphery, a movement that sought its natural expression in the traditional, contractual understanding of the monarchy as an organic community. Hints of such a response were discernible in areas of Spanish America before 1808, when various groups began to react against what they saw as ill advised and intrusive Bourbon reforms.[20] But the 1808 crisis was brought about by the absence, not the perceived abuse, of royal authority, hence the initial course of events was dictated by the search for legitimacy rather than any conscious aspirations after independence. In the absence of a legitimate monarch, it was natural that the reaction was to resort to a doctrine of popular sovereignty rooted in medieval Hispanic contractualism.[21] It is true that, in the process, many Spanish Americans became convinced that they had been rejected by the very community to which they felt themselves to belong, a conviction that encouraged those who had assimilated revolutionary notions of popular sovereignty to view the crisis of legitimacy as an opportunity to reconstruct the old order upon liberal foundations. But the common language remained rooted in the traditional framework of Spanish monarchy, and the fact that now the monarch was not the oppressor but the oppressed lent an "extra emotional element . . . to the fervour of loyalty."[22] This imbued the insurgency not with the anti-Spanish ethos of nationalist historiography, but with a subtle, essentially monarchical antiabsolutism that was part of a wider movement including Spain.[23]

It is unsurprising, in this context, that the organs of government that filled the vacuum of power from 1808–12 should have been the old regional *cabildos*—the municipal corporations also known as *ayuntamientos*. For it is clear that local, provincial elites chose to support the 1812 Cádiz constitution not because they saw it as a modern, forward-looking, liberal document, but precisely the reverse. The constitution was supported because it allowed traditional liberties to be preserved. Already in 1809, the Spanish Junta Central had declared, in Ferdinand VII's name, that "the Indies are not properly colonies, or *factorías*, like those of other nations, but an essential and integral part of the Spanish monarchy." Consequently, Spanish American kingdoms were to enjoy "national representation" and were to send representatives to the peninsula.[24] In all this, the framers of the constitution clearly "cherished a blind faith that Spain and America were afflicted by the same ills, and that a 'common cure' would do for both."[25]

This "blind faith" was shared by many influential Spanish Americans and reflected in the truly amazing diffusion and proliferation of elective *ayuntamientos* after 1812, one of the period's most remarkable political developments. The phenomenon fitted well into traditional forms of political organization and was facilitated by the way in which the Cádiz constitution was not only accepted but actively implemented by the existing authorities in Spanish America. This not only gave the constitution special legitimacy, but allowed it to filter down through the vivid, ritual, visual representations characteristic of traditional official and religious functions. As Annick Lempérière has shown, the development of republican institutions in Spanish America took place in a very traditional cultural framework, one to which she gives the evocative term "baroque," which was marked by a profusion of feasts, processions, symbols, allegories, and images of saints.[26] Indeed it is possible that the vitality of old expressions of monarchical and Catholic identity were revived and reinforced during this period, almost as if they were belated reactions to the Bourbon attacks against popular religious expressions.

My final "stop" in this survey is the mid-eighteenth century, a time when the Bourbon revolution in government, as Brading once called it,[27] began to jar with local traditions, even leading to open confrontation. And, just as Knight suggested for the *cristeros* and *tomochitecos*, it was often when Bourbon ministers meddled with religious *practice* and ritual (rather than belief) that matters came to a head.[28] An illustrative case is that of Antonio Pérez, an Indian shepherd whose activities would have been forgotten had they not been brought to the Inquisition's attention in 1761 by a priest called Domingo de la Mota. The case involved more than 100 Indians that De la Mota found engaged in "idolatrous practices": of these, he arrested 64 in Chimalhuacán, a locality in Chalco where Pérez declared himself "high priest." Mota was shocked to discover that the object of the Indians' devotion was a figurine "made of wood in the shape of a woman . . . seated on a chair, her shoulders covered with a shawl . . . and instead of a skirt she wore a yellow altar pallium." Although known to devotees as "Our Lady the Virgin of the Lily, the Palm and the Olive," this could not, according to Mota, be a true image of the Virgin because "her breasts were naked and monstrous and her face resembled more that of a man than of a woman." Testimonies revealed that Pérez denigrated the established Church. When hearing confession, Pérez tried to persuade his penitents that they were poor because they "went to church which was hell," "listened to the priests, who were devils," and "believed in the god of the priests, who was false." Pérez ridiculed church images and paintings as merely human works and advised his followers that they would "do better to commend themselves to drunkards" than to priests.[29]

Pérez's bitter attack contrasts sharply with earlier cases of heterodoxy, which were usually marked by misunderstandings and confusions. The message of this militant shepherd, by contrast, was clear. The Church and its priests were attacked, not because they were Christian, but because they sanctioned a system that contradicted Christianity's essential tenets. Indeed, the similarity between Pérez's deployment against the Church of the (thoroughly Christian) notion of the devil, and the Church's use of the same notion against Indians' alleged idolatries, is immediately striking. Pérez had clearly assimilated the essential tenets of Christianity. It is unsurprising that it was in Christianity that he found the means to voice his grievances: he celebrated Mass, heard confessions, administered baptism and the Eucharist, witnessed marriages, and insisted that worship be given to the one true God—represented by the image of the Virgin—and not to the evil "god of the priests." What Pérez was fighting, therefore, was not Christianity, nor even the Church that he knew through the preaching and ministrations of mendicant friars, but the increasingly detached intrusions of secular clergy, and the attack on corporate forms of religious expression inspired by the Jansenist and regalist sympathies of Bourbon ministers. Utilitarian and *dirigiste* in their political philosophy, these reformers disliked baroque popular religious expressions and resented corporate piety for its wasteful encouragement of sumptuous, elaborate liturgies; at the same time, they insisted on the importance of episcopal authority and the central role of the secular parochial clergy, thus inevitably coming into conflict with the corporate popular devotions that were at the center of local religiosity and communal identity.

This survey goes some way toward explaining the persistence of the constant that we highlighted at the heart of that "multiple variable" that religion seems to be. Religious practice and ritual are important because they go hand in hand with essential material needs like the alleviation of drought, of course, but much more so because they are inextricably intermingled with fundamental aspects of the self-understanding and identity of traditional communities. It is only by giving this constant the central importance that it deserves that we can begin to understand why, once independence was achieved, the emerging state—whether centralist or federalist, liberal or conservative—confronted an enormous collection of elective municipalities and autonomous groups that were intensely jealous of their sovereignty, suspicious of the center, and more attuned to traditional forms of popular piety and political representation than the secular political culture that the state eventually sought to foster.[30] It is surely not accidental that, as liberalism became more accepted and the state adopted a secularizing outlook, elective *ayuntamientos* were singled out as obstacles to progress that needed abolishing. The curious thing from our perspective is that, alongside *ayuntamientos*, went convents, confraternities, and brotherhoods.[31]

Without our constant, the fact that towns and rural municipalities incorporated, reinterpreted, and appropriated liberal institutions in order to defend their autonomy even (and at times, indeed, especially) against the liberal state might seem paradoxical. But in the context of the survival and persistence of this constant the development acquires a clear logic. As we have seen, the Cádiz constitution itself gave far more emphasis to the local community than the individual. Indeed, the constitution's very legitimacy depended upon the idea of fidelity to the monarch. Thus the constitution's promulgation ceremonies in towns and cities were roughly identical with the bulk of traditional ceremonies, and did much more to legitimize and revitalize the social order than threaten it. Towns and rural municipalities often read the constitution as a new form of contractualism between sovereign and subjects that harked back to Hapsburg times—a phenomenon that helps to explain why successful *caudillos* were those who managed to evoke modern liberal concepts alongside a deeply traditional and pseudo-monarchical language based on the old communal rights.[32]

At a popular level, our constant also helps explain the emergence of popular leaders, like the insurgent José María "Chito" Villagrán, whose personal trajectory has been memorably summarized by Eric Van Young: "from local delinquent and town bully, to criminal of passion, to rebel, to a figure of at least partial apotheosis among insurrectionary heroes after his death."[33] This is clearly not a character to whom one would naturally be drawn as a good example of the subtle interaction between religious tradition and political modernity. Yet Chito was the putative author of a fascinating letter denouncing Miguel Hidalgo's excommunication and the official condemnation of the insurgency. The letter is replete with religious ideology in political matters and is therefore well worth quoting at some length:

> If the Church does not hurl anathemas against the infamous Napoleon because, being a Corsican, he takes control of the kingdom of France, nor against his brother Joseph, who was crowned in Spain, nor against the Dutch who, renouncing their national government, acknowledge the intruder Louis Bonaparte, why does it hurl anathemas against a nation that, to maintain pristine the Catholic Religion it professes, takes up arms to demand and acquire the rights usurped from it so long ago, to throw off a tyrannical government, and to take unto itself the sovereignty of its King, Don Fernando, whom Napoleon and his emissaries . . . after persecuting and almost decapitating, are trying to despoil of his rights? I cannot persuade myself . . . that the anathemas fulminated by the Church fall on the defense we are making of religion and liberty, and thus I believe firmly that we are not comprehended in its penalties . . . Should we permit our religion and our liberty to perish, or should we not take up arms to defend both?[34]

The letter's content is so extraordinary that, as Van Young argues, although unquestionably signed by Chito, it is likely to have been written by a well-educated priest in his entourage, suggesting that such doctrines must have been "in the air," and that Chito and his followers "must have absorbed them at least to a minimal extent and that they may even have articulated in systematic fashion his own embryonic beliefs."[35] In the likes of Chito we witness a natural convergence between, on the one hand, a patriotic intellectual tradition that was bent on insisting that Mexico's Catholicism owed nothing to Spain, and, on the other, a more popular indigenous tradition that could not conceive of a past that had not been Christian. This curious indigenous state of mind can be discerned from several extant land titles written in Náhuatl in the late seventeenth and eighteenth centuries,[36] but it is fascinating to see it conflated here with the idea that Saint Thomas the Apostle was responsible for the Christianization of Mexico, in a way that we tend to associate more readily with Fray Servando Teresa de Mier. "Assume," the author of the letter writes toward the end, "that not St Thomas the Apostle but the Europeans brought the Faith to these regions, but seeing that they intend to destroy that which they have built, it is necessary to persecute them and drive them out"![37]

In his concluding assessment, Van Young describes Villagrán's letter as a "kind of quasi utilitarian, communalist view of political legitimacy," uniquely characteristic of the "sacrally- and ethnically-based communalism" that would become the norm in later expressions of "popular liberalism," and that "may even have had common roots in the socio-political structure and religious sensibility of Colonial Mexico." Our constant is in evidence again; once more it helps to make sense of the way in which "strands of religious and political thought" were "bound together in a sort of inseparable double helix at whose nether end lay the communal indigenous village and at whose apex stood the Spanish monarchy" (Van Young's phrases). At the nether end, moreover, community identities were anchored "not only in ethnic distinction but also in sacrality, so that a political struggle ipso facto became a religious one, and a religious struggle a political one."[38] Given this confluence of patriotism, religious ritual, and autonomy, is it so surprising to find that, in the 1920s and 1930s, Mexican Catholics formed a National League for the Defence of Religious Liberty in response to the public suppression of Catholic ritual practice and waged a rebellion in the name of Christ the King?

Colonial Origins

The recurring centrality of religious practice in these cases should make the special imaginative effort required of modern minds to understand the fundamental importance of religion more straightforward. It is important to reiterate that by "religion" we are not primarily concerned here with questions of belief, doctrine, interior piety, or even ethics. These questions were, of course, important to individuals in the past, just as they are important in the present. Where the modern world differs from the traditional communities that concern us is in its ability to separate religious from secular considerations. Now, any such separation would have been unthinkable in traditional communities and would also have posed a threat of unimaginable proportions to their existence and raison d'être, for it would have been perfectly clear to them that to conduct one's life without reference to religion was as irrational and dangerous as to cultivate the soil without reference to the course of the seasons.

This is likely to seem overstated. Our constant, it might easily be objected, is too monolithic to be credible as an effective historical cause. This kind of objection makes good sense in the context of a historiography that commonly regards the presence of Christianity in colonial Mexico as the result of an incomplete and generally unsatisfactory process, leading to the emergence of an essentially "syncretic" type of religion, replete with pre-Hispanic elements that constantly seek ways to escape from the official Church's stifling control. But this kind of historiography is clearly centered on the notion of conversion, understood as the result of the presentation and acceptance of a doctrine or a set of beliefs. Yet, we have throughout emphasized that this is not the most helpful approach, for it inevitably exaggerates the differences and incompatibilities between Christianity and indigenous religions, overstating their doctrinal and ideological rigidity by seeing them as mutually exclusive. Nor is it the most favored approach among current studies of colonial religion. The bulk of these in fact emphasize the reciprocal nature of the interaction between Europeans and Amerindians throughout the colonial period, leading to the incorporation of indigenous elements into the rituals and ceremonies of Christianity and vice versa. Although it is undeniable that official Christianity and native religious leaders often deplored and even actively discouraged such developments, it does not follow that the manifestations that emerged from the various processes of interaction were in any way heterodox. If their condemnation seems almost axiomatic in many contemporary sources, this is because the majority of such documentation was at pains to present the process of Christianization in unashamedly triumphant terms. The alleged clash between Christianity and "paganism" was deliberately presented as if fought out in heaven, complete with saintly and angelic interventions, and the narratives therefore tended to emphasize the almost instantaneous nature of the Christian victory over the native "gods" or "demons" associated with the destruction of a native temple and the establishment of a Christian church.

The otherworldly tone of such narratives, deliberately intended to help the native neophytes accept Christianity's inevitable triumph, overlooks the much more characteristic, slower, and piecemeal periods of transition and adjustment. In his analysis of a similar development in European Late Antiquity, Peter Brown has suggested that it is important "to set the vivid certainties of many Christian texts against a wider background." The Christianization that mattered most was the "imaginative Christianisation of the *mundus*"—the world of ordinary experience—a process that entailed the creation of a "common sense about the actions of the divine and the nature of the universe" which was very different from that held by the "cognitive majority." Thus "the ancient collective representation of the *mundus* gave to . . . Christians . . . as much as to pagans . . . imaginative room for manoeuvre. Its many layers reconciled faith in the One, High God with dogged, indeed reverential, concern for the *saeculum* that had once been ascribed, more frankly, to the care of the ancient gods."[39]

Brown's observations find truly striking parallels in colonial Mexico. In very much the same way as the collective representation of the *mundus* in Late Antiquity, the symbiotic interplay between Christianity and native religions in colonial Mexico cannot be adequately gauged through the writings and initiatives of missionaries and clergymen; it is essential to go beyond these, to the more sparsely documented contacts of Europeans of widely different backgrounds with indigenous peoples. There were in fact innumerable similarities and points of contact between the religious landscapes of the Mesoamerican and the Iberian worlds.[40] Take the saints, for instance. In Spain, the saints were widely regarded as resident patrons of their communities. Vows to the saints, as a rule, were made in response to some natural disaster and there was a widespread belief that the saints were capable of inflicting harm on communities if the latter did not observe their sacred contracts. Each village in Spain had its own calendar of sacred times marked on the village memory by natural disasters and other supernatural signs that had become solemn contracts with the saints; and everyone knew that it was a collective responsibility, going back in time and ahead into the future, to observe these contracts and that dire consequences could follow lapses.[41] Change the word "saint" for "tutelary deity" and we could well be describing "local religion" in pre-Hispanic central Mexico.

At the level of religious practice and ritual, therefore, it is unlikely that Christianity would have floated over Mesoamerican magic like a layer of oil over water.[42] Recourse to magic was in fact accepted by both cultures and put into effect in very much the same way. The average European or African arriving in Mesoamerica throughout colonial times would have felt no particular qualms about deferring to Indians, not only for their knowledge of the physical environment, but also for the manipulation of the local spiritual forces that they understood so much better. And the process did not flow only in one direction. Surprisingly soon after the conquest, native healing practices came to be accompanied by Christian prayers and invocations, and even hallucinogens are known to have been associated with Christian saints and angels.[43]

What is more surprising is that these processes were often most effectively accomplished through the unspectacular, often downright suspect, ministrations of itinerant preachers and wonder-workers. Indeed, the lure that missionaries exerted over native peoples was often the result of their power as healers, and the way in which their ministrations were requested in much the same way as those of former pagan healers, like the *naguales*, is a recurring trend. It can be detected even among representatives of the official position that had most reason to fear such "unholy" or "sacrilegious" mixtures. The indefatigable Jacinto de la Serna, for instance, one of the few "extirpators of idolatry" to flourish in colonial Mexico, left a particularly apt example of this process. Despite his insistence that Indians' healing powers were to be attributed to a pact with the devil, he nevertheless described how he himself, in an identical context, once performed a similar healing rite on a servant, after failing to find a suitable homely cure, with "a piece of bone from the saintly and venerable body of Gregorio López."[44]

It was precisely in this twilight world of ritual practices, of the cult of saints and of their relics and miracles, that the vital transfusion of Christianity with local indigenous religions was most successfully achieved. Much more than the distant bishops and priests, the presence of these religious practitioners, who became widely known as *venerables*,[45] must have impressed the native peoples with the sense of a new power that seemed stronger than the nature spirits of the local religious systems, but not for this reason dramatically different from their world view or religious faith. It was precisely the ministration of such *venerables* that formed the basis of the liturgical activities of the shepherd Antonio Pérez. As he condemned and vilified the greed and corruption of the secular clergy and the official Church, Pérez honored the memory of two mendicant friars, a Dominican and a Franciscan, who respectively taught him the art of healing and helped him to locate the images at the center of his devotions. Pérez's account of his early years as a healer is uncannily reminiscent of the world of hermits, ascetics, and wonder workers that populate seventeenth- and eighteenth-century hagiographical and missionary literature. Pérez recalls how the Dominican taught him to cure,

> advising me to use . . . eggs, soap, milk, cooking oil, mint or tomato skins. . . .
> He taught me cures for everything . . . For all my treatments I recite the *Credo*
> as the Holy Church teaches it . . . and I add these words: "in the name of the

Most Holy Trinity, of the Father, the Son and the Holy Spirit. Amen." I put my trust first in God, and only then in the herbs. When he is on his way to recovery, the sick man recites the act of contrition. I do all that because the Dominican friar told me to.[46]

Just like the holy men of Late Antiquity, these *venerables* functioned as facilitators of new allegiances and patterns of observance. In a comparatively mundane way they embraced, and gradually reduced to order, a large number of conflicting systems of explanation. As Brown writes, "placed between Christian and pagan clients, the holy man aided the emergence of a new distinctive 'religious common sense,' associated with a more all-embracing and exclusive monotheism."[47] So, although the activities of missionaries are presented in the bulk of our sources as exceptional and dramatic, they were in fact "nothing more than a highly visible peak in a spiritual landscape that rose gently upward from the expectations and activities of ordinary Christians." In very much the same way, the *venerables* became figures of "genuine supernatural power at a time when the holy was still stretched beyond the narrow confines of the Church."[48]

Clearly then, the spread of the Christian religion in Mexico was not so much the result of the teaching and acceptance of a new *doctrine* or a set of *beliefs*, as of the manifestation and realization of a new *power* that manifested itself most effectively in ritual symbolism and action. Christian ministers appealed to the native peoples because they were assumed to have access to the holy in its various manifestations, even to the point of being able to embrace and validate a wide range of potentially exclusive explanatory systems. At one level they were capable of identifying so closely with the local cultures that they could not fail to infuse them with the spirit of Christianity. The cult that had been paid to local nature spirits and tutelary deities was readily transferred to the saints; and although there can be no doubt that a large majority of pre-Hispanic deities and spiritual forces retained the devotion of the people, it is no less clear that they were consecrated to new powers and acquired new associations.

This is not, of course, to deny the importance of the process of conversion at a more personal and interior level. Here, Christian ministers made a strong impact because they represented a scale of values and a way of life that was fundamentally different to that of the old order. The emphasis on the interaction of free wills that the Christian idea of intercession entailed, for instance, brought the notion of mercy into a potentially impersonal cosmos. And with freedom came sin. To quote Brown again, "the holy man was not only a favoured courtier of his God: he was a preacher of repentance." Any dramatic change in the course of ordinary life could be "held to have registered the most amazing of all discontinuities—the stirring to contrition of the sinful human heart."[49] None of the evidence from chronicles or hagiographies or missionary accounts of Christian ministers in colonial Mexico leaves us in any doubt about this most basic of Christian narratives. The message of the new religion was primarily one of divine judgment and salvation, and it sought expression in the eschatological distinction of the present world and the world to come.

This stark aspect of the Christian message could not fail to make a deep impact upon a world where the effects of conquest had brought poverty and exploitation, illness and death to the forefront as unavoidable facts of daily experience. It goes some way toward explaining the intense asceticism and otherworldliness that are among the most striking characteristics of colonial religion. These qualities are often interpreted as the result of a mere imposition of the mendicant friars' ascetic way of life, but in the circumstances they clearly responded to a much more immediate and essential psychological need. An adequate appreciation of this development would require us to dissociate the notions of otherworldliness and asceticism from their modern pietistic connotations of individualism, subjectivism, and idealism. For the kind of Christianity that came to characterize most regions of colonial central Mexico was collective, objective, and realist. If it is true that the world to which it aspired was outside history and beyond time, it is no less true that it was firmly believed to be the ultimate end toward which both time and history were moving.

The central place that the Catholic liturgy occupied in this process would be impossible to exaggerate. The mendicant friars and their successors in the seventeenth and eighteenth centuries were above all good liturgists formed by their daily reading, psalm singing, and meditation of scripture.[50] And it was above all in the liturgy that they could claim to possess a corporate experience and communion with the eternal world. This was no mere collection of formulaic rites and rituals: it was a fully integrated cycle that was inextricably intermingled with the agricultural year and thus readily supplanted the old ritual cycle of sacrifice around which the life of the community had revolved. But additionally, the liturgy provided a clear principle of unity and a means by which the native neophytes could readily become attuned to a new view of life and a new concept of history. For all the articles of the Christian faith were historically situated, and consequently the liturgy over time developed into an historical cycle where the progress of humanity, from creation to redemption, unfolded. Thus the cult of the saints—which presented many similarities with the old sacrificial propitiation of tutelary deities—became inseparable from the Christian liturgy, and the commemoration of the feasts of the saints provided an element of corporate identity and social continuity by which every community found its liturgical representative and patron. Nowhere was this process better reflected than in the early mendicant constructions. Continuing the medieval tradition of surrogate Jerusalems, they became, in Jaime Lara's words, "part of a sacred landscape with topographical references to the real and ideal Jerusalem, confirmed by mimetic liturgical processions and conflated with pre-Hispanic sacral spaces."[51]

Although this liturgical religious culture was essentially medieval and rooted in the mendicant experiences of the sixteenth century, much of it survived intact into the Baroque and modern periods, notably in popular expressions like the feast of Corpus Christi.[52] But it is the fundamental role it has always played in the symbolism and ritual of local communal identity that has given it its particular resilience and persistence, not as a monolithic constant, but as one that continues to display a remarkable ability to adapt, and that modern historians can only ignore at their peril.

Notes

1. E.g., David Bailey, *¡Viva Cristo Rey! The Cristero Rebellion and the Church-State Conflict in Mexico* (Austin: University of Texas Press, 1974), Robert Quirk, *The Mexican Revolution and the Catholic Church: 1910–1929* (Bloomington: Indiana University Press, 1973).
2. Jean Meyer, *La Cristiada* (3 vols. Mexico City: Siglo XXI, 1973–74).
3. Matthew Butler, *Popular Piety and Political Identity in Mexico's Cristero Rebellion: Michoacán, 1927–29* (Oxford: British Academy/OUP, 2004), 6.
4. Francisco Bulnes, *Juárez y las Revoluciones de Ayutla y de Reforma* (Mexico City: H.T. Milenario, 1967); Charles Hale, *Mexican Liberalism in the Age of Mora* (New Haven and London: Yale University Press, 1968); Jesús Reyes Heroles, *El Liberalismo Mexicano* (3 vols. Mexico City: Universidad Nacional, 1957–61).
5. David Brading, *The Origins of Mexican Nationalism* (Cambridge: Cambridge University Press, 1985), 95.
6. Richard Sinkin, *The Mexican Reform, 1855–1876: A Study in Liberal Nation Building* (Austin: University of Texas Press, 1979), 37–9.
7. David Brading, *Haciendas and Ranchos in the Mexican Bajío* (Cambridge: Cambridge University Press, 1978), 157–63.
8. Fernando Cervantes, *The Devil in the New World* (New Haven and London: Yale University Press, 1994), 90–7.
9. Guy Thomson with David LaFrance, *Patriotism, Politics, and Popular Liberalism in Nineteenth-Century Mexico: Juan Francisco Lucas and the Puebla Sierra* (Wilmington: SR, 1999). Tetela was not an isolated example, as Jean-Pierre Bastian demonstrates for pockets of central Puebla/Tlaxcala, the Puebla/Hidalgo sierras, the district of Zitácuaro, and the Huasteca potosina: see *Los Disidentes: Sociedades Protestantes y Revolución en México, 1872–1911* (Mexico City: El Colegio de México, 1989); Jean-Pierre Bastian, "Las Sociedades Protestantes y la Oposición a Porfirio Díaz," *Historia Mexicana* 38 (1988): 469–512.
10. Alan Knight, "Popular Culture and the Revolutionary State in Mexico, 1910–1940," *Hispanic American Historical Review* 74, no. 3 (1994): 438.
11. Jennie Purnell, *Popular Movements and State Formation in Revolutionary Mexico: The Cristeros and Agraristas of Michoacán* (Durham: Duke University Press, 1999), 111–62.
12. Butler, *Popular Piety*, 9–10.
13. Alan Knight, "Rethinking the Tomóchic Rebellion," *Mexican Studies/Estudios Mexicanos* 15, no. 2 (1999): 382–3.
14. Ibid., 383.
15. Butler, *Popular Piety*, 84.
16. Ibid., 34
17. Ibid. For an excellent survey, Guy Thomson "Popular Aspects of Liberalism in Mexico, 1848–1888," *Bulletin of Latin American Research* 10, no. 3 (1991): 265–92. The illustrative case of Francisco Agustín (Cuetzalan) shows that a

genuinely popular defense of liberal constitutional rights emerged after the Indians were forced to sacrifice the control they traditionally exercised over their common lands. "Popular liberalism" here offered the Indians some autonomy.

18. Brian Hamnett, "Liberalism Divided: Regional Politics and the National Project During the Mexican Restored Republic, 1867–1876," *Hispanic American Historical Review* 76, no. 4 (1996): 660.
19. François-Xavier Guerra, *Modernidad e Independencias: Ensayos sobre las Revoluciones Hispánicas* (Mexico City: Fondo de Cultura Económica, 1993), 92–102.
20. John Leddy Phelan, *The People and the King: the Comunero Revolution in Colombia, 1781* (Madison: University of Wisconsin Press, 1978), ch. 13; Anthony McFarlane, *Colombia before Independence: Economy, Society and Politics under Bourbon Rule* (Cambridge: Cambridge University Press, 1993), 251–71; *Reform and Insurrection in Bourbon New Granada and Peru*, ed. John Fisher, Allan Kuethe, and Anthony McFarlane (Baton Rouge: Louisiana State University Press, 1990).
21. Mario Góngora, *Studies in the Colonial History of Spanish America* (Cambridge: Cambridge University Press, 1975), 68–79.
22. John Elliott, *Empires of the Atlantic World: Britain and Spain in America, 1492–1830* (New Haven and London: Yale University Press, 2006), 382.
23. Tamar Herzog, *Defining Nations: Immigrants and Citizens in Early Modern Spain and Spanish America* (New Haven and London: Yale University Press, 2003), 144–5.
24. Manuel Chust, *La Cuestión Nacional Americana en las Cortes de Cádiz* (Valencia: Fundación Instituto Historia Social, 1999), 32–3.
25. Elliott, *Empires*, 378; Demetrio Ramos, "Las Cortes de Cádiz y América," *Revista de Estudios Políticos* 126 (1962): 488.
26. Annick Lempérière, "¿Nación moderna o República Barroca? México, 1823–1857," in *Imaginar la Nación*, ed. François-Xavier Guerra and Mónica Quijada (Münster: Lit, 1994), 135–77. François-Xavier Guerra, "La Independencia de México y las Revoluciones Hispánicas," in *El Liberalismo Mexicano*, ed. Antonio Anino and Raymond Buve (Münster: Lit, 1993), 15–48.
27. David Brading, *Miners and Merchants in Bourbon Mexico, 1763–1819* (Cambridge: Cambridge University Press, 1971), ch. 1.
28. David Brading, "Tridentine Catholicism and Enlightened Despotism in Bourbon Mexico," *Journal of Latin American Studies* 15, no. 1 (1983): 1–22, is illuminating.
29. Archivo General de la Nación, Ramo Inquisición, tomo 1000, exp. 21, ff. 292r–293v. Serge Gruzinski, *Man-Gods in the Mexican Highlands: Indian Power and Colonial Society 1520–1800* (Stanford: Stanford University Press, 1989), ch. 5; Cervantes, *Devil*, 69–73.
30. Antonio Anino, "El Jano Bifronte Mexicano: Una Aproximación Tentativa," in Anino and Buve, *El Liberalismo*, 177–86.
31. This was the formal disposition of the 1856 Ley Lerdo.
32. John Lynch, *Caudillos in Spanish America, 1800–1850* (Oxford: Clarendon, 1992), 3–34, and passim.
33. Eric Van Young, "Popular Religion and the Politics of Insurgency in Mexico, 1810–18212," in *The Politics of Religion in an Age of Revival*, ed. Austen Ivereigh (London: Institute of Latin American Studies, 2000), 85.

34. Ibid., 86. Van Young's translation.

35. Ibid., 88.

36. James Lockhart, *The Nahuas after the Conquest: A Social and Cultural History of the Indians of Central Mexico, Sixteenth through Eighteenth Centuries* (Stanford: Stanford University Press, 1992), 229, 257.

37. Van Young, "Popular Religion," 87.

38. Ibid., 112.

39. Peter Brown, *Authority and the Sacred: Aspects of the Christianisation of the Roman World* (Cambridge: Cambridge University Press, 1995), x–xi, 4–14.

40. See the interesting comments by Jaime Lara, *City, Temple, Stage: Eschatological Architecture and Liturgical Theatrics in New Spain* (Notre Dame: University of Notre Dame Press, 2004), 6–7.

41. William Christian Jr., *Local Religion in Sixteenth-Century Spain* (Princeton: Princeton University Press, 1981), 33, 97, 124, 142, 174–7.

42. Nancy Farriss, *Maya Society under Colonial Rule: The Collective Enterprise of Survival* (Princeton: Princeton University Press, 1984), 297.

43. Cervantes, *Devil*, 60–1.

44. Jacinto de la Serna, *Manual de Ministros de Indios para el Conocimiento de sus Idolatrías y Extirpación de Ellas*, in *Colección de Documentos Inéditos para la Historia de España* (Madrid: Academia de la Historia, 1842–95), 104: 58. Cervantes, *Devil*, 59; Osvaldo Pardo, "Contesting the Power to Heal: Angels, Demons and Plants in Colonial Mexico," in *Spiritual Encounters: Interactions between Christianity and Native Religions in Colonial America*, ed. Nicholas Griffiths and Fernando Cervantes (Birmingham: University of Birmingham Press, 1999), ch. 6.

45. E.g., the descriptions of miracles and cures by the Dominican Francisco de Burgoa, *Palestra Historial de Virtudes y Ejemplares Apostólicos* (Mexico City, 1670); the Augustinian Matías de Escobar, *Americana Thebaida: Vitas Patrum de los Ermitaños de N. P. San Agustín* (Mexico City, 1924); and the Jesuit Andrés Pérez de Ribas, *Historia de los Triunfos de Nuestra Santa Fe entre Gentes de las Más Fieras y Bárbaras del Nuevo Orbe* (Madrid, 1645). On Franciscans, see the ms. compiled by order of Bishop Juan de Palafox, giving details of 15 *venerables* in the first decades of the seventeenth century: "Informaciones de Quince Religiosos Venerables de esta Provincia de San Diego de México," Archivo Generale dei Frati Minori, Rome, MS. T. 10.

46. Gruzinski, *Man-Gods*, 105–6.

47. Brown, *Authority and the Sacred*, 60.

48. Ibid., 64.

49. Ibid., 74–5.

50. Lara, *City, Temple, Stage*, 42, laments that scant attention has been paid to the mendicants' "liturgical imagination."

51. Ibid., 109.

52. Ibid., 191–5, and Richard Trexler, *Reliving Golgotha: the Passion Play of Iztapalapa* (Cambridge, Mass.: Harvard University Press, 2003).

Chapter 3

Protestants, Freemasons, and Spiritists: Non-Catholic Religious Sociabilities and Mexico's Revolutionary Movement, 1910–20[*]

Jean-Pierre Bastian

Among recent interpretations of Mexico's 1910 revolutionary rupture are those emphasizing the phenomenon's above-all political nature as a "passage from being subjects to citizens," a process through which "political initiative passed into the hands of the citizenry and ceased being the privilege of the few."[1] This reading suggests an abandonment of the idea that the *carran-cismo* of 1915–20 was a reversal or retreat. Indeed, it suggests that 1910 culminated in 1917, and fully valorizes two of the period's achievements: the 1917 Constitution and the return of the rule of law. I wish here to return to the beginnings of the "citizen-making" process and examine this view. This means following trails that are relatively unexplored but fundamental, if we are to understand the emergence of a liberal-democratic project that could voice sociopolitical concerns better than nineteenth-century liberalism.

This way of understanding the 1910 revolutionary rupture requires us to take seriously the declarations of historical actors defined largely by masonic, Spiritist, or Protestant ties. According to Bulnes, the revolution was the "anarchistic apostleship of primary school masters, Mexican Protestant pastors, impoverished journalists, backwoods lawyers newly-spawned in diseased classrooms, [and] greasy, beat-up masons."[2] For his part, Valadés noted that "more than any written ideological manifestations, what gave wings to new political thinking [was] measured discussion in masonic and spiritist societies; for though these neither directed nor conspired in public affairs, they did maintain the spirit of debate over what they called political and social free will."[3]

Taking these statements seriously requires us to explore the world of modern religious sociabilities—of lodges, Spiritist circles, and Protestant societies. These formed a space counter to the regime throughout the Porfiriato, and led their members to respond to Madero's call in 1910. Their action did not end with Madero's victory. Rather, the revolutionary process gave them new impetus; this is worth exploring to the extent that these socially minoritarian but ideologically active sectors participated in the world of public opinion, itself largely driven by the associational press they produced. Taking non-Catholic religious sociabilities as a specific object of study thus contributes to our understanding of the societal and civic dimensions of revolutionary rupture and process.

To consider these associative networks is also to point out the revolution's religious dimension. This dimension has been deemed secondary, compared with more radical (social, labor, agrarian) factors. Yet we can argue, on the contrary, that religion should be taken as a structuring factor, across the *longue durée*, in the struggle for Mexico's political and social transformation. The religious rupture inscribed in individuals' deliberate adherence to non-Catholic religious societies implied an individual wish to break with a tenaciously corporate social structure, whose sacred canopy was the Thomist conception of society inherited from the colony. As José María Luís Mora stressed, many of Mexico's problems stemmed from the need to substitute a spirit of association for an *esprit de corps*. In political terms, this meant replacing a social order where religion was an essential attribute of collective identity with a space of free opinions woven in civil society. Separating Church and state was a necessary but insufficient step. Indeed, by inventing the state as a secular institution, the Church was created. This Church opposed any secularizing principle head-on and believed that the common good was a religious and not merely a political, question. As it rejected separation, so it refused its reduction to private spaces. By separating from its customary civil support, therefore, the state was forced to build a pluralist society independently, against the Church. This was demonstrated, from Lerdo de Tejada onward, by the diffusion of modern, especially religious sociabilities that depended on the freedom of worship enshrined in the Reform Laws.

In order to build independently of the Catholic ideological apparatus that dominated civil society, modern actors adopted opposing, if parallel, discourse and practices. In order to secularize state and society an attempt was made to break with a public culture rooted in Catholicism, especially after Catholicism was structured against liberalism with the encyclical *Quanta Cura* and the 1864 *Syllabus*. The break with the Catholic universe, therefore, worked through dissident religions, principally Protestantism and Spiritism. Other options, for example, the creation of national Catholic Churches, failed because they did not demarcate the symbolic fields sufficiently. Of course, the symbolic rupture was not always religious. Some became free-thinkers, but in this deeply rural society a complete break with the religious conception of life interested only a few urban, highly educated sectors. On the other hand, freemasonry offered an ambiguous space where individuals could break with Catholicism or adopt a distant symbolic position without rupture. For this reason, there were liberal Catholic masons who were not Protestants, Spiritists, or freethinkers; and masons "of convenience," who were private Catholics but anticlerical in their lodges. This option was not open to those who chose Protestantism and Spiritism. This explains why the identification of the principle leaders in 1910 as Spiritist (Madero) and Protestant (Orozco, Gutiérrez Gómez) was decisive, for in leaving the Catholic universe, they demonstrated greater radicalism. By individual choice, members of these sociabilities symbolized what the revolution *was:* an attempt to leave the sacred canopy of Thomist corporativism and enter a pluralist civil society, paving the way for representative democracy.

The point that interests us when rescuing this type of revolutionary actor is that anti-Catholicism, whether religious or antireligious in form, was a structuring element of the political universe. Likewise, conciliation with the Church or calls for the strict application of the Constitution were key elements in demarcating political and social positions. Porfirian conciliation, meanwhile, was a way of returning to the Catholic civil base without paying the price of democracy and pluralism. Therefore, the members of dissident religious societies who could not accept this type of compromise necessarily found themselves involved in a radical liberalism that drew them into revolution.

I will try to show that these minoritarian religious actors—the civil base of an embryonic democratic process—were a permanent presence in Mexico's revolutionary process. I shall do so by referring principally to Protestant sociabilities, which formed a more important and structured network than Spiritist societies. Spiritist circles have not, as yet, been studied as networks, unlike Protestant societies. The same is true of lodges, whose role is also difficult to interpret: yet because we know that the majority of Protestants were freemasons, studying the former is a way of following the progress of the latter. In what follows, I shall point to significant actions and moments that refer us to the civilian dimension of this radical liberalism within the revolutionary process.

A Radical Liberalism

In the Porfiriato's authoritarian context, Protestant, Spiritist, and masonic sociabilities emerged as means of socialization whose organizing principle required members to shed a corporatist reality and transform themselves into individuals, members of a society of equals. The associative practice, as well as ideology, that characterized these societies was founded in an optimistic vision of the individual, who was rescued from a global corporate society perceived as corrupt. The creation of religious societies that broke with Catholicism's corporate religious tradition reveals a genuine movement in civil society. This was especially true in "fragile areas" on the periphery of political and religious centers where increased demands for political autonomy were made at a time of increasing centralization: the Huasteca, the Tabascan Chontalpa, south-central Tlaxcala, the Sierra de Puebla, western Chihuahua, and the Zitácuaro and Chalco districts were ideal areas for such expansion, and were additionally areas where the Catholic Church's presence was weaker, and which had forged popular liberalisms.[4]

Here, masonic lodges, liberal clubs, and Spiritist, Protestant, patriotic and mutualist societies engaged in slow political work using a radical liberal pedagogy. This pedagogy was applied as much in the societies' religious celebrations as in liberal-civic acts, and was driven by a lettered minority in terms of its civic discourse and the pedagogic models instilled in students; it invoked new principles that broke with traditional society, and caused a progressive displacement of the circles of power within civil society, benefiting private social initiative; above all, it articulated a constant critique of conservative liberalism, which was perceived as conciliatory and a betrayal of the constitutional principle of abstract democracy. Consequently, the expansion of new forms of association led to the development of new networks of power, woven by civil society and outside state control. Through the denial of traditional social values and the affirmation of the abstract equality of individuals (society members were already constituted as such), a potential *pueblo* of electors—modern democratic actors—was being built. The appropriation of democratic models by certain social sectors occurred throughout the Porfiriato, especially via the description and naming of what, according to these societies, was harmful, undemocratic, and opposed to the common good. This meant not only the Catholic Church and its agents in particular, but also its allies: those whom *mestizos* sometimes considered to be "Spaniards," and the holders of economic and political power (*hacendados*, the owners of businesses or factories; the *porfirista* political class).

By describing what was harmful through an anti-Catholicism exacerbated by the Church's recovery of social space, these societies formed part of the liberalism that was forged in Mexico by uprooting itself from the Catholic tradition. However, Mexican liberalism swung between two attitudes toward Catholicism and religion: on the one hand, the denial and eradication of religion, as with *magonismo*, and on the other, conciliation, as with *porfirista* conservative liberalism; meanwhile, modern religious sociabilities, and with them a defeated liberal faction classed by *científicos* as "metaphysical," sought a third way, which consisted of detaching themselves from Catholicism in order to eradicate it and replace it with secularized religious and moral values. These values, inspired by a purified Christianity, would create morally and socially responsible individuals, the subjects of the modern state's sociopolitical action. One aspect of this shift was the development of a true civic religion displayed in civic acts where metaphysical liberalism and popular patriotism flourished in opposition to *porfirista*, nationalist, and centralizing patriotism.

Maderismo

Madero's strength was to have integrated radical liberal and Catholic democratic actors in the anti-reelectionist process and thus momentarily to have broken metaphysical liberalism and its representation of a dual society in matters of religion. The parade in Puebla (May 1911) of students from the Methodist College, the Palafox Seminary, and the state's Normal School in support of the *maderista* campaign was symbolic in this regard. The political-religious fields separating Catholics and radicalized liberals that the Porfiriato helped to demarcate appeared to vanish with Madero's victory.

The religious actors who participated in Madero's victory entered the new regime's administrative structures. In particular, several Protestant school-teachers and pastors became governors' secretaries, such as teacher Braulio Hernández (Abraham González's secretary in Chihuahua) and former Methodist pastor and mason, José Rumbia (secretary to Antonio Hidalgo in Tlaxcala); some even became state governors, such as Cándido Navarro, a former student of Puebla's Methodist College and governor of Guanajuato (October 1911); other Protestants became directors of state education in Guanajuato, Hidalgo, Sonora, and elsewhere. Continuing their anti-reelectionist militancy, many threw themselves into electoral contests and became deputies.[5] However, none entered the highest levels of the *maderista* administration, which remained largely in the hands of the Porfirian elites.

In fact, late autumn 1911 saw a democratic explosion, with the creation of numerous parties following the creation of the National Catholic Party (PCN) that May. The *maderista* project had been extremely modern, both in its political organization (propaganda tours, election meetings, candidates' designation via clubs and conventions) and in its concept of representation. In the first months of the new regime, such democratic practices were again put into operation and the actors associated with the old radical liberalism entered the electoral process enthusiastically. At the same time, after the *porfirista* machine's collapse, what was initially a division between elites ended up mobilizing the rest of society. The number of armed groups multiplied, and a type of legitimacy with no electoral basis reappeared: that of an oppressed people being represented by those who had arms to defend them, which was the classic mechanism for producing *caudillos*. Thus, there reappeared a type of actor whose disappearance had been one of Díaz's constant objectives, just as it would be later of the Constitutionalist and postrevolutionary governments.

The coalition that Madero built against Díaz did not survive power and the uncertainties of electoral democracy. In a context where legitimacy was being undermined, the frustrated pluralism of the electoral struggle quickly gave way to the old opposition between liberals and Catholics. The PCN, whose motto was "God, Nation, and Liberty" named itself God's party. This party used the national Catholic symbols as electoral weapons, while its political platform included the abolition of the Reform Laws; conversely, the PCN defended freedom of religion and education, no reelection, and the reconciliation of capital and labor.[6] Numerous PCN electoral victories were annulled in Congress for political reasons, causing it to pull away from Madero. However, with one party monopolizing the mantle of God's legitimate representative and enfeoffing the Catholic Church, the religious question erupted again in a political context where democratic legitimacy was contested by the interests of regions and *caudillo*. Spiritists, Protestants, freethinkers, and masons now reactivated the combative anti-Catholicism they had momentarily kept quiet. On 14 October 1911, two days before the announcement of Madero and Pino Suárez's electoral victory, 15,000 *maderistas*—most of them members of anti-reelectionist clubs—demonstrated in the capital's streets against conservatives who mocked the Reform Laws, the PCN, the clergy, the *científicos*, and those who supported De la Barra as vice president. As PCN influence grew after the June 1912 elections, a liberal reform block was created in the chamber of deputies against the party.

In this context of polarization, the arrival in August 1912 of the Spanish polemicist Belén de Sáraga—representing the International Freethinking Committee in Mexico—hardened the opposition of rival political camps over the religious question. Sáraga's lectures provoked indignant reactions to "her open opposition to the Catholic religion."[7] The government was thought to be behind these events as they discredited the PCN and strengthened the Progressive Constitutional Party for which Madero stated he had voted in the June elections. Sáraga was taken round masonic and Spiritist circles. After her last lecture, the permanent junta that emerged from the Second Spiritist Congress (1908) invited "the leaders of the different liberal factions, the members of masonic lodges, the heads of workers' groupings, and the presidents and members of philosophical societies, to form a committee which would carry out a great public demonstration" in *doña* Belén's honour.[8] The committee was made up of *La Nueva Era*'s editor, the Partido Liberal president, two students, two well-known spiritists, and Carlos Herrera y López— president of Mexico City's *ayuntamiento* and the Spiritist Junta—and Rogelio Fernández Güell, another junta member. The act that took place on 8 September near the Juárez monument strengthened the rupture between Madero and the PCN.[9] After Sáraga's appearance, the government accentuated its anti-Catholic posture and dislike of the PCN. Consequently, the government's enemies began to conspire against it.

This confrontation can also be seen at regional level, where popular intellectuals emerged from the ranks of Protestant networks to join the struggle against Catholic interests linked to hacienda owners. Such was the case of José Rumbia, ex-Methodist pastor and leader of the Río Blanco strikers, and of the Methodist pastors and schoolteachers who opposed Tlaxcala's Liga de Agricultores.[10] Other ex-pastors supported radical agrarianism, such as the Methodist José Trinidad Ruíz, who drew up the Plan of Ayala with Zapata and Otilio Montaño in November 1911, or the Protestant schoolteacher and Chihuahua's secretary of state, Braulio Hernández, who was radicalized against a landowning coalition along with Pascual Orozco in February 1912.[11]

I am not claiming that the religious societies unanimously supported revolutionary radicalization, but that disillusionment with *maderismo*'s moderate politics led them to reprise a radicalized discourse that now mixed radical liberalism's anti-Catholicism with regional, particularly agrarian, demands. After Huerta's coup d'état and alliance with the Catholic Church, religious persecution affected Protestants. These denounced "the clericalism that is attempting to take control of the highest spheres of government."[12] In January 1914, they anxiously pointed out that "throughout the country there are ceremonies to consecrate the Republic to the Sacred Heart of Jesus and to proclaim Jesus Christ the King of all Mexicans."[13] León's Methodist Chapel was stoned in June 1914 "during a demonstration organized by high society ladies," and Mexico City's Presbyterian Seminary was set alight in late 1913.[14] *Huertista* antiliberalism was met by *carrancista* anti-Catholicism. In 1914, anticlerical violence reached unprecedented levels. As a Methodist newspaper stated that September, "in Querétaro, Guadalajara, Jalapa and elsewhere, the confessionals and *santos* have been thrown into the streets and burned in the crowd; in other communities in Puebla, the revolutionaries penetrated the sanctuaries on horseback, took out the alms box, opened it and shared [alms] among the people; elsewhere they dragged nuns from their convents; in Monterrey most Catholic churches were closed and confession banned, as was the case in Querétaro and Guadalajara. In Zacatecas, some priests were shot because they were found with guns in their hands."[15] Although they did not condone these actions, Protestants excused them in light of circumstances. In such a context, the *carrancista* struggle was seen as a return to the Reform Wars, culminating in the confiscation of clerical property and priestly deportations. This struggle was waged with the military and ideological participation of those members of Protestant societies who made up the *carrancista* armies and constituted one of the civil bases of the revolutionary movement.[16]

Preachers of the Revolution

In late 1914 the revolution split between Constitutionalists and *villistas* while the *zapatista* rebellion continued. More than ever, Carranza now needed to spread the Constitutionalist movement systematically, both in and outside the country. Yet Carranza knew to mistrust intellectuals linked to Díaz and Huerta. He knew, too, that the Catholic clergy had become the enemy of Constitutionalism, especially after Constitutionalist armies unleashed anticlerical campaigns. It was logical, then, that he should incline toward young, popular intellectuals from Protestant backgrounds; these had been trained as pastors and teachers in the schools founded by United States missionaries and, crucially, supported him. Here he found cadres willing to help spread Constitutionalism, insofar as they shared an exaggerated anti-*huertismo* and an anti-Catholicism derived from the radical liberalism of their background social contexts. In late 1914 in Veracruz, Carranza entrusted the leadership of the Central Office for Revolutionary Information and Propaganda to Gregorio A. Velásquez, a Methodist pastor from Nuevo León. This office was initially created (June 1913) in Hermosillo, under the direction of Herminio Pérez Abreu.[17] Pérez Abreu's brother, Adolfo, organized anti-*huertista* espionage in Mexico City and sent information to Hermosillo via Douglas, Arizona. He also "received information [concerning the Constitutionalists' plans] from the [Hermosillo] office," and redistributed it in the capital, secretly and in great danger. On 16 April 1914, Pérez Abreu received his credentials as a revolutionary secret agent and opened another espionage branch in Veracruz, leaving

Victorio Góngora, an engineer, as the Constitutionalists' secret agent. From Mexico City and Veracruz, both men now organized "active propaganda in all the States of the South East and in Veracruz itself" through the *El Dictamen* newspaper. Various Protestants collaborated with Pérez Abreu, both in Mexico City and Veracruz. In December 1914, the Veracruz office became the central office after Carranza's government set up in that city. At this point, Velásquez became leader, regrouping his nationwide Protestant contacts in Veracruz and appointing José Velasco, also a Methodist pastor, second-in-command.[18] As one missionary pointed out, "it was quite a Protestant center," insofar as Velásquez "enlisted as many Protestants as possible, [because] they understand true democracy better than others and can be relied on for their character and consistency."[19] Pedro Navarro, Conrado Morales, and Jacinto Tamez, former students of Coyoacán's Presbyterian College, were speakers for this office. Four pastors and/or teachers of the Presbyterian Church—Moisés Sáenz, Luis Torregrosa, Lisandro Cámara, Benjamín Celaya—also lent their services. Velásquez published a daily bulletin reporting military events and news relating to Constitutionalist appointments and activities in Veracruz. The office's most important work was to organize teams of pro-revolutionary speakers, commissioned to go from village to village disseminating Constitutionalist literature and the grand principles that Carranza defended. Thus, from April until late June 1915, Cámara, Celaya, and Trinidad Beltrán Pérez toured Veracruz, Tabasco, Oaxaca, and Chiapas. In villages where the Constitutionalist Army was established they assembled the population, made speeches about Constitutionalism, and reported military victories. They also founded Constitutionalist propaganda clubs, as in Tonalá (Chiapas) on 30 April 1915. Likewise they organized a network of offices and agents, for example, by appointing Fidel F. Cortés as representative of the Revolutionary Propaganda Office in Tehuantepec (Puebla) on 21 May 1915. In Oaxaca, Cortés had installed the Free Oaxaca Club and in Tehuantepec he founded and chaired the Jesús Carranza Revolutionary Club. Lisandro R. Cámara, in particular, helped him in the capital, and the telegraphists "who left Mexico to bring information" included Protestants such as Ezequiel Quiñónez and Nicolás Cámara. From his appointment, Cortés published articles in Tehuantepec's *Pueblo Istmeño* newspaper exhorting the population "to take up arms in favor of Constitutionalism and against the Jesuit Dávila and the *felicistas*," and presenting himself "as a loyal friend and staunch supporter of the *pueblo*, that humble people which has always been used as the magnates' beast of burden and the whipping boy of *porfirista-huertista* despots and landowners."[20]

By mobilizing popular intellectuals, the propaganda office waged an ideological struggle based on a discursive model that had been, and was, that of Protestant societies. It is no surprise, then, to see Luis Torregrosa speaking for the office in a Veracruz park about the "role that religious principles may play in the work of reconstruction."[21] With the *carrancista* victories, some Protestant pastors and teachers returned to work. Others continued to lend their services to Constitutionalist journalism: Velásquez directed the *carrancista* newspaper *El Pueblo* (Mexico City) and José Velasco *El Demócrata*

(San Luis Potosí).[22] Many others went into public education. In this sphere, too, Carranza decided to rely on Protestants.

Carrancismo and Education

The Carranza government's decentralized education policy left only federal territories under the direction of the secretary of public education. Félix Palavicini was the official in charge of education from August 1914 to September 1916.[23] A topographical engineer and graduate of Tabasco's Instituto Juárez, Palavicini was a *maderista* deputy who stayed on under Huerta and allied himself to Carranza on the eve of victory. This, perhaps, is why Carranza mistrusted him, and named his friend Andrés Osuna director general of public education for the Federal District and Territories. Educated in Methodist missionary schools and North American universities, Osuna had been Coahuila's director of public education during Miguel Cárdenas's government; obliged because of his liberalism to leave this post during the Porfiriato's final years, he had done a stint in Nashville, Tennessee, studying at Vanderbilt University and working for Methodist missions. He had been an active advocate for *carrancismo* in Washington and the southern United States, until Carranza called him to occupy the post in early 1916.[24] Tension grew rapidly between Osuna and Palavicini. The latter, treating Osuna as his secretary and a pro-Yankee, did everything to get rid of him. In a letter to Carranza on the eve of his resignation (July 1916), Palavicini accused Osuna of finding posts in the administration for relatives and coreligionists. The real problem, though, was Palavacini's bitterness at having no real power, since "in the Ministry of Public Education's reduced jurisdiction, two-thirds of posts on the payroll correspond to the Directorate of Primary, Normal, and Preparatory Education, of which Señor Osuna is in charge."[25] The divergence between the two was more related to politics than to education. Both rejected Porfirian educators' hierarchical vision of a society directed by scientific laws of evolution, a model that had led, they thought, to the accumulation of wealth in a few hands and to the nonparticipation of the masses.

In its place, they wanted an education system directed toward the people, which would create new men with initiative, ability, and democratic spirit. It was exactly what Protestant missionary schools had promoted since their beginnings in Mexico. Along much the same lines, Osuna proposed creating a secondary school to link primary and preparatory school, thus allowing the "humble classes" access to higher education. He criticized the formerly elitist education harshly:

> The most knowledgeable revolutionaries affirm, without hesitation, that the intellectuals were always on the side of the *porfirista* dictatorship and Huerta's usurpation, with very rare exceptions that we are the first to acknowledge. The normal schools, for example, have been destined for the privileged classes and have not been the guiding element of a society which truly cares for the education and social improvement of the masses.[26]

In his first year in charge, Osuna created the Technical Board of Education that permitted "personal ideas and interests to be completely eliminated, so

that we may give ourselves to the explanation of purely technical questions."[27] He put in motion a school medical service for the first time, and
promoted the development of industrial schools, using Methodist industrial
schools in Mexico City as his model. He invited Paula Sotres de Rivera, a
teacher in Mexico City's Sarah L. Keen Methodist College, to help found an
industrial school, which was similar to one created for the poor in Santa Julia
by the missionary Laura Temple. Osuna also recruited a teacher, Concepción
Pérez, from the same college to preach on temperance, morality, and hygiene
in Mexico City's prison and many of its factories.[28]

Osuna campaigned to clean up education by removing corrupt teachers
and raising recruitment standards. He organized a commission to purge directors who drew a salary despite running no school. In order to carry out his
education policy, Osuna surrounded himself with Protestant teachers. From
1916–20, Moisés Sáenz, a graduate of Coyoacan's Presbyterian Preparatory
School, took the reins of the National Preparatory School, first as secretary,
then director; Alfonso Herrera Mendoza (1870–1948), a former teacher in
Puebla's Methodist College, became National University secretary (1916–20)
after serving as the Directorate of Technical Education's chief administrative
officer (August 1915).[29] The Presbyterian Eliseo García headed the Normal
School, while his coreligionist, Lisandro R. Cámara, led the school's boarding
section; many Protestant teachers took up less important posts.[30] This drew
strong attacks on Osuna, led by Palavacini himself, by late 1916.[31] But
Osuna's friendship with Carranza—who considered him "exceptionally apt
and a good teacher"[32]—kept him in post until May 1918, while the schools
passed into *ayuntamiento* control with the new constitution.

Events in the Federal District were replicated in states with Protestant (or
pro-Protestant) governors and a strongly Protestant school presence. In
Coahuila, the Presbyterian Espinoza Mireles appointed José María Cárdenas,
a Presbyterian teacher, as public education director. In Guanajuato, the
Presbyterian military governor, Miguel A. Peralta, named Moisés Sáenz to
the same post in 1915, while governor José Siurob later appointed the
Methodist Rodolfo R. Ramírez director of the state's preparatory school;[33] in
Hidalgo, the Methodist José Velasco was director general of public instruction from June 1915, having been secretary of the Federal District's Normal
School in 1914.[34] In Tlaxcala, Governor Máximo Rojas, a strong Protestant
sympathizer, employed the Methodist Leopoldo Sánchez as education director
in 1918. Governor Cesáreo Castro of Puebla, a close friend of the director of
the Mexican Methodist Institute, placed grant holders in that institution, while
in Yucatán, Salvador Alvarado, whose program was backed by Protestant
missions, recruited Protestant teachers.

What is most notable is these teachers' dual—revolutionary and religious—
militancy. Osuna gave lectures in the Methodist Church on the Calle de Gante,
and would invite the Rector of the University, Alfonso Pruneda.[35] Sáenz did
likewise in Guanajuato and, besides running the National Preparatory School,
assumed important duties in a Protestant youth organization, agreeing, in
early 1919, to direct a Protestant magazine (*El Mundo Cristiano*).[36] In these

years, Sáenz created an active pedagogy that he would develop as subsecretary in the Ministry of Public Education (SEP) in the 1920s. This pedagogy, inspired by his teacher, John Dewey, allied active schooling principles to the Protestant ethic. In 1917, Sáenz argued that evangelical schools were superior to official ones because they offered "something so important that every man who thinks but a little will not hesitate in considering it the key to success in life. This something . . . is their tendency . . . to foment character formation."[37] For the young Mexican educator, "integral education must educate men at the intellectual and physical, as at the moral, level." Men combining these three levels of education would be the country's future leaders, an elite that would allow the Mexican nation to proceed toward a new order whose axis was the school. Indeed, Mexico cried out for "upright men of conscience and ideals who heard the call of the age and lent themselves to the fight."[38]

At Querétaro, the constituents' debate over education (article 3) revealed the ambiguity of the Protestant position. Protestants wished to destroy education by Catholic clergy but without laicizing education altogether, thus leaving space for the religious schooling that had, in them, created an ethic of duty, initiative, and integrity. Osuna publicly opposed article 3 in a statement to journalists in which he defended the option for religious education.[39] In the assembly, the staunchest critic of the Protestants was Palavicini. Basing his argument on the fact of Protestants' dual—religious and public—militancy, and stirring in anti-Americanism and anticlericalism, Palavicini expressed himself thus:

> the Protestant minister has organized sports clubs which have all the English terminology; he has organized the Young Men's Christian Association where there is music, where bad verse is recited, where the one step is danced, and where from time to time the epistles of Saint Paul are read; but the Protestant minister doesn't stop there . . . he infiltrates all the official establishments masked as a radical revolutionary . . . he collects with the right hand the salary of a lay teacher, while with his left hand he receives money from the Protestant missions the North American Republic. This is the price of the evangelization of the Mexican Republic and is an aspect of conquest.[40]

Carrancismo's Clientelist Network

The importance of the Protestant network inside the *carrancista* regime explains Palavicini's head-on, reiterated attack. Religious actors' presence in Constitutionalism was not the fruit of some religio-imperialist collusion, however, but of Protestantism's associative practice alongside radical liberalism. This, as I have shown elsewhere, developed since the Porfiriato.[41] This practice explains Protestants' involvement in the revolution, in which they participated by abandoning their churches and schools and taking up arms in 1910–11 and 1913–15. Madero's sympathies toward Catholicism's democratic faction, as well as his merely incipient agrarian and labor reforms and maintenance of Porfirian structures, alienated his Protestant supporters and many other revolutionaries who expected radical change. The *decena trágica*, Huerta's rise—due partly to the Catholic hierarchy's support—and the consequent repression of radical liberals and Protestants, brought about the latter's alliance with Carranza in the struggle against Huerta. In this way, many leaders and members of Protestant congregations rose quickly in the *carrancista* forces. During the Aguascalientes Convention, an attempt was made, at Gregorio A. Velásquez's initiative, to form a Protestant *carrancista* military lobby. It is significant, too, that the president of the Convention's Permanent Commission, General Martín Espinoza, and its secretary, Colonel Miguel A. Peralta, were respectively a member and pastor of Protestant congregations.[42]

Hence it is not the case, as Baldwin suggests, that for Protestants the Revolution was an opportunity to make propaganda.[43] On the contrary, they were part of a movement whose goals were to combat the Catholic Church's influence, establish genuine democratic practices, and extend education throughout the population. Protestants participated in a revolution, which to them represented the culmination of years of struggle, dating from the early Porfiriato. They hoped that with Carranza it would finally be possible strictly to enforce Church-state separation, to end the alliance "of *beato* and bourgeois," to propagate education and "destroy ignorance and fanaticism," to build up agrarian smallholdings against the hacienda, and to establish labor laws like those of the mutualist societies in which they had participated. Protestants understood the revolution as the possible extension to all civil society of what they had experienced in their religious societies and schools. This is why the best cadres were no longer pastors and teachers but *carrancista* officers seeking posts in the revolutionary administration. Protestants did not come to control the Constitutionalists' Information and Propaganda Office by chance. They had years of experience as public orators, which they acquired by dint of leaving their pulpits and going to the public squares to speak in liberal civic-religious acts in which they praised the Constitution and the rights of the citizen while denouncing clericalist violations of the Reform Laws. The Constitutionalism that they spread in 1914–15 was the same as the one they defended against *porfirista* conservative liberalism.

On the other hand, it is important to remember that Protestants in the *carrancista* bureaucracy had woven personal links with Carranza and his family long before the revolution. Andrés Osuna became a friend of Carranza's when he began teaching in Coahuila; he and his brother, Gregorio, supported Carranza's failed campaign for Coahuila's state governorship in 1909; Gregorio Osuna was one of the first soldiers to bear arms alongside Pablo González in 1911, and then was Carranza's principal agent in his gubernatorial campaign that summer.[44] In Coahuila, both Osuna and Carranza belonged to the same radical liberal networks that were attempting to combat the center's influence in the state. The presence of high-ranking Protestant officials, therefore, brings us back to a much more concrete explanation: they were secure and loyal clients for Carranza. For this reason, they contributed to the regime's exercise of military, political, and ideological authority. Andrés

Osuna Hinojosa was successively director general of public education (January 1916–May 1918) and provisional governor of Tamaulipas (May 1918–June 1919). His brother, General Gregorio Osuna Hinojosa, was superintendent of the Constitutionalist Railway (1915), military governor of Aguascalientes (June 1916–January 1917), president of the Mexico City *ayuntamiento* (September 1917–January 1918), and interim governor of Tamaulipas (April–June 1917). Their nephew, General Carlos Osuna León, was Durango's military governor (April 1917). Another Protestant from the Coahuilan networks was Gustavo Espinoza Mireles, Carranza's private secretary from 1914–16, and Coahuila's provisional (October 1916–April 1917) and constitutional governor (from September 1917).[45] Lieutenant-colonel Alfonso Herrera Mendoza (1870–1948), an ex-Methodist pastor from Campeche, had close ties to General Jesús Carranza for whom he was private secretary (1914–15) before becoming National University secretary (1916–20).[46]

Carranza's surrender of the regime's ideological compass to members of a northern network extending along the Coahuila-Nuevo León-Tamaulipas axis, or to other networks close to his family, is confirmed in the person of Gregorio A. Velásquez, a former Methodist pastor in Coahuila and Nuevo León who redoubled his *carrancista* political activities on appointment as director of the Higher School of Commerce and Administration (September 1915–April 1917). He acted as Carranza's chosen man in 1916 to set up the Liberal Constitutionalist Party (PLC), whose secretary was another Presbyterian schoolteacher, Lisandro R. Cámara. Organized by Carranza himself to elect the deputies that he had designated for the Querétaro Convention, the PLC made an about-turn after July 1917 and became a national party controlled by those disenchanted with Carranza's policy.[47] Henceforth, Velásquez was characterized by his totalizing *carrancismo* and combative opposition to the PLC, a position he solidified by founding the First Liberal Constitutionalist Party (PPLC). As party head, he doubled his efforts to support the regime and Carranza. Furthermore, Velásquez was able to deploy all his support for the regime when appointed (from February 1918) director of the national *carrancista* newspaper *El Pueblo* (1916–1920).[48]

Moisés Sáenz (1888–1941), a Nuevo León Presbyterian, belonged to these same networks, as did his brother Aarón. Giving key posts to these officials involved the secondary participation of many Protestant officials at lower levels of the administration, particularly in public education, as Palavicini complained.[49] In fact, public education in the Federal District remained in Protestant hands throughout the regime under secretaries Andrés Osuna (January 1916–May 1918), Eliseo García (August 1918–March 1919), and Moisés Sáenz (June–August 1920).

Not all Protestants in the administration came from this northern axis. The Presbyterian and mason (Level 33) Juan Neftalí Amador (1873–1916), who was subsecretary of the interior in Veracruz (1914–15), a *carrancista* secret agent in Washington (1915), and subsecretary for foreign affairs until his death in August 1916, was originally from Zacatecas and belonged to a family of Presbyterian pastors and *comecuras* (priest-baiters) from Villa de

Cos whose religious dissidence went back to the beginnings of liberal reform and the expansion of such societies in the region.[50] It is possible to multiply the number of examples at state level, particularly in states where Protestant networks and schools had been strong, such as Tlaxcala or Aguascalientes, where the Methodist Santiago G. Paz was *oficial mayor* in 1916.[51]

A question that arises when the existence of such links is revealed is whether from 1915–20 there was an attempt on Carranza's part to manufacture a northern clan capable of holding in check those from Sonora who were competing for power. If such a hypothesis is true, then the Protestant networks in the *carrancista* administration acted as the clients and the politico-administrative base of a failed project.

Tension grew between *obregonistas* and *carrancistas* following the constitutional debates of 1916–17. The debate over article 3, concerning religious schools and religious education in public schools, served to entrench opposing positions inside the revolutionary clan. The *carrancistas* were reformists and moderates while the *obregonistas* adopted radical anticlerical positions. Carranza's draft of article 3 was rejected and the final wording evidenced an intransigent Jacobinism, the consequences of which damaged the revolution insofar as this led, some years later, to the *Cristiada*. Protestants began to be denigrated in public debates, apparently for their beliefs, but really because they constituted a network in Carranza's service.[52] This occurred to such an extent that calling *carrancistas* "Protestant ministers" became a leitmotif for discrediting them. Even Ignacio Bonilla, put forward by Carrranza as his successor, was accused of "having been a sheriff for some time in Arizona, then a Protestant minister in Texas."[53]

Alvaro Obregón's coup ended the *carrancista* project, but not the influence of dissident religious actors in the revolutionary process. Enfeebled as a network and clientele by *obregonismo*, Protestants were reborn politically in *callismo*'s networks, although they carried much less weight than they had during the Constitutionalist movement.[54] Their fall can be confirmed if we observe that Andrés Osuna was unable to find state employment from 1920–24; Moisés Sáenz's candidacy as director of public education in the Federal District was opposed in July–August 1920, meanwhile, and he was later pushed out of the country, returning only in August 1924 as a high-ranking SEP official. But this was after Vasconcelos's resignation and the dismissal of the teachers who supported him.[55] A violent anti-Protestant wave was unleashed both by the Catholic Church and the *obregonistas* who were fighting *carrancismo*'s influence. An *obregonista* expressed this with clarity in June 1920 when he wrote that "the golden age of Protestantism in Mexico passed with the death of Carranza, because no longer will there be fifty Protestant priests in public posts . . ."[56]

Conclusion

Reading the revolution as the awakening of people in the cities and the countryside to modern politics, and as their demand for effective civil rights, does not mean rejecting a social reading, but it does mean articulating the social and the political by investigating where and how such a demand was experienced. In a society in transition, as Mexican society was, non-Catholic religious sociabilities—with their strong regional roots and provincial actors who burst forth alongside the urban *criollo* elites—are worthy of being rescued in an archaeological sense. Such an archaeology points to a religious logic connected to the liberal democratic logic that was required along with economic modernization. With these sociabilities, political action passed from the elites to the middling social sectors. These networks thus contributed to the "passage from being subjects to citizens." Their presence in the revolutionary process on the side of democratic struggle was a constant from 1910–20, first for Madero and later for Carranza. However, the actions of the leaders of those sociabilities were not free of contradictions. If an emphasis on education as a creator of citizenship and a commitment to democracy formed part of their discourse and actions, in political practice they could not escape the clientelistic logic that conditioned access to recognition and to public space. The linking of Protestant actors with a regime that used them as a clientele shows the difficulty of transforming an ingrained political culture and its practices.

On the other hand, the rebirth of the religious question in the revolutionary process highlights the extreme difficulty in privatizing the sacred and consigning it to the private sphere. Religion and nonreligion entered the public debate forcefully and defined political positions there. This resulted in part from the Catholic Church's resistance to secularization, which led it to support Huerta. Consequently, the question of regulating the religious sphere politically was posed in a radical way in constitutional debates. In the discussion over constitutional articles, the dominant position was one of exacerbated, combative anticlericalism, as defended by a considerable number of masons. This threw the limits of Mexican secularization into relief. Imposed by anticlerical revolutionaries from within the political apparatus, the secularization process took place against religion and not with it, because the Catholic Church rejected any notion of privatization. Protestant actors were in a different position. They aspired to act with greater moderation in religious matters, thinking, conversely, that religion should not be combated, but limited, and that it would thus contribute to democratization as an essential part of a civil society moving toward pluralization.

Notes

*   Translated by Paul Rankin and Matthew Butler.

1. Alicia Hernández Chávez, *La Tradición Republicana del Buen Gobierno* (Mexico City: El Colegio de México, 1993), 32.

2. Francisco Bulnes, *El Verdadero Díaz y la Revolución* (Mexico City: Editorial Hispano-Mexicana, 1920), 407.

3. José Valadés, *El Porfirismo, Historia de un Régimen* (Mexico City: Editorial Patria, 1970), 58.

4. Jean-Pierre Bastian, *Los Disidentes: Sociedades Protestantes y Revolución Social en México* (Mexico City: El Colegio de México, 1989). Guy Thomson with David G. LaFrance, *Patriotism, Politics, and Popular Liberalism in Nineteenth-Century Mexico: Juan Francisco Lucas and the Puebla Sierra* (Wilmington: Scholarly Resources, 1999).

5. Bastian, *Los Disidentes*, 293.

6. Moisés González Navarro, *Masones y Cristeros en Jalisco* (Mexico City: El Colegio de México, 2000), 31.

7. Cited by Yolia Tortolero Cervantes, "Un Espírita Traduce sus Creencias en Hecho Político: Francisco I. Madero (1873–1913)" (PhD diss., El Colegio de México, 1999), 254.

8. Cited by Tortolero, "Un Espírita," 259.

9. Tortolero, "Un Espírita," 263.

10. Jean-Pierre Bastian, "Itinerario de un Intelectual Popular Protestante, Liberal, y Francmasón en México: José Rumbia Guzmán, 1865–1913," *Cristianismo y Sociedad* 92 (1987): 103–5.

11. Bastian, *Los Disidentes*, 300n106. Deborah J. Baldwin, *Protestants and the Mexican Revolution: Missionaries, Ministers, and Social Change* (Chicago: University of Illinois Press, 1990), 118.

12. *El Abogado Cristiano Ilustrado* (henceforth *ACI*), 25 Sep. 1913.

13. *ACI*, 19 Jan. 1914.

14. *ACI*, 11 Jun. 1914, and 9 Jul. 1914.

15. *ACI*, 17 Sep. 1914.

16. Cf. Samuel G. Inman, cited by Jean Meyer, *La Révolution Mexicaine* (Paris: Calman-Lévy, 1973), 70: "there were entire congregations led by their pastors who volunteered in the Revolutionary Army."

17. Condumex, Fondo XXI, Archivo del Primer Jefe del Ejército Constitucionalista, 1889–1920 (henceforth Condumex), c. 125, leg. 14103.

18. *Actas de la Iglesia Metodista Episcopal de México* (henceforth *AIMEM*), 1908–14.

19. Cited by Baldwin, *Protestants*, 139.

20. Condumex, c. 35, legs. 3743, 3765; c. 36, legs. 3896, 3936; c. 37, legs. 4001, 4028, 4077–8; c. 39, legs. 4197, 4206–7, 4213; c. 40, legs. 4384, 4389, 4391, 4416; c. 42, leg. 4565.

21. Wallace to Presbyterian Missionary Board, 10 Jun. 1915, cited by Baldwin, *Protestants*, 303.

22. Velásquez also received the Constitutionalist forces' propaganda concession in the United States, which was taken from him in Dec. 1918 and granted to the "Sonora News Co." Cf. Condumex, c.128, leg.14608. José Velasco directed *El Demócrata* in 1916; on 2 May 1916 he asked Carranza to support him in offering his services to Espinoza Mireles in Saltillo. Condumex, c. 76, leg. 8299.

23. Félix F. Palavicini, *La Patria por la Escuela* (Mexico City: Linotipografía, 1916); Félix F. Palavicini, *Mi Vida Revolucionaria* (Mexico Ciy: Ediciones Botas, 1937).

24. Andrés Osuna, *Por la Escuela y la Patria, Autobiografía* (Mexico City: Casa Unida de Publicaciones, 1943), 133.

25. Condumex, leg. 87, leg. 9756.

26. Osuna, *Escuela*, 182.

27. Ibid., 159.

28. *AIMEM*, 1916, 28.

29. *ACI*, 17 Sept. 1914.

30. "What the Mexican Revolution has done for Protestantism," *Christian Advocate*, 22 Jul. 1915: "Appointment of Juan (G. A.) Velásquez, A. Osuna, A. Herrera, and José Velasco to Important Post in the Reorganization of the Country's Education System," *Journal of the 27th Delegated Conference of the Methodist Episcopal Church, 14 May 1916, Saratoga Spring* (New York: The Methodist Book Concern, 1916), 1028. *El Faro*, 22 Sep. 1916. On Moisés Sáenz, Director General of Public Instruction of the State of Guanajuato, cf. *ACI*, 10 Nov. 1915. On Cesáreo Castro, cf. *AIMEM*, 1917, 85; on Sáenz, director of the National University Preparatory School, cf. Samuel G. Inman, *Intervention in Mexico* (New York: Association Press, 1919), 191; on Salvador Alvarado and Protestant churches, cf. Baldwin, *Protestants*, 300–1. On L. Sánchez, cf. *ACI*, 5 Sep. 1914, and 19 Sep. 1918. On A. Herrera, *ACI*, 26 Aug. 1915, 4 Nov. 1915, 7 Sep. 1916.

31. Condumex, c. 105, leg. 12017; c. 106, leg. 12083.

32. Note by V. Carranza in Condumex. José Pintador et al. to Carranza, Mexico City, 26 Dec. 1916.

33. *El Pueblo* (henceforth *EP*), 28 Jan. 1916. *ACI*, 12 Oct. 1916. *EP*, 13 May 1917.

34. *ACI*, 26 Feb. 1914; 17 Jun. 1915.

35. *ACI*, 22 Jul. 1916; *AGI*, 6 Jul. 1916.

36. *ACI*, 20 Jan. 1916; *El Mundo Cristiano*, 3 Jul.–9 Oct. 1919.

37. On Sáenz's Protestantism, cf. Jean-Pierre Bastian, *Protestantismo y Sociedad en México* (Mexico City: CUPSA, 1983), 155–67.

38. *El Faro*, 2 Feb. 1917.

39. Osuna, *Escuela*, 194. E.V. Niemeyer, *Revolution at Querétaro: The Mexican Constitutional Convention of 1916–1917* (Austin: University of Texas Press, 1974), 71.

40. Cited in Niemeyer, *Revolution*, 71–2.

41. Bastian, *Los Disidentes*.

42. *EP*, 7 Mar. 1915; Marianne E. McKechnie, "The Mexican Revolution and the National Presbyterian Church in Mexico, 1910–1940" (PhD diss., The American University, 1970), 126. Besides those mentioned, Colonel Gregorio Osuna, General Enrique W. Paniagua, Colonel Isabel P. Balderas, and others, were in Aguascalientes.

43. Baldwin, *Protestants*, 302.

44. Osuna, *Escuela*, 102–32. *La Actualidad*, 12 Aug. 1911.

45. Osuna, *Escuela*, 216. For a biography of Gregorio Osuna, cf. *El Evangelista Mexicano*, 15 Feb. 1941; see also *EP*, 18 Apr. 1916; 14 Jun. 1916; 14 Jan. 1917; 2 Feb. 1918; 13 Apr. 1917; 28 Jul. 1917; 4 Apr. 1917.

46. *ACI*, 17 Sep. 1914.

47. Hence Carranza ordered Andrés Osuna to refuse the PLC Presidency in Jul. 1917. Cf. Charles C. Cumberland, *La Revolución Mexicana: Los Años Constitucionalistas* (Mexico City: FCE, 1975), 327, 328n5.

48. Gregorio A. Velázquez, *Horizontes Políticos, Continuación de "Mi Campaña contra el PLC"* (Mexico City: Oficina de Información Política, 1918); *ACI*, 2 Feb. 1915; *EP*, 26 Oct. 1916; *EP*, 9 Feb. 1918.

49. Palavicini, *Vida*, 214; Condumex, c. 87, leg. 9756.

50. *EP*, 11 Sep. 1916. *EP*, 30 Mar. 1921. Flores Zavala, *El Grupo Masón en la Política Zacatecana, 1880–1914* (Mexico City: Estampa Arte Gráficas, 2002), 173, 213, 237–8. Bastian, *Los Disidentes*, 20–30, 258, 293.

51. *ACI*, 17 Oct. 1918; *ACI*, 27 Nov. 1913; Raymond Buve, *El Movimiento Revolucionario en Tlaxcala* (Mexico City: UIA, 1994), 333. On S.G. Paz cf. *ACI*, 16 Nov. 1916.

52. This came later. "La Intransigencia en la Cámara de Diputados," *ACI*, 27 Dec. 1917.

53. Cumberland, *Revolución*, 366. *El Mundo Cristiano*, 5 Aug. 1920. Protestant Deputies constantly had to respond to accusations that they were "Protestant bishops." Cf. *EP*, 7 Nov. 1917; 19 Jun. 1918.

54. Osuna, *Escuela*, 232–97. Osuna discharged various functions from 1924. Aarón Saenz, a friend, correligionist, and governor of Nuevo León from 1927, named him director of public education (1927–32).

55. Osuna, *Escuela*, 245; Ernesto Meneses Morales, *Tendencias Educativas Oficiales en México, 1911–1934* (Mexico City: Centro de Estudios Educativos, 1986), 275, 280, 451; *El Mundo Cristiano*, 5 Aug. 1920.

56. *El Mundo Cristiano*, 22 Jul. 1920, 1 Jul. 1920. Polemics surrounding "Protestant infiltration" of *carrancismo* continued. Cf. Alfonso Junco, "Protestantes y Revolucionarios," *Excélsior*, 19 Sep. 1927, and "Carrancismo y Protestantismo," *El Universal*, 11 Apr. 1942.

Chapter 4

Ethereal Allies: Spiritism and the Revolutionary Struggle in Hidalgo

Keith Brewster and Claire Brewster

When rumors of Marcial Cavazos's death began to reach the people of Pachuca, they refused to believe it. During de la Huerta's rebellion (1923–24), he had seemed invincible. The local newspaper, *El Observador*, suggested that not until *pachuquenses* saw Cavazos's body with their own eyes would they accept this "stunning news." The national press received reports from Hidalgo with equal astonishment. Articles giving details of his final moments merged into obituaries as they reflected upon the illustrious past of "the most romantic figure in the revolutionary history of the Republic," and "the inheritor of the mantle of 'Pancho' Villa."[1] As much as half the population of Pachuca filed past Cavazos's coffin to pay their last respects before he made his final journey to San Luis Potosí. Given such accolades it is surprising that the figure evoking such sympathies had spent the last days of his life in rebellion against the federal government. Twice in as many months, Cavazos's men had taken control of the state capital; throughout early 1924, their lightening raids had thrown commerce, transport, and federal military authority in Hidalgo into chaos. Clearly, newspaper editors found it hard to reconcile the disparaging official portrayal of rebel leaders with that emanating from those in Hidalgo touched by Cavazos's actions. Quite simply, many people in Pachuca could not accept that "*el General Fantasma*" ("the Ghost General") was dead.[2]

For federal and state authorities, Cavazos's death brought relief that a formidable opponent had been eliminated. Their attention quickly switched to the bundle of papers found among Cavazos's few possessions when he was killed. Military intelligence officers were confident that these blood-stained pages would reveal vital information about the identity and whereabouts of the rebel's remaining allies.[3] In the event, they were to be thwarted one more time by their adversary. Offering little practical information, the documents appeared to be nothing other than a collection of communications with the dead. While they may have provoked speculation over the state of Cavazos's mind, they were soon discarded and archived away as a bizarre but ultimately insignificant detail of the *delahuertista* rebellion in Hidalgo.[4]

In this chapter, we revisit the documents found on Cavazos's body as a means of investigating the role of Spiritism in times of combat.[5] Using comparative material, we outline how a heightened sense of mortality felt by those in combat conditions could stimulate diverse searches for spiritual answers. Yet for many Mexican revolutionaries, their usual source of succor, the Catholic Church, was hostile to their petition. Within this context, we explore the extent to which Spiritism may have acted as a credible alternative—a means by which military leaders could rally their men—and how ordinary soldiers may have viewed it as a source of spiritual comfort in times of conflict. In order to do this, we offer a textual analysis of the documents found on General Marcial Cavazos's body. The absence of hard evidence confirming the religious composition of Cavazos's troops makes firm conclusions impossible. Yet by matching the tenor of the various spiritual messages to the rapidly changing circumstances that rebel troops endured during a critical period in the campaign, we provide tentative conclusions concerning how these messages might have been received and what comfort, if any, could have been derived from them. We suggest that for Cavazos and many of those fighting under his command, messages from the spirits bore several benefits: they directed and often reaffirmed the political agenda of their cause; constantly reinforced morale and discipline; offered the spiritual strength to continue fighting in the face of adversities; and most importantly, provided strong reassurance that by following God's instructions, their future life in the spiritual world was assured. The combination of these benefits may have persuaded Cavazos and his men to continue their struggle toward its suicidal conclusion.

Spiritism and Other Beliefs

Before gauging its significance within prerevolutionary Mexican society, it is important to clarify misconceptions surrounding Spiritism's belief system and relationship to other secular religions. The tendency to see Spiritism and Spiritualism as synonymous was partly caused by the late nineteenth-century practice of labelling any interest in the paranormal as "Spiritualism." In the case of Mexico, this convergence was reinforced by officials within the Catholic Church who met all attempts to rationalize religion by science with contempt and condemnation. To understand which groups might have been attracted to Spiritism, however, it is necessary to deconstruct such generalizations. In this respect, it is useful briefly to consider the divergence of interest in the paranormal outside Mexico, and then apply such understanding to similar developments in Porfirian society.

A frenzy of public curiosity in the afterlife emerged in 1848 when Margaret and Catherine Fox claimed that spirits could communicate with them through "rapping" tables and other inanimate objects in their house in

Hydesville, New York. As David Cannandine points out, European responses to this Atlantic import were diverse. At a popular level, the activities of Spiritualists included the whole gamut of moving tables, tapping, and apparitions. Its popularity no doubt reflected the eternal concern over life after death, spiced with varying measures of intrigue, adventurism, and sheer entertainment.[6] Simultaneously, scientific investigations into the phenomenon were conducted in different parts of Western Europe. Most pertinent to our understanding of Mexico were the activities of the French educator, philosopher, and member of the Royal Academy of Arras, Hipólito León Denizard Rivail. Under the pseudonym, Allan C. Kardec, he began to apply scientific rationale to the paranormal and in 1857 published his preliminary findings in *The Spirits' Book*, the first of seven volumes on the subject that he wrote before his death in 1869.

The work of Allan Kardec provides a link to Spiritism in Mexico and helps distinguish it from Spiritualism. *Kardecismo*, as his particular interpretation of Spiritism is commonly known, was championed in Mexico by a military man, General Refugio I. González, who translated Kardec's books into Spanish. In 1872, González became a founding member of the Central Mexican Society of Spiritists, with circles in Mexico City, Guadalajara, Guanajuato, San Luis Potosí, Monterrey, and Tampico.[7] Reflecting Kardec's own educational background, Spiritism became a preoccupation for those among the intellectual elite who sought to apply scientific rationale to religious faith. As such, it was quite separate from the religious practice of the Iglesia Mexicana Patriarcal Elías, which in Mexico would become known as Spiritualism. The founding father of this faith, Roque Rojas Esparza, (Padre Elías) viewed his followers as members of the ten lost tribes of Israel, and saw Mexico as the New Jerusalem. Significantly, Padre Elías believed that Mexico's indigenous ancestors protected and guided the faithful. By incorporating indigenous spiritual healing into its belief system, Spiritualism underscored its local nature and helped to construct deep and durable inroads into popular religion.[8] In many respects, therefore, the European division between intellectual and popular interests in the paranormal was replicated in Mexico and distinguished by whether one was a follower of Kardec (that is, a Spiritist) or Padre Elías (in other words, a Spiritualist).

What was it about Spiritism that proved so attractive to its followers and so threatening to others, particularly the Catholic Church? In 1875, the Creed of the Central Mexican Society of Spiritists set out the tenants of the faith. It stated that Kardec recognized the existence of one supreme God, who was the Creator of all things. While the Catholic Church would have no argument with such sentiments, Kardec's thoughts on the nature of God's relationship with humans ran foul of Catholic teaching. Spiritists acknowledged the two known Laws of God, brought to man by Moses and Jesus Christ, yet they also argued that a Third Revelation was conveyed by a multitude of intermediaries—the spirits.[9] Such thoughts were anathema to the Catholic Church because they embraced notions of reincarnation and the ability of humans to summon the spirits.[10] Equally threatening was the

Spiritist notion that man did not need temples or priests to worship God as "the heart [is] the best altar of the virtuous man, while unquestioning morality [is] his best cult."[11] Little wonder, then, that in 1898 the Vatican and the Congregation of the Holy Office gravely condemned the practice of Spiritism. In 1917 they went further by issuing a categorical statement that no-one should ever attend a Spiritist session of any kind.[12]

Growing interest in Spiritism within Mexico coincided with Porfirio Diaz's gradual courtship of the Catholic Church in the late nineteenth century, a move which had the effect of suppressing discussion of religious affairs that were deemed to be anti-Catholic.[13] Within this environment, the Church refused to recognize any distinction between Spiritism and the Spiritualism practised by the Iglesia Mexicana Patriarcal Elías. Furthermore, the Church viewed Spiritism as one of an avalanche of foreign philosophies that sought to weaken its links with the Mexican people. The fact that Spiritists applied science to explain connections between celestial and material worlds encouraged the Church to see them as the fourth column of an assault launched by positivists, liberals, and social Darwinists, all of whom sought to replace faith with experimentalism.[14] Yet this generalization ignored the incompatibility of such philosophies. Social Darwinists, for example, ridiculed notions of reincarnation, and wondered whether Spiritist sessions brought believers into communion with their primate ancestors.[15] Equally, Spiritists viewed Positivist notions of reason as religiously bankrupt: scientific reason could never reach the point of questioning the existence of God. Their insistence on the presence of God but the redundancy of Church institutions made Spiritists the target of the pious and the skeptic alike.

Spiritism in Times of Turmoil

As Jean-Pierre Bastian's chapter on modern religious associations correctly highlights, there is a paucity of academic research into the network of Spiritists in Latin America. In its absence, we are left to speculate on the correlation between the faith and broader sociopolitical influences. There is no doubt, however, that during the early twentieth century the search for new ways to God had gathered pace within Latin American intellectual circles. In this respect, the tentative conclusions of Eduardo Devés Valdés and Ricardo Melgar Bao offer tantalizing avenues for future investigation. They explore possible links between members of Latin America's intellectual elite whose individual search for spiritual answers had led them beyond Catholicism.[16] This loose network contained illustrious members such as José Vasconcelos, Víctor Haya de la Torre, Gabriela Mistral, and César Augusto Sandino. Together they comprised an eclectic bunch: besides being Theosophists, they could be autodidacts, masons, Catholics, socialists, freethinkers, Protestants, even anarchists and communists. In the cases of Mexico and Brazil, in particular, Spiritism added to the concoction of spirits.[17] Beyond a common belief in reincarnation, these figures all shared a conviction that their individual destiny would be determined by their efforts to improve the lives of others.

Valdés and Boa suggest that for some individuals, among them Francisco Madero, Vasconcelos, Sandino, and Haya de la Torre, this sense of mission fostered a charismatic, even messianic, form of leadership.[18]

Given the theological and philosophical environment within which Spiritism developed, we can construct an image of those who might be drawn to beliefs such as Spiritism. Reflecting Spiritism's growth in Mexico during the *Reforma*, it is reasonable to suppose that Spiritists were influenced by a political rhetoric that questioned the privileged position of the Catholic hierarchy. It is also reasonable to assume that, along with Protestants and masons, Spiritists comprised part of a loose coalition that was ideologically opposed to Porfirio Díaz's rapprochement with the Catholic Church.[19] By the same token, Spiritists retained sufficient religiosity to reject the more radical notions proposed by other critics of the Catholic faith. It might be more accurate, therefore, to view Spiritists as religious and political moderates. While questioning the need for wealthy religious infrastructures, they were not atheists; while possessing a humanitarian mission, they were not communists. Although the ethos of Spiritism was based on demonstrating benevolence and rectitude toward one's fellow man, this was not tantamount to proposing wholesale social equity. From this perspective it becomes easier to understand why members of the middle class might be attracted to such a philosophy. Spiritism did not question the right to make money from one's own industry. Furthermore, having challenged the Catholic Church's role as the provider of moral guidance, Spiritism acted as their social conscience.

Many of these attributes resonate in the case of Francisco Madero, the most famous Spiritist of the Mexican Revolution. While he never overtly championed his beliefs in public, his writings make it clear that communications with the spirits instilled in him a sense of mission. Although this mission included improving conditions for peons within the family hacienda, it neither questioned the status of the peon nor the institution of the hacienda. When the spirits of Benito Juárez and Madero's deceased brother, Raúl, urged him to write *La Sucesión Presidencial en 1910*, it was not a programme of social revolution. Similarly, the Plan of San Luis Potosí called for political reform and respect for the 1857 Constitution, not a manifesto for wholesale social change. In her study of Spiritism's political influence on Madero, Yolia Tortolero reveals other influential figures who were attracted to the doctrine: José Juan Tablada, Antonio Mediz Bolio, and Félix Palavicini. Each of them sympathized with Madero's political objectives: significantly, all were educated men from comfortable backgrounds.[20] Equally, available evidence of Spiritism within the military suggests a similar social composition as former *maderista* political activists exchanged rhetoric for rifles. Among those cited by Tortolero are Ezequiel Padilla, Plutarco Elías Calles, Miguel Alemán (father of the future president), and Juan Andreu Almazán.[21] Like Madero, their religion remained predominantly private and was not explicit in their civic or military actions. For this reason, perhaps, little research has been attempted on the applications of Spiritism among the armed forces. In the absence of such evidence, our reconstruction of how spiritual factors may have governed the interaction between officers and troops is greatly aided by comparisons with developments elsewhere.

Mexico's history shows how the path toward spiritual clarity can often take unexpected turns under the duress of combat. Eric Van Young offers examples of late colonial movements led by charismatic leaders who promised a better future for their troops. The case of "the mad messiah," José Bernardo Herreda, combines aspects of messianic thought and millenarianism; indeed, Herreda promised to lead his people to a new phase in which a previously lost harmony would be regained.[22] In the different indigenous uprisings in Chiapas and Yucatán during the eighteenth and nineteenth centuries, inanimate objects, such as stones and wooden crosses, "spoke" to the troops, conveying spiritual and practical instructions regarding the proper conduct of the rebellion. Guy Thomson's study of late-nineteenth-century militarism in the Sierra Norte de Puebla reveals how Nahua soldiers bestowed supernatural powers upon the charismatic leader, Juan Francisco Lucas.[23] During the revolution, the followers of Primo Tapia bestowed similar mystical attributes upon him.[24] Admittedly, in all of these cases we are talking about indigenous troops who were drawing on their own sense of the spiritual world and transmitting their hopes and fears into the physical essence of a particular leader. However, if we were to apply a dispassionate, atheistic gaze, then the Virgin, crucifix, or battlefield sermons of the *cristero* rebellion could be viewed as performing a similar role for *mestizo* soldiers in times of danger.

The resurgence of religiosity during times of social dislocation and turmoil is a common phenomenon.[25] Studies of the American Civil War, for example, reveal a growing interest in Christianity among combatants on both sides. Confederacy generals were particularly keen for chaplains to take an active role in maintaining the morale of the rebel forces.[26] Similarly, Christian missionaries within the Union armies remarked on the difficulties of coping with the enormous demands of those seeking spiritual guidance.[27] A significant feature of this growth of religiosity was its millenarian nature. The Unitarian *Monthly Religious Magazine* published the impressions of Christians among the Union ranks who believed they were giving their lives for the "dawning age of God" and that by wearing "the sacred armor" they were fighting "not for conquest or vainglory, but for the entrance of the glorious day."[28] The need to feel a part of a far more worthy spiritual struggle appears to have been a common reaction to the seemingly reckless disregard for humanity that soldiers witnessed on a daily basis.

In many respects, the experiences of American troops were present in the trench warfare of the First World War. In 1917, a committee headed by the bishop of Winchester was set up to assess the likely future consequences of prolonged warfare on religious life in Britain.[29] Based on questionnaires completed by clergy and combatants, the report began by putting the experiences of fighting men into context: they had all, voluntarily or otherwise, been swept into a life radically different from any they had ever imagined possible; they had all given up their freedom and submitted to a life regulated by military discipline and warfare. As with combatants in the American Civil War, the report observed that "the impact of danger awakens the religious consciousness of the most unlikely men," helping them to endure situations that were "beyond the limits of human strength."[30] Of more relevance to our analysis of Spiritism, however, are the thoughts of combatants regarding immortality. The report noted the widespread sentiment that soldiers "do not argue much at all about life after death. The feeling is that death (they have seen it so often) cannot be the end, or there is no God." As one brigadier-general put it, "I think the greatest change in men's views on social and religious questions after the war will come from the fact that not only a belief but a perfect faith in life beyond death will be almost universal among men who have actually taken part in the fighting."[31] While by no means a common attitude, one observer noted that "a very dangerous belief in spiritualism is gaining ground, and a tendency towards dabbling in it."[32] For some combatants at least, this reflected a feeling that conventional intermediaries between heaven and earth were inadequate: "We have lost faith in the power of our clergy to clear up the mystery. We have considerably more faith in the powers of such men of science as Sir Oliver Lodge or Sir William Crookes to elucidate them—not that we have too great faith in them."[33] The sense that soldiers were taking ownership of their own path to God was seen as a threat by the ecclesiastical authorities. Indeed, at a conference at Lambeth Palace in 1920, the Church of England pointed out the grave dangers that Spiritism posed as it implied the subordination of the mind and will to unknown personalities or forces.[34] It should be remembered that only three years earlier, the Vatican had banned Catholics from attending Spiritist sessions for very similar reasons.

While their cultural and religious backgrounds differed from their British contemporaries, Mexican combatants would have shared their feelings of dislocation, of physical and mental hardship, and their exposure to mortal danger and violent death. It is also reasonable to suppose that Mexicans experienced a similar search for spiritual answers. Perhaps the most natural source of such guidance was the Catholic Church. Yet many revolutionaries would have found that the Catholic God was not on their side. Following news of Madero's death, for example, the Catholic newspaper, *El País*, reported that the faithful gave thanks to their holy patrons for having conceded the salvation of the republic.[35] Just as British troops had gained religiosity while losing "faith in the power of [their] clergy to clear up the mystery," similar trends may have developed in Mexico. Could it explain, for example, why *zapatistas* could quite happily sack churches and imprison clergy while still bearing arm patches and banners declaring their faith in the Virgin of Guadalupe?[36] Or, as was the case with some *villistas*, did it move men to show profound loyalty to a charismatic leader? Could it inspire others to show equal devotion to military leaders who offered a combination of strong physical, moral, and spiritual guidance? We suggest that it was exactly this desire for human and spiritual answers that convinced soldiers to follow a leader such as Marcial Cavazos.

Textual Analysis of the Spiritual
Communications

It is clear from Cavazos's military career that he should not be dismissed as a misguided, even deranged, individual who managed to convince sufficient people that he had a central role within the grand scheme for the future. Marcial Cavazos was no "mad messiah." Born in Coahuila, he became a successful trader in Parral, Chihuahua. He was an active *maderista* who later joined Villa's División del Norte under the immediate command of Maclovio Herrera. Later switching to the *carrancista* cause, Cavazos offered ostensibly loyal service until siding with the *aguaprietistas* in 1920. After various short-term postings, he and his forces were eventually sent to Hidalgo in October 1923, where he assumed command as chief of military operations. Less than two months later, however, news came that he had led his troops over to the *delahuertista* side. Even as he did so, communities touched by his presence offered written testimony of his military professionalism and his troops' rectitude. Cavazos could not be accused of conducting warfare for personal gain. Indeed, he was a reluctant soldier who, at various times during his brief military career, had shown contempt for the corruption and intrigues of the military hierarchy by seeking to resign his post and resume a civilian life.[37]

Cavazos's rebel campaign in Hidalgo was largely determined by topography and military logistics. His main advantage was that he possessed a highly proficient, mobile cavalry division, which he deployed to maximum effect. The broad sweep of the Huasteca *hidalguense* provided excellent protection for those who knew it well, and it was from here that Cavazos could run the federal army ragged, launching lightning raids in different locations before withdrawing to the safety of the hills. People in Pachuca began to talk of his invincibility and it was with considerable admiration that he soon became known locally as "*el General Fantasma*." The continued professionalism of his troops did much to counter official propaganda portraying him as an unprincipled criminal. Despite considerable state government censorship of the local press, no newspaper ever printed a report that was highly critical of Cavazos's actions.[38] A possible reason for this was that they empathized with his plight: the newspaper editors belonged to a provincial middle class that had greeted Madero's political campaign with great enthusiasm; a sector of provincial society that, as Bastian argues, would have included Protestants, freemasons, and fellow Spiritists.[39] While not all these individuals would have shared the depth of Cavazos's despair with the trajectory of the revolution, they may nonetheless have looked benevolently on the actions of the respected former *maderista* general.

What were the origins of Cavazos's military professionalism, bravery, and, it must be said, good fortune? It is at this point that a closer look at the bundle of papers found on Cavazos's body becomes interesting. An important initial observation regarding the texts is that the communications do not seem to address Cavazos's troops directly. None of the documents takes the form of a sermon directed specifically at the troops: these are always referred to in the third person, and their subordination to those being addressed in the messages is either directly or implicitly assumed. This means that Cavazos or at least one of his close advisors—or both—were present at sessions when the spirits guided the hand that wrote the messages.[40] The communications were all written in perfect Spanish, consistent with the social background of those sending and receiving them. Some of the authors of the messages are easily recognizable: they include former president, Benito Juárez, and Cavazos's military commander during the revolution, General Maclovio Herrera. The identity of others, such as Allan Kardec and General Refugio I. González, would not generally be known outside Spiritist circles.

Many of the communications are dated, although in some the date is either illegible or missing. The time-span stretches from 2 January 1924 to 8 April 1924; that is, from days after Cavazos joined the *delahuertista* rebellion to days before his death at Pozuelos. Yet one should resist the temptation to deduce that the spirits were *delahuertistas*, as Cavazos had been a long-time Spiritist and it is therefore reasonable to presume that he would have received Spiritist messages before the rebellion.[41] A more logical explanation for this concentration of Spiritist messages is that during this highly mobile rebel campaign, Cavazos's saddle bag became the bureau for important documents. Significance can, however, be drawn from the fact that these communications were the only documents that he held close to him during the last, desperate days of his life.

All the communications, to a greater or lesser extent, begin with a preamble that marks them out as distinctly religious. Typical is a communication dated in Meztitlán, 26 February 1924: "May the blessing and peace of God fall upon you. I appear giving an oath before the Supreme, Eternal, and Almighty God to be the spirit of Francisco I. Madero who is present among those who travel on Earth." The fundamentally religious context is established even before the body of the message is conveyed. In the face of Catholic condemnation of Spiritism, the messages constantly underline that God is at the heart of their campaign and their faith, and that contact between earthly and ethereal beings is only possible through his grace and blessing.

Several interesting points arise from the military aspects of the messages. Firstly, the majority of the communications offer explicit military information and many respond to specific questions asked of the spirits by Cavazos or others with him. On 5 February 1924, for example, the spirit of Allan Kardec made contact at the Hacienda de Vaquerias: "Know that your enemy is advancing—do not be caught off-guard. Your enemy hopes to deliver a decisive blow. Be alert!"[42] Another communication from Allan Kardec, dated 26 February 1924 and received at Meztitlán, merges information with encouragement:

> The enemy hope to catch up with you. They have no other intentions, but they do not have the resolve to venture to this place because they fear defeat. This is why they have stopped pursuing you. They cannot work out your tactics, and

are baffled and worried . . . When you leave this place, do not head for the South or the West, where there are many enemy forces as a result of the most recent actions. Take the northern route until you come to a place that you deem secure.[43]

While nonspiritual confirmation of accurate advice is rarely seen in the documents, there was an uncanny correlation between federal troop movements and the information given by the spirits. As a note of caution, it should be acknowledged that Cavazos was a professional soldier with many years of combat experience: the information conveyed in the above message would not have been beyond any prudent military officer with surveillance operations in place.

A second observation regarding these communications is that military information was not sent only by dead soldiers. As the above examples show, far from concerning himself purely with spiritual matters, Allan Kardec's spirit took an active interest in the day-to-day issues of warfare. However, the majority of communications from Cavazos's former commander, Maclovio Herrera, fall into two main categories: those offering specific information regarding troop movement and tactics, and those offering encouragement, particularly at times when the morale of Cavazos's men may have been low. The close bond between former comrades-in-arms is apparent in the informal, personal nature of the following communication:

> You (*ustedes*) have no idea how much pleasure it gives me to give you advice and know that I will always be by your side. And you (*tú*), my dear brother who is Commander of the Column, do not forget how great your responsibility is, how great your efforts and sacrifices must be in order to overcome the many hurdles (1000 shackles). But remember also that these sacrifices will bring you a better life. I will never tire from recommending this same point: be professional although prudent; be far-sighted in your affairs; take every precaution to overcome the difficulties that you will encounter on the way. Resolve them with help from your invisible brothers. When you cannot cope, ask them to guide you. Do not succumb to doubt. This is what your protector and friend recommends to you.[44]

Herrera underlines that, even in rebellion, the professionalism displayed by Cavazos and his troops was essential. Certainly as a rebel leader conducting a guerrilla war against superior enemy numbers, it was important to obtain the cooperation, if not outright support, of the local population.

The changing nature of the messages mirrored the ongoing political and military developments in the *delahuertista* rebellion. Earlier optimistic predictions that the "just cause" would soon lead to victory were replaced by others of a different mood. On 11 March 1924, Adolfo de la Huerta headed for exile in the United States. National newspapers reflected the rapid erosion of *delahuertista* resolve and speculated that Cavazos was on the point of laying down his arms. During this period, Cavazos received intimations from Mexico City that the federal government was disposed to accept his surrender;

indeed, Obregón publicly said as much to the people of Hidalgo. To many observers, including Cavazos's allies in Hidalgo, to continue the rebellion was both pointless and suicidal. Yet while his allies negotiated terms of surrender, Cavazos decided to fight on; moreover, he convinced the majority of his men to do likewise.

Cavazos must have been aware of the dire consequences of refusing Obregón's terms of surrender. Although Cavazos never publicly stated his reasons for doing so, the spirit of Allan Kardec was emphatic in its counsel:

> Do not accept the proposals that these men make. They do not have good intentions, they have criminal intent. Do not believe promises that are untrue as they will lead you to the abyss. Remember that Christ said "Only God is true; men are deceitful."—Do not accept proposals that are founded upon perversity.[45]

Evidence that the strains of a failing campaign were impinging on the otherwise strong bond of trust and discipline between Cavazos, his officers, and his men can be seen in the nature of communications from the spirit of Cavazos's former commander:

> I cannot allow any rift between you two. I cannot allow any disagreement between you two, who are like sons to me. No, my beloved sons, see yourselves as true blood brothers in order that you might receive the blessings and prize of God.[46]

In a lengthy communication, Herrera refers to the desertion of some of Cavazos's troops and offers moral support:

> Men often experience moments of weakness in life. Do not despair in those who drift away . . . some will go, but others will come. This is how humans are. Those who withdraw today are bad. Tomorrow they will pay dearly for their disloyalty.[47]

At this point, when Cavazos and his men had spent a month in the hilltop refuge of Yahualica in the Huasteca, the tone of the messages once more changed. Most notably, the neat handwriting of earlier communications was replaced by a semi-legible scrawl, as if the writer was in a hurry or in a distressed state. Gone are the direct references to the political situation in Mexico and the imminent success of the "just cause." Gone, too, are the references to disunity among Cavazos's troops. By this time, those left with Cavazos had resigned their fate to that of their leader. It was at this seemingly lowest point in Cavazos's campaign that the communications adopted a distinct millenarian tone. Perhaps the most direct of these is from the spirit of Allan Kardec dated 19 March 1924:

> The spirits that dwell in the celestial planets are among you men on Earth. The spirits that live in the community of worlds above us come to bring great things. They come to initiate you in the Truth because the clock of time strikes

the hour in which the darkness fades and is replaced by light (The Truth). The free spirits come to you to help in the Concert of souls, anxious that you play the lyre and sing songs of Glory to the Lord of Lords. Come without suspicion, without fear of doubts, Oh men of Earth! We give Voice! We invite you because God opens the gates of his celestial palace and celebrates the arrival of his prodigal sons to the paternal home.

I will be your path,
I will be the hand that guides you
I will be the intermediary . . .
God calls you through his emissaries (The spirits).
Hear the voice of your Father who asks for your return.
Respond to his call.[48]

On 31 March 1924, the spirit of Allan Kardec advised Cavazos and his men to break cover and begin their assault on the state capital, Pachuca. A footnote later added to the communication drew great significance from the fact that the date coincided with "the resurrection of our venerable master, Allan Kardec." The lengthy communication included tactical instructions, but sustained the millenarian edge:

You will not be detained in this land; it is only a short journey to where the soul must disperse . . . and, guided by the compass of Universal thought, continue the march towards its destiny . . .[49]

Cavazos's seemingly suicidal attack on Pachuca on 19 April 1924 was significant for two other reasons. Firstly, it may have been timed to coincide with the anniversary of Maclovio Herrera's death nine years earlier. Secondly, the millenarian messages coincided with Easter commemorations of the resurrection of Christ. In the event, Cavazos and the small band of cavalry who raided Pachuca survived. They then joined the rest of his forces and beat a retreat to the nearby Hacienda Pozuelos. Two days later federal troops caught up with the elusive rebels and took up positions on the hills overlooking the isolated hacienda. The following day Cavazos's men were awoken by the sound of airplane engines, followed by explosions as planes and field artillery rained missiles down upon them. The bombardment made Cavazos's position untenable and at 5 a.m., he and his men broke cover and attempted to break the federal stranglehold. They almost made it. Cavazos and several of his soldiers covered considerable ground before a federal detachment led by Lieutenant Pascual Zamorrón caught up with them. Cavazos mortally injured Zamorrón in a close exchange of fire, shortly before the latter hit Cavazos with three bullets, the last to the head killing him instantly.[50] The battle at Pozuelos left 74 rebels killed or executed; 96 were taken prisoner. Most of the dead were buried in a common grave near the hacienda along with their horses and obsolete equipment. Only the bodies of Cavazos and his leading officers were brought back to Pachuca. Cavazos's body was put on public display to convince doubting citizens that the rebel leader was dead.[51]

Some Tentative Conclusions

From the early beginnings of Mexican Spiritism, the religious philosophies of its followers were inextricably linked to contemporary political movements. Spiritism, along with Protestantism and freemasonry, flourished among groups marginalized by the Porfirian system. It was no coincidence, Bastian argues, that there was a broad correlation between regions that fostered radical liberal groups in the Porfiriato and those that gave immediate support to Madero's revolution.[52] Yet such sympathies were predominantly confined to the middle classes and to provincial intellectuals. Spiritism was less likely to gain currency in rural areas where the authority of the Catholic faith was either fully accepted or selectively embraced. Furthermore, even where there was significant support for Spiritism, it remained a minority faith regularly subjected to public ridicule.

From this perspective, it seems unlikely that many of the rank and file fighting in the revolution and the conflicts that followed were practising Spiritists. Certainly, in the one military unit for which documental material exists, there is no evidence to suggest that the spirits were in communion with the entire battalion. In the absence of corroborating evidence, we can only speculate how these messages were translated to Cavazos's men. As in the case of Madero's political actions, Cavazos may have concealed the source of his inspiration and merely led his troops in a manner expected of a professional officer. In this scenario, Spiritist principles of humanitarianism, professionalism, and an utmost conviction of following a just cause, may have been covert, but nonetheless central to the relationship Cavazos had with his men. Alternatively, Cavazos may have been more open regarding his Spiritism. For those who did not share his beliefs, repeated examples of how Divine Providence had saved them from the enemy during the de la Huerta campaign may have made his doubters reconsider. As their military situation became increasingly desperate, the courage to continue may have come from the distinctly millenarian message that Cavazos offered.

Let us again remind ourselves of the human emotions that Cavazos's men would have experienced: extreme fear, the trauma of witnessing the violent death of friends and comrades.[53] Before them was a man who seemed steadfast in the cause they were pursuing and who might even have reassured them of the one thing that played most on their minds; what would happen to them and their comrades when they died. Far from the theological knockabout between the Catholic hierarchy and its critics, there was nothing in the messages Cavazos received that would alienate Catholics among his followers. The talk of a divine God, heaven, and the salvation of the soul, would have been familiar and comforting. Those of Cavazos's men whose Catholic convictions had waned or become confused, may, like their British counterparts, have constructed alternative ways to God. In such circumstances, a charismatic leader such as Cavazos may have proved an attractive option.

We should not forget that the professionalism of Cavazos and his troops was one of the enduring qualities that made them stand out from their contemporaries. That their individual and group actions were exemplary suggests a deep tie of loyalty and obedience to their commander. Such a relationship does not, of course, prove divine intervention: all professional fighting units aim to foster an environment in which good leadership, camaraderie, and pride become self-perpetuating. Yet for Cavazos to have retained such loyalty throughout the years of the Revolution—and even more so during an increasingly unsustainable revolt against the federal government—suggests something more. Whether Cavazos appeared before his men as an ordinary commander or as one who had received spiritual guidance, his deep convictions, his bravery, tenacity, and his amazing luck in campaigns may have been sufficient for his troops to believe that their leader had exceptional qualities.

A possible scenario, therefore, is that Spiritism proved attractive among combatants at certain junctures; during troubled times when more orthodox religious beliefs proved inadequate to explain life experiences. Spiritism offered a spiritual alternative to those whose religious and cultural backgrounds were heavily influenced by Catholic doctrines of divine intervention, supplication, and communion, but who could no longer sustain an unquestioning faith in the Catholic Church or papal authority. More specifically in the case of combatants, Spiritism performed a function that would have been less crucial in civilian life—it offered moral support and meaning to the world of death and destruction surrounding them.

As an epilogue, the Calles-Torreblanca archive provides a fascinating postscript to Cavazos's rebellion in Hidalgo. Among a collection of confidential reports on regional security is one, dated 17 November 1924, concerning rebel activity in the village of Siguilucan in Tulancingo. A group of men, who identified themselves as having belonged to the forces of Cavazos, demanded horses and money from local residents before heading for a location where, they believed, the late Cavazos had buried a cache of arms and ammunition. They said that they were planning to establish the "Cavazos Brigade" and, on 1 December, to launch a campaign against federal targets. When asked why they were mobilizing, they said that they were following orders from the "Jefatura Suprema." They did not indicate to whom they referred.[54]

Notes

1. *El Observador*, 21 Apr. 1924; *Excélsior*, 21 and 22 Apr. 1924; *El Universal*, 22 Apr. 1924.
2. *El Observador*, 10 Apr. 1924. Local people and the press referred to Cavazos as *General Fantasma*, due to his apparent ability to elude pursuers and be seen in two places at the same time.
3. *Excélsior*, 24 Apr. 1924.
4. Archivo General de la Nación, Fondo Obregón-Calles (hereafter AGN/OC), 101-R2-I-1, anexo 4.
5. We are extremely grateful to Ana Gray for the hours she spent deciphering the least legible sections of the text.
6. David Cannandine, "War and Death, Grief and Mourning in Modern Britain," in *Mirrors of Mortality: Studies in the Social History of Death*, ed. Joachim

Whaley (London: Europa Publications, 1981), 187–242; Geoffrey K. Nelson, *Spiritualism and Society* (London: Routledge, 1969), 101.

7. Yolia Tortolero Cervantes, "Un Espírita Traduce su Creencia en Hechos Políticos: Francisco I. Madero (1873–1913)" (Ph.D. diss., El Colegio de México, 1999), 52.

8. Paloma Escalante Gonzalbo, "Spiritism and Spiritualism," in *Encyclopedia of Mexico: History, Society and Culture*, ed. H. Werner (2 vols. Chicago: Fitzroy Dearborn, 1997), 2:1369–70.

9. *Enciclopedia Universal Ilustrada (Europa-Americana)* (Madrid: Espasa-Calpe, 1924), 22:259.

10. Totolero, "Un Espírita," 70–4.

11. Ibid., 74.

12. *Enciclopedia Universal Ilustrada*, 261.

13. Tortolero, "Un Espírita," 92.

14. Jean-Pierre Bastian, "Las Sociedades Protestantes y la Oposición a Porfirio Díaz en México, 1877–1911," in *Protestantes , Liberales y Francmasones: Sociedades de Ideas y Modernidad en América Latina, Siglo XIX*, ed. Jean-Pierre Bastian (Mexico City: Cehila, 1990), 140. As Bastian argues, Spiritists were viewed as part of an anti-Catholic liberal religious front that included Protestants, masons, and religious dissidents.

15. Tortolero, "Un Espírita," 70.

16. Eduardo Devés Valdés and Ricardo Melgar Bao, "Redes Teosóficas y Pensadores (Políticos) Latinoamamericanos, 1910–1930," *Cuadernos Americanos* 78 (1999): 137–52.

17. Guillermo Cook, *The Expectation of the Poor: Latin American Basic Ecclesial Communities in Protestant Perspective* (Maryknoll, N.Y.: Orbis, 1985), 35. For studies on Spiritism in Brazilian society see: Roger Bastide, *The African Religions of Brazil* (Baltimore: John Hopkins University Press, 1960); David J. Hess, *Spirits and Scientists: Ideology, Spiritism, and Brazilian Culture* (Pennsylvania: Pennsylvania State University Press, 1991).

18. Valdés and Bao, "Redes Teosóficas," 146–52.

19. Bastian, "Las Sociedades Protestantes," 153.

20. Although there is some evidence to suggest that Spiritist circles were active in rural communities, insufficient research prevents us from determining how widespread such beliefs were, whether they were fostered by local elites, or whether these incidents should more correctly be seen as Spiritualist in nature.

21. Tortolero, "Un Espírita," 22.

22. Eric Van Young, "Millennium on the Northern Marches: The Mad Messiah of Durango and Popular Rebellion in Mexico, 1800–1815," *Comparative Studies in Society and History* 28 (1986): 385–413.

23. Guy Thomson with David G. LaFrance, *Patriotism, Politics, and Popular Liberalism in Nineteenth-Century Mexico: Juan Francisco Lucas and the Puebla Sierra* (Wilmington: Scholarly Resources, 1999).

24. Paul Friedrich, *Agrarian Revolt in a Mexican Village* (Englewood Cliffs, N.J.: Prentice-Hall, 1970).

25. Nelson, *Spiritualism*, 76. See, for example, the Cargo cults of Melanesia and the Ghost-Dance Religion of North American indigenous peoples.

26. Sidney Romero, *Religion in the Rebel Ranks* (New York: University of America Press, 1983), 113–22.

27. *United States Christian Commission. Fourth Annual Report, 1 January 1866* (Philadelphia, 1866).

28. Gardiner H. Shattuck Jr., *A Shield and Hiding Place: The Religious Life of the Civil War Armies* (Marcon, GA: Mercer University Press, 1987), 15–16. The nascent Spiritualist movement had yet to register in the religious thoughts of soldiers. Nelson, *Spiritualism*, 83; Steven E. Woodworth, *While God is Marching On: The Religious World of Civil War Soldiers* (Kansas: University Press of Kansas, 2001), 22–3.

29. *The Army and Religion: An Enquiry and its Bearing upon the Religious Life of the Nation* (London: Macmillan, 1919).

30. Ibid., 7, 11.

31. Ibid., 17.

32. Ibid., 19–20.

33. Having lost his own son in battle, Lodge became a leading proponent of Spiritualism among the British elite.

34. Stacey R. Warburton, *Church History in Enc. Brit. XXX* (1922).

35. Jorge Vera Estañol, *Carranza and His Bolshevik Régime* (Los Angeles: Wayside Press), 24–5; *El País*, 26 Feb. 1913, quoted in Ernest Gruening, *Mexico and its Heritage* (New York: The Century Co., 1928), 212–13; John Rutherford, *Mexican Society during the Revolution: A Literary Approach* (London: Clarendon Press, 1971), 286.

36. Rutherford, *Mexican Society*, 284; John Mason Hart, *Revolutionary Mexico: The Coming and Process of the Mexican Revolution* (Berkeley and Los Angeles: University of California Press, Berkeley, 1987), 306.

37. For details of Cavazos's early life and military career see: Archivo de la Defensa Nacional (hereafter ADN), c. XI/III/3–2015. For specific details of his military campaigns, ADN, c. XI/III/3–2015, tomo 1, ff. 5, 45–6; see also Condumex, Fondo XXI, Manuscritos V. Carranza, docs. 1/142, leg. 15273, car. 133/152, Chapoy to Carranza, San Luis Potosí, 19 May 1919; ADN, c. XI/III/3–2015, f. 66, Chapoy to Guerra y Marina, San Luis Potosí, 30 Oct. 1918; ADN, c. XI/III/3–2015, f. 559, Cavazos to General de División José Amarillas, Tehuacán, 30 Apr. 1922. See also, Primo Feliciano Velázquez, *Historia de San Luis Potosí, Vol. IV* (San Luis Potosí: Academia de Historia Potosína, 1982), 286–9; Friedrich Katz, *The Life and Times of Pancho Villa* (Stanford: Stanford University Press, 1998), 591.

38. For specific examples of this professionalism, see: Mexico; Suprema Corte de Justicia de la Nación, Casa de la Cultura Jurídica de Hidalgo, Pachuca, Penal, Exps. 262/23, no. 2, 227; *Excélsior*, 22 Apr. 1924.

39. Bastian, "Sociedades Protestantes," 154.

40. Cavazos was not present at all these sessions: at least one message makes it clear that those receiving communication were seeking advice on how to cure Cavazos from an unidentified illness.

41. The only documents suggesting Cavazos to be a Spiritist are those found on his body, but supporting evidence suggests that family ties had introduced him to influential Spiritists, including Madero, during his early life in Coahuila. Interview with Jorge Lara Rubio, Pachuca, 26 Aug. 1999.

42. AGN/OC, 101-R2-I-1, from Allan Kardec, Hacienda de Vaquerias, 5 Feb. 1924.

43. AGN/OC, 101-R2-I-1, from Allan Kardec, Meztitlan, 26 Feb. 1924.

44. AGN/OC, 101-R2-I-1, from Maclovio Herrera, Meztitlan, 26 Feb. 1924. Continuation of the Communication—6 p.m.

45. AGN/OC, 101-R2-I-1, from Allan Kardec, Yahualica, 17 Mar. 1924.

46. AGN/OC, 101-R2-I-1, from Maclovio Herrera, Meztitlan, 26 Feb. 1924.

47. AGN/OC, 101-R2-I-1, from Maclovio Herrera, Yahualica, 15 Mar. 1924.

48. AGN/OC, 101-R2-I-1, from Allan Kardec, Yahualica, 19 Mar. 1924.

49. Kardec died on 31 Mar. 1869. AGN/OC, 101-R2-I-1, from Allan Kardec, Yahualica, 31 Mar. 1924.

50. By a strange coincidence, the remains of both men lie within meters of each other in San Luis Potosí's Panteón Saucillo.

51. ADN, c. XI/III/1–80, tomo 5, f. 1193; ADN, c. XI/III/I-606, tomo 2, f. 477; Alfonso Taracena, *La Verdadera Revolución Mexicana* (Mexico City: Jus, 1963), 10:10, 97–100; Archivo Plutarco Elías Calles-Fernando Torreblanca (hereafter, ACyT), Pérez, Francisco R., gav. 71, exp. 120. inv. 5407, leg. 5/16.

52. Bastian, "Sociedades Protestantes," 161–2.

53. Instituto Mora, 972.061.MIS.8; Isaac Grimaldo, *Apuntes para la Historia* (San Luis Potosí: Talleres de Imprenta de la Escuela Industrial Militar, 1916), 43–5.

54. ACyT, Informes Confidenciales, gav. 43, exp. 35, inv. 2900, leg. 3/6, ff. 102–157/313 (1924–25). Memorandum dated 17 Nov. 1924.

Chapter 5

The Regional Dynamics of Anticlericalism and Defanaticization in Revolutionary Mexico

Adrian A. Bantjes

Between 1914 and 1938, anticlericalism and defanaticization constituted central aspects of a nationwide cultural revolution that had deep roots in the Enlightenment, liberalism, the Bourbon reforms, and Jansenism. This revolution sought to forge a secular Mexican nation by deploying an intricate symbolic, ritual, and discursive matrix aimed at breaking the people's shackles to clergy and religion.[1] As Emilio Portes Gil put it, "The struggle didn't begin yesterday. The struggle is eternal. The struggle originated twenty centuries ago."[2] Religious conflict spanned nearly a quarter century, affected most regions, and sparked widespread resistance, not just the *Cristiada*, but also less spectacular forms of resistance, such as clandestine masses, legal challenges, petition drives, boycotts, demonstrations, riots, guerrilla activity, and defiant new forms of popular religiosity.[3]

However, while there were waves of persecution, antireligious campaigns were never implemented uniformly or simultaneously. Some states witnessed conflict early, while others remained untouched until the 1930s. Implementation varied from brutal to lukewarm, while Catholic responses ranged from mass mobilization and armed resistance to apathy or negotiation. To understand why, when, and where conflict arose, it is necessary to explore the cultural matrix's interaction with structural and contingent dynamics. The goal of this chapter is first and foremost to offer a national overview of revolutionary defanaticization, and, at the same time, to examine the variables that may have triggered cycles of local and regional religious violence.

Cycles of Irreligiosity, 1914–38

Anticlericalism had deep roots in Mexican history, dating back to the Bourbon and liberal reforms. During the waning days of the *Porfiriato*, liberals, especially radical *magonistas*, combined with a "heterodox nebulosity" of freemasons, Protestants, spiritists, and mutualists to deepen Mexico's Jacobin tradition.[4] Yet the first wave of revolutionary anticlericalism during 1914–15 caught Church and laity unawares. Alan Knight maintains that this anticlericalism reflected the Constitutionalists' outrage at a perceived alliance between Church, Catholics, and the Huerta dictatorship.[5] Personalist and arbitrary, and lacking symbolic and legal structure and popular support, Constitutionalist Jacobinism involved the desecration and closure of churches, the confiscation of clerical property, the arrest, extortion, and expulsion of priests, the exclaustration of *religiosas*, vandalism, and iconoclasm, attempts to close Catholic schools, and the prohibition of rites and sacraments. In Yucatán and Jalisco, elements of a systematic policy appeared, foreshadowing the campaigns of the 1920s and 1930s. Anticlerical outrages affected not just the clericalized center, but also many southern and northern states.[6]

The intellectual authors were generally *carrancista* revolutionaries from Coahuila and Sonora. However, in the Gulf region, homegrown radicals of the Chontalpa army, such as Carlos Greene, also showed early signs of Jacobinism.[7] Though anticlericalism is often portrayed as an urban, middle class phenomenon,[8] early anticlericals often had lower or lower-middle-class origins. Some were organic intellectuals, peons, miners, or railway men.[9] Others had petit bourgeois backgrounds as storekeepers, farmers, journalists, civil servants, or schoolteachers.[10]

However, Jacobinism did not characterize the main popular movements. *Zapatistas* practised folk Catholicism, maintained ties with the clergy, and rolled back Constitutionalist anticlerical measures when they occupied Puebla and México.[11] *Villismo* has a more ambiguous history, and anticlerical atrocities tainted its early phases. But Villa's respect for popular beliefs as well as strategic calculations prevailed, and he emerged as "the defender of the faith."[12] After *villista* forces captured Guanajuato, they reopened the churches, permitted bell ringing, and restored the jewels that the Constitutionalists had taken from the Virgen de la Concepción.[13]

In 1916–17, revolutionary delegates held a constitutional convention at Querétaro, where, as Knight reminds us, religion featured more prominently than the social issue.[14] Jacobins incorporated strict anticlerical articles into the constitution of 1917, setting the nation firmly on course toward conflict. article 3 provided for secular education, article 24 outlawed public worship (*el culto externo*), article 27 declared churches to be property of the nation, while article 130 denied the Church legal personality, provided for federal intervention in matters of worship, outlawed monastic orders, prohibited the clergy from teaching, voting, or owning property, forbade confessional political parties, and allowed states to regulate the clergy's numbers and activities.[15] As Catholic opposition increased, President Venustiano Carranza came to fear the conflict's potential for violence and quietly moderated official anticlericalism. After his death at the hands of rebel forces in 1920, his successor, Alvaro Obregón, was also conciliatory to the Church, though he condoned regional anticlericalism.[16]

A second wave of persecution hit Mexico during the 1920s, as the federal government required states to enact laws in order to implement the constitution's anticlerical articles. Anticipating the *cristero* rebellion, from 1920–26 numerous states waged campaigns to decapitate the Church through the expulsion of prelates; the imposition of severe legal restrictions on the numbers of priests; the expulsion, incarceration, and assassination of nonregistered priests; the encouragement of schismatic clergy; and the exclaustration of *religiosas*. The Church's infrastructure was seriously degraded by the confiscation of seminaries, convents, *curatos*, charities, schools, and episcopal residences. Catholics also faced purges in education and the bureaucracy, censorship, the suppression of demonstrations, and, of course, the brutal military campaign against the *cristeros*.

The revolutionaries responsible for the second wave belonged to a new breed of politicians allied with President, later *Jefe Máximo*, Plutarco Elías Calles. They were governors and congressmen, many trained at the National Preparatory School or law school, who had established populist power bases by mobilizing coalitions of *rojos* (*agraristas* and workers). Inspired by liberalism and freemasonry, and increasingly by Marxism, these second wave anticlericals were not merely interested in persecuting the clergy and privatizing religion: on the contrary, they also sought to establish a secular national culture and, according to one observer, "extirpate the Catholic Faith from the soil of Mexico."[17] Their associates included both external agents, especially federal teachers and officers, and local actors: mayors, police, *agraristas*, masons, and members of the Mexican Anticlerical Federation.

In 1925, conflict spread to heretofore peaceful states. By 1926, Campeche, Coahuila, Jalisco, Sonora, Tabasco, and Durango had long passed legislation limiting numbers of priests. From 1926–29, an additional 20 states followed suit,[18] leaving only half a dozen states *without* restrictions on the clergy. Such legislation was highly controversial. In response to a 1923 law, Durango Catholics attacked the governor's palace, killing a guard. Soldiers opened fire, killing and wounding many demonstrators.[19] Calles's crackdown on the Church in 1926 caused the bloody *cristero* rebellion in central-western Mexico. According to Jean Meyer, as 50,000 *cristeros* engaged 100,000 federal troops, the federal Army became "an active agent of anticlericalism and the antireligious struggle" that pursued "its own war of religion" in Mexico.[20]

In central-western states in the 1920s, we find a pattern of strong anticlericalism and fierce lay resistance. After Governor José María Elizalde of Aguascalientes handed over the San Marcos church to the schismatic Iglesia Católica Apostólica Mexicana (ICAM) in 1925, military suppression claimed several lives and left 256 wounded.[21] Catholics rallied by organizing a strong Unión Popular Aguascalentense, but faced harsh repression. Some fell into the clutches of Zacatecas's infamous zone commander, General Eulogio Ortíz, who devised bizarre forms of intimidation, such as locking up prisoners overnight in the company of a flea-ridden sow bear.[22] In Colima in 1926, Governor Francisco Solórzano Béjar, a lawyer in the Calles family's sugarcane business at El Mante,[23] was implicated in the brutal suppression of a demonstration at the *palacio de gobierno* on Easter Monday, when state representatives, police officers, and, it is said, the governor himself, opened fire on the crowd, killing several demonstrators.[24] In July 1925, Governor José Guadalupe Zuno of Jalisco launched raids on Guadalajara's churches, provoking Unión Popular demonstrations that ended with 600 casualties and 600 arrests.[25]

Anticlericals thus faced a formidable opponent. In the diocese of Léon, for example, we find a powerful Church and highly organized laity: here there were 8 "social" Catholic *patronatos* and cooperatives, 6 unions, and 5 temperance societies, with a combined membership of 6,500; there were also 8 councils of the Knights of Columbus, and 15,000 pupils attended 40 parish schools for poor children and 27 private colleges for the children of better-off families. Vigorous pious associations, such as the Apostleship of Prayer (with 5,000 members) flourished as late as the 1930s. The Vassals of Christ and the Adorers of the Blessed Sacrament also remained active, as did workers' schools and circles, and academies of the Juventud Femenina Católica Mexicana. Catholic Action, with a membership of 5,637, provided catechism, organized women's unions, launched moralization campaigns, and headed the Red Cross.[26]

In some states, such as Claudio Tirado's Puebla, governors and politicians understood the depth of Catholic beliefs and soft-pedaled anticlerical measures.[27] In San Luis Potosí, likewise, Governor Rafael Nieto, an old-style anticlerical and friend of Calles, preached respect not confrontation: "Do not needlessly harass the believers; do not unnecessarily close the churches; do not touch religious objects; do not enter the sanctuary of conscience . . ."[28] His successor, Aurelio Manrique, an old *magonista*, seemed eager to confront the Church; yet, when Calles asked him to promote the schismatic Church, Manrique refused, later criticizing the 1926 religious conflict as an unnecessary provocation. Subsequently, Governor Abel Cano (1925–27) plunged the state into a sectarian conflict that reached its nadir with the removal of the widely venerated image of the Virgen del Carmen.[29]

In the south, far from the Catholic heartland, conflict was also felt in the 1920s. Tabasco's governor, Tomás Garrido Canabal, expelled the bishop, arrested priests, and handed churches over to the schismatic ICAM or converted them into schools. Garrido's League of Atheist Teachers propagated rationalist education, while his protégé and successor, Ausencio Cruz, demolished the Cathedral and expelled priests who refused to marry.[30] In Veracruz, Governor Adalberto Tejeda, a member of Calles's inner circle, unleashed a similar wave of persecution that included the torching or dynamiting of 20 churches.[31] In Yucatán, Governor Felipe Carrillo Puerto promoted rationalist education and socialist rituals (*lunes rojos*, "red" baptisms).[32] Yucatán's 1926 *Ley Reglamentaria de Cultos*, issued by Alvaro Torres Díaz, prohibited burials inside church, the kissing of religious images, the use of holy water in fonts, religious funerals in public cemeteries, processions with religious images, and sermons that criticized the government.[33]

By 1929, the senseless religious violence of the *cristero* war had exhausted Mexico. After lengthy Church-state negotiations, the so-called *arreglos* announced the resumption of services and the nonenforcement of anticlerical legislation. An estimated 90,000 soldiers and *cristeros* had died, as had many civilians. Most of Mexico's 3,600 priests had fled their parishes, while another 90 were killed.[34]

Yet a final wave of defanaticization followed almost seamlessly on the conflicts of the 1920s. The *arreglos*, which Catholics and Jacobins alike viewed as an ignominious defeat, merely resulted in a brief reprieve. Subsequently, there was a short-lived resurgence in both Church activity and anticlericalism. In 1929, the hierarchy established an effective lay organization, Mexican Catholic Action (ACM), which grew rapidly, reaching 365,088 members by 1942.[35] Jacobins, meanwhile, worked to sabotage the *arreglos* and promote radical educational reform, as Calles demanded in his infamous Guadalajara *grito* (1934). According to Meyer, the government also quietly eliminated some 5,000 former *cristeros*.[36] As early as 1931, and generally by 1932, conflict erupted again. *Pace* Reich, from 1931–36 more states than ever witnessed religious conflict. Draconian laws drastically limiting the number of priests appeared in many states in 1931, with most states following suit by 1934. All priests, or all but one or two, were expelled from Tabasco, Veracruz, Campeche, Chiapas, Chihuahua, Sonora, Sinaloa, Querétaro, Aguascalientes, and Colima, with Colima stipulating that its one priest be married and 50 years old.[37]

This time only a few states, notably Tlaxcala, Saturnino Cedillo's San Luis Potosí, or Morelos, saw modest restrictions or considerable tolerance. As Reich points out, legislation did not always mean enforcement.[38] Yet religious tolerance was fragile, based on short-term political calculation and susceptible to external pressure. While politicians might derive benefits (Catholic quiescence or electoral backing—the so-called "*voto morado*") by promising tolerance, their opponents could accuse them of being "soft" on the clergy.

Puebla's governor, José Mijares Palencia, resorted to a double game: his *secretario de gobierno* did the dirty work, preferably during Mijares's absences. Though a 1934 law reduced the number of priests to 23, moreover, 223 unregistered priests remained active due to "a modicum of tolerance."[39] In tolerant Tlaxcala, meanwhile, only external pressure threatened to bring conflict: in 1935, the National Revolutionary Party (PNR) identified the state as one of the clergy's last redoubts, and the governor promised a special investigation.[40] The diocese of Oaxaca was also relatively unscathed; only 4 priests out of 64 were registered here, but the rest remained in their parishes, where they continued to officiate "with a degree of freedom."[41]

Yet such negotiation was risky. In Zacatecas, *callista* Governor Matías Ramos may have been amenable to the occasional private agreement ("*arreglo privado y personal*"), as when he assured Father Francisco de B. Reveles, an old family friend, that registered priests would be allowed to officiate. However, nonregistered priests could not be tolerated because Romero had "political enemies," such as the federal education inspector, who denounced the governor as an ally of the clergy and a "*cardenista a última hora*." A Jacobin "mentor," imported from Sonora, monitored the governor's activities and dictated orders to which he "prostrated himself humbly."[42]

In many states, therefore, we find scant evidence of negotiation. Some governors, moreover, relished their anticlerical role. In Jalisco, the *callista* governor, Everardo Topete, committed an egregious breach of etiquette in 1935 during a tour for foreign diplomats of Guadalajara's Hospicio Cabañas. As diplomats viewed adjacent portraits of the Hospicio's founders—Bishop Juan Ruiz de Cabañas and Sor Inés Osorio—Topete joked that one portrait showed the founder and the other "the Bishop's woman and lover." The Uruguayan ambassador's wife, shocked by the governor's coarseness, responded: "Sir, these words do no honor to the office you represent."[43]

Conflict also consumed Querétaro under Saturnino Osornio, a strongman who earned the *Jefe Máximo*'s "unconditional protection." Osornio was implicated in the savage murder of three Catholic youths accused of "seditious propaganda," who, according to the diocese, were forced to take a drive with the governor, his brother Fidencio, the mayor, and a police officer. The youths were then tied behind the vehicle and dragged to the outskirts of Pedro Escobedo, where, still alive, they were tortured, mutilated, and buried. Their remains were found in a shallow grave after dogs were spotted carrying pieces of human flesh. The father of one of the victims embarrassed Fidencio Osornio during his induction into Congress by venting his outrage from the gallery.[44]

Conflict extended to many northern states. In 1930s Chihuahua, Governor Rodrigo M. Quevedo, a staunch *callista*, closed all churches, changed religious nomenclature, and allowed only five priests to officiate.[45] Under Rodolfo Elías Calles, son of the *Jefe Máximo*, Sonora witnessed dramatic acts of iconoclasm that sparked demonstrations and Mayo and *serrano* rebellions.[46] Baja California's anomic, spiritually heterodox border society, however, failed to challenge official anticlericalism. Baja California Norte permitted only one priest, who promptly crossed the border, giving the coup de grâce to an already fragile clerical infrastructure.[47] The Church was so weak in Baja California Sur that only in 1948 did Combonian missionaries arrive to take charge of this forgotten corner of Christendom.[48]

Much of the south also witnessed radical, third-wave defanaticization. In Tabasco, persecution continued unabated under Governor Víctor Fernández Manero. Campeche's legislature banned religious nomenclature and holy festivals, including the fiesta of the Virgen del Carmen in Palizada.[49] However, in Yucatán—one of the first states to experience defanaticization in the 1910s and 1920s—the campaign was muted: cultural missions steered clear of attacking religion, as did the Normal School near Valladolid, a town noted for its religiosity. Yet campaigns were more pronounced in the *pueblos*.[50]

Despite occasional tolerance, most priests experienced considerable difficulty. According to Meyer, by 1935 only 305 priests were authorized to officiate in all Mexico.[51] Unregistered priests officiated in secret, often facing hefty fines, denunciation, arrest, and, not infrequently, death. Many left for the relative safety of Mexico City, while others fled the country, leaving the Church unable to fulfill its most elementary spiritual responsibilities. Priests were often arrested for minor offenses, such as adorning church doors, ringing bells, failing to place the *pabellón nacional* in church, or staging civil indigenous processions.[52] The Sierra Norte de Puebla, Sonora, and other regions were purged of all priests.[53] In Quintana Roo, the ever vigilant General Melgar deported the few brave pastors who attempted to visit the faithful from neighboring states.[54]

Priests feared imprisonment and death. In 1935, 31 priests from the archdiocese of Guadalajara were arrested on suspicion of aiding Catholic rebels, but were later released after paying fines of a thousand pesos.[55] In Durango that year, three priests suffered a mock execution.[56] Colima's zone commander, having concentrated unregistered priests in Tepic, warned the *cura* of San Pedro Lagunillas that he could choose between staying in the city and "losing his head."[57] The assassination of Father Buenaventura Montoya, suspected of maintaining contact with Zacatecas rebels, was notorious. Soldiers dumped his body in Villa Guerrero's plaza in 1936 warning fellow priests that "today it was his turn and tomorrow [yours]."[58] That same year in Chihuahua, Governor Talamantes ordered the arrest of the defiant priest of Santa Isabel, Pedro Maldonado. The padre went into hiding, but a year later was found beaten to death.[59]

In 1932, Pius XI denounced renewed anticlericalism in the encyclical *Acerba Animi*. States responded by expelling most prelates.[60] The Archbishop of Guadalajara, Franciso Orozco y Jiménez, was exiled to the United States from 1932–34.[61] In October 1935, soldiers cordoned off his Tlaquepaque residence and fruitlessly searched the church of La Soledad for arms.[62] Confidential sources asserted that Jalisco's civil and military authorities considered a sinister fate for the Archbishop, whom they considered a principal instigator of the "Second" *Cristiada* (*La Segunda*): a contrived assassination plot in which troops would first stop the Archbishop's car to search for ammunition and then "answer fire" from his vehicle.[63] When Orozco died of natural causes, however, Guadalajara's municipal authorities refused to allow his body to be transferred to the Cathedral for burial, and only acquiesced after the interior ministry intervened. Eighty-thousand mourners accompanied his body.[64] Disguised as a *ranchero*, Bishop Juan Navarrete of Sonora fled to the mountains, where he founded a clandestine, arcadian seminary in the Sierra de Bacadéhuachi. Navarrete condoned, and was probably in contact with, Catholic rebels.[65] When the Bishop of Zacatecas, Ignacio Placencia y Moreira, was arrested in 1934, a crowd of 3,000 demanded his freedom and, after his release, guarded him night and day in the Cathedral.[66]

Churches closed in many states—Colima, Guanajuato, Querétaro, Chihuahua, Sonora, Sinaloa, Tabasco, Veracruz, Chiapas, Campeche—often for years.[67] Treasury officials, federal troops, and state and municipal authorities raided and confiscated ecclesiastical and private properties. In 1934, the governor and mayor of Aguascalientes, Enrique Osorio Camarena and Ricardo Mainero, directed raids on the bishopric and seminary.[68] In Guadalajara, secret police (*los secretas*) searched Catholic properties, including the convents of the Sisters Adorers (Religiosas Adoratrices) and the Noviciate of the Franciscan Tertiaries, sending the novices fleeing over the rooftops.[69]

Increasingly, education became the bone of contention. As education minister, Narciso Bassols (1931–34) made a renewed effort to implement constitutional article 3 and launched an ill-fated experiment in sex education. The Apostolic Delegate, Archbishop Ruiz y Flores, made it clear that Catholics were not to accept the regulations. Campaigns by the Unión Nacional de Padres de Familia (UNPF) and the ACM shut down official schools in Mexico City in 1934, precipitating Bassols's resignation. In 1933, the PNR's Six Year Plan introduced a "socialist" form of public education, which ultimately proved to be more antireligious than socialist. Presidential candidate Lázaro Cárdenas, a dedicated anticlerical, supported the initiative, implemented in 1935. Federal teachers, whom the clergy denounced as "*anti-curas*," played a key role in the defanaticization campaigns; Catholic schools were now largely eliminated or pushed underground.[70]

Many states also carried out a large-scale *depuración ideológica*, as in Guanajuato, where 150 "suspect" teachers lost their jobs.[71] As governor of Michoacán (1928–32), Cárdenas cancelled all teachers' appointments and made their renewal contingent on acquiring PNR membership and demonstrating a belief in "revolutionary ideology."[72] Discrimination sometimes extended to all state employees. Sinaloa's governor, Manuel Páez, demanded that bureaucrats sign a personal declaration that "conclusively demonstrates support for the government's revolutionary program," particularly socialist education, which "attacks fanaticism and religious prejudice."[73]

Mass Catholic protests frequently caused dramatic drops in school attendance. Half of Guanajuato's secondary school population dropped out as a result of campaigns organized by Catholic *damas* and the UNPF, forcing some federal schools to close. Only 15 percent of federal school teachers in the state signed a *compromiso* to teach the "socialist" curriculum. To fill the gap, Catholics founded 170 *escuelas hogar* (home schools), many operated by Catholic Action, where dismissed teachers taught up to half the school population.[74] In Aguascalientes, teachers resigned en masse. On 4 August 1934, police arrested 300 UNPF demonstrators. Communities such as Ojuelos resorted to violence when teachers taught their pupils that God did not exist ("*que no hay Dios*") and introduced sex education. When one student ran out of class in 1935 crying that the female teacher was "*encuerada*" (naked), villagers armed with clubs and stones for two days besieged teachers and the mayor, who sensibly took to the roof. After one teacher denounced the priest of Bajío de San José, parishioners beat him with clubs, tossed him into a ravine, and ran him out of town.[75] Overall, some 100 teachers lost their lives in terrorist violence and another 200 were wounded or mutilated (*desorejados*).[76]

Catholics resented sacrilegious provocations; the antireligious festivals, "defanaticizing" cultural missions, the desecration of sanctuaries, and iconoclastic outrages, all touched raw spiritual nerves. In Tepic, the *síndico*, the treasurer, and a health department official harassed Bishop Hurtado by "serenading me with religious parodies and highly immoral songs, hurling terrible insults at me, and brutally banging on my door while dancing and making a huge scene . . ."[77] On May Day 1936 in Chihuahua, union members, schoolchildren, and students of the Instituto Científico donned red and black uniforms and marched through the streets carrying antireligious placards.[78] In 1935, Garrido Canabal brought his *camisas rojas* from Tabasco to Mexico City, where they provoked street fights in Tacuba and a bloody confrontation outside Coyoacán's San Juan Bautista church.[79] In the dioceses of Oaxaca, Huajuapam, and Tehuantepec, school inspectors demanded the death penalty for the priests of Villa Alta, staged open air *reuniones culturales*, and sponsored a scandalous "exposition of paintings that denigrate the Church, the Supreme Pontiff, the Prelates and the Priests." In 1936, three revolutionary blasphemers entered Oaxaca's Cathedral during an exposition of the Blessed Sacrament and, refusing to remove their hats, "uttered a blasphemy out loud in front of the faithful." There were attempts to undermine Oaxaca's *mayordomías* and cancel religious fiestas. The widespread belief that schismatics had poisoned Presbítero Fortino Velasco sparked a riot in Minatitlán in 1936.[80]

Cases of iconoclasm in Sonora, Chiapas, Veracruz, and Tabasco triggered violence. On 10 May 1935, members of Sinaloa's Bloque Revolucionario Socialista attacked the Church of the Colina de Culiacán—the *Tepeyac culiacense*—hurling stones at the image of La Guadalupe, tossing out the altar slab, and smashing paintings of the Via Crucis. Miraculously, the face of the Virgin survived intact. Three thousand Catholics protested by praying the rosary at the sanctuary.[81] Under *callista* Victórico Grajales, Chiapas witnessed widespread iconoclasm and the closure of all churches. In Tuxtla Gutiérrez and elsewhere, *quemasantos* incinerated pyres of saints' images and crucifixes, profaned churches, and held anti-Catholic conferences. In a theatrical apostasy, one priest renounced his faith by burning his cassock. In response, Catholics spirited away the miraculous images of San Pascualito and El Señor del Pozo. When teachers burned images at Rincón Chamula and confiscated the church to serve as an Indian boarding school, Tzotziles from San Juan Chamula hid their saints and mobilized a militia.[82] An iconoclastic gathering staged by the normal school of Hecelchakán, Campeche, provoked Mayan villagers of Nunkuní to drive out the Jacobins.[83] In Guadalajara, too, federations of revolutionary students and the Anticlerical League served as the agents of defanaticization. In 1936, students vandalized the church of San Felipe Neri, draped the *rojinegro* banner over its façade, and threw a tear gas canister into the congregation, which had assembled for spiritual exercises.[84]

The guerrilla resistance of *La Segunda* continued stubbornly through the mid-1930s, though it lacked the cohesion of the first *Cristiada*. According to Meyer, 7,500 *cristeros* took up arms in some 13 states in central and western Mexico, as well as Sonora and Oaxaca, in rare cases fighting until 1941.[85] More commonly, Catholics resisted with demonstrations and riots. When Catholics in Puerto México (Oaxaca) learned that their church had been converted into a *casa de campesinos* in 1935, they retook it by force and returned its images. The rioters received help from Catholics in Tabasco, from where the miraculous image of Nuestro Señor de la Salud had been smuggled for safekeeping after an earlier iconoclastic attack. Images were burned in

Nejapa, and an attempted burning in Juchitán sparked a riot.[86] Another scare, in Oaxaca City, led Catholics to mobilize in defense of the Virgen de la Soledad.[87] In Irapuato (Guanajuato) in 1935, Catholics almost killed an anti-clerical woman who claimed she was the "Protestant Virgin" and beat the assassin of their *cura* to death in the sanctuary.[88]

On Sunday 29 March 1936, Catholics in San Felipe Torresmochas (Guanajuato) attacked a cultural brigade. The incident took place when *brigadistas* and *agraristas* staged a meeting in the gazebo in front of the parish church and began "denouncing fanaticism and religious beliefs." As teachers assailed churchgoers, "one of the peasants, an old man of 70, who could no longer stand those insults, dealt a terrible *machete* blow to the person who was offending him, cutting off a good part of his skull and causing a massive hemorrhage . . ." The teachers then "riddled him [the assailant] with bullets." When Catholic bystanders pelted *brigadistas* with stones, the anticlericals opened fire, killing 19 and wounding at least 22 rioters (unofficial sources spoke of 100 casualties). According to a Catholic witness, the violence was "simply the natural venting of a people whose most sacred possession had been offended: their beliefs." President Cárdenas, however, blamed the violence on the clergy when he arrived that afternoon:

> From this spot, where the masses have been incited against the self-sacrificing teachers; from this spot, where they say the truth is preached but where lies are practised (because it is a lie that socialism deprives children of the love for their parents); . . . from here I would . . . like to identify those who are truly guilty . . .

Having pointed his finger at the clergy, Cárdenas gave them 24 hours to leave town. Some have suggested, however, that this sobering experience led him to the conviction that the anticlerical campaigns were a serious threat to the stability of the nation.[89]

In Ciudad Camargo (Chihuahua) later that year, three civilians and two soldiers died when union members opened fire on Catholic demonstrators. Twenty Catholics were arrested and confined with the corpses. Uniquely defiant judges granted *amparos* to priests and demonstrators, leading Governor Quevedo to dismiss the judge of the second district.[90] In 1934, the Puebla government suppressed a demonstration of Catholic women and workers, several of whom were shot inside the *palacio de gobierno*.[91] In 1937–38, the future *sinarquista* leader, Salvador Abascal, led a ragtag army of Indians carrying the image of the Virgin of Guadalupe on a crusade to reopen the Tabascan churches, but shock troops initially drove them out, pistol in hand.[92]

Not all resistance was violent. In most states, Church and laity organized mass petition drives demanding freedom of religion, the reopening of churches, and the return of priests. Catholics boldly sought audiences with governors and congressmen. *Damas católicas* from Colima even visited President Cárdenas, who made vague promises but stressed that it would be difficult to overturn the reforms, "So difficult, that it can only be achieved by a revolution." Embarrassed aides tried to hide the ladies from a curious *New York Times* correspondent.[93]

The situation improved markedly from 1936, as Cárdenas purged *callista* governors, toned down the regime's anticlerical rhetoric, and ordered the education ministry to abandon defanaticization. Cárdenas was eager to forge alliances, often unholy ones, with anti-*callistas*, including conservative elements, such as the *cacique* of Puebla, Maximino Avila Camacho, who promptly declared himself a Catholic, reestablished the clergy, and generally ignored the *Ley de Cultos*.[94] In 1936, the Bishop of Zacatecas was welcomed home with "acclamations, vivas, literary soirées, etc." That summer, as rebel activity dropped off, the head of state education declared "socialist" education a failure and called on purged teachers to head the new schools.[95]

In Guanajuato, Governor Melchor Ortega responded to opposition with soft-pedaling and an "extra-official and reserved" pledge that "socialist" education would be voluntary.[96] After Ortega's fall, Bishop Emeterio Valverde y Téllez celebrated his *bodas de oro sacerdotales* in style. Easter services in the *rancherías* saw "an outpouring of the faithful as never seen before." Catholic Action launched a successful moralization campaign that resulted in more than 600 marriages. By 1936, the diocese boasted 634 cathechismal centers attended by 1,829 catechists, who cared for the spiritual needs of 29,049 children and 6,275 adults. A solemn Mass was held in the *Cristo Rey* basilica in October, while 5,000 faithful joined a diocesan pilgrimage to Tepeyac.[97]

Improvement was not always the result of Church-state *arreglos*. In Yucatán, priests took advantage of the improving climate to resume their still illegal activities.[98] In March 1936, throngs reopened the Campeche churches by force.[99] In October 1935, Querétaro Catholics drowned out the inauguration speech of Governor Ramón Rodríguez with calls for religious freedom.[100] In Chiapas, with Grajales removed from power in 1936, Catholics jubilantly celebrated the *fiestas guadalupanas* and Christmas *posadas* (which *grajalistas* had rebaptized *fiestas de invierno* or *fiestas comerciales*).[101] And, despite his campaign pledge that "I will not take a step back when it comes to . . . the defanaticization of the masses," Governor Gustavo Talamantes of Chihuahua allied himself with Cárdenas and initiated a process of conciliation.[102]

In some states (Tabasco, Veracruz, Jalisco, Guanajuato) conflicts persisted into the late 1930s and beyond. Chiapas's churches finally reopened in 1937, though the clergy did not return until 1938.[103] In February 1937, Catholics in Orizaba, and later the entire state of Veracruz, responded to the violent death of a young girl by reopening churches by force.[104] Similar popular movements emerged in Sonora, Campeche, Tabasco, and elsewhere.

Geographical and Sequential Patterns
of Impiety and Resistance

Is it possible to map regional patterns of impiety and resistance? What were the variables that determined how, when, and where defanaticization campaigns were implemented? Both Knight and Meyer identify broad patterns dependent on variables such as Church organization, local religiosity, and revolutionary mobilization. However, Meyer cautions that physical geography was a factor, but a less decisive one than may be imagined.[105] Conflict and resistance were seemingly strongest in what Knight identifies as the "white" zone: the central-western Catholic heartlands, where an elaborate clerical infrastructure and conservative Catholic cultures persisted. Meyer and Knight agree that the cradles of Mexican anticlericalism were the northern *frontera bárbara*—where religious heterodoxy flourished in a weakly clericalized, liberal, often Protestant and masonic, economically dynamic, environment—and the "pioneering areas" of the Gulf. Knight dubs these regions of frontier (northern and coastal) radicalism the "red zone." Finally, in the heavily indigenous ("pink") south, where Church and state were traditionally weak, autonomous, syncretic forms of folk Catholicism flourished.[106]

However, such sweeping analysis runs the danger of relying on essentializing views of religion and regional cultures. The north, it seems, was more clericalized and more deeply religious than previously thought. Likewise, the Oaxacan dioceses, notably Mixtec Huajuapam, displayed a stronger clerical and lay organization and a more sacramentalized religiosity than its "pink" designation might lead one to believe.[107]

Reich, on the other hand, dismisses regional generalizations entirely and instead posits a national cooperation thesis that denies the existence of a true religious conflict during the 1930s, and even before. "[I]f anything, pervasive compromise was the rule";[108] the anticlericalism of the 30s was "merely superficial."[109] Our evidence tends to disprove this thesis, while Meyer wisely reminds us that "It would be puerile to suppose that this modern state was committed to anticlericalism for all time; . . . it never failed to compromise whenever it could."[110]

What do our findings add to this inconclusive debate? A 25-year panorama indicates that conflict was widespread and almost continuous, arising in many states not generally recognized as religious hotspots. From 1914 onward, there is not one year of complete religious peace during the entire revolutionary period. There is no doubt that the central-western "white" zone witnessed profound conflict. However, in several states with "white" characteristics, notably Puebla and San Luis Potosí, the strength of Catholicism occasionally convinced the state to avoid needless provocation. In *zapatista* regions (Tlaxcala, Morelos, México), which Knight identifies as zones of primary revolutionary mobilization, conflict was either muted or the result of external pressure.[111] Both northern and southern states demonstrated high levels of conflict, especially if we interpret resistance broadly to include, say, demonstrations, boycotts, and petitions. Thus, we may confidently speak of a *nationwide* revolutionary *Kulturkampf*, not simply a regional conflagration involving the *cristero* belt of the Bajío and western highlands.

State level center-periphery dynamics are also evident, but caused divergent outcomes. Anticlericalism is often considered an urban phenomenon, whereas weakly clericalized rural areas are viewed as less Jacobin.[112] However, we should remember that urban centers were not just the seat of revolutionary government and "poles" of modernity, but also served as centers of deeply entrenched Catholicism. Many state capitals and some towns were also diocesan sees, with all the ecclesiastical apparatus that this entailed (Cathedrals, *cabildos*, seminaries, diocesan lay chapters). Any rural/urban dichotomy, therefore, must be carefully nuanced. In Puebla, for example, anticlerical governors were reluctant to confront Catholics in the state capital, whereas campaigns developed unchecked in the Sierra Norte. In Yucatán, likewise, villages felt persecution more severely than Mérida and Valladolid, where a "calculated moderation" prevailed.[113] In Coahuila, Saltillo Catholics opposed educational reform, while the *agrarista* Laguna was supportive.[114] Ultimately, what is most significant is the extent to which regions were characterized by legacies of radical liberalism, revolutionary insurrection, or pervasive lay Catholicism. Identifying the regional juxtaposition of radical bulwarks and deeply religious societies—whether the Catholicism that they practised was more sacramentalized or "popular" in character—is the key to understanding these otherwise contradictory regional patterns.

What seems to cause the timing of these cycles? National political dynamics, especially factional strife, played an important role. However, we should not overlook the contributions of less visible local actors—teachers, agrarianized peasants, mayors, officers, and masons. In Zacatecas, for example, Jacobinism, on its way out at the national level by 1936, was "extemporaneously" driven by "local elements."[115]

Anticlericalism was first unleashed in response to *huertismo* in 1914–15, then coincided with efforts to implement the anticlerical Constitution, starting in 1920. There was an almost seamless continuity between the violence of the 1920s and the conflicts of the 1930s, when Mexico witnessed more widespread conflict than ever. However, Cárdenas acknowledged the risks of staying the course. More importantly, he took advantage of Catholic antipathy toward his arch-enemy, Calles, to purge the revolutionary family in 1935–36. These purges were motivated by *realpolitik*, not ideology, and allowed for the rise in many states of conservative factions, some of which courted Catholic support. After the fall of *callismo*, Cárdenas denounced extreme antireligious campaigns and watered down socialist education. The situation then improved markedly.[116]

Motivating Factors of Defanaticization and Resistance

Mexican Jacobins were first and foremost inspired by ideological considerations, and viewed the clergy and, frequently, religion itself, as obstacles in the path toward modernity.[117] However, ideological considerations were naturally influenced by calculation and greed. Ben Fallaw offers a nuanced political reading of defanaticization that emphasizes collusion between the laity and often tolerant revolutionary officials, with the *voto morado* often employed as a bargaining chip.[118]

Besides political calculation, pure greed contributed to the campaigns. When troops seized the *curato* of San Pedro Lagunillas (Nayarit), they lifted the floorboards in search of hidden treasure. Soldiers were suspected in the disappearance of a monstrance, two chalices, a crown, and a dagger of Our Lady of Sorrows from the church of San Juan Peyotán (Nayarit).[119] After a raid on the bishopric of Aguascalientes, the wives of the mayor and a Treasury official were seen carting off the spoils.[120] The murders of Padre Nicolás González of Fresnillo (Zacatecas) and his servant, who was stabbed 18 times, were seemingly motivated by a desire to appropriate the *cura*'s lands.[121] Catholics interpreted the theft of religious objects as sacrilege and responded accordingly. When a "naked individual" attempted to rob items from the church of Talajal (Jalisco), passers-by shot him dead.[122]

Priests often faced extortion. In Oaxaca, garrison commanders, municipal authorities, postmasters, and treasury collectors exacted spurious "professional taxes" from nonregistered priests in return for permission to officiate, or as happened in Ojitlán, to celebrate the feast of the patron saint (which cost the priest 300 pesos). In the diocese of Tehuantepec, too, "*mordidas* [we]re a fact of daily life."[123] Sums could be substantial. The authorities of Catemaco and Otatitlán appropriated parish alms totaling 20,000 pesos per year.[124] Exacting illegal rents from the clergy for the occupation of nationalized buildings was also common.

During the 1930s, Mexico witnessed a massive, nationwide transfer of Church property and private real estate owned by Catholics to federal and state institutions and popular organizations.[125] This revolutionary nationalization of Church property—a successor to the liberal *Reforma* that remains to be studied—provided an inexpensive means to develop the educational, agrarian, and bureaucratic infrastructures, to debilitate the institutional Church, and to reward populist constituencies.

What motivated some communities to resist, while others presented only lukewarm opposition or acquiescence? Here the nature of local culture, religion, and identity was crucial. Meyer dramatically argues that the *cristeros* were peasants steeped in a traditional culture who sought to defend Church and religion, and, ultimately, a way of life—an "ethical and mythical kernel of humanity"—against a totalitarian Leviathan state become God that exhibited "a radical, summary, and brutal anticlericalism."[126] Jacobin "aggression profoundly disturbed the psychological, affective, and existential equilibrium of the population." This attempted "process of deculturation . . . inevitably led to violent conflict."[127] In some regions the *Cristiada* was generated by Christians who practised a highly sacramentalized religion dependent on the parish priest, "the keystone of rural society," whose elimination brought about "the death of the soul" and constituted a "radical rupture in individual lives and in the history of the community."[128] Cut off from the sacraments, peasants desperate to coax back a God driven from the temples offered up the ultimate collective sacrament of self-sacrifice.[129] Where priests were scarce and sacramental Christianity an illusion, "simple, primitive" Christians exhibited similar patterns of resistance. Ethnicity did not dictate reactions, as both indigenous and *mestizo* communities shared similar forms of religiosity or indifference.[130]

Matthew Butler has recently developed Meyer's early cultural approach by linking the independent cultural determinants of religion and radicalism with material factors (land tenure, economics, ethnicity), to produce an excellent model for the analysis of patterns of religious conflict, in the process clearly identifying its highly localized nature.[131] Our findings suggest that a cultural model is generally applicable to the revolutionary period. Patterns of resistance depended less on Church organization per se than on the diverse nature of local societies and identities, and on their relationship to religion in its various forms. Levels of clericalization were far from being the only source of resistance. As Butler argues, the localized construction of religious culture was the underlying constant.[132] Overall, resistance tended to be strongest where Catholicism was highly sacramentalized and the laity well-organized (and not just in the center-west); *or* where popular or folk Catholicisms had deep roots that significantly defined local, including indigenous, identities.

On the other hand, resistance tended to be weaker where religiously anomic societies prevailed, as in Baja California, the *agrarista* settlements of the Yaqui Valley, or the Laguna; these were often areas of recent settlement with large floating populations of rural proletarians susceptible to *agrarismo*. Knight identifies these as zones of secondary revolutionary mobilization, where new social movements sought alliances with the state and "the agrarian-anticlerical tandem" was part of the "revolutionary package deal."[133]

Conclusion

This overview leads to several conclusions. The religious conflict affected most regions of Mexico and spanned nearly a quarter century. Though anticlericalism and defanaticization reflected cultural origins in the Enlightenment, campaigns were *triggered* (not caused) by regional and national sociopolitical dynamics. External agents frequently played a leading role. However, Calles did not create the regional Jacobins. A new generation of local populist politicos required little prompting. Others engaged in tactical anticlericalism, and, at times, negotiations and secret *arreglos*. While ideological motivations featured prominently, political calculation, populist mobilization, or, not infrequently, outright greed, were also contributing factors.

In February 1936, Cárdenas finally denounced the excesses of defanaticization, stating that "anti-religious campaigns will only provoke a prolonged resistance, and will definitely retard economic growth."[134] Anticlericalism was largely abandoned by 1938. *Realpolitik* had prevailed over cultural concerns. The manner in which local histories and cultures *interacted* with conjunctural trends determined the process and outcome of defanaticization. The institutional strength of the Church was less important than the vitality of lay religiosity. Despite the establishment by the late 1930s (*not* 1929) of a successful *arreglo* between Church and state, the patterns of conflict that had been drawn during the Revolution, or well before, would continue to haunt Mexico into the twenty-first century.

Notes

1. See my "Idolatry and Iconoclasm in Post-Revolutionary Mexico: The Dechristianization Campaigns, 1929–1940," *Mexican Studies/Estudios Mexicanos* 13, no. 1 (1997): 87–120.
2. Cited in Antonio Dragón, *María de la Luz Camacho. Primera Mártir de la Acción Católica* (Mexico City: Buena Prensa, 1937), 82.
3. See my "The War against the Idols: The Meanings of Iconoclasm in Post-revolutionary Mexico, 1910–40," in *Negating the Image: Case Studies in Iconoclasm*, ed. Anne McClennan and Jeffrey Johnson, (Aldershot: Ashgate), 41–65.
4. Jean-Pierre Bastian, "Jacobinismo y Ruptura Revolucionaria durante el Porfiriato," *Mexican Studies/Estudios Mexicanos* 7, no. 1 (1991): 30. Jean-Pierre Bastian, *Los Disidentes: Sociedades Protestantes y Revolución en México, 1872–1911* (Mexico City: Colmex, 1989), 17, 304–5, 308.
5. Alan Knight, this volume and *The Mexican Revolution* (2 vols. Cambridge: CUP, 1986), 2:203.
6. Ibid., 206–7, 246.
7. Carlos Martínez Assad, *Breve Historia de Tabasco* (Mexico City: FCE, 1996), 118.
8. Knight, *Mexican Revolution*, 2:184.
9. E.g., Eulalio Gutiérrez, Manuel Diéguez, Francisco Murguía, Juan José Ríos, Pablo González.
10. Gabriel Gavira had some schooling; Antonio Villarreal, Calles, and Francisco Múgica were teachers.
11. Leonardo Lomelí Vanegas, *Breve Historia de Puebla* (Mexico City: FCE, 2001), 312; María Teresa Jarquín O. and Carlos Herrejón Peredo, *Breve Historia del Estado de México* (Mexico City: FCE, 1995), 122–3.
12. Jean Meyer, *The Cristero Rebellion: The Mexican People between Church and State, 1926–1929* (Cambridge: CUP, 1976), 12–13; Samuel Brunk, *Emiliano Zapata. Revolution and Betrayal in Mexico* (Lincoln: University of Nebraska Press, 1995), 68–9; Friedrich Katz, *The Life and Times of Pancho Villa* (Stanford: Stanford University Press, 1998), 446–8; Knight, *Mexican Revolution*, 2:205, 288.
13. Monica Blanco, Alma Parra, and Ethelia Ruiz Medrano, *Breve Historia de Guanajuato* (Mexico City: FCE, 2000), 177.
14. Knight, *Mexican Revolution*, 2:476.
15. Peter Lester Reich, *Mexico's Hidden Revolution: The Catholic Church in Law and Politics since 1929* (Notre Dame: University of Notre Dame Press, 1995), 11–12; Meyer, *Cristero Rebellion*, 13–14.
16. Meyer, *Cristero Rebellion*, 16; Knight, *Mexican Revolution*, 2:489.
17. Meyer, *Cristero Rebellion*, 40.
18. Reich, *Mexico's Hidden Revolution*, 92.
19. José de la Cruz and Pacheco Rojas, *Breve Historia de Durango* (Mexico City: FCE, 2001), 226–9.

20. Meyer, *Cristero Rebellion*, 41–2, 52, 159.

21. Beatriz Rojas, *Breve Historia de Aguascalientes* (Mexico City: FCE, 1994), 176; Meyer, *Cristero Rebellion*, 36–7.

22. Archivo del Secretariado Social Mexicano, Mexico City (ASSM), Conflicto Religioso por Diócesis, 1926–37, (CRPD), Contestación Aguascalientes (CA), May 1935.

23. Roderic Ai Camp, *Mexican Political Biographies, 1884–1935* (Austin: University of Texas Press, 1991), 207.

24. José Miguel Romero, *Breve Historia de Colima* (Mexico City: FCE, 1995), 182.

25. Meyer, *Cristero Rebellion*, 37.

26. ASSM, Informes Cuestionario Religioso (ICR), Puntos León, 1936, Informes Cuestionario Religioso.

27. Lomelí, *Breve Historia*, 344–5.

28. María Isabel Monroy and Tomás Calvillo Unna, *Breve Historia de San Luis Potosí* (Mexico City: FCE, 1997), 258.

29. Ibid., 264–71; Meyer, *Cristero Rebellion*, 46.

30. Carlos Martínez Assad, "Tomás Garrido Canabal," in *Encyclopedia of Mexico: History, Society, and Culture*, ed. Michael S. Werner (2 vols. Chicago: Fitzroy Dearborn Publishers, 1997), 1:556–7; Camp, *Biographies*, 58, 95.

31. Camp, *Biographies*, 209; Bantjes, "Idolatry," 101.

32. Sergio Quezada, *Breve Historia de Yucatán* (Mexico City: FCE, 2001), 199–203; Ben Fallaw, "Felipe Carrillo Puerto," in *Encyclopedia*, 203–5.

33. *Diario Oficial del Gobierno Socialista del Estado de Yucatán*, XXIX: 8605, 13 Apr. 1926.

34. Meyer, *Cristero Rebellion*, 64, 74–5.

35. Reich, *Mexico's Hidden Revolution*, 102.

36. Meyer, *Cristero Rebellion*, 202.

37. Reich, *Mexico's Hidden Revolution*, 36, 92; CRPD/ASSM, Decreto 138, 16 Aug. 1934.

38. Reich, *Mexico's Hidden Revolution*, 39, 92.

39. CRPD/ASSM, Contestación Puebla, 10 Sep. 1936; Lista Puebla, 9 Jul. 1935.

40. CRPD/ASSM, Lista Puebla, Oct. 1935; Elsie Rockwell, "Reforma Constitucional y Controversias Locales: La Educación Socialista en Tlaxacala, 1935–1936," in *Escuela y Sociedad en el Periodo Cardenista*, ed. Susana Quintanilla and Mary Kay Vaughan (Mexico City: FCE, 1997), 206–7, 211–14, 218, 222–3.

41. ICR/ASSM, RO, [1934].

42. CRPD/ASSM, Informe Zacatecas (IZ), Feb., Nov., and 4 Dec. 1935.

43. CRPD/ASSM, Informe Guadalajara (IG), Sep., Oct., 1 Nov. 1935.

44. Marta Eugenia García Ugarte, *Breve Historia de Querétaro* (Mexico City: FCE, 1999), 221; CRPD/ASSM, Personas, Querétaro, June 1935; Corrupción, Querétaro, 26 Jun. 1935.

45. ICR/ASSM, Informe Chihuahua (IC), Jan. 1936.

46. Adrian A. Bantjes, *As if Jesus Walked on Earth: Cardenismo, Sonora, and the Mexican Revolution* (Wilmington, DE: SR, 1998).

47. Paul Vanderwood, *Juan Soldado: Soldier, Rapist, Martyr, Saint* (Durham: Duke University Press, 2004), 127–30.

48. Ignacio del Río and María Eugenia Altable Fernández, *Breve Historia de Baja California Sur* (Mexico City: FCE, 2000), 200–1.

49. Ben Fallaw, "Anti-priests and Catholic-Socialists: Federal Teachers, Religion, and the Consolidation of the Postrevolutionary State in Campeche, 1934–1940," NECLAS paper, 2004, 3, 7–9.

50. CRPD/ASSM, Contestación Yucatán (CY), 9 Sep. 1935.

51. Meyer, *Cristero Rebellion*, 205.

52. CRPD/ASSM, Datos Querétaro, 1 Mar. 1935.

53. CRPD/ASSM, Respuesta Puebla, 4 Jun. 1935; Bantjes, *As If Jesus*, 11.

54. CRPD/ASSM, Informe Yucatán, 5 Jul. 1936.

55. CRPD/ASSM, IG, 1 Nov. 1935.

56. CRPD/ASSM, Respuesta Durango, 6 Aug. 1935.

57. CRPD/ASSM, Informe Tepic (IT), 9 Mar. 1936.

58. CRPD/ASSM, Circunstancias . . . Montoya; IZ, Aug. 1936.

59. ICR/ASSM, IC, Jan. Apr. 1936; Luis Aboites Aguilar, *Breve Historia de Chihuahua* (Mexico City: FCE, 1994), 152–3.

60. CRPD/ASSM, Respuesta Durango, 6 Aug. 1935; Información Aguascalientes, Mar. 1936; ICR/ASSM, Respuesta Oaxaca (RO), [1934].

61. CRPD/ASSM, Archbishop Orozco to Cárdenas, 25 Jun. 1935.

62. CRPD/ASSM, IG, Oct., 1 Nov. 1935.

63. CRPD/ASSM, Autoridades . . . , Guadalajara, 30 Oct. 1935.

64. ICR/ASSM, IG, Feb. 1936.

65. Bantjes, *As If Jesus*, 25–6, 46–50.

66. CRPD/ASSM, Respuesta Zacatecas, 20 Jul. 1935.

67. ICR/ASSM, Puntos León, 1936; Informe Religiosas, Guadalajara, 30 Oct. 1935; CRPD/ASSM, Informe al V. Comité, Colima, Nov. 1935–Jul. 1936.

68. CRPD/ASSM, CA, May 1935.

69. CRPD/ASSM, IG, 1 Dec. 1936.

70. CRPD/ASSM, CY, 9 Sep. 1935.

71. Bantjes, "Idolatry," 108; CRPD/ASSM, Director General Educación Guanajuato, 1 Aug. 1935.

72. CRPD/ASSM, Informe Morelia, Apr. 1936.

73. CRPD/ASSM, Circular 27, Sinaloa, 25 Oct. 1934.

74. ICR/ASSM, Puntos León, 1936; CRPD/ASSM, Respuesta León (RL), 7 May 1935.

75. CRPD/ASSM, CA, May 1935.

76. Meyer, *Cristero Rebellion*, 205.

77. ICR/ASSM, IT, Mar., Apr.

78. ICR/ASSM, IC, May, Aug., Sep., Dec. 1936.

79. Carlos Martínez Assad, *Breve Historia*, 177.

80. ICR/ASSM, RO, 8 Jan., 20 Apr. 1936; CRPD/ASSM, Informe Tehuantepec (ITc), Jan. 1936; ITc, Dec. 1936; Benjamin Thomas Smith, "Anticlericalism and Resistance: The Diocese of Huajuapam de León, 1930–1940," *Journal of Latin American Studies* 37, no. 3 (2005): 484–6.

81. CRPD/ASSM, Informe Culiacán, 10 May 1935.

82. Gustavo Montiel, *Tuxtla Gutiérrez de Mis Recuerdos* (Mexico City: Costa-Amic, 1980), 109; Bantjes, "War against the Idols," 54.

83. CRPD/ASSM, Datos Yucatán, 13 Jul. 1935; Fallaw, "Anti-priests," 2–3.

84. ICR/ASSM, IG, 12 Jan. 1935, Apr. 1936.

85. Jean Meyer, *La Cristiada* (3 vols. Mexico City: Siglo XXI, 1973–74), 1:375; 2:375.

86. CRPD/ASSM, Complemento Tehuantepec, 15 May 1935.

87. Interview with Luis Castañeda Guzmán, Oaxaca, 14 Jan. 2002.
88. CRPD/ASSM, RL, 7 May 1935.
89. ICR/ASSM, Informe León. La verdad . . . Ciudad Manuel González, 1936; Meyer, *Cristero Rebellion*, 205–6.
90. CRPD/ASSM, IC, Dec. 1936.
91. CRPD/ASSM, Respuesta Puebla, 20 Mar. 1935.
92. Martínez Assad, *Breve Historia*, 173.
93. CRPD/ASSM, Documentation Decreto Colima, 16 Aug. 1934. See massive documentation in the Archivo General de la Nación (AGN).
94. Lomelí, *Breve Historia*, 359–60, 364, 369.
95. CRPD/ASSM, IZ, 14 Mar., 17 July, Aug. 1936.
96. CRPD/ASSM, RL, 7 May 1935.
97. CRPD/ASSM, Reseña . . . Fiestas León; Datos . . . corresponsal León, 10 Dec. 1936; Jornadas, León.
98. ICR/ASSM, Informe Yucatán, 31 Dec. 1935.
99. Fallaw, "Anti-priests," 13–20.
100. CRPD/ASSM, Acontecimientos Querétaro, Oct. 1935; Reich, *Mexico's Hidden Revolution*, 82.
101. ICR/ASSM, Ma. Del Carmen Natarén to Consejo, 1936.
102. CRPD/ASSM, IC, Dec. 1936.
103. Julio Ríos Figueroa, *Siglo XX: Muerte y Resurrección de la Iglesia Católica en Chiapas. Dos Estudios Históricos* (Mexico City: UNAM, 2002), 106.
104. Meyer, *La Cristiada*, 2:364.
105. Meyer, *Cristero Rebellion*, 84.
106. Alan Knight, "Popular Culture and the Revolutionary State in Mexico, 1910–1940," *Hispanic American Historical Review* 74, no. 3 (1994): 432–3, 437–8; Meyer, *Cristero Rebellion*, 24–9, 113.
107. Bantjes, *As If Jesus;* Smith, "Anticlericalism and Resistance."
108. Reich, *Mexico's Hidden Revolution*, 90.
109. Ibid., 113.
110. Meyer, *Cristero Rebellion*, 32.
111. Knight, "Popular Culture," 427, and this volume.
112. Knight, *Mexican Revolution*, 2:184.
113. CRPD/ASSM, CY, 9 Sep. 1935.
114. María Elena Santoscoy, *Breve Historia de Coahuila* (Mexico City: FCE, 2000), 315, 322.
115. ICR/ASSM, IZ, 14 Mar. 1936.
116. Meyer, *Cristero Rebellion*, 205–6.
117. Bantjes, "Iconoclasm."
118. Ben Fallaw, "Kulturkampf or Collusion: Catholics and the Postrevolutionary Mexican State, 1929–1940," NECLAS Paper, 2003, 10–12, 21–2, 40.
119. ICR/ASSM, IT, Jan., Mar., Apr., 7 Jun. 1936.
120. CRPD/ASSM, CA, May 1935.
121. ICR/ASSM, IZ, 14 Feb. 1936.
122. CRPD/ASSM, IG, 1 Sep. 1936.
123. CRPD/ASSM, ITc, May 1937.
124. Ibid.
125. See massive documentation in the AGN.
126. Meyer, *Cristero Rebellion*, 209, 213, 218.
127. Ibid., 189.

128. Ibid., 187.
129. Ibid., 193, 197–8, 200.
130. Ibid., 195–7.
131. *Popular Piety and Political Identity in Mexico's Cristero Rebellion: Michoacán, 1927–29* (Oxford: OUP, 2004), 213–21.
132. Ibid., 216. Compare Jennie Purnell, *Popular Movements and State Formation in Revolutionary Mexico: The Agraristas and Cristeros of Michoacán* (Durham: Duke University Press, 1999), 95.
133. Knight, "Popular Culture," 427. Also this volume.
134. Cited in Meyer, *Cristero Rebellion*, 205.

Chapter 6

"The First Encounter": Catholic Politics in Revolutionary Jalisco, 1917–19

Robert Curley

Los constituyentes del 17 . . . discutieron y deliberaron frente a un pueblo ateo y por tanto ficticio, imaginario, imposible.

Anacleto González Flores

In 1918, Jalisco's lay Catholic associations organized a lockout of their churches to protest legislation designed to limit the Church's role in society.[1] With clerical support, students, workers, employees, mothers, and domestic servants used their churches to focus Catholic anger against the state government. These confessional organizations successfully established a radical discursive and political polarity between Catholics and revolutionaries, couched in terms of *pueblo* and tyrant, good and evil. The views held by Catholic political activists, both clerical and lay, were repeated by many different groups who demanded the repeal of laws they considered offensive. Through such polarization, these groups succeeded in associating a particular practice of Catholic worship with the liberal concept of individual liberty, despite the fact that the Church was neither "liberal," nor had a strong tradition of defending individual liberties in Mexico.

In another respect too, the events of 1918 were unlike earlier Church-state conflicts. The revolution had destroyed the old regime, and the postrevolutionary state was only just being constructed. In the absence of effective central government, power dispersed to the regions and did not necessarily emanate from Mexico City. In Jalisco, the most aggressive anticlerical legislation derived not from the 1917 Constitution but from its local application. Likewise, Jalisco's Church-state conflict was resolved in the local Congress with the encouragement of Manuel M. Diéguez, then at the tail end of his tenure as governor of Jalisco (1914–17, 1917–19). Probably Carranza convinced Diéguez that Jalisco's religious problem was likely to have repercussions elsewhere: nevertheless, the dynamic remained locally rooted up to this point. The fundamental conflict concerned the politically charged question

of religious liberty, on the one hand, and the revolutionary program for con-
structing a secular society on the other.[2] This clash was one aspect of the revolutionary process that rapidly affected—and mobilized—large sectors of
society, crossing differences of class, sex, ethnicity, and generation, and forging a distinctly religious political identity. Although conflictual, the process
was interactive; as Jalisco's Catholics resisted the revolution, they articulated
a discourse of "sacred" rights and a mass-based political practice reflecting
wider social developments.

Local Politics and the 1917 Constitution

Church-state tensions were refocused in Mexico by the 1917 Constitution.
Disagreement centered on the following areas: article 3, which prohibited
religious schools; article 5, which equated religious vows with servitude and
established that the state would not recognize them; article 13, which denied
legal status to religious organizations; article 27, which prohibited religious
associations from owning property and established that churches were property of the Nation; and article 130, which established that the state would
exercise final authority above and beyond any other institution regarding religious worship.[3] The episcopate responded in a pastoral letter of February
1917 signed by 14 exiled bishops in Texas and published that April. The episcopate protested against the restriction of religious liberty, but ended on a
conciliatory note, arguing that the Church was not interested in power and
would cooperate with government if an air of tolerance and mutual respect
were restored in Church-state relations: "We are persuaded," the prelates
concluded, "of the benefits of a healthy exercise in democracy, as the only
way to bring to our nation a firm and stable government that balances and
moderates, respecting the rights of all and giving to each that which belongs
to him."[4]

The archbishop of Guadalajara, Francisco Orozco y Jiménez, did not sign
the collective pastoral because he had only recently returned from exile.[5] His
return incognito to Jalisco is chronicled in a 10-page journal written at the
time.[6] Orozco did not arrive at Guadalajara, and there were no welcoming
processions. Rather, he arrived privately, disguised by a long beard and trav-
eler's clothes, from the north: via Aguascalientes and the sparsely populated
south Zacatecas sierra, until reaching Totatiche. Like the bishop of *zapatista*
Cuernavaca, Orozco could move around with some security, confident that
the region's country-folk did not share the anticlericalism of urban revolutionaries.[7] He began his pastoral visit unannounced in Totatiche, and continued town-to-town, following the sierra southward before moving into the
highland region of northeast Jalisco known as *Los Altos*. Orozco almost certainly learned of the collective pastoral weeks after publication. At about the
same time—May 1917—he received a supportive letter from the Vatican's
secretary of state, Cardinal Gaspari, relaying a greeting of Benedict XIV.[8]
Shortly after, on 4 June, Orozco seconded the April letter in a pastoral written from an unidentified parish in the archdiocese. Orozco's short letter

protested against the 1917 Constitution but instructed his faithful to abstain from seditious acts that would play into the hands of the Church's enemies. At the same time he advised his supporters that circumstances did not warrant a retreat into idle lamentations; rather, Catholics should take advantage of their suffering in order to build religious unity.[9]

On 1 June 1917, Manuel M. Diéguez assumed office as Jalisco's constitutional governor, initially to general indifference.[10] Diéguez immediately adopted a hard-line position in religious affairs, however, and embodied a Constitutionalist intransigence bred partially of uncertainty. Both he and his interim governor, Manuel Aguirre Berlanga (part of 1914, most of 1915–16), were outsiders: Diéguez, a former employee of the Cananea copper mines, was a Sonoran, while Aguirre belonged to Coahuila's coterie of *carrancistas*. In certain other respects too, Diéguez resembled Carranza's proconsuls to the Mexican south.[11] Like Alvarado, Castro, or Múgica, he had "plebeian" origins and saw privilege, hierarchy, and entrenched officialdom—both secular and clerical—as enemies; he also lacked local connections and popular support, but was driven by a "powerful blend of idealism and ambition" rooted in his *magonismo*, his nationalism, and his anticlericalism; and, as Jalisco's governor and military commander, Diéguez operated in accordance with a binary vision pitting liberal against conservative, reform against "reaction."

Diéguez's attacks on entrenched—particularly Church—privilege were received as open hostility by militant ("political") Catholics. The likes of Anacleto González Flores, already engaged in Catholic politics, viewed the Constitutionalists as descendents of the French Jacobins who treated Jalisco as "conquered" territory. In his 1920 essay on Jalisco's religious persecution, González Flores wrote: "The revolution . . . has neither understood nor recognized the *pueblo* . . . [but] reduced it to a meaningless word, and tortured it with the guillotine of the Terror."[12] Diéguez's "reactionaries" also comprised intellectuals, therefore, who produced written propaganda and availed themselves of a comparative historical vision reaching back to the French revolution. This distinguished them from Catholics who probably saw revolutionary hostility toward their customs in more immediate terms.[13] All this points to a basic paradox of the Mexican revolution: while *carrancistas* saw themselves in a struggle to rid the country of the old regime, political Catholics saw a people persecuted by alien revolutionaries for their religious customs. Although divergent in their goals, both sides labored to forge a "new" citizen from the mire of revolution.

Three days after Diéguez took office, on 4 June, Archbishop Orozco's pastoral was read out in Mass at several Guadalajara churches, where it could most easily be distributed. In response, Diéguez ordered the state attorney to close these churches and arrest their priests on charges of rebellion. In all, eight churches were closed, including the Cathedral and Our Lady of Guadalupe, popularly known as *El Santuario*. Charges of sedition were filed against Orozco and priests who read the letter at Mass, resulting in several arrests.[14] On 12 July, the recently founded Association of Mexican Catholic Youth (ACJM) organized its first public protest, inviting Catholics to march from *El Santuario* to the governor's palace in exercise of their constitutional right (article 9) to protest. The marchers were composed of men and women of varied ages and classes, carrying banners that read "We Protest Energetically Against the Apprehension of Priests," and "We Protest Against Criminal Searches of Church Buildings." In González Flores's account, the march progressed southward through the artisan neighborhoods near *El Santuario* to the city center. Passers-by watched with surprise, and people came to doors and windows to observe the march.[15] As the marchers passed University Gardens, four blocks from the governor's palace, they were cut off by police reservists with pistols drawn: many marchers were beaten up and two dozen men—including the organizers—and a group of women were arrested. The U.S. consul reported that some women had fought with police.[16]

González Flores, among those arrested, referred to the clash as "the first encounter." The women were eventually scolded and told to go home, suggesting officials considered them less threatening than the men, and perhaps misled. The male detainees—law, medicine, and engineering students, high-schoolers, and a *cargador*, or carrier (the only working-class detainee mentioned)—were jailed. González Flores mused on the irony of their imprisonment: the mayor's office, as well as the local jail, was installed in the former archbishop's palace, confiscated by revolutionaries in 1914. Locked up in the palace basement, the 24 detainees continued their protest, praying the rosary aloud, singing songs, and reciting a poem—"*Los Pueblos Tristes*"—by nineteenth-century Cuban poet and independence champion Bonifacio Byrne, which exhorts the God of pity to take the side of the downtrodden.[17]

Next day, the detainees were marched before the mayor, Luis Castellanos y Tapia, who censured their protest. Particularly reprehensible, in his eyes, was the fact that young women had been involved in public protest; here was an indicator that gender relations and a particular construction of women as being "outside" the political were changing.[18] Fines were set at 200 pesos per head, at which point the carrier asked that his fine be set in accordance with the law: no more than a week's wages. When this petition was denied, all of the detainees refused to pay, and thus served 15-day sentences.[19]

Alarmist newspapers reported an imposing protest, a clear indication of Catholic discontent.[20] Two days later, archdiocesan secretary Miguel Cano was arrested and charged with rebellion.[21] For several months afterward, Guadalajara's liberal press—*El Gato*, *El Occidental*, and *El Independiente* in particular—ran stories of the alleged criminality, rebelliousness, and lawlessness of priests in Guadalajara and its rural towns. For his part, González Flores wrote in 1920 that "the first encounter" gave Jalisco Catholics an important lesson in the limitations of legal protest: article 9 did not guarantee Catholics the right to peaceful protest, and the Constitution was a lie.[22]

Following the 12 July march, Catholic attention in Guadalajara focused on reopening the churches. Organized across and within parish structures, two mass petitions circulated in the diverse neighborhoods affected by the closures. The petitions comprised some 3,000 signatures in all. One third corresponded to neighborhoods north and west of the city center, which demanded the reopening of the churches of Dolores, Mezquitán, San Diego, Santa María, San José, and Our Lady of Guadalupe; the remaining two thirds of petitioners focused solely on the parish church in Mexicaltzingo. The first petition included churches from two different parishes—Our Lady of Guadalupe and Sweet Name of Jesus—which covered the city's entire north and northwest; Mexicaltzingo was the parish seat of a broad artisan and Indian neighborhood south of the city center.[23]

The petitions' most significant aspect, other than their broad appeal, is perhaps their independently constructed identity. These are not the standard, community-based petitions one might find in many rural towns. Indeed, the signatories' only commonality was their rejection of a government policy affecting their local customs; otherwise, they did not necessarily have much in common with one another. It is difficult to unpack the signatories' social demographics except in rudimentary terms, but two-thirds were women, and—judging from the churches cited—most were artisans, *mestizos*, and Indians. This does offer a tentative hypothesis: that Guadalajara's lower-middle and lower sectors did act politically, and in ways that a social scientist might consider "modern," even though their objective was the preservation of customs that might be considered "traditional," conservative, or reactive. If the petitions are further considered in light of the ACJM's July march, the threads binding this incipient social movement were parish-based and organized through lay associations. The local press certainly compared this new Catholic social movement to the National Catholic Party (PCN) success of 1911–14; the 1917 protests were organized in the same way, and with similar success, as an early exercise in a Catholicized mass politics.[24]

Church Property and the National Interest

The 1917 Constitution dominated Church-state relations and the strategies of political Catholics for the next 10 years. Initially, however, religious conflicts were played out regionally between state and diocesan governments. This was partly because Carranza, as president, was inclined to play down Church-state antagonisms through nonenforcement of the Constitution's anticlerical articles. Similarly, the episcopate sought conciliation and cooperation. Among *carrancista* governors as well as bishops, though, there were widely divergent positions. In this regionally defined context, the first important confrontation occurred in Jalisco in 1918 between Governor Manuel Bouquet Jr. (Diéguez's interim replacement from February 1918 to January 1919) and Archbishop Orozco.[25] The episode's historical significance was to involve the same issue (indeed many of the same actors) that triggered the *cristero* rebellion, with the difference that Church and state came to a political solution after months of coordinated Catholic protest. In 1926, this would no longer be possible. Possibly the resolution in 1918–19 inflated Catholic expectations of a later settlement and encouraged dangerous brinkmanship.

The 1918 conflict centered on the state government's decision to survey churches for expropriation and to apply constitutional article 130, which gave the state authority to regulate religious worship—and even to license clergy—while stipulating that this authority should be exercised respectfully of local circumstances. In February, public works department director Rafael Sálazar surveyed Guadalajara's churches in order to decide which should be closed and expropriated under article 27. Sálazar targeted 32 of the city's 54 churches for expropriation: 21 were projected for use as elementary schools, 5 as museums, 4 as artisan workshops, and 2 as drawing academies; 16 churches would be preserved as places of worship, while 3 still under construction were not evaluated, and 2 more, characterized as ruins, would disappear.[26] The larger churches serving Guadalajara's popular artisan and Indian neighborhoods were singled out as centers of "fanaticism," in particular Mexicaltzingo and El Santuario: both were parish seats and at the center of large, deeply religious neighborhoods. The churches of La Merced in the city center and San Martín to the northeast were also singled out. All the churches described as centers of propaganda and "fanaticism" were active promoters of Catholic Social Action.

Sálazar's report offers a fascinating glimpse into a mind convinced of the existence of scientific utopias. An engineer, he seems to have had little empathy with religion, which he described as completely superfluous to progress. Sálazar's vision was evolutionist, with primacy placed on material and intellectual progress. Like many revolutionaries, Sálazar was driven by a view of progress rooted in education. As far as religion was concerned, his mentality was curatorial: churches and their possessions were to be inventoried as objects belonging to the fine arts department, as part of the nation's natural history.[27] For Sálazar, expropriated Church property should serve

a higher order than the simple devotion that enervates the individual with illusory expectations of imagined miracles, which have never contributed anything to humanity's intellectual, moral, or material progress; for none of the knowledge to which we owe the inventions and discoveries that have allowed our societies to enjoy well-being [is] in any sense . . . due to religious devotion. Clearly, religious dogma has not guided men towards the discovery of a single truth useful to humanity; it is not religious dogma to which we owe the many inventions of machines and methods for producing artifacts, which in their different applications to industry and human activity have facilitated life and increased wealth; nor is it religious dogma to which we owe the discovery of Laws, either in the moral or physical order. . . . These inventions and discoveries . . . and all that has enabled mankind to prosper and flourish, are due to science.[28]

After surveying Church property, Jalisco's state legislature prepared a legal framework for expropriation based on a bill introduced by Jorge Villaseñor.[29] The legislation, eventually known as decree 1913, would restrict all religious denominations to one priest and church per 5,000 faithful, while requiring all religious "professionals" (that is, priests and ministers) to be licensed by the state. For the licensing, photographs of practising priests would be collected in an official registry along with a description of each priest's physical appearance, place of work, residence, earnings, and so on.[30] Similar registries had been used previously, as far back as the Intervention, to keep track of prostitutes and prisoners. Porfirian bureaucrats had also used such measures to track domestic servants and unskilled laborers. But priests had never been considered for such demeaning treatment, and the law was met with widespread anger and rejection.[31]

On 31 May 1918, Congress approved a law limiting the number of churches and priests;[32] on 3 July the governor published decree 1913, permitting one church for every 5,000 citizens or fraction thereof, based on the 1910 census. With approximately 110,000 inhabitants in 1910—176,000 in 1918 by Salazar's own estimates—the 16 churches designated for religious use in Guadalajara would not cover half of the city's recognized needs. Each would be staffed by one priest, no more, and according to the 1917 Constitution, only Mexicans by birth would be permitted to work as priests.[33]

The Church-state problem was not simply legal, but political, as Diéguez seems to have recognized. Two days after decree 1913's publication, Archbishop Orozco y Jiménez was arrested in Lagos de Moreno by soldiers acting on orders from Diéguez. The following day, General César López de Lara arrived at Lagos by train from Michoacán, and escorted the archbishop to Tampico.[34] At several stops along the way, the archbishop's defenders presented *amparos*, legal restraining orders against his detention and forced exile; but each time the military refused to abide by the injunctions. In Tampico, Orozco was charged with treason and strongly advised to leave the country, which he did.[35] In Chicago for the next year, Orozco was the distinguished guest of Monsignor Francis Kelley, author of the 1915 diatribe against Mexico's revolutionaries, *El Libro de Rojo y Amarillo, una Historia de Sangre y Cobardía*.

Petitionary Politics and the Public Sphere

If the old regime's disintegration and the PCN's disappearance in 1914 disarticulated Catholic politics, then the Constitutional Congress and establishment of a new regime in 1917 reenergized the movement, mobilizing large numbers of Catholics in opposition to the restrictions placed on the practice of religious worship. The 1918 movements against decree 1913 and in support of Jalisco's exiled archbishop were characterized by various organizational forms. Some were parish-based, others were at the same time community-based; but all were articulated through lay Catholic organizations such as the ACJM and the Catholic Women's Association of Guadalajara (ADCG). All engaged with civil government at different levels, from the town council to the state congress, from the governor's office to President Carranza. The campaign was waged through petitions, public demonstrations, mass pilgrimages, economic boycotts, and civil disobedience. This

diversity of protest forms is of considerable importance because it underscores the broad appeal of the demands and the formation of a Catholic political identity. These were the strategies of a "public Catholicism" that was
highly politicized and willing to challenge the regime in spheres that the state
considered proper to the revolution.[36]

Petitions became important from June 1918, prior to the archbishop's
exile, when Guadalajara Catholics petitioned Carranza. Their petition was
devised as an expression of popular support for an April *memorial* sent by the
archdiocesan vicar general, Manuel Alvarado, to Carranza; the April document recounted the aggressions committed by the military government
against Catholics prior to the reestablishment of Constitutional rule
(1914–17).[37] While the *memorial* was detailed and lengthy, the petition was
brief and alluded to the principal complaints of those affected: church closures; the authorities' refusal to comply with court orders that churches
reopen; the confiscation of corn under the pretext that it was tithe; the arrest
of newspaper vendors who sold Catholic dailies; the detention and fining of
faithful for publicly wearing Ash Wednesday crosses on their foreheads; the
confiscation without due process of private property allegedly belonging to
the Church.

Significantly, the petition focused less on Catholic *complaints* regarding
the Constitution than on constitutional articles protecting religious worship
and Catholics' rights of assembly and protest. In particular, Catholics pointed
to article 130's prescription concerning the regulation of religious practice,
which stipulated that priests and churches should be licensed in numbers
according with local needs. Finally, the signatories argued that, as Mexicans,
they had a fundamental right to protection under the new laws. Speaking in
their own name, for Guadalajara's lay Catholic organizations, and for the
Catholics of all Jalisco, they demanded that the laws reflect the desires of
"public opinion."[38] Rather than a negative litany of complaints, therefore,
Catholics here outlined a positive discourse of politico-religious rights. As the
petition circulated, however, decree 1913 was published, making the situation considerably tenser. The petition was sent to Carranza with the signatures of more than 4,500 Guadalajara Catholics—both men and women—as
Orozco y Jiménez was driven into exile.

Following the June petition, considerable numbers of lay Catholic organizations in Guadalajara began circulating signed protests in the form of pamphlets, flyers, and open letters to the "authorities." These constructed a
Catholic identity on the basis of group affiliation, through the various lenses
of youth (catechists, students, minors), gender (middle to upper class
women, unmarried women, non-mothers), occupation (workers, servants,
teachers, employees), and church congregation. The role of young women
catechists is relevant, as catechism teachers likely formulated worker and servant petitions. For example, the protest sent by the catechists, servants, and
workers of the Santa Zita Association started with the surnames of some of
Guadalajara's elite families, and concluded with 100 surnames belonging to
servants and workers (this should not be interpreted as bourgeois manipulation

of the lower classes).[39] Many protesters simply decried their circumstances, demanding respect for their customs, religion, and archbishop. Energetic legal protest was generally signified as virile or manly for young Catholic men. In contrast, for women in the ADCG protest was articulated in terms of female suffering and selflessness:[40] one women's protest stated that

> There are moments when a woman, naturally resigned to suffering, cannot but make herself heard. Such is the case when she is aggrieved with respect to that which she most loves and which is most deserving of her love. She will remain silent confronted with offenses made toward her person; but confronted with assaults on her Faith, her life's force and vigor, woman must always respond with the sublime cry of protest.[41]

In general, this image of unselfish suffering recurs across the social hierarchies, providing a common or unifying construction of Catholic feminine identity. Catholic victimhood also pervades Alvarado's 1918 *memorial*, which in this sense provides the millenarian master-narrative for a Catholic reading of the Mexican Revolution as a reliving of ancient Rome, with martyrdom and sacrifice as the fruits of the faith:

> The Church was born on the Cross, grew up in the Catacombs, and has always lived combated and persecuted: its true children have never lifted a hand against their persecutors, nor committed offense against their executioners, nor caused aggression, but rather [have lived] suffering, [granted] pardon and [accepted] martyrdom . . . [S]till, when a law has favored them or their Church, they have not missed the chance to defend themselves by it.[42]

Unlike the June petition, the July petitions carried the signatures of organization members, ranging from a few who signed on behalf of the group to a few hundred. In all I am aware of 24 protests circulating in Guadalajara, mostly in July 1918. These were generated by specific groups, often tied to parishes; between them they carried some 1,300 signatures (roughly 25 percent of the June signatures); and were more often signed by women than men (the ratio was about 8 to 1). This bias may reflect official intimidation. In mid-July, 120 signatories—mostly young men—were arrested and sentenced by the criminal court.[43]

Meanwhile, the ADCG called for action. In a meeting with members of the ACJM and the Cervantes Academy (a Catholic school), Catholic women agreed to print signs denouncing decree 1913 and the archbishop's enforced exile, and to place them in all homes in the city.[44] Black bows also appeared over doors and in windows of Catholic homes as a sign of mourning. The ACJM distributed thousands of fliers inviting city Catholics to congregate peacefully on the afternoon of 22 July at Diéguez's house. The text of the invitation, attributed to González Flores, is telling:

> To the Catholics of Guadalajara: You are invited, without distinction of class or sex, to gather on Monday the 22nd at 5 p.m., in the plaza of the train station, in

order to demonstrate to General Manuel M Diéguez, in response to indications that he made to a commission of Catholic women, that the majority of Guadalajara is Catholic and does not agree with Decree 1913.—Order is requested, and employers are asked to give leave to their employees.[45]

Crowd estimates ranged from 10,000 to 60,000, and a Catholic publication cited one eyewitness who offered a breakdown made by a man named Angel Corsi: 35,000 in the plaza and gardens, 15,000 along Calle Ferrocarril, and 10,000 along the plaza's side streets.[46]

From his balcony, Diéguez addressed the crowd; after a resounding "yes" to his inquiry as to whether the demonstrators were Catholic, he told them that he was well aware of their religious affiliation and never questioned it. Diéguez told the crowd that their priests had misled them, for which he received loud cries of "no" and catcalls; and he continued by telling demonstrators that their priests were unwilling to abide by the law. Diéguez finished by warning the crowd that if they were Mexicans they had but two choices: abide by decree 1913, or leave the state as pariahs.[47] Interestingly, this challenge parallels the conversation between Calles and the bishops of Morelia and Tabasco on the eve of the *cristero* rebellion in 1926. Then, Calles told prelates Díaz and Ruíz y Flores that the Church had only two choices, to petition congress to amend the Constitution or rise up in arms. In 1918 and 1926, thousands of Catholics opted not to abide by the law, but with very different results.[48] In Jalisco in 1918, the response was legal protest and peaceful noncooperation. This experience was surely in Church leaders' minds in 1926 when they once again decided to close the churches, this time nationally.

Following his encounter with the crowd, Diéguez withdrew from his balcony. Shortly afterward, mounted police attacked, creating space in the plaza for a larger police contingent on foot. In the ensuing chaos, many Catholics were beaten. An eyewitness reported seeing Police Commissar Borrayo severely wound two women, both of whom died subsequently.[49] Another protester ran from Borrayo and took shelter in the Bolivian consulate. A woman named Herrera was reportedly killed by a saber-blow to the neck, while petty merchants lining the train station's entrance were arrested on charges of concealing weapons for the crowd. Writing to his old friend Miguel Palomar, Marcelino Alvarez Tostado ended with the following irony: "we have two more martyrs to add to the many victims of the most glorious [revolution]."[50]

In Antonio Gómez Robledo's interpretation, this was the moment the government lost any moral authority it might hitherto have held over Jaliscan society. For his part, González Flores wrote that

> the ire of Caesar was felt, when police on foot and horseback threw themselves against the unarmed crowd, as if they were attacking an army at war. Women, children, elderly, and young, all who had the misfortune of finding themselves within the reach of those cossacks, were beaten, trampled under charging horses, and struck with machetes.[51]

Despite the repression, the protest generated a feeling of Catholic victory. Newspapers were warned not to report the incident; in protest, *La Epoca* left its front page blank, except for a caption of Lamennais: "*Le silence est, après la parole, la seconde puissance du monde.*"[52] In Guadalajara, mused Gómez Robledo, there was no need to put the story in writing because the locals could read not only between the lines, but without them.[53]

After the violent dispersal of the 22 July protest, Jalisco's legislature published an amended version of decree 1913, called decree 1927, which repealed the first. Decree 1927 retained its predecessor's basic content, but specified fines of 10 to 200 pesos and 1 to 11 months' imprisonment for priests who did not comply.[54] Compliance meant that priests must be licensed by the state in order to minister. The Archdiocese's response was to end priest-led worship in the churches. If priests did not exercise their vocation, they would not need state licenses. And, while much worship went underground during the following months, as of 1 August, Mass would not be given in any Guadalajara churches.[55] For the rest of the state, the same would be true as of 1 September.[56]

In Guadalajara in the final July days, church attendances swelled under the pressure of those who wished to confess, marry, receive baptism, or receive the Eucharist, an important, if impressionistic, indicator of popular interest in the orthodox aspects of Catholic worship.[57] The same pattern was repeated outside the capital in the days before 1 September. From August, a state of mourning that entailed two distinct forms of protest was rigorously observed. The first was inward, recalling the practices of abstention observed during Advent and Lent: black ribbons appeared in windows and over doors in homes across the city; Catholics refrained from recreation; made purchases of basic necessity only; abstained from music and celebration; and boycotted the use of carriages, cars, and the city's trams.[58] The symbolism of mourning was widespread in the city, in addition to the discontinuation of all church-based activity or religious practice. From September, the mourning protest was extended throughout the state. The empty church buildings were converted into symbols of resistance across the archdiocesan landscape; at the same time, Catholic homes statewide became clandestine churches, a move consciously modeled on the catacombs of antiquity. The self-imposed distance between worshippers and their formal places of worship, and the relocation of the cult to primitive Church settings, served to strengthen Catholic resolve.

On 14 August, the Archdiocese published a circular for the faithful that declared two days of holy obligation for all clergy and laity, respectively falling on 22 and 23 August in the Zapopan Basilica and *parroquia* of San Pedro Tlaquepaque.[59] As customary pilgrimage sites just outside Guadalajara's city limits, these two churches temporarily became the material and symbolic focus of Catholic identity. The faithful created en masse a modern-day pilgrimage for religious liberty, which served as a point of union and a reaffirmation of Catholic identity in the struggle against civil authority.

The Catholic newspaper, *El Futuro*, published the following note:

> Things continue without change in the city; the Government sustains its
> campaign of persecution and the Catholics [continue their] passive resistance,
> protesting with extreme piety, during these final days of worship in the towns
> near Guadalajara; more than three quarters of the population has been to
> San Pedro and Zapopan; of course, the majority make the trip on foot, there
> and back.[60]

The article went on to comment, with a certain irony, that decree 1927 was
a blessing in disguise and had sown a "miraculous crop" that the Church
would harvest.

The second part of the mourning protest was directed as much outwardly
as inwardly. Its principal target was the pro-government daily, *El Occidental*,
which was held by Catholic laity systematically to misreport the news pertain-
ing to government repression of their movements. González Flores referred
to the protest as an assertion of "economic sovereignty," a term echoing the
language used by Gandhi in his struggle against the British in India. The campaign consisted of a boycott of the newspaper, not only in terms of consumption but of pressuring those who used the newspaper for advertising purposes.
The pro-Catholic newspaper, *La Epoca*, published a list of city businesses that
advertised in the newspaper. According to Camberos Vizcaíno, *La Lucha* did
likewise and also included a list of prominent masons in the city, whose businesses were boycotted.[61] The boycott was effective: in a matter of weeks, *El
Occidental* was forced to discontinue circulation, and never again reappeared.

Concurrently with the August boycott, the state governor and legislature
were bombarded with protests from Jalisco's rural towns and secondary
cities. Between mid-August and mid-September, I have counted 45 protest
letters representing 32 different towns. Although a few were sent directly to
Carranza, most went to the state legislature or governor. In at least one-third
of towns, the ACJM was directly involved in the petition campaign. In all,
these protests carried approximately 35,000 signatures. Unlike the July petitions, men now signed more often than women. Protests signed exclusively by
men generated nearly 19,000 signatures; over 9,000 accompanied protests
sent exclusively by women; and another 6,000 accompanied petitions signed
by men and women. Most petitions came from towns that were also parish
seats. For example, 600 *vecinos*—"Mexican citizens of Ciudad Guzmán in
full exercise of their Constitutional rights" (read men)—petitioned the
Governor; three days later, over 200 Damas Católicas of Ciudad Guzmán
protested in a separate petition to the state congress.[62]

What do the petitions reveal about Jalisco's towns? As might be expected,
there is a loose correlation between town size and the numbers signing the
petitions. Many towns sent separate petitions for men and women, a reflection of the sexual division observed by lay organizations. In two cases—
Arandas and San Miguel el Alto, important highland parishes that became
vital centers of *cristero* resistance—3 petitions were sent. In the case of San

Miguel, women and men circulated separate petitions, the latter signed by more than 1,100 *vecinos* and sent to the governor, who answered. On receiving the governor's reply, the men of San Miguel formulated a response, which was again signed by over 1,000 Catholics. Similarly, in Arandas, separate men's and women's petitions were sent to Carranza, the first with over 900 signatures, the second with over 3,000; at roughly the same time, a third petition circulated among the men of Arandas, which was also signed by over 3,000 *vecinos*. Hence the 1918 petitions were in some cases good religious predictors of future *cristero* militancy.

Elsewhere in Los Altos, for example, Encarnación de Díaz and Mexticacán pledged civil disobedience and refused to obey decree 1913/1927.[63] In Mexticacán on 21 August 1918, over 800 men and almost 1,000 women exercised their constitutional right to petition the authorities (article 8) by signing a joint protest. Instead of petitioning the president, the governor, or state congress, however, they directed their demands to the municipality. Specifically, they asked that decrees 1913 and 1927 be repealed; that no other decrees of similar nature substitute them; and that their local representatives make use of the constitutional right of municipal governments to send bills to Congress. The Mexticacán *ayuntamiento* supported the petition, in turn sending an accord to Congress. In a four-point agreement, the *ayuntamiento* unanimously applauded the townspeople's pacific attitude; approved the protest, as Catholic citizens pledging to "honor the favor of God before that of the State"; formally petitioned Congress on the town's behalf, asking it to take up the issue of repeal; and requested a formal response from the authorities in Guadalajara. The *ayuntamiento*'s president, vice president, legal counsel, and secretary signed the petition. Following their signatures, an exclamation read: "These are the actions of those who are, and know how to be, true representatives of the people!"[64] Some 10,000 copies of Mexticacán's petition were printed and distributed en masse in Guadalajara and each of Jalisco's more than 100 municipal governments.[65]

Conclusion

In December 1918, the U.S. Consul in Guadalajara, John Sillman, called on Carranza in Mexico City. Carranza received him cordially, asking if Mrs. Sillman had made the trip and suggesting they have dinner soon at the president's home. Regarding the religious question in Jalisco, Carranza remarked that he saw no reason for the ongoing conflict, and that he trusted it would soon be resolved. He was pushing legislation in the Federal Congress that would put an end to the troubles in Guadalajara, and also hoped to abolish the 1917 Constitution's provision that prohibited foreign-born priests and ministers in Mexico. Sillman filed a positive report on this occasion, and although he was somewhat vague on the measures to be taken, the conflict was indeed soon resolved.[66]

Concurrently, in late 1918, a new state legislature and governor were elected in Jalisco, clearing the way for a repeal of decree 1913/1927.

Following his 16-month leave of military absence, Diéguez returned to office on 31 January 1919 in order to give his final address as governor. Anacleto González Flores credits Diéguez with recognizing the need to repeal Jalisco's anticlerical legislation, and with taking the proper action before handing over power.[67] On 4 February 1919, the state's legislature rescinded decree 1927 in a vote of 15 in favor to 5 against.[68]

Following the repeal of decree 1927, Archbishop Orozco y Jiménez wrote to Interior Minister Manuel Aguirre Berlanga, in Mexico City, to request a passport along with guarantees for his return to Guadalajara. Prior to responding, Aguirre Berlanga consulted with Luis Tapia Castellanos, recently elected governor of Jalisco. Tapia responded that if and when the opportunity presented itself, he would arrest Orozco y Jiménez on an outstanding warrant dating from 1914. Notwithstanding the eventual threat of a new arrest, Aguirre Berlanga notified the archbishop that he had been granted permission to travel to Mexico, provided that he go first to Mexico City in order to consult with federal government officials. Thus Orozco y Jiménez set out for Mexico City in August. Meanwhile, his legal counsel in Guadalajara, Jalisco's former PCN head, Manuel F. Chávez, won an important battle when a district judge threw out the remaining warrant for the archbishop's arrest.[69] On arrival at Mexico City, Orozco y Jiménez wrote President Carranza and Governor Tapia. The letters are self-consciously diplomatic; the archbishop informed Carranza and Tapia of his arrival, said that he would remain in Mexico City for some time, declared himself a servant of both, and promised to communicate his travel plans prior to departing for Guadalajara.[70] When finally the archbishop arrived at Guadalajara in October, the celebrations were noisy and public. Men, women, and children of all classes lined the streets to greet him and shouted victory slogans; for days thereafter, Orozco y Jiménez received countless commissions from every corner of the archdiocese.[71]

There is a marked contrast embedded in this conflict that ought to be clarified. On the one hand, Church representatives like the archbishop of Guadalajara, as well as state agents like the interior minister and even general/governor Diéguez, sought out a delicate status quo in which both institutions might back away from conflict. On the other hand, in 1919 both Church and state were underwritten by highly mobilized social bases. The repeal of decree 1927 and Orozco y Jiménez's return were celebrated loudly and publicly, signaling a new Catholic offensive. Anticlerical violence would soon follow, initially through informal channels and eventually through a newly articulated state policy. Neither Church nor state leaders could then be counted on to control their social bases; furthermore, it is not always clear whether they wanted to.

There is another significant question in all of this, which should be of general interest to historians: to what extent did conflicts between groups of revolutionaries and Catholics forge a new politico-religious Catholic identity, shape revolutionary practice, or construct the political sphere of postrevolutionary Mexico? The conflicts analyzed in this episode suggest all of the above. Firstly, the events of 1917–19 proved to be a catalyst for a nationally based movement, sustained by a coalition of lay organizations such as the ACJM, the Mexican Union of Catholic Ladies (UDCM), and the various Catholic labor unions, both rural and urban, that formed the Confederación Católica Obrera (CCO).[72] These organizations assumed that Catholicism was a basic component of identity and compatible within the framework of other special interest constituencies (women, workers, youth). Secondly, as I have attempted to demonstrate, people of different backgrounds and localities—and surely with different expectations—were able to band together in a clear, militant expression of confessional identity politics for a limited period of time. In so doing, they reached two basic goals: on the one hand, they forced a political retreat from their civil authorities, and on the other they created a situation in which all of their ecclesiastical authorities could return from exile—the archbishop from his forced expatriation, and the parish priests from a self-imposed separation from their Church.

The role of lay Catholic organizations in the political battle was central, and their victory was significant. During the following six years, groups of Catholic women, youth, and workers would grow, constituting themselves as parallel organizations in competition with the state for its constituencies and exercising a major influence in the public sphere. This final point is particularly relevant. Although weak and internally divided, the Mexican state did claim for itself a legitimacy and an authority conferred by revolution. In practice, however, Mexico's religiously inspired political movement questioned both this authority and its fundamental legitimacy.

Notes

1. Biblioteca Pública del Estado de Jalisco (henceforth, BPE), Miscelánea 783.7, "Apuntes para la Historia: La Cuestión Religiosa en Jalisco," 1918; J. Ignacio Dávila Garibi and Salvador Chávez Hayhoe, *Colección de Documentos Relativos a la Cuestión Religiosa en Jalisco* (2 vols. Guadalajara: Tip. J.M. Yguíniz, 1920); Anacleto González Flores, *La Cuestión Religiosa en Jalisco* (Mexico City: ACJM, 1920).

2. See Guillermo Raúl Zepeda Lecuona, *Constitucionalistas, Iglesia Católica, y Derecho del Trabajo en Jalisco (1913–1919)* (Mexico City: INEHRM, 1997), Laura O'Dogherty, *De Urnas y Sotanas: El Partido Nacional Católico en Jalisco* (Mexico City: Conaculta, 2001).

3. *Carta Pastoral del Episcopado Mexicano sobre la Constitución de 1917* (Acordada, 1917). "La Actitud de los Prelados Mexicanos ante la Nueva Constitución Política de la República," *Jalisco*, 20 Jun. 1917. Cf: Luis C. Balderrama, *El Clero y el Gobierno de México: Apuntes para la Historia de la Crisis en 1926* (2 vols. Mexico City: Editorial Cuauhtémoc, 1927), 19–32.

4. *Carta Pastoral*, reprinted in J. Ignacio Dávila Garibi, *Apuntes para la Historia de la Iglesia en Guadalajara* (Mexico City: Editorial Cultura, 1977), 5:310–21.

5. Orozco y Jiménez was born in Michoacán in 1864 and served as archbishop of Guadalajara from 1912 until his death in 1936. The Jesuit historian, José Gutiérrez Casillas, referred to him as an activist, *luchador*, and "Good Shepherd" who resisted the Revolution's anticlerical surge through his leadership or simply by hiding out in the mountains and rural towns of the archdiocese

during periods of persecution so as not to abandon his flock. *Historia de la Iglesia en México* (Mexico City: Porrúa, 1974), 455.

6. Francisco Orozco y Jiménez, "Breve Relación," in Dávila, *Apuntes*, 7:300–10.
7. Cf: Jean Meyer, *La Cristiada* (3 vols. Mexico City: Siglo XXI, 1998), vol. 2.
8. Dávila, *Apuntes*, 5:323–4.
9. *Cuarta Carta Pastoral que el Ilmo. Y Rmo. Sr. Dr. y Mtro. D. Francisco Orozco y Jiménez, 5ᵗᵒ Arzobispo de Guadalajara, Dirige a sus Diocesanos*, 1917, 1–5.
10. SD 812.00.20974, John Sillman to State Department, Guadalajara, 2 Jun. 1917; Mario Aldana Rendón, *Del Reyismo al Nuevo Orden Constitucional, 1910–1917. Tomo I. Jalisco desde la Revolución* (Guadalajara: Gobierno del Estado/Universidad de Guadalajara, 1987), 327.
11. Alan Knight, *The Mexican Revolution* (2 vols. Lincoln: University of Nebraska Press, 1986), 2:236–51.
12. González Flores, *Cuestión Religiosa*, 291, 317.
13. Cf. Adrian A. Bantjes, "Burning Saints, Molding Minds: Iconoclasm, Civic Ritual, and the Failed Cultural Revolution," in *Rituals of Rule, Rituals of Resistance: Public Celebrations and Popular Culture in Mexico*, eds. William H. Beezley, Cheryl English Martin, and William E. French (Wilmington: Scholarly Resources, 1994), 273.
14. San Miguel Mezquitán, San José, Mexicaltzingo, Sweet Name of Jesus, San Francisco, and El Carmen were also closed. The detained priests were Miguel Cano, the archdiocesan secretary, and Lorenzo Altamirano. *Jalisco*, 12 Jul. 1917; *El Occidental*, 12 Jul. 1917; González Flores, *Cuestión Religiosa*, 298.
15. González Flores, *Cuestión Religiosa*, 299–300. Vicente Camberos Vizcaíno, *Un Hombre y una Epoca: Apuntes Biográficos* (Mexico City: Jus, 1949), 251.
16. SD 812.00.21115, Sillman, Guadalajara, 13 Jul. 1917.
17. González Flores, *Cuestión Religiosa*, 300.
18. See Denise Riley, *"Am I that Name?": The Category of Women in History* (Minneapolis: University of Minnesota, 1988).
19. González Flores, *Cuestión Religiosa*, 297–304; Camberos Vizcaíno, *Un Hombre*, 251.
20. *Jalisco*, 13 Jul. 1917; *El Occidental*, 13–14 Jul. 1917; *El Gato*, 19 Jul. 1917.
21. *El Gato*, 15 Jul. 1917; *El Occidental*, 17 Jul. 1917.
22. González Flores, *Cuestión Religiosa*, 302.
23. AHJ, Ramo G.4.917, c. G-340, exps. s/n, Catholics to governor, 15 Sep. 1917, and Sector Juárez residents to governor, Sep. 1917.
24. *El Radical*, 16 Sep. 1917; *El Paladín*, 16 Jun. 1918.
25. See Mario Aldana Rendón, *Manuel M. Dieguez y el Constitucionalismo en Jalisco (Documentos)* (Guadalajara: Gobierno de Jalisco, 1986).
26. Churches in villages east/northeast of the city (San Andrés, Tetlán, Huentitán el Alto, and Huentitán el Bajo) were presumably left open for worship. Archivo Municipal de Guadalajara (hereafter AMG), 1918, exp. 139, Gobierno to Municipal President Rivera Rosas, 1 Feb. and 5 Mar. 1918.
27. AMG, 1918, exp. 669, Gobierno to municipal president, 27 May 1918.
28. AMG, 1918, exp. 139.
29. Jorge Villaseñor, "Importante Iniciativa sobre la Reglamentación del Artículo 130 Constitucional," *El Occidental*, 20 Feb. 1918.
30. *Colección de Leyes y Decretos Relativos a la Reducción de Sacerdotes y la Persecución Religiosa en Méjico desde el Punto de Vista Jurídico*, ed. Félix

Navarrete and Eduardo Pallares (Mexico City, n.d.), 241–54; Dávila, *Apuntes*, 5:354–8. On 15 Jul. 1918, 47 Catholic lawyers filed a lawsuit appealing Decree 1913.

31. On this, see Robert Curley, "La Democratización del Retrato: Registro de Empleados Domésticos, 1888–1894," in *El Rostro de los Oficios*, ed. Arturo Camacho Becerra (Guadalajara: Editorial Amate, 2006), 23–36; Sergio González Rodríguez, *Los Bajos Fondos: El Antro, la Bohemia y el Café* (Mexico City: Cal y Arena, 1990).
32. *El Occidental*, 1 Jun. 1918.
33. Dávila and Chávez, *Documentos*, 1:64–7.
34. *El Informador*, 9 and 11 Jul. 1918.
35. BPE, Miscelánea 783/7, "Apuntes," 7–15; González Flores, *Cuestión Religiosa*, 310–12; Antonio Rius Facius, *De Don Porfirio a Plutarco: Historia de la ACJM* (Mexico City: Jus, 1958), 103–6; Camberos Vizcaíno, *Un Hombre*, 254–5.
36. See David O'Brien, *Public Catholicism* (New York: Macmillan, 1989). José Casanova, *Public Religions in the Modern World* (Chicago: University of Chicago Press, 1994).
37. Alvarado is the first of 435 signatories, of whom over 90 percent are arch-diocesan clergy; BPE, Miscelánea 783/7, "Memorial del Cabildo Metropolitano y Clero de la Arquidiócesis de Guadalajara, al C. Presidente de la República Mexicana, Dn. Venustiano Carranza; y Voto de Adhesión y Obediencia al Ilmo. y Revmo. Sr. Arzobispo, Dr. y Mtro. Dn. Francisco Orozco y Jiménez," Apr. 1918.
38. Dávila and Chávez, *Documentos*, 2:45–9; *El Informador*, 10 Jul. 1918.
39. Dávila and Chávez, *Documentos*, 2:36.
40. See María Teresa Fernández-Aceves, "The Political Mobilization of Women in Revolutionary Guadalajara, 1910–1940" (PhD diss., University of Illinois-Chicago, 2000), 110–13. Gabriela Cano, "El Porfiriato y la Revolución Mexicana: Construcciones en Torno al Feminismo y al Nacionalismo," *La Ventana* 4 (1996): 39–58.
41. Dávila and Chávez, *Documentos*, 2:27.
42. BPE, Miscelánea 783.7, Memorial, 31.
43. *El Informador*, 19 Jul. 1918.
44. González Flores, *Cuestión Religiosa*, 315; Rius Facius, *De Don Porfirio*, 104.
45. Rius Facius, *De Don Porfirio*, 108.
46. Fondo Palomar y Vizcarra (henceforth FPyV), 41.297.3207, Alvarez Tostado to Palomar y Vizcarra, 22–23 Jul. 1918; BPE, Miscelánea 783.7, "Apuntes," 19. *El Informador*, 23 Jul. 1918, estimated more than 10,000.
47. FPyV, 41.297.3206, Alvarez to Palomar, 22–23 Jul. 1918; González Flores, *Cuestión Religiosa*, 321–23.
48. Archivo General de la Nación (AGN), Presidentes, Estado Mayor Presidencial, 340(72)58.
49. Borrayo is still remembered by locals for his violence. A school on the plaza now carries his name. Interview with Roberto Hernández, 23 Apr. 1996.
50. FPyV, 41.297.3207, Alvarez to Palomar, 22–23 Jul. 1918.
51. González Flores, *Cuestión Religiosa*, 322; Antonio Gómez Robledo, *Anacleto González Flores: El Maestro* (Mexico City: Jus, 1947), 72.
52. "Silence, after words, is the second power in the world." Félicité Robert de Lamennais (1782–1854): French philosopher-priest who advocated democracy

and Church-state separation. When Rome condemned his ideas, Lammenais published *Thoughts of a Believer* (1834) and left the Church. This choice itself suggests that Guadalajara Catholics were not blind followers of pro-Roman bishops.

53. Gómez Robledo, *Anacleto González Flores*, 73.
54. Dávila and Chávez, *Documentos*, 1:64–7, 74–8; *Colección de Leyes*, 241–54.
55. Rius Facius, *De Don Porfirio*, 111.
56. Decree 1913 stated that the legislation would first take effect in Guadalajara (1 Aug.), then in the rest of the state (10 Sep.); *Colección de Leyes*, 243.
57. These were not Anita Brenner's syncretic faithful with idols stashed behind altars; or, if they were, they also had a conventional interest in the sacraments that is generally downplayed in the writing of Brenner's generation. See Anita Brenner, *Idols behind Altars* (New York: Payson and Clark, 1929).
58. González Flores, *Cuestión Religiosa*, 331.
59. Dávila, *Apuntes*, 5:380–5.
60. BPE, Miscelánea 783.7, "Apuntes," 21.
61. González Flores, *Cuestión Religiosa*, 332.
62. Dávila and Chávez, *Documentos*, vol. 2.
63. González Flores, *Cuestión Religiosa*, 333.
64. BPE, Miscelánea 783.7, "Apuntes," 91–2; Dávila and Chávez, *Documentos*, 2:200–6.
65. González Flores, *Cuestión Religiosa*, 333.
66. SD 812.00.22456, Sillman, Guadalajara, 28 Dec. 1918.
67. González Flores, *Cuestión Religiosa*, 337.
68. *El Informador*, 5 Feb. 1919.
69. Francisco Barbosa Guzmán, *La Iglesia y el Gobierno Civil. Tomo VI. Jalisco desde la Revolución* (Guadalajara: Gobierno del Estado, 1988), 231–3.
70. The text of both messages is reprinted in J. Ignacio Dávila Garibi, *Apuntes para la Historia de la Iglesia en Guadalajara* (Mexico City: Cultura, 1977), 5:420–1.
71. Antonio Rius Facius, *De Don Porfirio a Plutarco: Historia de la ACJM* (Mexico City: Jus, 1958), 113–14.
72. The CCO was formed in 1919 and renamed the Confederación Católica del Trabajo (CCT) in 1920. In 1922 it was expanded and renamed the Confederación Nacional Católica del Trabajo (CNCT). From 1921–22, another CCO—a women's organization called the Confederación Católica de Obreras—also existed. This eventually united with the CNCT, which included both men's and women's unions.

Chapter 7

Trouble Afoot? Pilgrimage in *Cristero* Mexico City

Matthew Butler

From 1926–29, thousands of Mexicans gave their lives for *Cristo Rey* (Christ the King), avatar of a new devotion that proclaimed Christ's temporal kingship in the person of the Sacred Heart enthroned. The cult was particularly strong around Mexico City, where a Catholic rebellion waged under the same banner—the *cristero* revolt, or *Cristiada*—was paradoxically weak.[1] Though there was no *capitalino* crusade, Christ's worldly authority was proclaimed annually on the last Sunday of October in mass pilgrimages to the mountain of Tepeyac. These sacred marches, organized by lay leaders and endorsed by clergy, attracted hundreds of thousands of pilgrims in the years 1926–28. Yet biblical multitudes, including priests, also coalesced around spontaneous peregrinations, such as the tumults that followed the funerals of Padre Pro (1927) or José de León Toral (1929). These formal and informal pilgrimage modes were connected in a metanarrative of militant piety, shared a symbolic repertoire (*Cristo Rey* imagery), and depended upon a lay foot soldiery. Both were conceived as spiritual plebiscites against state anticlericalism. To some extent, however, these cycles differed in terms of their meaning and character, and thus give us an insight into the dynamism and richness of revolutionary devotionalism.

We can conceptualize this difference by utilizing Victor and Edith Turner's celebrated pilgrimage theory and William Christian's "local religion" thesis.[2] Thus we may distinguish, following the Turners, between structural and "liminoid" pilgrimage forms: here, between ordered pilgrimages whose purpose, fundamentally, was the legalistic defense of the institutional Church and the inculcation of orthodoxy; and comparatively destructured, saint-centered pilgrimages, which generated religious meanings semi-independently of the structure and produced intense feelings of intercommunion (what the Turners call *communitas*). Rather than expressing a set of rigid religious oppositions based on class or caste, this pattern corresponds to a localized religious formulation as described by Christian: that is, a territorially bounded setting in which "high" and "low," universal and parochial, religious elements jostled for space, usually without significant friction.

During the *Cristiada*, indeed, prescribed and lived religion was often close enough to prevent real conflict; when it came to celebrating secret masses and fomenting "lay" sacraments, for example, priests and parishioners collaborated.[3] Moreover, rifts, when they developed, could follow ideational categories encompassing different estates/classes. This was true, say, of the growing schism between the majoritarian, pacifist episcopate and Catholics (including bishops) who sympathized with the *ultras* of the National League for the Defence of Religious Liberty (LNDLR), an armed group founded in 1925. For the former, *Cristo Rey*'s monarchy denoted a secure Church, sovereign in its sphere and free to Christianize socioeconomic relationships. Persecution, meanwhile, was divine punishment for Mexico's devotional sloth—especially its tolerance of godless revolutionaries—and was best remedied by prayer. This providential touch aside, this vision differed little from Rome's conception of Christ's temporal Kingdom, prescribed universally in 1925. While sharing this outlook, *ligueros* and their clerical allies took this antisecularism much further, sanctifying the victims of persecution and theologizing the complete and violent overthrow of Mexico's postrevolutionary regime. From late 1928, this tactical and doctrinal contradiction could no longer be accommodated within a localized religious form, so became damaging.

Cristo Rey's official cult was celebrated in mass processions to the Basilica of Guadalupe. Besides reclaiming the streets, these regimented events channeled a mass of devotional energy in support of the episcopate's politico-theological vision. Thus, pastorals outlined a sacralized political economy in which divine mercy—God's removal of his providential scourge, Calles—could be won with penitential offerings to *Cristo Rey* and prayers to the Virgin. Pilgrimage was therefore a didactic, as well as an instrumental form designed to teach the laity that redemption lay in Christ, accessible via Mary at the foot of the cross. The pilgrim's mimetic hardships—bloodied feet, thirst, wearing crowns of thorns and black garb—would reinforce this ultimately Christocentric lesson. While mobilizing for this national Calvary, however, the episcopate necessarily surrendered control of public religion to the laity, creating new cadres of specialists to manage the devotion site and officiate at the festival. Even orthodox manifestations of the *Cristo Rey* cult, then, to some extent reflected the pressures for widening social participation that shook Mexico in 1910.

Informal pilgrimages additionally showed a *communitas* spirit, an intense commingling that corroded distinctions of class, caste, and gender. There were collective outbursts of free-form religion—a frenzied clamoring for relics, the kissing of martyr's bodies—in which the social roles of women and children, rich and poor, were turned upside-down. Such cultic inversions, however, worried the Church less than threats to its monopoly over doctrine (what Jaffary calls control of "theological production"),[4] the most serious of which occurred after León Toral assassinated president-elect Obregón in 1928. Henceforth, LNDLR radicals and their clerical apologists moralized armed struggle by invoking the doctrine of tyrannicide and lioniz-ing León Toral's heroic Catholicity. This was too much for the dominant episcopal faction, which clamped down on the militants. Over time, then, informal pilgrimage cults trespassed into the taboo realm of doctrine, not merely practice, in the process adding a revolutionary element (politico-spiritual violence) to the equation. The stirrings of a revolt against revolu-tionaries *and* episcopal concordatories underscored the risks of religious disintermediation and help explain why episcopal moderates hurriedly signed the *arreglos* that ended the *Cristiada* in 1929.

As William Christian also finds in the case of Spain, there was tension in Mexico between pilgrimages to holy places, and those celebrating people. Unlike pilgrimages to established shrines, such as Tepeyac or Chalma, "anthropological" peregrinations occurred in improvised settings, not Church-controlled contexts, and during post-traumatic moments (typically, the after-shock of public executions); they also left tangible evidence (corpses, relics), vividly humanizing the sacred. Proto-martyrs' still-cooling remains were hence more conducive to displays of religious, shading into political, excess. Indeed, it is this primordial, affective quality—the early fizz of unstructured devotion—that *communitas* denotes, for all that critics deny the concept's historicity or exaggerate its universalizing claims.[5] In the case of Mexico's "*cristero* martyrs," efforts to routinize the cult have followed official endorse-ment, but the initial, open-ended fervor, also imprinted on the sources, was palpable. The absence of *communitas* from choreographed *Cristo Rey* pilgrimages does not mean, conversely, that such resacralizations were rote, mechanical performances. As Ruth Harris reminds us (likewise Rulfo's "Talpa"), pilgrimage has a raw physicality that inscribes meaning on minds and bodies: it is not just discourse.[6] The difference here lies in the fixity of practice and ethos. Some pilgrims advanced in ordered battalions, grimly determined to fight the Church's fight; others wept in exultant throngs that were more free-wheeling in religious terms but prone to stampede into ecstatic, violent frenzies.

These pilgrimages are also worth studying because analyses of postrevolu-tionary ritual usually focus on civic reenactments (revolutionary flag days, beauty pageants, sports matches). By contrast, processional sacra, after the colony, are ignored.[7] This *patria*-building exclusivity, besides reinforcing a semantic link between modernity and secularism, belies the fact that pilgrim-ages constituted many of the biggest (indeed most "patriotic") gatherings after 1910. The Sacred Heart Consecration (1914), the Eucharistic Congress (1924), and the Marian centennial (1931), were the most prominent, but there were endless smaller *romerías*, as at Iztapalapa or Juquila.[8] In such events, as in Europe,[9] laypeople marched in unprecedented numbers to thwart religion's confinement to the private sphere. The mass assertion of a laicized public religiosity also forms an important part of the revolution's sacred history, and creates a link between religious and broader social change. These sacred journeys may help us to see postrevolutionary Mexican Catholicism as more than a sheer, counterrevolutionary monolith, revealing instead the ways in which it was transformed by the wider social drama of 1910–40.

Hail, King! *Cristo Rey*
Pilgrimages, 1926–28

The *Cristo Rey* feast entered the universal liturgy in Pius XI's *Quas Primas* (11 December 1925).[10] Pius departed from the premise that since God was the origin of authority, societies could not simply emancipate themselves from divine law. Christ's temporal Kingdom would exist, Pius went on, when the Church was sovereign in its sphere and empowered to "perfect" the secular arm, ensuring mundane justice and otherworldly salvation. At heart, the cult called for re-Christianization under the aegis of a Church independent in the ecclesiastical and social spheres. In Mexico, Christ's social imperium was proclaimed in March 1913, when the episcopate sought Rome's blessing to enthrone the Sacred Heart as *Cristo Rey*. This coronation would renew Mexico's colonial compact with Christ, which liberals had ruptured, causing God to unleash the neo-Aztec butchery of revolution in punishment. Rashly, this teleology was articulated just weeks after the "tragic 10 days" (*decena trágica*)—the violent seizure of power in Mexico City by General Victoriano Huerta in early 1913, casting a providential halo round Huerta and forever associating *Cristo Rey* with reaction in revolutionary minds. The ostentatious coronation (January 1914) saw a gold crown and scepter placed beneath the Sacred Heart in the metropolitan Cathedral. Controversy erupted again in 1923, when the apostolic delegate, Ernesto Filippi, consecrated a hilltop monument to *Cristo Rey* at Silao in front of 50,000 pilgrims, outraging revolutionary anticlericals.[11]

The *Cristo Rey* cult took shape during the *Cristiada* as routines (novenas, home-altar consecrations) were devised for it.[12] A September 1926 pastoral stated that the cult opposed "Christ's expulsion from the home, education, institutions, and the law," and affirmed that "terrible secularism" had ruptured Mexico's historic contract with God, bringing divine chastisement. Yet God would restore peace if offered prayer and penitence.[13] As this binary method implied, in practice the *Cristo Rey* devotion evidenced a more composite character than its Christocentric name suggests. Indeed, the cult was deliberately juxtaposed with a secondary Marianism, coopting Mary's followers and channeling their devotions in the struggle against *callismo*.

On the one hand, devotees were to become Christ's "living image," imitating *his* Passion by "crucifying" *their* passions with abstinence.[14] Mortification using rods and cilices was allowed—spiritual athletes like Conchita Cabrera doubtless took up scourges and red-hot irons—and Pius even gave indulgence to those who died shouting "*¡Viva Cristo Rey!*"; their "steaming hearts," torn beating from the breast by Calles-Huitzilopochtli, were like the Sacred Heart.[15] The devotion thus incorporated the mimetic brutalism of France's *Sacré Coeur*, transposed into a Mexicanized historical teleology of election, transgression, and atonement (Conquest, Reform/Revolution,

Christ's Kingdom). The flock was told to show true love of Christ and take up the cross, thus erasing an historical debt and appeasing a vengeful monarch.

The devotion was further Mexicanized by association with the Guadalupe, the afflicted nation's "Mother and Queen." Prayer campaigns were devised to work "sweet violence" on Mary, swaying her heart with a spiritual tribute of accumulated sorrow. Pastorals reminded the faithful that Christ was the *source* of grace, but Mary as co-dispenser could help restore "religious liberty" if properly entreated. *Cristo Rey*'s sanguinary demands were thus triangulated and moderated in an intercessionary relationship involving the faithful, Mary, and Christ. Indeed, contemporary pastorals posited a syncretic religious mode—"To Jesus, then, by Mary!" as one put it—which mixed collective sacrifice (reparatory cult to the Sacred Heart) with votive intention (solicitous prayer to Mary).[16] This Marianism was perhaps a failsafe, in case the *Cristo Rey* cult failed to take root: but probably it was intended to increase the devotion's efficacity by gift-wrapping the flock's sacrificial gifts in Mary's gentle advocacy. It also served a didactic function by underscoring the asymmetrical relationship between saintly intercessors and Christ: Mary could plead for persecution to end, but only *Cristo Rey* could decide when. A final (local) element was the cult's somber, funereal tone, inverting any formal triumphalism (Christ the *King*). Indeed, persecution dictated that Mexico's *Cristo Rey* feast be experienced not as a coronation but as a black fiesta mourning Christ's enforced abdication of his throne.

Once this image was fixed, the godly infantry prepared for the first pilgrimage.[17] Some priests attended incognito—the archbishop of Mexico was spotted in civvies—but logistical and ritual organization fell to lay groups: the Our Lady of Guadalupe Academy, the LNDLR. These activists urged Catholics to journey to the Basilica for a consecration and later to enthrone *Cristo Rey* at home. At dawn on 23 October 1926, some 200,000 pilgrims—perhaps a *fifth* of the capital's population—set out for Tepeyac from the pilgrimage's starting line at Peralvillo, an hour's walk from the sanctuary. Many crammed into trams or cars, but the majority went on foot (and many of these barefoot), forming columns 10-abreast and marching up the Calzada de Guadalupe and Misterios, the parallel approaches to the shrine. A "contagious fervor" reigned along the Calzada, with marchers singing *Cristo Rey* hymns and intoning the national anthem to Catholicized lyrics. The stone prayer-stations along Misterios were covered with flowers as people stopped to recite the Rosary. In the only violent incident, mounted police charged, causing fleeing pilgrims to cut their bare feet scrambling over a railway line. Yet sheer numbers swept the *montada* aside, and the pilgrims advanced irresistibly toward the *santuario* further north.

The first ranks appeared at Tepeyac in the early morning gloom, still singing the Rosary. Most had arrived by noon, when throngs filled the atrium. The pilgrimage was orderly: as devotees reached the sanctuary on their knees, they were directed in through the west door and out by the south; while inside, devotees surged toward the Guadalupe image along the east nave, then receded along the west. Pilgrims passed the miraculous *yate* in ranks of 10, genuflecting as they went, while "commissions" of activists, identified by green armbands, policed the traffic. *Acejotaemero*[18] Luis Rivera del Val and acolyte Miguel Pardinas were among those who regulated this groaning influx. Accounts testify to a circular flow in and out of the Basilica— the building itself pumped like a heart. At mid-morning, lay leaders performed solemnizations. The consecration's laicism—it would be "directed by the faithful"—was well advertised. Moreover, LNDLR representatives were chosen beforehand to recite their state's consecration. This liturgy started at 9.40 a.m., when Rafael Ceniceros y Villareal, LNDLR president, read the consecration from a podium in the Basilica's center. State delegates then read their oaths, before people knelt for the Creed and prayers to *Cristo Rey* and the "Indian Virgin." People in the atrium also knelt down. At 11 a.m., another layperson performed a kind of "white" Mass consisting of a sermon and spiritual communion. This preacher first stated that the Extremaduran Guadalupe, "after whom our Virgin took her name," was being crowned simultaneously in Toledo. In the absence of the Eucharist, the service ended in spiritual communion with this Mass. The lay leader recited a prayer to this effect from the presbytery, which the congregation repeated, as if "tuning in" to a shortwave sacramental frequency from abroad. Throughout the day, candles flickered and there were cheers to *Cristo Rey* and the Virgin. Police were powerless to prevent singing and praying (a "festival of liberty") in the streets. A few profane activities were noted, but a somber atmosphere prevailed, with "roulettes, lotteries, or *cantinas*" closed. The absence of "the embarrassing spectacles of drunkenness, common on 12 December" was noted with interest by pro-government reporters.

Mexico's *Cristo Rey* cult therefore boomed,[19] reflecting traumatic persecution and clerical/lay exhortation. The pilgrimage, however, was surprisingly ordered. Indeed, the evidence suggests a rather unproblematic enactment of *Cristo Rey*'s social Kingdom: the ritual conjuring—by home, parish, and state—of a resacralized community; the use of approved liturgies (the consecration act "must be"—indeed *was*—"that written by Pope Leo XIII"); the deployment of massive columns to displace secular authority; the pilgrims' Christian restraint and embrace of physical pain (no drinking, walking on bloodied feet and knees, the passive meeting of a cavalry charge); and Mary's positioning relative to *Cristo Rey* (a glimpse of La Guadalupe, then consecration to Christ); all dramatized the official message of a nation under Christ's divine captaincy, comforted by the Indian Virgin.

Doubtless the experience was not uniform: there may, for example, have been a disjuncture between those whose pilgrimage effectively ended under Juan Diego's cloak,[20] and those in the "inner circle," consecrated as *Cristo Rey*'s vassals. But if this *was* a divergence—many people in the atrium also joined in the consecration—it nonetheless reflected the cult's binary construction. Pilgrims' recitations of the Rosary and hymns to *Cristo Rey*, meanwhile, and the spiritual communion, also point to a subtle interaction here between lay and clerical religious outlooks.

The most innovative aspect was the laicization of religious authority. Such consecrations were usually clericalist pageants, yet this was organized by individual parishioners and the LNDLR. League militants also performed quasi-sacramental, priestly functions (sermons, spiritual communions, consecrations). To those present, this transfer of sacred authority must have seemed fairly radical. Yet these were not renegade acts, and occurred within defined parameters; the rites bore a clerical imprimatur, and even the choreography of lay ceremonials—performed in the Basilica's center or in the presbytery—accorded with episcopal norms reserving certain holy precincts, such as the altar, to clergy. If liberating in one sense, then, militants' auxiliary efforts were also didactic; desirable behavior was encouraged, for example, while "private" cult that disrupted or delayed the mass accumulation of religious tribute (personal prayer beneath the Virgin) was prevented. Lay mediation thus ultimately accentuated the event's orthodox character as a national civico-religious penance to Christ, backed by Mary.[21] The event was resoundingly patriarchal, too, with a male directorate and Catholic women consigned to the rank and file.

Thus the Church honed a mass pilgrimage format, putting stripes on a lay officer class in the process. The formula's success was shown in the fact it could be repeated, but this was not a static festival and there were accretions/refinements year on year. The 1927 feast, for example, was preceded by a week of penitential exercises and a Rosary month, both premised on the belief that persecution was divine punishment and repentance, as with Jonah, the remedy. The episcopate thus plunged the faithful into the whale's belly, prescribing "corporal punishments" (cilices, flagellation, fasting) and prayers (the Via Crucis and Rosary) in church.[22] According to Bishop Miguel de la Mora, episcopal subcommittee president,[23] this mortification and prayer campaign was an "astounding success." There were even reports—and here hagiographical excitement got the better of him—of "fasting by breast-feeding children, whose mothers did not give them the breast until noon."[24]

The 1927 *Cristo Rey* pilgrimage, coordinated by Basilica-based "religious associations," attracted a crowd bigger than any assembled for a Guadalupan fiesta, *El Universal* insisted. At 8 a.m. on 30 October, an "endless procession" of pilgrims began, with buses and trams overtaking those who walked. "Many thousands" made the journey in the "greatest composure," carrying wreathes of flowers but no religious insignia. Mounted police lined the route to keep the peace and at various points diverted pilgrim cohorts to reduce traffic, but there was no violence. Police riders also thinned the crowd into lines near the atrium in order to prevent crushes. Inside the monument, lay associations again "took charge of ordering the procession." A pilgrim-route was signposted inside the Basilica, and pilgrims who stopped before the image of Mary were told by lay leaders to pray on the hoof. There was no "special ceremony" of consecration, and Catholics "restrict[ed] themselves to saying their prayers in more or less numerous groups, or to singing religious hymns." Crowds were still arriving at 2 p.m.; by this time the Basilica's *altar mayor* was ablaze with candles, its base and stairwells buried under white roses.[25]

In many respects, this was a copy of the 1926 pilgrimage. Lay leaders ran the show, Christ's altar—bearing the legend *¡Viva Cristo Rey!*—remained the object of reverence, and the fiesta served its instrumental purposes of flexing Catholic muscle and tilting providence's scales. The main differences were the absence of LNDLR activists (busy organizing a revolt); the protracted build-up of spiritual exercises; and the absence of a national consecration rite. The last point—which could imply this was a Marian homage by another name—looks more significant than it is, and probably reflects the prevalence of individual consecrations and the absence of League agents. For the event was very different, in terms of mood and constituency, from the Marian *fête*: while *Cristo Rey* was a mournful feast, on 12 December 1927 "fairground trade" ("wheels of fortune, merry-go-rounds, whirligigs") sprang up at Tepeyac, and there were drunken punch-ups and arrests. Pilgrims also came in smaller numbers than for *Cristo Rey*, and mostly from indigenous *pueblos*, such as Iztapalapa and Xochimilco. Thus the new cult was sufficiently differentiated to suggest real commitment among devotees; conversely, by 1927 the Guadalupan feast was seemingly Indianized, *Excélsior* reported, as *Cristo Rey* became the avatar of religious patriotism.[26]

The 1928 pilgrimage was more elaborate. Again, pastorals urged penitence as a prelude to Christ's "solemn festival"; as before, the cycle climaxed with "ordered pilgrimages," testifying that "the Mexican *patria* adores Christ the King, and from Him awaits salvation";[27] and again, new observances were incorporated. After two years of persecution, the episcopate now lamented that many children ("angels of their families") were growing up ignorant of Christ in a "lethal atmosphere of paganism, repulsive nakedness, [and] insatiable pleasure." To escape this *callista* Sodom, the faithful must now recite the standard penitences, but also catechize, recite a novena and triduum, and confess to a priest. "Fervent pilgrimages" to Tepeyac, any Sacred Heart sanctuary, or failing that, any church, must follow, and a Holy Hour by the Peruvian ecclesiastic Mateo Crawley-Boevey (a Vatican-endorsed, international exponent of Sacred Heart enthronement) was prescribed and sold at 10 *centavos*.

On 28 October, 200,000 pilgrims went to Tepeyac. Again the *cantinas* stayed closed and lay militants formed devotees into lines in the atrium. "Vigilance cordons" now lined the naves to ensure that "none of the believers could stop for long to recite their prayers," and that "all prayed walking." This had been done before, but now laypeople led the singing of canticles and cries of ecstasy. Groups of choristers (*voceadores*) stood at the Basilica doors, singing praises (*alabanzas*) and responses to Mary, and handing out floral crowns (*coronitas de Cristo Rey*). An orator whipped devotees into a frenzy and urged pilgrims to hurry to the holy spectacle ("Let us go, sinners, and see what we have not seen: the Sacred Heart on the Mountain of Christ!"). The emphasis on sacred music continued inside with choirs of confrères singing prayers of supplication (*plegarias*). There was a curious priestly simulacrum, too, in the form of a statue of Porfirian prelate Labastida y Dávalos; placed before the Sacred Heart's throne,[28] this marble figure interrupted the laity's view of *Cristo Rey*, visualizing the need for clerical mediation. The altar was adorned with a massive floral arrangement and paper flags bearing the *¡Viva Cristo Rey!* slogan.[29]

The evidence again suggests a rather close fit between clerical/lay religion, as lay leaders organized mass events that fixed persecution's meaning as a providential evil, remediable by mass appeals to God and better living of the Christian life. The routinization and embellishment of a basic festive structure probably reflected growing lay self-confidence as well as clerical officiousness. The event even acquired a certain liturgical splendor (music, Holy Hours) and a clearer division of labor (specialized roles of *cantor*, commissar, orator). Ritual props—crowns, flags—were also standardized. The front-loading of prayer campaigns, finally, meant that the pilgrimage became the closing act of a devotional cycle: in this process, *Cristo Rey*'s feast became associated with, to some extent an elongation of, catechesis (note the pedagogic emphasis) and the sacraments (penance, communion). Most people did not object to this creeping institutionalization. What mattered was that the laity stepped into the breech in response to revolutionary persecution, showing that it, too, was the Church. There was, within these limits, a feeling of self-discovery echoing wider social change. As one Catholic wrote, "The *pueblo* desired to show its faith to the government . . . The procession, without priests, without *santos*, without bishops, without candles, was simply magnificent. *It was the march of a people*."[30]

Days of the Dead: *"Cristero"* Pilgrimages, 1927–29

On 23 November 1927, Miguel Agustín Pro was executed in the shooting gallery of the Inspección de Policía (now the Lotería Nacional building), arms outstretched and crying *¡Viva Cristo Rey!* A Jesuit, Pro was shot with three others for alleged involvement in a plot to murder president-elect Obregón. That same day, Bishop Mora proposed purifying *callismo*'s "Dantesque" atmosphere by erecting a national *Cristo Rey* basilica.[31] Events now outstripped the episcopal subcommittee, however, and something like spontaneous canonization occurred next day when the bodies of Miguel and his brother, Humberto, left the Pro home in the Colonia Juárez for the Panteón de Dolores. The previous night, the house became an "ardent chapel," and thousands of mourners "of all social classes" passed through to touch the coffins with medals, rosary beads, or their lips. At the request of the Pros' father, don Miguel Pro, the Host was placed on Miguel's coffin in a scene reminiscent, a witness wrote, of "the catacombs at Christianity's beginnings." There were Holy Hours and requiem masses. As the sun rose, "unimagined" crowds filled the house. The deceased's father now knelt between his sons' coffins, proclaiming Miguel an apostle and Humberto an angel.[32] A dozen laypeople and priests—including the Jesuit, Méndez Medina—put the coffins on hearses. The crowd knelt as the horses started, and a solitary cry of *¡Viva Cristo Rey!* rang out. Calles is said to have looked

down from Chapultepec as 40,000 weeping Catholics processed along
Reforma; others threw flowers and recited the Rosary, and everywhere
crowds pressed forward in a bid to touch the caskets. When the route became
impassable for horses, the boxes were unlimbered and carried. Another
20,000 Catholics waited at the cemetery waving palm branches and praying.
As these multitudes dissolved into one, the funeral "acquired the aspect of an
apotheosis," a witness wrote, with people singing the National Anthem and
praising *Cristo Rey*. Silence fell as the bodies were lowered into graves in the
Jesuit crypt. In the absence of an ordained celebrant, don Miguel Pro threw
the first soil over his sons, and said, "We have finished. *Te Deum Laudamus.*"
The Creed was then recited, the mourners weeping as gravediggers topped
off the sepulcher. Though improvised and laicized, "the solemnity of this
burial was indescribable," according to the Mitre's awestruck informant.[33]
Soon the tomb was covered in flowers and candles. Sick pilgrims also started
to arrive, removing candle stubs and droplets of holy oil. Miracles were
announced, starting that November, as these minute traces of sacrality scattered like pollen across the land: a child's blindness cured in Guadalajara; a
Chihuahuan who quit boozing; a thief who returned ill-gotten gains in
Zacatecas; a reformed adulterer here; a Lazarus there, and all after touching
Pro's image or artifacts.[34] On the first anniversary of his death, Catholics
placed flowers on Pro's grave. Significantly, however, prayers were also said
for Juan Tirado and Luis Segura Vilchis, the *ligueros* who dynamited
Obregón's cavalcade and died alongside Pro. Moreover, LNDLR material
was found in the crowd, and the singing of canticles gave way to seditious
shouting. There were scuffles and arrests as tempers rose.[35]

This pilgrimage cycle, clearly, was articulated in a different idiom, with
social homogenization and collective, even frenzied, grief being notable
features (the Turners' "likeness of lot and intention" yielding "commonness
of feeling").[36] Besides this ecstatic destructuring, the pilgrimage was infused
with religious meanings produced within a Catholicized field, but semi-
autonomously: these included claims of sanctity (Miguel the apostle,
Humberto the cherubim) and "miracles," typically reversing physical and
moral decay. Then there was the ad hoc burial and "charging" of devotion-
alia by touching Pro's casket or garments. In short, this was a cult in which
supernatural agency (miracles, relics) and sainthood (martyrdom) played
significant parts, not just prayer and penitence; there was a belief, accordingly, that persecution and social collapse could be prevented or eased by
individuals' violent deaths, or others' exposure to the religious radioactivity
of blessed artifacts. This was different to the stoic martyrdom and prayer
campaigns of the hierarchy, but was more a case of popular, perhaps
Jesuitical, fervor, than anything else. Pro's martyrdom was *passive*, above all,
and placed the clergy firmly in the middle of the story as *Cristo Rey*'s favored
sacrificial lamb. Pro's cruciform immolation—probably the *Cristiada*'s iconic
moment—encouraged such Christ-like associations, and his funeral too, was
something of a Via Crucis; if the emotional pitch and signifiers differed from
those of the October pilgrimages, then they nonetheless remained within

orthodoxy's fold—unlike, say, the Juan Soldado cult that emerged under *cardenismo*.[37]

Here, then, the laity gave vent to emotive and thaumaturgical (at worst credulous) aspects of the faith; yet, priests too shared in much of this localized religion.[38] More worrying to the Church were devotions that upped the political ante on the basis of freelance exegesis, particularly those that inverted the terms of benign self-immolation, turning this sacrificial economy upside down to sanctify not merely passive submission to violence but killing itself. As seen, this shift had occurred by late 1928, when *liguero* militants associated Pro with dead LNDLR *pistoleros* as fast as the Church disentangled him. Prayer cards also promoted Segura Vilchis and Tirado as "brave, unconquered Christians," who would be fêted by the "Mother Church" and crowned in heaven with "green laurels."[39] For Bishop Manríquez of Huejutla—confirming the attitude was of temperament, not estate—Segura Vilchis was an "athlete of Christ," one of the Church's greatest saints.[40]

The pilgrimages that concretized such beliefs were more liminal, crossing a variety of socio-sacred thresholds. Juan Tirado, for instance, was buried after the Pros at Dolores. His shack in the Colonia Obrera was adorned with floral crowns and blood oozed from his body, prompting devotees to moisten cloths with sacrificial juice; some even "moved the corpse to make more blood seep out," the archdiocese's spy lamented. A large crowd—"the humble working classes alternating with the high aristocracy"—also assembled, and as the pilgrimage progressed, the poorest women became equals of the rich, their weary, half-naked children placed in a truck, and the women themselves carried in "luxury cars" by "high ladies." "Poor children" carrying flowers formed the pilgrimage vanguard, while behind them, a "courageous woman of the *pueblo*," brandishing a cane decorated with flowers, took the lead. First, she ordered the men to doff *sombreros*, and policemen their kepis. She then led responses to *Cristo Rey*, signaling for quiet as the pilgrims neared Chapultepec Castle, then ordering a shattering cry of *¡Viva Cristo Rey!* for Calles's benefit: "She then shouted three times, 'Lord, deign to defeat the enemies of Your Holy Church!,'" the archdiocesan record shows, "and the multitude answered, 'We beg You, hear us!'" In the cemetery, "illustrious ladies" officiated at Tirado's graveside, and another woman organized a collection for his widow, passing a basket through the crowd. When gendarmes arrested her, the crowd gave chase, stormed the police barracks (*comisaría*), fought with police, and freed her.[41]

This event, too, evidenced opposition to Mexico's *estado laico* as well as personal grief. Yet it was distinctive in its commemoration of tyrannicide (Tirado's anticipated sanctity), violent *dénouement*, and the extent to which women directed proceedings. Indeed, women acted as celebrants (at the burial) and sacred orators (the responses), as well as political-religious agitators, and did so without class distinctions. This social leveling and feminization created an aggressive mood, furthermore, culminating in actual violence: the smashing of the *comisaría* door, the assaulting of (male) state agents. These female socio-religious interlocutors thus exceeded women's prescribed roles within the

Church, yet probably saw themselves not as usurpers but as embodiments of a "true," "virile" Catholicism, whose defense could not be left to others. Defense justified any secondary transgressions, even if the subtext of this credo was that enemies of the faith could be killed. As true faith's custodians, women were not spiritual rebels but Lady Macbeths urging Catholics to screw their courage to the sticking-place and fight an unclean state in the streets.[42]

Such moral distinctions became crucial after the middle-class *beato* José de León Toral emptied a borrowed revolver into Obregón's face in August 1928. As Toral hung by his thumbs for interrogation, Bishop Mora distanced the clergy from the "sensational crime" and tried to nip a belief in immaculate homicide in the bud. Mora blamed the murder on Toral's deluded belief that he was "an envoy of God," and significantly, used the inquisitorial term *iluso*—denoting bogus mysticism—to discredit him. Mora thus interpreted events in terms of a *doctrinal* challenge to proper authority: for him, Toral was a fraud whose "strange," "suggestible" nature made him a creature of Madre Conchita, the nun who encouraged his mad adventure. The killing, plainly, was criminal, and the Church condemned it and its deluded author.[43] This was a fierce attack, yet apologetic literature urging Catholics to form "Pro-José de León Toral" Defense Committees soon appeared.[44] The LNDLR also understood what such comments meant for its rebellion and made a polemical riposte in *Points of Canon Law*, a pamphlet provocatively dedicated to Bishop Manríquez. This text (by "Arquimedes") described the killing as a "national good," with Thomist theology, natural justice, and national interest in its favor. Toral was no murderer, as his motive was not passion. On the contrary, his was a justifiable tyrannicide, on grounds set out by Aquinas,[45] because it furthered the religious interest, hence the greater good. Bishop Mora, meanwhile, was tyranny's accomplice, hiding "censurable fearfulness" behind "erroneous doctrine." His brand of "national pseudo-Catholicism" would warm Satan's cockles, moreover, given that the intended beneficiaries of the armed struggle turned out to be "cowardly adulators" of Calles.[46] Pro-LNDLR clergy, such as Regis Planchet, also disseminated theological treatises on tyrannicide.[47]

As Toral and Conchita's trial began, therefore—fittingly enough, on *Día de Muertos*—episcopal moderates became embroiled in a politico-doctrinal struggle with their *liguero* advocates. Meanwhile, a morbid ceremony developed outside court as pilgrims brought *cempasúchitl* flowers, candles, and offerings, which were placed on a shrine for the accused.[48] This "popular fair" was nothing, however, compared to the scenes after Toral's execution on 10 February 1929. That night, his house was besieged by thousands of devotees hoping to kiss the glass-topped coffin; people "absolved" him of Obregón's death, and thought him a "hero." His burial in the Panteón Español triggered intense mourning and hair-trigger violence. Huge crowds assembled in order to throw flowers and cry *vivas* to Toral and *Cristo Rey*, causing soldiers to surround the house, bayonets fixed, to keep order. Angry mourners, fearing a desecration, tried to remove the corpse by force. Soldiers beat devotees with rifles and firemen used hosepipes to force them into the

Espíritu Santo Church. Mourners tore up the streets and threw rocks. When a semblance of calm returned, the cortège set off behind police outriders and a convoy of vehicles. There was more violence when a policeman, identified as the man who delivered Toral's coup de grâce, was attacked and beaten by women pilgrims. Violence flared up at the cemetery too, when mourners were denied access to the "the hero's tomb." Police fired pistols and slashed with sabers, pilgrims stoned and clubbed: one man rallied the faithful with a "great cross of white flowers"; a woman on a balcony told people to "follow Toral's example," and a rooftop preacher urged people to pray the "hero" heavenward; the crowd chanted, "*A Dios rogando, y con el Mauser dando*" ("Praying to God, with the Mauser firing").[49]

This bloody peregrination—for the first time, there were fatalities— revealed a growing divergence between sectors of Catholic opinion. There were constants, such as significant social mixing and women's participation (black-clad *beatas* fighting police, automobiles suggesting a wealthy Catholic presence); but the pilgrimage's politico-theological rationale was radicalized, even if Toral was viewed as a crusader, not a saint. This mundanity contradicted his professed vocation as God's avenging angel, but lionizing the soldier Toral was really the point for the LNDLR. Indeed, Toral's hero cult was more dangerous than any mystical halo-seeking because it gave others' this-worldly religious violence a theological glow and could be used to press the Church to back the *cristeros*. Such a soldier theology was politically and canonically intolerable to the episcopate, which wanted to end the revolt but now saw its authority challenged by Catholics making independent doctrinal defenses of Toral. Disputations aside, the question of whether it was licit to kill, as well as die, for Christ, received a frighteningly concrete answer in Toral's wake. Indeed, Catholic *romerías* in Mexico City now seemed to claim, not just commemorate, the dead.

This revolutionary use of Catholic theology, to the LNDLR, was a way to bang the drum and coerce the Church into falling in behind those who believed that they fought in its name. The League, in short, wanted to offset, rather than cause, a schism, by forcing the Church off the fence in the matter of armed resistance. Moreover, LNDLR chiefs believed that they were manifesting the faithful's view. The episcopate understood things differently, and in February 1929 rounded on Catholics who set "the sons of the Church against one another." Outrageous writings that "attack the Ecclesiastical Authorities . . . and spread immoral doctrines" were circulating; these included the "Arquimedes" broadside and a "badly written" "Prayer to San Juan Tirado,"[50] which violated canons prohibiting independent doctrinal interpretation. Their promoters were "exploiters without conscience," guilty of "treason to the just cause." The subcommittee made the issue one of disloyalty. Yet the stamp of the *arreglista* Church, which yielded to the regime while cracking down internally, was apparent: the faithful were reminded that "Catholic action," if tilting at the heavens, must be an "auxiliary of sacerdotal action . . . [to be] regulated by Ecclesiastical Authority."[51] The path to salvation would not be forged by *cristeros*.

Conclusion

Pilgrimage was a dynamic mode, an arena in which different visions of Catholic Mexico could be enacted. The episcopate wanted *Cristo Rey* pilgrimages to be disciplined resacralizations of the commonwealth as well as prayer accumulators and a kind of sacramental action pedagogy; vast numbers of Catholics participated in such events, which applied a universal model in a Mexican context. Such events were nonetheless innovative in that they brought hundreds of thousands on to the streets to pressure the regime and devolved power to new lay actors. Pilgrimage was thus part of a wider, if temporary, pattern of decentralization by which a persecuted Church leased a significant degree of authority to the laity, including conditional powers to baptize and marry. The dangers of laicization became apparent in 1928. Spontaneous canonizations encouraged a sense of lay wonder, free assertions of sanctity, and a veneration of actual, not symbolic, martyrdom—religious flourishes that might ordinarily have concerned the hierarchy. Such pilgrimages became highly transgressive, however, when they evidenced this degree of religious slippage, and additionally, a political militancy that brought them into conflict with both the regime and an increasingly dominant sector of the episcopate.

For as long as the Church equivocated about the *cristeros*—arguing that rebellion was a matter of conscience—this politico-religious tension was latent, and subsumed in a model of "local" religion synthesizing particular and universal concerns. The slaying of Obregón changed the situation, however, by forcing the hierarchy to oppose violence or wager everything on the *cristeros*. Lay radicals responded to this shift. Henceforth, informal pilgrimage events evidenced not just "baroque" spiritual trappings but a sharp politico-theological edge, which cut across the episcopate's stance on the basis of autonomous appeals to holy writ. Toral's condemnation by the majoritarian episcopate forced *ligueros* to open a new front against episcopal treachery. For the League, this revolutionary invocation of Catholic theology was less a willing spiritual revolt than a futile (perhaps disbelieving) attempt to coerce a "*callista*" hierarchy to support it. Nonetheless, Catholic unity crumbled at this point as a local religion of militant piety, which until then accommodated diverging devotional styles and political outlooks, separated into constituent parts.

The Church did not forget this "interrupted revolution" in Mexican piety when signing the *arreglos* and restoring public cult in June 1929.[52] Catholic Action, a successor movement to organizations like the LNDLR but with greatly reduced autonomy, was founded that December.[53] Simultaneously, militant aspects of the *Cristo Rey* cult were buried. The 1929 feast occurred with masses in the Basilica and La Profesa (in lieu of the Cathedral, still sequestered): but the processional emphasis was first scaled down ("thousands [not hundreds of thousands] of pilgrims" now went to Tepeyac)[54] then shifted to the uncontentious Marian feast (12 December). As preparations for the 1931 Guadalupan centennial began, *Cristo Rey* was sidelined. By

1930, the festival focused on catechism, work, and sacrifice; Christ's sociotemporal Kingdom was now established through education and prayers in church.[55] The 1931 feast of divine royalty was a triduum and communion;[56] the *Cristo Rey* Apostleship, founded in 1933, would "diffuse religious education within the home," while first communion was the theme for 1934. The festival's character—now consisting of agapes, lessons, and prayers—had been emasculated, privatized. References to battling hosts persisted in the litany, but metaphorically.[57] As *Cristo Rey* was demobbed and dethroned, endorsement of his proto-martyrs—Pro, González Flores, et al.—was also put off for better times.

Notes

1. Jean Meyer, *La Cristiada* (3 vols. Mexico City: Siglo XXI, 1973–4), 1:136.
2. William Christian Jr., *Local Religion in Sixteenth-Century Spain* (Princeton: Princeton University Press, 1989). *Local Religion in Colonial Mexico*, ed. Martin Austin Nesvig (Albuquerque: University of New Mexico Press, 2006). Victor and Edith Turner, *Image and Pilgrimage in Christian Culture: Anthropological Perspectives* (Oxford: Basil Blackwell, 1978).
3. Matthew Butler, "Revolution and the Ritual Year: Religious Conflict and Innovation in *Cristero* Mexico," *Journal of Latin American Studies* 38, no. 3 (2006): 465–90.
4. Norah Jaffary, *False Mystics: Deviant Orthodoxy in Colonial Mexico* (Albuquerque: University of New Mexico Press, 2004), 76.
5. "A pilgrimage's foundation is typically marked by visions, miracles, or martyrdoms. The first pilgrims tend to arrive haphazardly, individually, and intermittently, though in great numbers . . . their devotion is fresh and spontaneous. Later there is progressive routinization and institutionalization of the sacred journey. Pilgrims now tend to come in organized groups, in sodalities, confraternities, and parish associations, on specified feast days . . . [Thus] religious specialists have attempted to domesticate the primitive, spontaneous modes of peregrination, with their freedom of communitas, into orderly pilgrimage, more susceptible to ecclesiastical control. Their model is the structured ritual system. Individual Catholic pilgrimages have in the course of time been transformed into extended and protracted forms of such sacraments as penance and the Eucharist. Their voluntaristic, even miraculous, essence has been subjugated to doctrinal and organizational edict. Their charism has been routinized; their communitas, structured." Turner and Turner, *Image and Pilgrimage*, 25–6, 32. For anti-Turnerian critiques, *Sacred Journeys: The Anthropology of Pilgrimage*, ed. Alan Morinis (Greenwood: Greenwood Press, 1992); *Contesting the Sacred: The Anthropology of Christian Pilgrimage*, ed. John Eade and Michael Sallnow (London: Routledge, 1991).
6. Ruth Harris, *Lourdes: Body and Spirit in a Secular Age* (New York: Viking, 1999), xix.
7. E.g., David Lorey, "The Revolutionary Festival in Mexico: November 20 Celebrations in the 1920s and 1930s," *The Americas* 54, no. 1 (1997): 39–82. Cf. Linda Curcio-Nagy, *The Great Festivals of Colonial Mexico City: Performing Power and Identity* (Albuquerque: University of New Mexico Press, 2004).

8. David Brading, *Mexican Phoenix: Our Lady of Guadalupe. Image and Tradition across Five Centuries* (Cambridge UK: Cambridge University Press, 2001), 288–310. Richard Trexler, *Reliving Golgotha: The Passion Play of Iztapalapa* (Cambridge, Mass.: Harvard University Press, 2003). Edward Wright-Rios, "Piety and Progress: Vision, Shrine, and Society in Oaxaca, 1887–1934" (PhD diss., University of California, 2004).

9. Raymond Jonas, *France and the Cult of the Sacred Heart: An Epic Tale for Modern Times* (Berkeley: University of California Press, 2000). David Blackbourn, *Marpingen: Apparitions of the Virgin Mary in Nineteenth-Century Germany* (New York: Alfred Knopf, 1994). William Christian Jr., *Visionaries: The Spanish Republic and the Reign of Christ* (Berkeley: University of California Press, 1996).

10. Eamon Duffy, *Saints and Sinners: A History of the Popes* (New Haven: Yale University Press, 2001), 333–40.

11. Andrés Barquín y Ruiz, *Cristo, Rey de México* (Mexico City: Jus, 1967), 9–27, 67–176. Valentina Torres Septién and Yves Solís, "De Cerro a Montaña Santa: La Construcción del Monumento a Cristo Rey (1919–1960)," *Historia y Grafía* 22 (2004): 113–54.

12. Condumex, 2.164, "Pida Mucho a Cristo Rey por México, Oración." P.G. Goñi, *¡Viva Cristo Rey! Explicación de la Fiesta de Cristo Rey, que Se Celebra el Día 30 de Octubre* (El Paso, 1927).

13. AHAM, c. C, "Instrucción Pastoral en la Fiesta de Cristo Rey," 1926.

14. AHAM, c. C-G, *Boletín Eclesiástico de la Diócesis de Querétaro* 51 (1926), "Exhortación Pastoral a los Fieles de la Diócesis de Querétaro."

15. Condumex, 5.115, "*Rex Sum Ego:* Gracia Singularisima para Todo México." Cf. Javier Sicilia, *Concepción Cabrera de Armida, La Amante de Cristo* (Mexico City: FCE, 2001).

16. AHAM, "Instrucción Pastoral"; c. 46/exp. 44, "La Sma. Virgen María, Medianera Universal de Todas las Gracias después de Jesucristo," 1926.

17. "¡Viva Cristo Rey y Nuestra Reina la Virgen Sma. de Guadalupe!", Condumex, 9.790; *Excélsior*, "Una Multitud Enorme, Ayer, en La Basílica" (22 Oct. 1926), "Solemne Fiesta Religiosa Será Celebrada Hoy: No Habrá Sacerdotes" (23 Oct. 1926), and "Peregrinación de Católicos a Guadalupe Ayer" (23 Oct. 1926); *La Controversia*, "La Consagración Nacional a Cristo Rey Fue Esplendorosa en Toda la República" (24 Oct. 1926); Luis Rivera del Val, *Entre las Patas de los Caballos* (Mexico City: Jus, 1992), 73–4; Antonio Dragón, *Vida Intima del Padre Pro* (Mexico City: Buena Prensa, 1952), 165.

18. Mexican Catholic Youth Association (ACJM) militant.

19. By comparison, the 1914 coronation attracted 12,000 pilgrims. Barquín, *Cristo*, 172.

20. The image was replaced by a copy from 1926–29. Brading, *Mexican Phoenix*, 317.

21. John Eade, "Order and Power at Lourdes: Lay Helpers and the Organization of a Pilgrimage Shrine," in Eade and Sallnow, 51–76.

22. Condumex, 5.394, "Convocatoria del Subcomité Episcopal a una Semana de Penitencia y Oración," 1927.

23. Joaquín Antonio Peñalosa, *Miguel M. de la Mora, el Obispo para Todos* (Mexico City: Jus, 1963).

24. AHAM, c. 58, exp. 76, Mora to Archbishop Mora y del Río, 17 Nov. 1927.

25. "La Peregrinación de Ayer a la Basílica de Guadalupe," *El Universal*, 31 Oct. 1927.

26. "Peregrinación a la Basílica de los Indios," *Excélsior*, 13 Dec. 1927.

27. Condumex, 9.824, "¡*Viva Cristo Rey!*," 17 Oct. 1928.

28. The statue was placed in a nave crypt in 1895. Brading, *Mexican Phoenix*, 294.

29. "200,000 Personas en Imponente Manifestación Visitaron Ayer La Basílica," *El Universal*, 29 Oct. 1928.

30. Cited in Meyer, *La Cristiada*, 3:276. My emphasis.

31. AHAM, c. 76/exp. 22, Mora to Mora y del Río, Mexico City, 23 Nov. 1927.

32. Eugenio Garcés Obregón, *Vida del P. Miguel Agustín Pro de la Compañía de Jesús* (Mexico City: Buena Prensa, 1931), 186–92. Francisco B. de Smartzj, *Heraldos de Cristo Rey: El Rev. P. Miguel A. Pro, S. J., y sus Compañeros Víctimas de la Persecución Religiosa en México* (El Paso, 1928). Rivera, *Entre las Patas*, 164–75. Dragón, *Vida*, 251–3.

33. AHAM, c. 46/exp. 36, "Algunos Detalles Acerca del Asesinato de los Sres. Rev. Miguel Pro, S.J., Humberto Pro, Luis Segura Vilchis, y Juan o Antonio Tirado, y de su Triunfo." Rivera, *Entre las Patas*, 176–7.

34. Garcés, *Vida*, 193–213.

35. "Ocho Católicos Detenidos Ayer en el Panteón de Dolores," *El Universal Gráfico*, 24 Nov. 1928; "Manifestación de Católicos Disuelta en Dolores," *La Prensa*, 24 Nov. 1928.

36. Turner and Turner, *Image and Pilgrimage*, 13.

37. Paul Vanderwood, *Juan Soldado: Rapist, Murderer, Martyr, Saint* (Durham: Duke University Press, 2004).

38. For a parallel phenomenon in an earlier period, see William Taylor, "Between Nativitas and Mexico City: An Eighteenth-Century Pastor's Local Religion," in *Local Religion in Colonial Mexico*, ed. Martin Austin Nesvig (Albuquerque: University of New Mexico Press, 2006), 91–117.

39. Condumex, 10.949, "Himno a los Innumerables Mártires que Han Muerto por la Sagrada Causa de la Religión en Nuestra Patria," 1929.

40. David Bailey, *¡Viva Cristo Rey! The Cristero Rebellion and the Church-State Conflict in Mexico* (Austin: University of Texas Press, 1974), 170.

41. AHAM, c. 46, exp. 36, "Algunos Detalles."

42. Cf. Jaffary, *False Mystics*, 5–6, 77.

43. "Declaraciones de Mons. de la Mora en Nombre del Subcomité Episcopal," *Excélsior*, 6 Aug. 1928.

44. AMPV, 81.620.680, "Se Han Repartido Manifiestos en Favor de Toral," 6 Aug. 1928.

45. For Aquinas, tyrannicide was legitimate if an act of last resort and the lesser of two evils.

46. Condumex, 7.548, Arquimedes, *Puntos de Derecho Católico. Controversia. A la Iglesia y a la Patria* (1928).

47. Condumex, 7.543, "De Si Es Lícita la Defensa Armada contra los Tiranos: Doctrina de Algunos Santos Padres," 1928.

48. "Un Movimiento Popular, Como Si Fuera una Feria," *El Universal*, 3 Nov. 1928.

49. "Escenas Frente a la Residencia de la Familia Toral," *El Universal*, 10 Feb. 1929; "Funerales de J. de León Toral," *La Prensa*, 11 Feb. 1929; AHAM,

c. G-L, "Imponente Manifestación durante los Funerales de José de León Toral," 11 Feb. 1929. Cuauhtémoc Fernández, *León Toral No Ha Muerto* (Mexico City, 1945).

50. Unfortunately I have been unable to locate this text.

51. Condumex, 10.947, "Instrucción del Subcomité al V. Clero y a los Fieles del País, sobre los Cultos de la Semana Mayor, y sobre la Previa Censura de los Escritos que se Publiquen," 1929.

52. I appropriate the well-known phrase of Adolfo Gilly, *La Revolución Interrumpida* (Mexico City: Era, 1994).

53. Martaelena Negrete, *Relaciones entre la Iglesia y el Estado en México, 1930–1940* (Mexico City: Colmex, 1988), 241–67.

54. "Grandes Actos Religiosos el Día de Mañana," and "La Celebración Religiosa Ayer," *Excélsior*, 26 and 28 Oct. 1929; "Ceremonia en la Basílica de Guadalupe," *El Universal*, 28 Oct. 1929.

55. AHAM, c. 34/exp. 2, "Catequismo de Cristo Rey y de Santa María de Guadalupe, de la Sociedad Católica de Moralización," 1930; c. 8/exp. 34, "Acto de Consagración a Cristo Rey que Deberá Rezarse con los Fieles en Todos los Templos del Arzobispado de México el Domingo 26 de Octubre, Fiesta de Cristo Rey," 1930.

56. AHAM, c. 8/exp. 23, circular, 15 Oct. 1931.

57. AHAM, c. 56/exp. 79, circular, 8 Mar. 1933; c. 8/exp. 76, circular, 18 Oct. 1934; c. 55/exp. 75, "Letanías de Cristo Rey," 1935.

Chapter 8

Revolutionary and Not-So-Revolutionary Negotiations in Catholic Annulment, Bigamy, and Divorce Trials: The Archdiocese of Mexico, 1929–40

Kristina A. Boylan

In January 1932, the archbishop of Mexico, Pascual Díaz y Barreto, issued a circular to archdiocesan priests concerning ecclesiastical marriage. Díaz reminded the clergy of their duty to familiarize themselves with, and instruct the faithful in, the parameters of sacramental marriage, beginning with the definition of "ordinary marriage" found in canon law (canon 1094). Díaz then bemoaned the "situation to which we [priests] have been reduced" and exhorted the clergy to remedy it.[1] The "situation" to which he alluded was a web of legal, social, and historical changes affecting the concept of marriage, and more specifically, the status of the Church and sacramental marriage in Mexico. Indeed, Díaz's phrase encompassed Church leaders' anxieties as they addressed the irregularities in religious practice and record-keeping associated with the Revolution, later anticlerical harassment, and the *cristero* rebellion. Díaz's anxiety was further provoked by growing migration, both internally and to the United States, which made it difficult to locate people when ascertaining their eligibility for marriage. Most seriously, the revolutionary Divorce Law (1917) and Civil Code (1928) constituted serious conceptual and practical threats to Catholic marriage. The legislation applied principally to civil marriage, an institution created during the 1850s Reform: but, when compounded with constitutional assertions of state supremacy over the Church—not to mention changing gender roles, forms of socialization, and social mobility—Díaz concluded that there was a crisis. The evidence lay in the irregular, if not immoral, practices of the laity concerning Catholic marriage.

This chapter explores the relationship between Catholic religious practice and social revolution in 1930s Mexico from two perspectives. Firstly, it briefly surveys Church leaders' ideals and fears concerning marriage, and the problems commonly associated with ecclesiastical marriage in 1930s Mexico.

Secondly, it presents case files from the archdiocese of Mexico's Matrimonial Provisorate (*Provisorato Matrimonial*)[2] in order to assess lay litigants' understandings and expectations as they articulated their concepts of marriage, rights, and personal happiness, and their institutional expectations of Church and state. These cases suggest that some lay Catholics in the 1930s sought to transpose revolutionary notions of individual happiness onto the institutional and ideological structure of Catholic marriage, or to use the power of the state as a lever for furthering their marital demands *within* a Catholic framework. The conclusion contrasts litigants' views with hierarchical anxieties in order to assess what changes occurred in Catholic views of marriage and personhood in 1930s Mexico—in sum, to see whether the situation was as dire as Díaz feared.

Catholic Marriage, Revolutionary Mexico

The Church's sense of post-*Cristiada* crisis should be interpreted in light of the boundaries of universal Catholicism concerning marriage as an institutional and ideological structure, and the significant tensions generated by conditions on the ground. Regarding the former, most significant was Pius XI's 1930 encyclical *Casti Connubii*, which was composed in response to liberalizing marriage trends that originated in the Reformation, continued in the French Revolution, and reemerged in the nineteenth and twentieth centuries (resistance to such legislation was even taught in Rome, where many Mexican bishops studied).[3] Intended as the standard for Catholics to measure their conduct with regard to marriage, the family, and sexuality, *Casti Connubii* reiterated the indissolubility of marriage and its first purpose—procreation and the raising of children.[4] Pius XI borrowed from the earlier pronouncements of Pius X (1903–14), who was likewise concerned about state interference in marriage, leading to interruptions and irregular documentation. The 1930 encyclical cited Pius X's *Ne Temere* (1907), which emphasized careful record-keeping as a way to defend marriage and also limited authorization to perform marriages to bishops, ordinaries, or parish rectors.[5]

Secondly, Church leaders were committed to enforcing doctrinal compliance via adherence to the newly codified Code of Canon Law (1917). Considered an achievement for the Church, the code collected, classified, and organized the body of laws that had been generated over centuries. The project grew out of the First Vatican Council (1870), was convened under Pius IX, undertaken under Pius X, and made public under Benedict XV (1914–22).[6] Yet, as the Mexican cases show, greater knowledge of the law at times created or accentuated problems. Very soon after the *arreglos*, petitions arrived regarding irregularities in sacramental practice, particularly for the verification or dissolution of marriages performed between 1926–29.[7]

Indeed, Catholic marriage as an institution faced a series of problems in the 1930s. The greatest affront, for the hierarchy, was absolute divorce. Marriage had been defined as a legal relationship instituted by civil authority—completely separate from any religious bond—with the creation of the

Civil Registry (1859) and introduction of the 1870 and 1884 Civil Codes. These liberal regulations also included a form of legal separation. Revolutionaries like Venustiano Carranza and Felipe Carillo Puerto later introduced absolute divorce in areas they controlled; divorce was then codified, along with marriage's mandatory civil character, in the 1917 Law of Family Relations and 1928 Civil Code. These provisions are often analyzed with respect to their expansion of the legal personhood of single women, or their perpetuation of married women's unequal status compared to married men.[8] For Catholics, however, these laws signaled newer and larger threats to the importance and respect accorded to the sacrament of marriage, and were part of a broader anticlerical attack on the Church. Add to this the disorganization reigning in and between parishes and the growing gaps in documented sacramental practice, and the reasons for episcopal panic become more apparent. These fears reached their highest pitch in the 1930s, when bishops responded by denouncing the "dangers" posed by civil laws and social trends.[9]

A particular problem in the 1930s, clergy complained, was that parishioners were harder to locate than before when it came to assessing the eligibility of a prospective bride and groom (*los novios*). Some confusion could be blamed on anticlerical campaigns, which hindered effective parish notarization. But population movement also increased during the Revolution, as rebellions and ecological crises drove people to leave unprotected villages. Immigration to the United States also rose; the legal migrant worker (*bracero*) program was instituted during the First World War, and droughts and civil unrest spurred northward migration in areas affected by the *Cristiada*.[10] And just moving from one parish to another was sometimes sufficient to cover an individual's tracks, as some of the case studies reveal. The Church bureaucracy struggled to keep pace with revolutionary social changes, and some Catholics became adept at exploiting communications delays, or the ambiguity surrounding sacramental marriages performed during the Revolution or the *Cristiada* to their own advantage.

Yet the Church itself contributed to this problem by suspending public worship in protest against the 1926 Calles Law.[11] Provisions were made in dioceses across Mexico to continue private sacramental practices. Bishops authorized clergy to officiate masses and perform other sacraments in private homes, and laypeople were authorized to store cultic objects normally reserved to consecrated buildings. Clandestine ceremonies were supposed to be conducted only after obtaining the bishop's permission, and participants were expected to keep accurate records for transferal into parish archives once normality was restored.[12] Church leaders tried to return their jurisdictions to normalcy following the June 1929 *arreglos*. In the hope that compliance with the law would result in lenient application, Apostolic Delegate Leopoldo Ruiz y Flores and Archbishop Díaz ordered clergy to register with the government and follow standard procedures when petitioning for the reopening of churches. Prelates assured officials that they would urge parishioners to support civil law, for instance by celebrating civil marriages before engaging in Church weddings.[13] Overall, Church leaders hoped to return the ecclesiastical bureaucracy to pre-*Cristiada* levels of efficiency, which included conscientious record-keeping as a way of ensuring good practice among the faithful.[14] However, it is apparent that from 1926–29 proper procedures were often disregarded by laity and clergy alike.

Provisorato Cases, 1929–40

Mexico's postrevolutionary regime trumpeted civil divorce among its successes, and growing numbers of the country's citizens sued for divorce as a means to transform their personal lives and strive for individual liberty and happiness.[15] Why, then, did some Mexicans still consider the Church the ultimate arbiter of marital problems, with exclusive authority to nullify marital relationships? As Silvia Arrom notes, ecclesiastical divorce was overwhelmingly employed by women in early independent Mexico, when liberal reforms created male citizens in part by rendering female adults like dependent minors. This period also saw a pronounced feminization of religion.[16] In postrevolutionary Mexico too, ecclesiastical divorce appeals followed a gender division dominated by women. A majority of Provisorate cases (54 percent) were initiated by women, showing that gendered divorce patterns endured during the Revolution. However, a significant number of men—supposedly more alienated from the Church, but here representing 32 percent of cases—now sought recourse within the institution. It is important to ask what had happened in postrevolutionary society—which was allegedly keener to empower men as citizens and productive laborers—to lead these men to initiate petitions to the Provisorate. Given that both spouses initiated an additional 14 percent of cases, it is also worthwhile analyzing the factors that led these people to choose the Church as a recourse for the resolution of their domestic problems, and to see how they fared.[17]

Superficially, one could dismiss these litigants—and the number is small, 150 people out of a diocesan population of one million[18]—as Porfirian remnants, unaware (or unconvinced) of the state's supremacy in the religious sphere, despite its defeat of the *cristeros*. Conversely, it is tempting to identify litigants and their "dissident" practices (bigamy, divorce, adultery) as "counter-hegemonic" voices, counterposed to the hierarchy.[19] However, the incidence of civil marriage increased from 1920–40, stabilizing thereafter; and it became common for Mexicans to marry in civil and religious ceremonies, indicating growing acceptance of both institutions' requirements.[20] When litigants approached the Provisorate, moreover, they critically weighed each institution's requirements, procedures, rituals, and potential benefits. Collectively, the cases reveal that laity and clergy became involved in a dialogue regarding marriage as the Church struggled to adapt to state demands and ordinary Mexicans to changing ideas and social conditions.[21] While few in number, therefore, the cases demonstrate how the Revolution could affect everyday perspectives on religion, family, and gender, and how this might be interpreted by Church leaders, who adapted to pressures both from the faithful and the state. In sum, the qualitative value of the documents—which provide a rare glimpse into the intimate, even moral, history of postrevolutionary Mexico—outweighs any quantitative limitations, provided the conclusions are framed cautiously.[22]

Official enthusiasm for canon law did not necessarily mean heavy-handed application. Nearly half the Matrimonial Provisorate cases (49 percent) have no clear resolution, and some advance little beyond opening complaints for lack of evidence or cooperation. About a third of the marriages (33.3 percent) were upheld, indicating the Church's commitment to the "defense of the marriage bond"; this was further demonstrated by the fact that only ten of the marriages examined (17.5 percent) were nullified, usually when bigamy was proven. Canon law was also a double-edged sword: if Church leaders sought to regulate practising Catholics through canon law, the code enabled Tribunal lawyers and litigants to make their cases more easily.

The 57 Provisorate cases available for the period 1929–40 resemble the ecclesiastical divorces studied by Arrom terms of detail (from one to hundreds of pages) and duration (from several days to a decade of investigations and appeals); and again, not all cases ended definitively.[23] However, the cases lack some information available for Arrom's study: the Church no longer collected information on litigants' ethnicity, for example, and because the *depósito* (the assignation of women litigants to specific households, to cover their living expenses as well as monitor their conduct during investigations and trials) had been eliminated, little information about social class is available. Some petitioners came from identifiably working-class neighborhoods, or complained of having to work to support themselves and their children, but the information is uneven. Prices for Tribunal services indicate little; if annulments were expensive—200 pesos or more—a single document cost only several pesos and was within reach of poorer petitioners. More litigants asked for relief than shirked paying, even though the archdiocese had little power to enforce payment.[24]

The petitions' start-dates range from 1929–34; the majority proceed through the 1930s, and the latest closing date is 1944.[25] The cases also document events from the 1900s and the 1910s. Though irregularities in practice and documentation are evident, the enduring success of late nineteenth-century "re-evangelization" campaigns—in which clergy sought to catechize the populace in doctrinally sound worship and practice—is apparent, too, given that many litigants demonstrated a basic grasp of canonical regulations of marriage and annulment.[26]

For the Church, *mere* impediments (marrying a heretic, or at certain times of the year; marrying if bound by simple chastity vows or if previously engaged) prevented a marriage from taking place, but did not render it invalid if discovered subsequently. More serious *dirimentia*—which prevented a marriage and nullified it upon discovery—included mistaken identity (*error*); conditions imposed on one party (*conditio*); solemn chastity vows; public indecorum (nonconsummation, concubinage); crime (adultery, conspiracy to murder a spouse); difference of religion; lack of consent (*ex defectu consensus*); defect of age (16 for boys, 14 for girls); impotence; and kidnapping. The Tribunal worried particularly that *Cristiada*-era irregularities would be used to renegotiate the indissoluble bond, and indeed, almost 23 percent of cases involve the *diriment* of *ligamen* (bigamy); eleven women and two men filed this charge against their spouses. Unless certain that a first spouse was deceased, a person attempting to enter into a second marriage was committing bigamy and flouting the sacrament's sacred nature.[27]

While bigamy was not new, the ability to circumvent the Church's preventive requirements—searching archives for marriage records, posting banns—had increased greatly during the *Cristiada*. In one egregious case, Esperanza Cabrera sought validation of her July 1926 marriage as Sara González petitioned for annulment of her November marriage—both to the same man. Both women had tolerated Eustolio Hernández's absences (as a medical student, then to complete social service in Guerrero), but their discovery of his bigamy provoked Cabrera to confirm her *derechos de esposa* and González to sever the relationship.[28] When finally interviewed, Hernández equivocated, claiming that González was "only a friend," then accusing her family of pressuring him to marry in a clandestine ceremony. Asked whether he was aware that he had deceived González and the Church, Hernández replied that he knew marriage was indissoluble but did not believe that "this marriage with Señora Gonzalez [could] be considered Catholic." His posturing as a good Catholic husband may have helped him. Though he had clearly married twice, the Tribunal ordered González, as instigator of the second case, to pay the trial expenses.[29]

There is no evidence that the Archdiocese was particularly sympathetic to male or female petitions. Daniel Rodríguez reported his wife's immoral and antireligious conduct—which included filing for civil divorce—in support of his accusation of bigamy.[30] Francisco Arellano accused his wife, María Soledad Olvera, of falsely claiming widow status, but an examination of their marriage certificate soon revealed similarities between his handwriting and that found in other documents, including a 1908 marriage to Josefina Incháurregui. Olvera separated from Arellano on learning of his bigamy, and warned that he intended to marry again. The Tribunal validated Arellano's first marriage and exculpated Olvera.[31] Antonio Mata asked for a service typically requested by women—that the Tribunal verify the location or the death of a spouse (this use of the Tribunal, documented for the colonial and early national periods, clearly endured after the civil registry's introduction).[32] Mata married Margarita Olmos in 1926, after which, he claimed, she committed adultery, left Mexico with her new partner, and was killed in an automobile accident. The Tribunal inquired with archdioceses abroad, but curtly told Mata that the onus was on him to prove his wife's death should he wish to remarry.[33] If some men wanted to reshape their lives through marriage, then, the Tribunal would not assist them just because their wives misbehaved.

Historically, both parties' free consent to marriage was the Church's ideal; but this was not always the case in practice, particularly for women bound by familial, social, and economic pressures.[34] One of the most intriguing patterns here is that of the eight cases (14 percent) based on claims of marriage without consent (*ex defectu consensus*), seven were made by men. Two claimed that revolutionary partisanship had compromised them, though this did not elicit much sympathy. Jose Alvarez testified that his brother-in-law, a "*carrancista* colonel," forced him to marry in 1919. Conversely, Miguel Gómez claimed that his future mother-in-law attempted to prevent his 1913 marriage by notifying the authorities that he was a "*carrancista*." Escaping execution, Gómez maintained the animosity of his in-laws, who encouraged his wife to leave him. His case did not proceed, however, and the Tribunal also turned down Alvarez's annulment petition.[35]

Bernardo Castañeda also claimed coercion; he admitted to a "romantic" relationship with Carmen Ortiz Aceves—daughter of former president, Pascual Ortiz Rubio—but had no intention of marrying her until "secret police" threatened him with "disappearance." Following the 1932 marriage, Castañeda alleged, he discovered Ortiz was not a virgin; she first claimed to have been raped, but subsequently confessed she had worked as a prostitute *and* been sterilized. Thereafter, Castañeda did not consider the marriage "Catholic," though he initially declined Ortiz's request for civil divorce on moral grounds.[36] Despite Castañeda's pro-Catholic, antistate appeals, his bid for divorce was unsuccessful, a likely cause being his involvement with the daughter of a well-connected revolutionary (*blanco*).[37] The Tribunal summoned Ortiz and several family members to testify in May 1934. Her father never responded, and while Ortiz initially received written responses, she never testified and was not pressured to do so (other litigants received repeated summonses in response to no-shows). Finally, citing inconsistencies between Castañeda's claims of coercion and deception, the Tribunal questioned if the marriage was coercive. Castañeda's lack of strategy now led to failure: first, he was reprimanded for threatening Tribunal members, and later accused one judge of bias deriving from "a relationship of close friendship and spiritual kinship" with the Ortiz family. A decade later, the marriage was upheld.[38]

Three other men's petitions indicating that force was threatened produced no clear resolution. In 1933, Jesús Rosas claimed Virginia Casarez's family had kidnapped him in 1909 after he impregnated their daughter (Rosas admitted to a sexual relationship, but claimed he was not Casarez's only partner). Being 15 years old at the time, thus too young to marry canonically, he had complied because he was "uneducated" and frightened.[39] In 1934, Rodolfo Salgado petitioned for annulment of his 1928 marriage to Angela Beristaín on the basis of her father's violent threats, first forcing Salgado to fill in a matrimonial questionnaire, and three days later marching him to church (though, as he pointed out, no banns were read and there were no witnesses).[40] In 1933, María Tovar de Vargas petitioned the Tribunal on behalf of Pedro Legoretta, whom she wanted for a son-in-law and whom she claimed had been forced to marry another woman in 1928. The Tribunal invited Legoretta to corroborate, but when he refused to appear (because he was "working") the Tribunal responded that only Legoretta could file the petition. A subsequent request, cosigned by Legoretta's intended father-in-law, did not move the Tribunal; this case contrasts with others in which the Tribunal acted swiftly to investigate bigamy, perhaps because of the litigants' transparently questionable motives.[41]

Another unimpressive element of the case, in the Tribunal eyes, was Legoretta's simultaneous pursuit of a civil divorce. Indeed, in 19 percent of cases (11 out of 57), at least one party had obtained, or was seeking, a civil divorce—usually on the understanding that this would lead to an annulment or ecclesiastical separation—or else had enquired whether a civil divorce would perforce allow them to remarry.[42] While this proportion is too low to indicate that the institution of Catholic marriage and clerical hegemony had been "reduced" as lamentably as Archbishop Díaz worried, it does reveal that some conflation between the institutions of civil and ecclesiastical marriage was occurring in lay minds, in that obtaining civil divorce was increasingly thought, however optimistically, to be a precursor of ecclesiastical separation.

The only successful petition linking ecclesiastical to civil divorce was that of Carmen Mier y Terán, who in March 1933 filed for permission to separate from Antonio Caso López, whom she stated was an alcoholic, had given her a "tumor" (a sexually transmitted disease?), and threatened her and her children. Within a month, the Tribunal gave Mier permission to separate for one year and to file for a civil divorce (though there is no record of this happening). It is not clear whether Caso was notorious or Mier's petition particularly moving: but appealing to the Church *before* seeking civil divorce was possibly a superior strategy, as it implicitly affirmed the primacy of sacramental marriage.[43] In contrast, Ana Alvarez, who in August 1929 petitioned for an ecclesiastical divorce from her violent husband, fled rather than await the Tribunal's verdict and was punished with denial of the sacraments. The Tribunal did not restore her religious privileges until 1936, when it again exhorted her to "try to remove the causes of separation."[44]

Despite the Tribunal's harsh devotion to marriage bonds, two factors indicate a degree of adaptation to postrevolutionary cultural norms. Firstly, from 1934 the Tribunal asked if a civil divorce had been filed or obtained in the "interrogation" questions it prepared for litigants and witnesses. While citing civil divorce as the basis for ecclesiastical separation did not necessarily help, the documentation and chronology could prove useful, as with Amelia Murphy, who successfully divorced her husband, Adolfo de Leeuw (the first such case).[45] In another case, *cura* Francisco Escartín petitioned on behalf of Josefina Mora, whose fiancé, Ernesto Moreno, freely admitted in the matrimonial questionnaire to having been married before, albeit in a questionable private ceremony in 1927. While Moreno thought it sufficient to have obtained a civil divorce in December 1933, Escartín did not, and set an investigation in motion for Mora.[46] Secondly, litigants increasingly—though unsuccessfully—demanded that marriage provide them with personal happiness, not merely the institutional vehicle through which to avoid sin and form families. Church leaders saw this trend as a harmful outgrowth of the individualism associated with modernization, secularization, and Revolution. And this was something new: as a point of comparison, only 1 male litigant out of 81 in Arrom's survey of Tribunal cases was so bold; in almost one-quarter of the 1930s cases, however (14 out of 57), litigants cited their wish to marry a more desirable partner as part of their reason for seeking an annulment.[47]

At times, Church leaders unwittingly echoed anticlerical complaints about the population's untrustworthiness and naiveté. Circulars in ecclesiastical bulletins warned parish priests (by extension, parishioners) of individuals who attempted to enter second marriages when their first marriages were still valid, and of individuals who pretended to be priests. Notices of parishioners and priests being tricked by travelers' stories of fleeing persecution or having the bishop's permission to officiate in a particular diocese, were also published in diocesan bulletins, posted on church doors, and read aloud to parishioners during Mass. Archbishop Ruiz y Flores reiterated these warnings in 1935, and reminded Mexicans that emergency conditions no longer existed: only in a few, specific locations were exceptions to canonical procedures permitted—in the rest, strict obedience to archdiocesan and parish authorities was required.[48]

When churches were closed or clergy were not officiating in them, certain requirements of the marriage process—such as the reading of banns—were often waived, hence could not serve as a subsequent basis for annulment. This did not stop people from trying. Daniel Oseguera married Eustolia Fragoso Mayor in haste in 1921—having requested a dispensation from two weeks of banns before the wedding—and then unsuccessfully tried to leave her by accusing her of deception and moral flaws (*error*). Other husbands likewise alleged "deception," and hence argued that they had not truly consented. But these, too, were told that misjudging their wives' character did not constitute the *error* that, when proven, could nullify a marriage.[49]

Discoveries of improper procedure and record-keeping decided ten of the cases, and formed elements of others.[50] Fr. Pedro Castillo Villaruel, involved in six cases from 1929–32, exemplified the clergyman who believed he was living an embattled Church's ethos, but was later faulted by the Tribunal. When asked why he had married one couple outside his parish, he cited canon 1098, arguing that a spiritual emergency existed and that no authorized clergyman could be present; he also cited Archbishop Mora y del Río's *Normas Pro Sacerdotibus* (27 July 1926), which required written permission for extra-parochial sacraments but left room for on-the-spot decisions if records were kept. Unfortunately, record-keeping was not Castillo's forte; of six marriages, he could only produce notes regarding one, and written authorization for another.[51] His argument that he had "been distracted" by the Church strike was not accepted, and his claim that the auxiliary bishop, Maximino Ruiz y Flores, had given him verbal permission to marry another couple met with a sharp rebuke. Then Castillo claimed that Mora y del Río, on the eve of his exile, had told him to "work as much as you can," which he took as a blanket authorization to perform sacraments for Mexican Catholics. While this claim was questioned, only one marriage was nullified for defective form. The outcome of the other cases is unclear, but Castillo was found to have "acted in bad faith" and charged for the expenses of all six cases. The Tribunal would not accept Castillo's argument for noncompliance—poverty and fears of state reprisal—even though he had previously been arrested and fined 500 pesos.[52]

Julián Caraballo and Ana María Silva petitioned to validate their marriage performed in April 1928 by *veracruzano* priest Pedro Morales. Many priests from that troubled diocese were exiles in Mexico City. The Tribunal found that Morales was among them, but found fault with him on several counts: not documenting the marriage because he was "running late" and "fearful of the authorities" was inexcusable; he also lacked authorization to perform weddings in the Archdiocese of Mexico and should have sought it, as the couple's situation was not an "emergency" according to canon 1098 or archdiocesan guidelines. Morales was not charged the investigation fees; the continuing difficulties in Veracruz diocese may have inspired some leniency. The Tribunal also validated Caraballo and Silva's marriage; the ceremony was corroborated by witnesses, and it probably did not hurt that their petition was mutual.[53]

Father Jorge Assaf was also chastised for failing to obtain permission to marry Elena Barquet and José Serur. As canon 1094 dictated, archdiocesan authorization was required as priest and *novios* were Maronite Rite Catholics.[54] Assaf explained this requirement when visiting the Barquet home to complete the matrimonial questionnaire on 20 October 1928. However, Elena's father and uncles pressured him to return that evening to marry the couple because, in their eyes, the time she had spent alone with Serur endangered her honor. Assaf visited Secretary Benavides at his home at 10 p.m. that night, but neglected to bring the questionnaire. Benavides refused Assaf permission to marry an unnamed couple and demanded that Serur return with the information the following day. Nevertheless, Assaf returned to the Barquet home and performed the ceremony, citing "moral pressure" as justification. Benavides duly gave Assaf written permission next day, but when Assaf returned to the Barquet house a week later, the place was in uproar. Serur had disappeared, and henceforth concern for Elena's honor was superseded by her desire to remarry; she petitioned for an annulment on 17 May 1929. Serur did not respond to summonses; after the third, the Tribunal proceeded without him. Father Juan Kuri, the Maronite supervisor for Mexico City, claimed that he could do nothing to censure Assaf or alter the situation, given the "abnormal circumstances" of the *Cristiada*. It may be that the Maronites' unique status aided both Barquet—the marriage was nullified on 17 July 1929—and Assaf; he was not ordered to pay expenses, only never to act without authorization again.[55]

Though regularizing marriage ties and sacramental practice was of great concern, the Tribunal's treatment of mutually petitioning couples was more benevolent. Eliseo Cortés and Angela Quintero petitioned for validation of their marriage in October 1929. Cortés had been interned in the Hospital de Jesús in October 1920; at the time, he and Quintero were not married, though they had several children. As Cortes' condition temporarily worsened,

Dolores Villaseñor, a lay volunteer, and Father Jesús Basurto, the chaplain, encouraged them to marry for their spiritual well-being and their children's sake. Nine years later, however, neither Basurto's authorization from the *cura* of Azcapotzalco to perform the marriage nor any written record of the ceremony could be found. But, with consistent testimony from two witnesses— Basurto and Villaseñor—the Cortés-Quintero marriage was validated.[56]

In a proven emergency, clerical offices were not necessary for a marriage to be valid. María Bermúdez of San Lorenzo Cuapiaxtl (Puebla) traveled to Mexico City in August 1928 to visit her longtime companion, Otto Sanders, interned in the Hospital Americano. Her parish priest, Ruperto Méndez, told her that while he supported the belated legitimization of their union, he could not officiate in Mexico City, given canonical regulations. On 12 August, Bermúdez found a priest in the hospital neighborhood, José Troncoso, who agreed in principle but declined to come immediately due to illness. Sanders's condition also worsened, and as Bermúdez's two sisters and their children (aged 17 and 15) watched, the couple made vows and asked for God's blessing, promising that they would have a formal wedding ceremony once Sanders's health was restored. Sanders died at 4 a.m., as Troncoso discovered when he later arrived at the hospital. Father Méndez, writing on Bermúdez's behalf, thought there was a possibility that the marriage might be valid and the children thus legitimized. The Tribunal agreed: mutual consent was a component of the sacrament (as described in canon 1791), and their situation conformed to canon 1098, which specified that "in danger of death marriage is contracted validly and licitly in the presence only of witnesses."[57] Without witnesses, such petitions were unsuccessful; the only corroboration of Elvira Hernández's story of blessings exchanged at her sickbed was her husband, Otilio Olguín, who meanwhile had filed for a civil divorce. He denied the exchange, and the Tribunal ruled that no marriage had occurred.[58]

Thus emergency provisions worked in favor of some lay people, even though priestly claims to have acted under them were often rejected. Another factor helped in the Cortés-Quintero case: their son, Felipe Cortés Quintero, was studying in Tlalpan's Seminario Conciliar and wished to enter the priesthood. To do so, he would need to be legitimate—a precondition eliminated for state positions under the 1857 Civil Code, but still important for the Church. Tribunal members agreed to validate the marriage for the young seminarian's "spiritual well-being." They also backdated another dispensation for consanguinity (Cortés and Quintero were second cousins, a fact the seminary found problematic). Confronting decisions that could help perpetuate the Church or keep young people in it, the Tribunal used canon law to help resolve marital irregularities.

Conclusion

Many litigants in these cases, male and female, based their claims on a modern concept: that marriage should contribute to personal happiness, and can and should be reshaped if it does not. Yet in pursuing such happiness, these lay actors sought recourse with an institution whose opposition to this concept was explicit. The Church's position remained that of canon 1093: "Even if marriage is invalid because it was entered into with an impediment, the consent offered is presumed to remain until its revocation is proved."[59] And, though charged with rooting out irregularities, the Tribunal dedicated more of its energy to validating marriages, often disregarding the sentiments of involved parties. Examples of frustrated litigants who attempted to follow procedure—like Ana Alvarez—are particularly hard for contemporary readers to accept. Unsuccessful cases such as Bernardo Castañeda's make more sense to the student of Mexican Church-state relations; it is unsurprising that someone who aggravated Church officials, or cited modern concepts alongside canonical provisions, received little sympathy.

The clergy was dedicated to the letter and execution of canon law, but this was no mere reaction to "modernization" or revolutionary anticlericalism; rather, it was a key part of the clergy's vision of the Church's survival. Pascual Díaz y Barreto's explicit instructions to reject civil divorce and instruct the laity on principles of marriage, as well as the Tribunal's tendency to reinforce marriage bonds if demonstrably valid (and to refuse to act at all until such a point), stemmed directly from recent Church policies and declarations made over the past century to resist the onslaught of modern secularizing states and social trends. At the same time, the Church in Mexico engaged in dialogue with Mexican society and the consolidating postrevolutionary state, adapting as a result. Díaz Barreto's 1932 instructions reiterated earlier mandates to encourage Catholic compliance with state demands for couples to perform a civil ceremony, though ambiguity persisted regarding which ceremony should come first. The Church's shift toward cooperation with the state's civil marriage registry over the course of the 1930s, as part of the post-*Cristiada* modus vivendi, undoubtedly contributed to the increased incidence of combined civil and religious marriages.[60] The Tribunal's use of civil divorce records and proceedings, from 1934, also merits recognition, because it indicates a degree of adaptation to the realities of the laypeople that the Tribunal was charged to serve and of the society in which they lived; conversely, the Tribunal could use the documentation of civil divorce proceedings to establish marital validity.[61]

The Tribunal had to confront the disorder and tangled relationships created not only by the Revolution and *la persecución* but by the Church itself, both officially (the interruptions in regular sacramental delivery and documentation produced by the Church strike) and unofficially (the cultivation of a crisis mentality among clergy and laity). From litigants' testimonies, moreover, it appears that Catholics who pressed for quick action at the expense of following canon law—whatever instructions they received from their clerical leaders—did not earn recognition for their loyalty, but ultimately censure. Still, some male Catholics as described here seem doubly unfortunate. In allying themselves with the Church, some distanced themselves from the state (or at least rejected its authority to declare a marriage sound or severed). Moreover, their utilization of the Church as a mechanism for improving their lives vis-à-vis their spouses is similar to the instrumental approach of secular jurists and politicians who reined in revolutionary family laws that, while promising greater freedom for men and women, also threatened to destabilize gender and family hierarchies as they knew (or idealized) them.[62] In this way, these men's idea of "revolutionary citizenship" *included* being Catholic, rather than following the anticlerical mandate to reject all things Roman.

Female Catholics persisted in longstanding utilizations of the Church, but manifested "revolutionary consciousness" as they weighed up the institutional options offered by Church and state, combining elements that made most sense to them. Many women litigants found their husbands' behavior objectionable, and the Tribunal seemingly took them seriously, earning their attention: Fragoso Mayoral countered her husband's claims of immorality with accounts of his abusive behavior; María Soledad Olvera disproved her husband's claims and showed him to be the bigamist; and Dolores Padilla used a state resource—she had her husband arrested and fined by police for domestic violence—to corroborate ecclesiastical charges against him. Comparable petitions made by other women who accessed revolutionary politics and divorce proceedings, harnessing the language of family obligations and rights in the process, also indicate that women too, were transposing "traditional" Catholic concepts on to governmental structures.[63]

Did the "situation" in which Díaz Barreto believed exist? Many of the hierarchy's concerns are reflected in these cases, yet cases in which ignorance or malice eroded Catholic constructions of marriage constitute only a minority. The hierarchy's view of the laity's capacities and understanding was limited, as was its range of enforcement and self-correction, which may have contributed to the growth of the small but significant numbers of people who decided that Catholic rules were irrelevant, and who married in civil ceremonies only while seeking solutions to their problems elsewhere. The men and women involved in these cases sought the best options for negotiating their marital status and obtaining their individual happiness and rights. For many, despite the forceful demands of liberal and revolutionary civil reforms, the mixed and outright negative messages of Church leaders, and the Tribunal's weak closure or enforcement, Church traditions and laws regarding marriage remained a valid and valued option.

Notes

1. Archivo Histórico de la Arquidiócesis de México (henceforth AHAM), Pascual Díaz y Barreto, c. 2, exp. Circulares 148B, "INSTRUCCIONES que el Excmo. y Rvmo. Señor Arzobispo de México, Dr. D. Pascual Díaz, Dirige a los Señores Párrocos del Distrito Federal sobre la Forma en que los Fieles Deben Celebrar sus Matrimonios" (20 Jan. 1932). Edward N. Peters, *The 1917 or Pio-Benedictine Code of Canon Law* (San Francisco: Ignatius Press, 2001), 376.

2. Every diocese must establish a tribunal, of which the matrimonial tribunal or provisorate is a part. The diocesan bishop heads the tribunal and appoints judicial vicars and judges; advocates can be clerics or laypersons. For regulations at

the time, Peters, *Code of Canon Law*, 519–646 (tribunals, canons 1552–1998; marriage tribunals, canons 1960–1992).

3. Jean Meyer, "Una Historia Política de la Religión en México," *Historia Mexicana* 43, no. 3 (1993): 718–22.

4. Pius XI, "Carta Encíclica de Ntro. Smo. Señor Pío Papa XI sobre el Matrimonio Cristiano" (31 Dec. 1930), *Boletín Eclesiástico de la Arquidiócesis de Guadalajara* (hereafter *BEAG*) IV, II, 3 (1 Mar. 1931).

5. William Addis and Thomas Arnold, *A Catholic Dictionary* (London: Virtue and Co., 1928), 630–1.

6. Peters, *Code of Canon Law*; A. Boudinhon, "Canon Law," *The Catholic Encyclopedia* (New York: Robert Appleton, 1910), v. XI.

7. Matthew Butler, "Revolution and the Ritual Year: Religious Conflict and Innovation in *Cristero* Mexico, 1926–1929," *Journal of Latin American Studies* 38, no. 3 (2006): 465–90, indicates that irregular marriages were reported as early as 1927.

8. Julieta Quiledrán Salgado, *Un Siglo de Matrimonio en México* (Mexico City: El Colegio de México, 2001), 21, 95; Anna Macías, *Against All Odds: The Feminist Movement in Mexico to 1940* (Westport: Greenwood Press, 1982), 13, 15, 35; Stephanie Smith, "If Love Enslaves . . . Love Be Damned: Divorce and Revolutionary State Formation in Yucatán," in *Sex in Revolution: Gender, Politics, and Power in Modern Mexico*, ed. Jocelyn Olcott, Mary Kay Vaughan, and Gabriela Cano (Durham: Duke University Press, 2006), 99–111; Ann Varley, "Women and the Home in Mexican Family Law," in *Hidden Histories of Gender and the State in Latin America*, ed. Elizabeth Dore and Maxine Molyneux (Durham: Duke University Press, 2000), 242.

9. Ramón Calvo, "El Matrimonio Civil ¡Alerta Contra el Peligro!," *BEAG*, V, III, 7 (Jul. 1932), 397–400.

10. Fernando Saúl Alanís Enciso, *El Primer Programa Bracero y el Gobierno de México, 1917–1918* (San Luis Potosí: El Colegio de San Luis, 1999); José María Muriá, "Una Tierra de Hombres Ausentes," in J.A. Gutiérrez G., *Aguascalientes y los Altos de Jalico: Historia Compartida* (Zapopan: El Colegio de Jalisco, 1997), 73–81; Martha Cháves Torres, *Mujeres de Rancho, de Metate y de Corral* (Zamora: El Colegio de Michoacán, 1998).

11. Jean Meyer, *La Cristiada* (3 vols. Mexico City: Siglo XXI, 1973–74), 2:261–85.

12. AHAM, Mora y del Río, "Instrucciones sobre el Uso de los Privilegios Relativos a Matrimonios" (1927); encyclicals *Paterna Sane Sollicitudo* (Feb. 1926), *Iniquis Afflictisque* (Nov. 1926), and *Acerba Animi* (Sept. 1932); Butler, "Revolution and the Ritual Year," 465–90.

13. Pascual Díaz y Barreto, "Instrucciones," (20 Jan. 1932); *Estatutos del Primer Sínodo Diocesano de Guadalajara* (Guadalajara: Impresa Font, 1938), 98; "Circular Núm. 38: A los Sres. Párrocos y Vicarios Fijos del Arzobispado," *BEAG* V, XI, 11–12 (Nov.–Dec. 1940), 398.

14. Martaelena Negrete, *Relaciones entre la Iglesia y el Estado en México, 1930–1940* (Mexico: El Colegio de México, 1988), 36–7, 338.

15. Smith, "If Love Enslaves," 99–111.

16. Silvia M. Arrom, "Changes in Mexican Family Law in the Nineteenth Century," in *Confronting Change, Challenging Tradition: Women in Latin*

American History, ed. Gertrude M. Yeager (Lanham: SR, 2005), 99; Macías, *Against All Odds*, ch. 1. Cf., Suzanne Desan, *The Family on Trial in Revolutionary France* (Berkeley: University of California Press, 2004).

17. Ilene O'Malley, *The Myth of the Revolution: Hero Cults and the Institutionalization of the Mexican State, 1920–1940* (New York: Greenwood Press, 1986), 142; Jocelyn Olcott, "'Worthy Wives and Mothers': State Sponsored Women's Organizing in Postrevolutionary Mexico," *Journal of Women's History* 13, no. 4 (2002): 108.

18. S. Camposortega Cruz, "Demography of Mexico City: The Same Problems with Less Population," *Demos* 4 (1991): 23–4. Mexico City's 1930 population was 1,029,000.

19. For similar critiques, Wright-Rios (this volume) and Butler, "Revolution and the Ritual Year," 465–90.

20. Quiledrán Salgado, *Un Siglo de Matrimonio*, 143–6, 307–8.

21. Timothy J. Knab, *The Dialogue of Earth and Sky: Dreams, Souls, Curing, and the Modern Aztec Underworld* (Tucson: University of Arizona Press, 2004), 141.

22. Silvia M. Arrom, *The Women of Mexico City: 1790–1857* (Stanford: Stanford University Press, 1985), surveys 81 cases from the years 1800–57 (207).

23. Ibid., 206.

24. Ibid., 212. AHAM, Provisorato Matrimonial (henceforth AHAM/PM) exp. 132, Tomás Twaites notes, 5 Aug. 1930 (single document); exp. 140 bis, Caso Contreras-Sosa, "Resulta," 22 Nov. 1930, and exp. 218, "Resulta," 30 Jan. 1935 (annulment expenses/complaints). Exp. 346, "Resulta," 6 Sep. 1934; exp. 50, "Resulta," 13 Nov. 1930; exp. 028, "Resulta," 1 Oct. 1929, and related documents; exp. 44, "Resulta," 28 Jul. 1930 (neighborhoods). Exp. 10, Petra Castro to Tribunal, 6 Mar. 1929, and exp. 223, on Angela Beristaín-Rodolfo Salgado Medrano marriage, 8 Jan. 1935 (Colonia Industrial) and exp. 89, "Resulta," 22 Feb. 1935 (Capilla del Buen Tono). For women's finanical concerns, exp. 218, Interrogatorium of Amelia Murphy, 19 Apr. 1934, and exp. 223, Beristaín to Tribunal, 28 Feb. 1935.

25. The Pascual Díaz y Barreto files end at his death (1936) but there is no restriction on reading attached documentation postdating his death; however, the files of his successor, Luis María Martínez (1936–56) will not be opened until 50 years after his death.

26. Jorge Adame Goddard, *El Pensamiento Político y Social de los Católicos Mexicanos, 1867–1914* (Mexico City: UNAM, 1981), 220–1; *Manual de Doctrina Cristiana: Curso Medio* (Mexico City: Progreso, 1929), 123–4, and Pbro. J. Rafael Faria, *Curso Superior de Religión* (Bogotá: Voluntad, 1941), 439–51.

27. Canon 1036 §1–3 (Peters, *Code of Canon Law*, 359). Addis and Arnold, *Catholic Dictionary*, 445–7.

28. AHAM/PM, exps. 218 M bis. (Cabrera to Tribunal, 28 Jul. 1934); 218 U (Cabrera and González Interrogatoria, 11 Sep. 1934; Twaites to Leopoldo Díaz y Escudero, 7 and 26 Sep. 1934; Abraham Flores y Hernández to Twaites, 2 Oct. 1934).

29. AHAM/PM, exp. 218 U, Hernández, Interrogatorium, 1 Oct. 1934; "Resulta," 15 Feb. 1935.

30. AHAM/PM, exp. 121, Rodríguez Campos to Tribunal, 31 Jan. 1930.

31. AHAM/PM, exp. 28, "*Declaratione Super Nullitate Matrimonium*," 11 Oct. 1929.

32. Arrom, *Women of Mexico City*; Richard Boyer, *Lives of the Bigamists: Marriage, Family, and Community in Colonial Mexico* (Albuquerque: University of New Mexico Press, 2001).

33. AHAM/PM, exp. 155 bis, Mata to Tribunal, 30 Sep. 1930. For women's cases, exps. 10 (Petra Castro-Bartolo Torres), 132 (Jovita Vázquez del Mercado de Bañuelos), 118 (Margarita Núñez-Manuel San Román), 217 O (Elvira Hernández de Jiménez Rueda-Otilio Olguín), and 133 bis. (María Delgadillo-Juan Vázquez).

34. Georges Duby, *The Knight, the Lady, and the Priest: The Making of Modern Marriage in Medieval France* (New York: Pantheon, 1983); also Mary Jo Maynes and Ann Beth Waltner, "Women's Life-Cycle Transitions in World Historical Perspective: Comparing Marriage in China and Europe," *Journal of Women's History* 12, no. 4 (2001), 11–21. Arrom (*Women of Mexico City*, 208) notes that annulments were "almost impossible to obtain" in late-colonial/early-independent Mexico but laypeople still saw them as a recourse. Boyer, *Lives of the Bigamists;* Steve J. Stern, *The Secret History of Gender: Women, Men, and Power in Late Colonial Mexico* (Chapel Hill: University of North Carolina Press, 1995).

35. AHAM/PM, exps. 89 (Alvarez Rodríguez to Tribunal, 18 Jul. 1933, and "Resulta," 2 Oct. 1934); 51 (Gómez Reina to Tribunal, 24 Sep. 1929).

36. AHAM/PM, exp. 202, Castañeda, petition, 5 Jul. 1933.

37. On Ortiz Rubio's sympathies, Tzvi Medín, *El Minimato Presidencial: Historia Política del Maximato, 1928–1935* (Mexico City: Era, 1991), 86–7, 115.

38. AHAM/PM, exps. 202 ("Resulta," 3 Jul. 1934, and Tribunal to Castañeda, 4 Oct. 1934); 346 ("Resulta," 6 Sep. 1934; notes, 2 Jul. 1942; Evelio Díaz to Saturnino Pineda, 25 Jul. 1942; Oficialia de Morelia to Tribunal, decision, 6 Nov. 1944).

39. AHAM/PM, exp. 215 E, Rosas [Tejeda] to Tribunal, 27 Mar. 1933.

40. AHAM/PM, exp. 223, Salgado Medrano to Tribunal, 13 Dec. 1934; Salgado Medrano, Interrogatorium, 14 Feb. 1935.

41. AHAM/PM, exp. 215 Bis., M. Tovar de Vargas to Tribunal, 13 Mar. and 21 May 1933; Twaites, 23 Mar. 1933; Domingo Blancas, 22 May 1933; Eugenio Vargas and M. Tovar de Vargas to Tribunal, 23 May 1933.

42. AHAM/PM, exps. 51 (Gómez Reina to Tribunal, 24 Sep. 1929); 51 bis (Raúl Doria to priest of Mixcoac, 30 Sep. 1929, and petition, 25 Oct. 1930); 152 (Ignacio Torrescano, petition, 15 Jul. 1930, and Oseguera, Interrogatorium, 19 Dec. 1931); 202 (Castañeda, petition, 5 Jan. 1933); 215 (E. J. Tejeda, petition, 13 Mar. 1933); 215C (Carmen Mier y Terán, petition, 24 Mar. 1933); 218 (Murphy, Interrogatorium, 19 Apr. 1934); 223A (P. Francisco Escartín to Tribunal, 26 Nov. 1934); and 223 (Salgado Medrano to Tribunal, 18 Feb. 1935).

43. AHAM/PM, exp. 215C, Mier y Terán, petition, 24 Mar. 1933; Twaites, notes, 22 Apr. 1933.

44. AHAM/PM, exp. 33, Ana Alvarez to Tribunal, 12 Aug. 1929; Twaites, notes, 19 Aug. 1929 and 30 Jun. 1936.

45. AHAM/PM, exps. 218 (Murphy, Interrogatorium, 19 Apr. 1934). Though canon 1967 already allowed for tribunals to consider the effects of civil marriage when an "accessory" to a sacramental dispute (Peters, *Code of Canon Law*, 637), the archdiocesan tribunal's increased utilization of divorce data at this point is clear.

46. AHAM/PM, exp. 223A, Escartín to Tribunal, 26 Nov. 1934.

47. Arrom, *Women of Mexico City*, 249–258, 227.

48. AHAM, Pascual Díaz, c. 2, "Circular No. 48, A los Señores Vicarios Foráneos, Curas, Vicarios Fijos, y Capellanes del Arzobispado," 27 Nov. 1931; Leopoldo Ruiz y Flores, "Programa Nacional de Renovación Espiritual," *BEAG*, VI, 5, 1 May 1935, 237–47.

49. AHAM/PM, exps. 152 bis. (Oseguera to Tribunal, 20 Sep. 1930, "Resulta," 19 Dec. 1930); exp. 50 (Gonzalo Muñóz to Tribunal, 21 Sep. 1929, and "Resulta," 13 Nov. 1930).

50. AHAM/PM, exps. 218, 218 M, 218 U, and 215 bis, in addition to cases below.

51. AHAM/PM, exp. 140 bis, Caso Gutiérrez-Avila, Castillo Villaruel, statements of 27 Oct. 1929 and 18 Sep. 1930; Peters, *Code of Canon Law*, 378–79; AHAM, Mora y del Río, "Normas Pro Sacerdotibus."

52. AHAM/PM, exp. 140 bis., Caso Gutiérrez-Avila, M. Ruíz y Flores, to Tribunal, 20 Oct. 1930; Caso Furlong-Buitrón, Castillo Villaruel, to Tribunal, 5 Apr. 1932, and "Resulta," 12 Apr. 1932; Caso Contreras-Sosa, J. Gutiérrez García, Promotor Fiscal, to Tribunal, 10 Nov. 1930, and DF police receipt, 4 Jun. 1927.

53. Celestino Barradas, *Historia de la Iglesia en Veracruz: Vol. III, 1920–1990* (Xalapa: Ediciones San José, 1990), 76; AHAM/PM, exp. 217, "Resulta," 7 Jul. 1934.

54. Catholics who trace their history to the St. Maro monastery (Lebanon); their community reunited with the Church in 1216, retaining its patriarch, liturgical language, and unique rites (Addis and Arnold, *Catholic Dictionary*, 548–50).

55. AHAM/PM, exp. 21, Barquet to Tribunal, 17 May 1929; Información Matrimonial Barquet-Serur, 20 Oct. 1929; Benavides's authorization for Assaf, 21 Oct. 1929; Assaf to Tribunal, 21 Jun. 1929; Benavides to Tribunal, 22 Jun. 1929; Kuri to Tribunal, 26 Jun. 1929; "Resulta," 17 Jul. 1929.

56. AHAM/PM, exps. 217 and 58: 1929 communications to Tribunal by Cortés (16 Oct. and 12 Nov.), Benavides (21 Oct.), Basurto (26 Oct.), Quintero (12 Nov.), and Villaseñor (12 Nov.).

57. AHAM/PM, exp. 2, communications to Tribunal from Méndez (San Lorenzo Cuapiaxtl parish, 27 Dec. 1928); María Carmen Bermúdez (22 Jan. 1932); Ester Sanders Bermúdez (22 Jan. 1932); Carlos Sanders Bermúdez (22 Jan. 1932), Rebeca Bermúdez (22 Jan. 1932); "Resulta," 15 Jan. 1929.

58. AHAM/PM, exp. 217 O, Hernández de Jiménez Rueda to Tribunal, 3 Nov. 1933; Olguín to Tribunal, 1 Dec. 1933; "Resulta," 22 Feb. 1934.

59. Peters, *Code of Canon Law*, 376.

60. Quiledrán Salgado, *Siglo de Matrimonio*, 143–46.

61. E.g., AHAM/PM, exp. 221N (Conrad Elkisch-Efriede Meyer).

62. Desan, *Family on Trial*; Smith, "If Love Enslaves," 99–111.

63. AHAM/PM, 220 B bis, Dolores Padilla to Tribunal, 30 Oct. 1934; Smith, "If Love Enslaves." Olcott, *Revolutionary Women*, 97, 101, 191, and 99–111.

Chapter 9

Religious Conflict and Catholic Resistance in 1930s Oaxaca*

Jean Meyer

Oaxaca moved in step with the rest of Mexico from 1929–32 enjoying a religious respite during the presidency of Pascual Ortiz Rubio before suffering a relapse in the years 1932–37.[1] Renewed persecution was linked to conflicts inside the "revolutionary family" (over the *Maximato*, the presidential succession and Lázaro Cárdenas's arrival as president, and the subsequent elimination of Plutarco Elías Calles), and to the battle over "socialist education." The years 1935–36 were, perhaps, the hardest for Catholics and their Church, whose leaders followed the policy of passive resistance (*Resistenz*) ordered by Rome, and condemned, both out of conviction and obedience to the papal line, any form of armed struggle (*Widerstand*).[2]

In Mexico, the June 1929 *arreglos* saw the triumph of the moderate episcopal tendency, which Rome firmly supported until it could demonstrate—with the *arreglos*' reapplication circa 1938—that the art of snatching victory from the jaws of defeat actually worked. Meanwhile, in order to prevent any recrudescence of armed conflict, Rome and its agents in Mexico—the faction of governing bishops—demonized hardline elements in the National League for the Defense of Religious Liberty (LNDLR) and dismantled other organizations that had participated enthusiastically in the *Cristiada*, such as the Catholic Association of Mexican Youth (ACJM) and "Joan of Arc" Women's Brigades. Now Catholic energies were channeled into the hierarchically controlled Mexican Catholic Action (ACM). The archbishop of Oaxaca, José Othón Núñez y Zárate,[3] faithfully toed this Roman line from 1929 until final victory.

When a new wave of anticlericalism broke in 1932, Núñez y Zárate, like the other bishops, told Catholics to pressure the federal and local governments using peaceful, legal means, and to organize themselves within Mexican Catholic Action (ACM) and the National Parents' Union (UNPF). He banned the armed struggle, tirelessly repeating papal prohibitions, and in this was supported by all the diocesan clergy with the exception of one "Manuel García" (a pseudonym: the priest existed, but I have been unable to identify him). Thus was established an interesting dialectic between the empowerment of Catholic laypeople, charged with defending their Church, and a commanding and efficient clericalism, since it was really bishops and priests who dictated positive and negative forms of Catholic conduct (*Resistenz* but no *Widerstand*).

The official position was summed up in the declarations of the archbishop of Morelia, Leopoldo Ruiz y Flores, in his capacity as apostolic delegate, on 28 December 1929: "in the event of an armed movement or revolutionary movement, the Catholic hierarchy and clergy will play no future part in it, as they did not in the past; nor will they allow themselves to be associated, connected, or identified with any such revolutionary activity."[4]

The Church, at this juncture, was committed to strengthening the federal government and worked to calm Catholic dissidents, especially the faction of *ligueros* that rejected the 1929 *arreglos*. The Church went a long way down the road of conciliation: Father Miguel Darío Miranda—Catholic Action's first ecclesiastical assistant—even stated on Christmas Eve 1929 that Catholics were "disposed to cooperate with the Revolutionary Party in any programme beneficial to the moral and economic progress of the Mexican people."[5] The president of the republic, Pascual Ortiz Rubio, also worked sincerely toward Church-state reconciliation: as he explained to two envoys of the United States' Catholic Church, Father Burke and William Montavon (secretary of the powerful National Catholic Welfare Conference), he was a Catholic and proud to be a descendant of the former archbishop of Guadalajara, Ortiz.[6]

That the Church decreed violence was not a valid means of self-defense or a way of achieving Mexico's social transformation does not mean that it abandoned its positions or surrendered to the state. Rather, it calculated that the medicine of armed struggle was worse than the disease, and that the adventurism of a few might open a Pandora's box. This strategy did not signify the end of the religious conflict, because after a few years' truce the government again took the offensive on all fronts: limiting priestly numbers until the clergy and sacramental offices virtually disappeared, thus earning Mexico a rebuke from the League of Nations; fighting to introduce "socialist education" and "seize the soul of youth"; and launching "Red Saturdays" and campaigns against "fanaticism." For its part, the Church used every means at its disposal to conserve, develop, and mobilize both its social base and international opinion, which played an important role in the conflict: Vatican diplomacy was effective, as was the activity of Catholics across the world, from Latin America to Europe, and from the United States to Canada.[7]

Events in Oaxaca

The Modus Vivendi Observed (1929–32)

In Oaxaca, as in all the republic, news of the June 1929 *arreglos* was received with joy and bell ringing. The bureaucracy was not to be left out, and on

15 July, the state government outlined for "*Señor* Doctor Don José Othón Núñez, Archbishop of Oaxaca," the legal dispositions

> which regulate this field, on the occasion of the handing-over of churches devoted to the Catholic cult. This Government, in accordance with the terms of Interior Ministry telegraphic circular number 24, dated 28 June last, and at your request, has ordered that [churches] be handed over to those *señores sacerdotes* of the Catholic cult mentioned by you in your kind communications, one without date and number, one dated the first of this month.[8]

The archives of Oaxaca's archdiocesan and state governments are replete with the files of church hand-overs, parish by parish, municipality by municipality. The operation was completed without difficulty, albeit amid a flurry of paperwork caused by the regime's officiousness. Government documents (*oficios*), such as that dated 22 July 1929 in Magdalena Ocotlán and addressed to the "Supreme State Government's Secretary General of Dispatches," can be read in their hundreds:

> In accordance with the final part of your most worthy *oficio*, number 3925, issued by the Dep[artment] of State, Government Section, and dated 4 July of the current year, I have the honor of remitting, under separate, registered cover, the legal act and inventory which were recorded on the occasion of the delivery of the Catholic church of this place to Citizen Francisco Vidrio, a priest of the Catholic religion . . . EFFECTIVE SUFFRAGE, NO REELECTION, Roads and Schools, Municipal President, Pedro González.[9]

We see clearly from the documentation that Oaxacas's municipal presidents and *juntas de vecinos*[10] hastened to surrender churches to priests as soon as news of the *arreglos* was out. In July, August, and September, the state department asked for endless papers— "certified copies, in duplicate" of this and that—but we see neither bad faith nor sabotaging of the hand-overs. In the outlying dioceses of Huajuápam and Tehuantepec the operation took longer, in its legal dimension if not in practice, perhaps because of distance or because these regions experienced *cristero* violence, especially the former.[11] On 15 February 1930, the state's Official for Dispatches telegraphed Tehuantepec's bishop, Genaro Méndez, who was still in San Andrés Tuxtla (Veracruz):

> Informed [of] Fr. Alejo Hernández's designation [as] Tehuantepec parish priest. So as to authorize churches' hand-over, indicate aforementioned priest's permanent place of residence and specify communities [in] whose churches he will officiate . . . Inform him Government proceeds in strict adherence [to] relevant Law and measures issued by Interior Ministry, with difficulties concerning some churches [in] this diocese owing to [priests'] failure to fulfill legal requirements . . . You may not appoint priests to parishes without prior licence and receipt of the church inventory, which must be issued by this Government.[12]

In a second phase, Oaxacan Catholics petitioned the state Congress on 15 October 1929 demanding the abrogation of the decree of 30 January, which limited the number of priests to one for every 100,000 inhabitants. Every parish sent hundreds if not thousands of signatures, men's and women's separately, on printed forms. This happened in the archdiocese of Oaxaca and in the dioceses of Huajuápam and Tehuantepec.[13] The petition was not accepted, as might be expected, but contributed to the drafting by the state department's government section of *oficio* 7-092. This was dated 18 December 1929, and addressed to the archbishop of Oaxaca:

> In view of the fact that churches . . . were delivered on the basis of circular number 24 of 28 June last, issued by the Interior Ministry, without taking due note of the measures that the same Ministry communicated in circular 33 of 15 August . . . you must proceed at once to normalize church deliveries [again], in accordance with the measures in the aforementioned circular 33.

From 15 August to 18 December, the state had not been concerned to implement this law, but the Catholic petition obviously rankled, given that the same official continued thus:

> Regarding the churches in [Oaxaca] city, I should tell you that, by order of the President, and in conformity with the rules communicated in the aforementioned Interior Ministry circular 33, only one priest, with custody of two churches, is permitted, because the population does not reach 40,000 inhabitants.[14]

However, this display of official temper soon passed and 1930 and 1931 were quiet years for the Church and faithful. Indeed, change eventually came from the outside, with local politicians merely adapting to the new climate without acting independently. Thus, in April 1931, the executive committee of the Oaxacan Confederation of Socialist Parties, the local legislature, and the Confederation of Socialist Leagues, demonstrated their solidarity with "the anticlerical attitude adopted by General Plutarco Elías Calles, Minister for War and Marine."[15] The storm that would sweep away Ortiz Rubio and his policy of religious conciliation was brewing.

The Church's Troubled Times (1932–37)

In late 1931, parish priests in Oaxaca were again forced to surrender their churches to the custody of lay people;[16] and when a new policy of nonapplication of the *arreglos* prevailed from early 1932, there were rumors of Catholic rebellions. Both to protest against the Mexican government's new offensive and prevent another *Cristiada*, Pius XI published the encyclical *Acerba Animi* (29 September 1932). If the 1929 *arreglos* forced the League to resign itself to a fait accompli, the government's policy change in 1931–32 gave the radical *liguero* minority an opportunity to return to the field of battle. This is why the pope, before he firmly prohibited Catholics from resorting to violence, first protested against government violations of the accords: Pius recalled that it was the state that first expressed desire to reach an agreement ending Mexico's religious war; that Rome, accepting the regime's good faith, had lifted the suspension of public worship, disarming the insurgents; and that now the government had openly violated "the conditions stipulated in the truce," unleashing a "totally criminal persecution" whose aim was "completely to destroy the Catholic Church." Pius saw this as a "positive step for that revolution which atheism, God's enemy, promotes using all means." Notwithstanding their failure, Pius restated that the *arreglos* had been justified in order to allow priests to attend to the spiritual lives of Catholics. In conclusion, he reminded Catholics of their duty to remain peaceful and support Catholic Action, under the bishops' control.[17]

The encyclical was diffused throughout Oaxaca and all Mexico, and the federal government's first reaction was to expel the apostolic delegate, Ruiz y Flores, at Congress's express petition. The bishops in Oaxaca, Huajuápam, and Tehuantepec soon had to leave and the number of priests authorized to minister was drastically reduced. On 1 April 1933, in his annual report, Governor Anastasio García Toledo (1932–36) could say:

> In accordance with the dispositions of the General Constitution of the Republic in matters of religion, the Government—that is, the state authorities—are acting as auxiliaries of the Federation by overseeing the strict fulfillment of the Law. A detailed investigation to locate those priests of the Catholic cult who are dispersed in the State's extensive territory is currently being carried out, in order to prevent those who are not inscribed in the relevant registry, and who have not satisfied the legal requirements in each case, from exercising their ministry.[18]

Because statistical limitations now prevented priests from exercising their profession, many had to practise illegally, protected by the community, or go into exile. The governor continued:

> In view of the special conditions prevailing in the regions of Sola de Vega, Juquila, and Jamiltepec, which were created by the incursions of an individual named David Rodríguez, and by well-founded suspicions that Catholic elements in this zone provide moral and material support in favor of his agitation; and until the results of an official investigation are known; the Catholic priest of Teojomulco, Sola de Vega district, has been suspended in the exercise of his ministry. By virtue of the numerous complaints also received against the priest Rafael J. Hernández, *párroco* of Lachixio, Sola de Vega district, it was also necessary to cancel [this priest's] licences. In the same way, action was taken against the priest of Cacahuatepec, Putla district . . . Various parish priests were fined for infringing articles 2 and 3 of the Reglamentary Law of constitutional article 130, which prohibit the celebration of religious matrimony without prior evidence that civil bonds of marriage have been obtained.[19]

"The individual named David Rodríguez"—a *cristero* from La Montaña from 1927–29—was worthy of a second reference:

> Public order and tranquility remain unalterable. Even though the Sola de Vega, Juquila, and Jamiltepec region is marauded by a group of armed men headed by David Rodríguez, who was identified three years ago as a bandit in the service of the Revolution's enemies, these circumstances cannot the affect the situation of general quiet which the State enjoys.[20]

Nonetheless, the authorities needed the intervention of the federal army, under orders of the state's chief of military operations, General Federico R. Berlanga. Indeed, there were Catholics ready to bear arms in this western region of Oaxaca in 1932, just as there had been during the *Cristiada* risings of 1927–29, only now they also defied ecclesiastical instructions. Rebels were encouraged and marshaled by a League reduced to its simplest expression, poorer and more impotent than ever. Isolated in small foci dispersed across the republic, these "liberators"—the name they gave to themselves—could not invoke religious defense as a cause, because the Church, starting with the pope, prohibited them from doing so. In such conditions, the movement—known as the "Second" *Cristiada* (*La Segunda*)—could not prosper, still less in Oaxaca, a state that had no "true" *Cristiada* in the previous Church-state conflict.

The League's military inspector could rightly exclaim that "the clergy here [Oaxaca], as almost everywhere else when not attacking us, offers at least passive resistance."[21] Yet the authorities seemed unaware of this fact: while the governor believed that suspending Teojomulco's *cura* would finish off the "bandit" David Rodríguez, the department of education's inspector explained how "Fr. Aureo Castellanos denigrates our Institutions, their governors, and the Federal School . . . [saying that it is] preferable to leave children without education than to educate them in a school without God": he annexed a copy of the "seditious proclamation made by the rebel David Rodríguez, who is up in arms. I presume that the *cura* drafted this proclamation. The rebels have twice attacked the Tataltepec school."[22]

The Battle over Schooling
(1934–35)

Just as these miniscule guerrilla foci were being extinguished, in Oaxaca and everywhere else, "socialist education" suddenly fanned the flames of revolt, lending the risings a certain vigor in 1935.[23] *Jefe Máximo* Calles's famous "Grito de Guadalajara" (July 1934), which urged revolutionaries to "seize the consciences of youth," was a war-cry for radicals on all sides, and the League even dared hope that an opportunity to recover its 1925–26 strength had arisen. Tension immediately escalated. From March 1934, Pascual Díaz—primate of Mexico, architect of the *arreglos,* and a man particularly loathed by *ligueros*—invited Catholics to fight against the introduction of a state education program that was monopolistic in form and antireligious in content; as always, however, he invited them to use purely legal methods such as refusing to send their children to school. The National Parents' Association, the National Association for Freedom of Education, and other organizations worked effectively for a boycott of public schools; in any event, "socialist" and "rational" (that is, vigorously atheistic) education was frequently confused by ordinary people with its forerunner, "sexual education," an unpopular association that weighed heavily against state schools. Absenteeism, or more accurately, school strikes, hit the ministry of public education hard.

Although Catholics were unable to prevent the reform of constitutional article 3, which required that education provide a "rational" vision of the world, in November 1935 the Mexican episcopate published a collective pastoral inspired by Pius's encyclical *Divini Illius Magistri*.[24] The last of the six "consequences and practicalities" presented in the pastoral reads as follows:

> For as long as socialist education is compulsory, in accordance with reformed article 3 of the Constitution, it is not licit (that is, it is sinful) for Catholics to open and support state schools which are, or should be, in any way subject to this law, or to send their children to such schools, be they public or private . . . We warn parents whose children are in such schools that they are committing a very grave mortal sin, for which they cannot be absolved in confession until their children are removed from such establishments.[25]

For its part, the Oaxacan government toed the official line, as did all states in the republic. In his 1935 *Informe*, Governor García Toledo thus dedicated seven pages to the theme:

> Not exaggerating our ability, but clearly conscious of our duty, we have also created a Defanaticizing Committee to support the socialist school, whose program of action is rightly directed against all aspects of religious schooling . . . So that the programme which we are developing inside and outside school may be appreciated, I will allow myself to cite some of its themes now: religion, superstitions, the personality of Christ, history and philosophy; miracles and their incompatibility with scientific truth; the exploitation of credulity through the medium of indulgences; so-called sacraments and the immorality of auricular confession; manifestations of idolatry in the cult of images; religious taxes as proof of clerical greed; the erroneous virtues attributed to "celestial advocates" [saints]; the hypocrisy of ecclesiastical celibacy; the impossibility of God's justice given life's injustices and the exploitation of Man.[26]

Because of this action, many schools stayed empty and many teachers—both men and women (this was a largely feminine profession)—chose to resign. As the shocked governor reported:

> It must be reported that the methods employed by the Government to implant socialist education have provoked worrying situations in numbers of *pueblos*. Hundreds of fathers and mothers congregated recently in the town of Huajuápam and sent a petition to the Executive under my control demanding that no

socialist school be implanted, and that private schools be allowed to work freely. These parents' demands go further, in that they also propose to nominate the teaching personnel in the region's schools, and threaten that if they do not achieve this aim, which is discordant with constitutional precepts, then a state of strike will be maintained in all establishments in the region. The attitude of these *pueblos* is explained if we recall that Huajuápam was the see of a Catholic bishopric . . . and it is the clergy which has brought these tactics into play so as to further its particular aim of keeping the great masses in obscurantism, all the better to be exploited by the capitalist bourgeoisie . . . The Government under my control has already ordered the measures which this case demands and will proceed energetically, because those who have a responsibility to history to forge a true *patria*, winning the rights and happiness which are owed to the humiliated masses, must not vacillate in the face of a revolutionary conquest as important as the socialist school.[27]

By this time, the state government had closed all private schools that did not satisfy legal requirements—which was nearly all of them—and was creating Nocturnal Cultural Centres in order to "modify undesirable tendencies and habits, and principally to destroy the superstitions and fanatical ideas which abound in the generality of indigenous villages."[28] Governor García Toledo clearly differed from his predecessor, Genaro Vásquez (1925–28), who thought Indian beliefs should be respected as a matter of principle. The result was a protracted and serious "school strike" in the whole state, not just in Huajuápam.[29]

In such an atmosphere, it is not surprising that the government summoned all priests in Oaxaca on 3 September 1934, or that a week later (11 September) it published decree 213, fixing the number of Catholic priests in the state at 1 per 60,000 inhabitants. As a result of this decree, municipal presidents received a telegram on 27 December 1934 ordering "the cancellation of all licences for priests who have been ministering in state territory."[30] Priests were now obliged to "concentrate in the capital." The archbishop was outside Mexico—expelled and with no possibility of returning—as were the apostolic delegate and 16 other prelates. In his "Open Letter" to President Cárdenas of 2 February 1935, Monsignor Ruiz y Flores, writing as apostolic delegate, noted that "there are states, such as Oaxaca, in which only one priest is permitted, and even he can minister only in the cathedral, making it impossible that the 1.2 million inhabitants who make up the population are properly attended."[31] How different this was to the years 1926–29, when the curia, chapter, and seminary all functioned normally in Oaxaca and the sacraments were administered without difficulty![32]

In 1934 and subsequent years, the governor also reported, "in this capital City, the Government and the National Revolutionary Party [had] unite[d] to organize and develop 'Red Saturdays,' " held in the Macedonio Alcalá Theatre,[33] as well as watching out for the "abuses" of Catholic priests:

Proof of this close surveillance can be found in the cancellation of the licences of the priests Ignacio Colmenares and Aurelio Bautista, who officiated in

Nochixtlán and Pochutla; the cancellation, too, of the licences of the priests [serving as] bishops of Tehuantepec and Huajuápam . . . In circular number 10 of 6 June last [1934] categorical orders were issued to the Municipal Authorities, imposing upon them the obligation not to permit on any grounds the exercise of any minister not expressly authorized by the Government.[34]

In his *Informe* for 1935, Governor García Toledo also pointed out:

Five years ago, the exercise of the priesthood was regulated in the State, yet the upwards transformation demanded by the Revolution's new ideological currents requires the adoption of ever more drastic determinations to nullify any attempt at clerical supremacy.

For this reason, the Executive under my control, responding to true social necessity, was ready to sanction Decree 213 of 11 September last, as a result of which the number of priests for the Catholic and any other religion was reduced to one minister for every 60,000 inhabitants. A consequence of this Law was the cancellation of the licences of all priests who had been ministering . . . This shows the conviction with which the Executive under my control responds, in matters of religion, to the [historical] moment and to revolutionary ideology, not merely limiting itself to the application of the law, but also developing a vast defanaticization campaign . . . in order to combat fanaticism in all its redoubts. These ramparts are designed to halt the progressive march of the Republic at any cost, even that of endangering national liberty and autonomy.[35]

The Army of Popular Liberation (Widerstand)

The state's offensive renewed the hopes of the few *liguero* irreducibles that remained. So did the fact that in 1935 the Oaxacan government faced particularly serious political problems emanating from within revolutionary ranks, "agitation [which] showed special characteristics in the region of the Isthmus, where bad *oaxaqueños*, stirred up by foreign elements, tried to create an emergency situation by declaring themselves in open rebellion . . . with weapons in their hands." This rebel movement was quickly contained, however, by the Federal Army.[36]

In the archives of the League's Special Committee (CE), we see clearly that Oaxaca's Catholics decided against the armed struggle and followed the strategy outlined by the pope and the bishops: resistance based on legal and peaceful methods, and which had no political ambitions to change the government, or—still less—to seize power (the old *liguero* dream). The complete absence of an armed movement in Huajuápam, which had been a serious *cristero* enclave in the 1920s but was now in the vanguard of the peaceful struggle against the socialist school, is striking.[37] The League still tried. Correspondence between the League's Special Committee—in hiding between Mexico City and Toluca—and its local agents is generally cryptic, though easily deciphered. For example, in a CE letter to Margarita Nava dated 8 April 1935 we read that "our business in these towns (of Oaxaca) is almost nil . . . and new commercial trips must be considered . . . so that a cooperative can be formed."[38]

In November 1935, *cristeros* appeared in the Isthmus: Nicanor Díaz led 60 men between Tehuantepec and Salina Cruz, and Rito Cortés a band in Jalapa del Márquez; two more groups worked with José F. Martínez and Avelino Morales in the Juchitán region; and it was said that another operated in the Chimalapa sierra, near Chiapas. The report presented by the veteran David Rodríguez, acting as chief of military operations in Oaxaca, is plain enough. From 12 November 1934 to 8 April 1935, Rodríguez was on the run with a reduced number of "liberating" soldiers between Juquila, Juchatengo, Minas, Tlacotepec, Texmelucan, and Sola de Vega. Fighting several battles, he was later pursued by 300 *federales*. On 4 April, he wrote

> I shot Teodoro Aguilar in Tlacotepec, for being an enemy of the cause . . . on 8 [April] I shot Aurelio Escamilla, [municipal] secretary of Minas, because he requested a [federal] detachment and informed on 20 people accused of rebellion, doing them great harm. I have moved to the state capital to buy war materials.[39]

In May, the local agent reported that he counted 50 armed men in eastern Oaxaca. In the south, Benigno Rodríguez had armed another 50 and Pascual Carrillo as many again; near the Mixteca, Vicente Orozco Carrillo had more than 100, but there was no mention of David Rodríguez.[40] Active in May and June 1935, the "liberators" then recessed. We know of quarrels among the leaders: "the new foreman [*capataz*] was wounded by some of our own people, whom it is thought that Carrillo instigated," a report reads, concluding that "the matter [was] very confused." Doubts also grew about the "new foreman," alias Juventino Montaño, who called himself a brigadier general.[41] One League agent reported:

> The people were becoming deflated, so I had to move them. It all started with a rural chief, A. Irápaga of San Juan Chialteca, who died along with his *pistoleros*, his wife, and two daughters, virile women [*embras de pelo en pecho*] who fought at our side. In reprisal for the capture of one the rebel's father, [*cristeros*] captured some [government supporters], cut off their ears and the soles of their feet, and castrated them. As you will comprehend, it is not easy to avoid such terrible incidents with these semibarbarous people . . . We have other rural chieftains coming, since we need to get rid of our enemies in the sierra . . . because the valley is unsuitable.[42]

The League's military inspector, signing as "D. Nieto," reported on 14 September that "we can count on almost no armed groups in the south"; General Montaño had 50 armed men in San Miguel Peras, and brothers Alberto and Juan Juárez 100 in Ocotlán; Pascual Carrillo had 50 in Zimatlán, not all of them armed, and Raúl Martínez another 50—some without weapons—in Santiago Mixtepec; Manuel Avendaño (Ixtepeji), Enrique

Marcial (Tlacolula), Maximiliano González (Tlaxiaco), and Baldomero Díaz (near Peña Larga, Ejutla), were all in the same boat, giving a total of 400 men, not all of them armed, and almost all without ammunition.[43]

On 16 February 1936, the local representative wrote to military inspector Domingo Nieto in Mexico City:

> When you departed [in early 1935], our situation was favorable, and remained so slightly when Sr. Rendón arrived . . . But today all is so changed that one barely believes it, there is such indifferentism [*sic*] that one doesn't know to what it can be attributed. We think [the *cristeros*] have simply been deceived, and that if they only saw some [activity] perhaps their spirits would rise somewhat. Some anonymous chiefs have been arriving, telling us that we are a shameless gang, and that it's bad enough for the *pueblo* without [us] telling them lies in order to rob them. I beg you to pray to God for us, so that He remedies our situation.[44]

But there was no remedy,[45] partly because the League absolutely lacked resources and had no money to buy the "liberators" ammunition, but principally because of the Church's absolute, oft-repeated condemnation of armed struggle. The League thus felt obliged to state that "the personal opinions of some priests who are disaffected with our Institution cannot change its course," and that

> ecclesiastical dispositions cannot affect the life of our Institution if one takes into account that [the League] has been recognised by the HOLY SEE and the Episcopal Committee. This is because our activities do not depart from Christian morality, even if we find ourselves operating in a purely civic field, protected only by our inalienable natural rights.[46]

In summer 1936, the federal army intensified its war against the last "liberators" and in July killed one of the Juárez brothers. "We are without provisions, the *muchachos* have no clothes, some lack capes and others *guaraches*, there is no medicine or ammunition—we lack everything,"[47] wrote Captain A. Morales. Only David Rodríguez retained some followers near Amatengo, but "things are turning bad because the government knows where [his] people are . . . The *muchachas* [of the "Joan of Arc" Brigades, which provided logistical support] are angry and don't want to know, because of the lies and deceipt."[48]

On 1 September, Montaño and Morales took Ocotlán with 42 men—26 of them armed—but lost the money they collected there (5,500 pesos); on 22 November, Montaño entered Zimatlán and then Santa Cruz Mixtepec. In his *Informe* for 1936, the governor reported the presence of "evil-doers" along the coast, the Isthmus, and in Ejutla, and admitted that Ocotlán had fallen: "the region which has required constant attention from the civil and military authorities is the one bordering the district of Jamiltepec, near the state of Guerrero." As for religion, "17 Catholic priests and one Evangelical are registered and licensed."[49]

The bishop now figured among these authorized priests, further debilitating the armed struggle. A *liguero* admitted:

> The League is barely ready to reorganize because I find no supporters, still less now that the *Señor Arzobispo* is near and people are saying there is no more conflict in Oaxaca. Whatever one tries to do, the priests themselves say that there is no need to get involved or to disturb the tranquility of the *pueblo*. With the *Señor Arzobispo*'s departure three days after arriving here, there was some agitation among Catholic groups, but then calm returned and it was all over for them.[50]

In his 1937 and 1938 reports, the new governor, Constantino Chapital, made no references to "evil-doers": "Even personal [religious] beliefs, which sometimes have collective and fanatical repercussions, have not constituted a stumbling block for the Administration."[51] The League's 1937 correspondence also mentions no armed actions, only demoralization: one agent reported "an interview with one priest [who] told me that the League's efforts are not beneficial because its work has never prospered. In the end, he told me that none of [the League's] labors was good, because the pope had condemned them."[52]

At the end of the year, Oaxaca's League representative wrote to Mexico City that "our situation is becoming painful for us because we don't find workers for the task. If our comrades continue with this apathy, we are heading for the abyss. Even the young women have failed."[53] By 1938, only one chief was still active, and in the worst manner: "Our *amigo*, Sixto Fernández, wraps himself in our flag in Zimatlán in order to commit crimes and robberies, as the *señor cura* there says." Mexico City *ligueros* replied that "we are not ready to tolerate any harm caused to the *pueblo* that helps us."[54] The following document marks the liberators' end:

> Every day it gets harder. Nobody helps us. They say we're crazy [*nos tiran de lucas*], and all because the *pueblo* has its freedom, or at least has all those things—fireworks, calends, religious services in the churches, profane *fiestas*—which it believes mean liberty. On the other hand, our men are despairing because of all the waiting without hope . . . Here it has been said that the clergy does not go along with the work of the League.[55]

The Other Resistance (Resistenz)

Throughout the 1930s, the Oaxacan faithful followed the instructions given by Rome and the bishops; Archbishop Núñez y Zárate himself belonged to the moderate group that never saw armed struggle in positive light, even in 1926–29. The objectives of resistance that followed the Roman line were the maintenance, at any cost, of Catholic worship and the sacramental life, and the spiritual education of Catholics of all ages and social groups. The many branches of Catholic Action, discounting political and syndical activity, constituted the desired instrument.[56] Only the legal path was permitted, and Catholics trod it faithfully and in huge numbers. In all this, the laity's role was decisive, especially after the government banned the activity of nearly all Oaxaca's clergy. Resistance developed in different directions according to circumstances, countering the government's many offensives. Socialist education was answered first by petitions, then by a school strike when these were discarded; the multiplication of religious activities and the performance of catechesis by women was a riposte to the near total cancellation of clerical licenses; so, too, was the boom in liturgical activity in church—which included lay-led prayers, rosaries, and "white" masses (the reading of the whole office of the Mass without consecration of bread and wine)—to say nothing of clandestine masses, marriages, and baptisms celebrated by priests in private houses and hideaways.

Petitions forwarded by the municipal authorities constitute the best-documented form of resistance in Oaxaca's state archives. These petitions cover all aspects of the religious crisis, from protests against the suppression of *mayordomías*[57] to a priest's request for permission to celebrate a village feast, from school battles to registration of the clergy. For the years 1933–38, the state's archive is replete with documents from all districts, parishes, and Oaxaca's many *pueblos*. This ubiquity in itself explains the irritation of state governors who denounced the ancient and pernicious complicity that existed between the municipal authorities and the priesthood.

The researcher who leafs through the boxes for the ex-district of Villa Alta, for instance, will find abundant documentation. In 1933, the local authorities defended the priest Epigmenio Hernández, *párroco* of Camotlán, from accusations made by village schoolteachers. The affair ended unusually, with both sides agreeing to "a compromise, with the aim of proceeding by common agreement in future." The pact foresaw

> That the *señor cura* shall continue to lend the services corresponding to his mission, but on condition that the bad customs, superstitions, and other needless expenditure which are made on the pretext of both profane and religious festivals, and which encourage alcoholism, be suppressed.[58]

In 1934, Tlahuitoltepec, Atitlán, and Zacatepec de Choápam defended their priest against rural schoolteachers (*maestros rurales*) who protested that "on 4 [June] at nine in the morning, a great number of men, women, and children followed Angel Martínez—who was carrying a 'fetish' with great humility—to the walls of the Catholic church." The denunciation was made in the hope that "priests do not continue in this absurd fashion to exploit the Mixe race of our State." The priest was immediately summoned by the governor to answer "a matter of an administrative character," and a "detailed investigation" was ordered into "the acts which have been denounced, so as to prove or discredit them." The municipal authorities argued that "*profesor* I. now seeks to prejudice us by surprising the State Government and the Interior Ministry with a report that is at cross-purposes in every way. In this community as in the whole region, there are persons devoted to the Catholic religion, but these believers celebrate their Cults without exceeding the existing Laws."[59]

In 1935, in the context of the educational battle, *maestros rurales* made abundant denunciations of conniving priests and municipal authorities who between them violated the laws, celebrated festivals and processions, and supported *mayordomías*. This happened

> despite the legal prohibitions—Camotlán's mayor was scolded—made on various occasions with the aim of abolishing this class of acts, which are so prejudicial to the *pueblos* themselves . . . By agreement of the Citizen Governor, energetically I order you to prevent the continued celebration of the aforementioned "*mayordomías*" which occasion the economic ruin of those charged with such fruitless tasks, and infringe the aforementioned dispositions.[60]

Throughout the year, *maestros* tirelessly denounced "violations of the Laws of Worship" and the presence of "unauthorized priests"; in parallel fashion, Oaxaca's villages never tired of presenting collectively signed petitions asking the government for a priest when the famous decree 213 (September 1934) allowed only 1 priest per 60,000 inhabitants. Thus, in Etla, the petition carried the signatures of 1,200 women.[61] Some demands proved irresistible. When the population and traders of Juquila asked for *cura* José Cao Romero to be allowed to exercise his ministry in the *santuario*—the most famous in the state—during its main feast, the interior ministry issued a permit, albeit limiting its validity from 4–13 December 1935.[62]

In the files relating to the ex-districts of Etla, Juquila, Ocotlán, Nochixtlán, Sola de Vega, Zimatlán, Huajuápam, Teposcolula, Tlaxiaco, Putla, Pochutla, Miahuatlán, and Tlacolula, the same kinds of petition endlessly recur, whether the exact details concern a temporary permit for the priest to celebrate, a "licence to effect a procession in the cemetery with certain images," or the sending of "documents requesting, on the basis of the *Ley de Cultos*, an authorization for a Catholic minister to officiate in the zone comprising our *Pueblos*, which fall within the Law's scope" (as sent by 13 Ocotlán villages in May 1935).

Conclusion

Juquila's Regional Workers and Peasants' Federation could justifiably complain in 1936 that "fanaticism is still practised with the authorities' full knowledge and tolerance," since "*mayordomía* festivals which openly contradict the postulates of the Revolution are constantly celebrated."[63] As in Juquila, so it was everywhere in Oaxaca. Curiously, Archbishop Núñez y Zárate exhibited similar pessimism after returning to Oaxaca:

> With immense sadness, we consider that the advance of evil in all its many forms has reached such a point that a general apostasy seems to be occurring. It is not that we are unaware of the many Catholics who still fulfill their religious

duties; but at the same time, it is a terrifying reality that those who live in complete religious indifference, devoted to immorality in its most odious forms, are now legion.[64]

It is worth asking why the archbishop should so lament. As he wrote, the religious conflict was coming to an end, as President Lázaro Cárdenas's signals and concrete acts suggested: state by state, parish by parish, Catholics were recovering their churches and *curas*. In Oaxaca, Catholics won the battle, or ended it on the offensive, and did so in the most orthodox way in the world. They had not heeded the calls for armed struggle. As in 1926–29, they had preferred—in union with their clergy—*Resistanz* to *Widerstand:* that is, they opted for the long and patient struggle of civic action and a renewed religious life, not guns. One could even argue that there was greater merit in the conflict's second phase, given that the 1930s Oaxacan Church could not count on the modus vivendi that Governor Genaro Vásquez respected in the 1920s. In the 1930s, Oaxaca would not see this salutary experience repeated, nor enjoy "special" government, and at any given moment was left practically without priests or subjected to the same onslaught as the rest of Mexico. The *Cristiada* had not spread through Oaxaca in the 1920s, in large part because the religious life was not seriously affected. Again, the *ligueros'* insurrectionist calls found little echo in the 1930s as lay people as well as ecclesiastics chose the slow, patient, and arduous digging of a civic struggle. They won, and emerged confirmed in the rightness of their enterprise.

Notes

* Translated by Matthew Butler.

1. For an outline, Jean Meyer, *La Cristiada* (3 vols. Mexico City: Siglo XXI, 1973–74).
2. I follow the distinction made by German historian Martin Broszat to categorize resistance in Nazi Germany. *Resistenz*—a medical-biological concept—denotes an organism's defensive response, its development of immunological resistance; *Widerstand* refers to open (here political, ultimately armed) resistance.
3. Núñez y Zárate (b. Oaxaca, 1867–1941) was a brilliant priest, promoted by Archbishop Eulogio Gillow. As bishop of Zamora from 1909, Núñez became famous for promoting "social" Catholicism, protecting Indians and peasants, and organizing the Zamora Diet (1913). Archbishop of Oaxaca from 1922 until his death.
4. Flyer, 28 Dec. 1929, containing Leopoldo Ruiz y Flores's declarations (author's collection).
5. William Montavon, quoting Fr. M.D. Miranda, 1 Sep. 1930: cited in Servando Ortoll, "Catholic Organizations in Mexico's National Politics and Internacional Diplomacy (1926–1943)" (PhD diss., Columbia University, 1987), 110. Also papal declarations in audience with Mexican Catholics (2 Jun. 1931): "Catholic Action, in Mexico, too, and in spite of all the suffering and tremendous persecution which have happened there, does not, must not, and will not involve itself in politics. Its objective is a religious objective: its seeks

always to form more, and better, Christian consciences." *Discorsi di Pio XI*, ed. Domenico Bertetto (Turin: Societa Editrice Internazionale, 1960), 2: 556.

6. William Montavon, 24 Jan. 1930, cited by Ortoll, "Catholic Organizations," 106.

7. From 1932–37, the pope dedicated various texts to Mexico referring directly to the country in the encyclical *Divini Redemptoris* (1937), which condemned communism.

8. Archivo Histórico del Arzobispado de Oaxaca (henceforth AHAO), Autoridades Civiles, oficio 4158, 15 Jul. 1929.

9. Archivo General del Poder Ejecutivo del Estado de Oaxaca (henceforth AGEPEO), Asuntos Eclesiásticos, Ocotlán, municipal president to Gobierno, 22 Jul. 1929.

10. Groups of lay people, 10-strong, charged as a result of the 1926 Calles Law with administering the fabric of churches in the clergy's absence. Theoretically under government control, these municipal committtees were modelled on the *associations cultuelles* created after the 1905 Church-state separation in France.

11. AGEPEO, Revolución, leg. 213.15, Tehuantepec, telegram, 14 Feb. 1930; AHAO, Correspondencia, Bishop Luis Altamirano of Huajuápam to archbishop of Oaxaca, 9 Aug. 1929.

12. AGEPEO, Revolución, leg. 213.5, Tehuantepec, 15 Feb. 1930.

13. AHAO, Diocesano, Parroquias, petitions, 15 Oct. 1929.

14. AHAO, Diocesano, Autoridades Civiles, oficio 7-092, Gobernación to Archbishop Núñez, 18 Dec. 1929.

15. Archivo Plutarco Elías Calles, inv. 496, 4 telegrams, Apr.–May 1931.

16. AGEPEO, Asuntos Eclesiásticos, Etla district (1931).

17. *Acerba Animi*, 29 Sep. 1932, in *Acta Apostolicae Sedis* 24 (1932): 321–32.

18. AGEPEO, *informe*, Governor A. García Toledo, 1 Apr. 1933, 9.

19. Ibid., 10, 16.

20. Ibid., 5.

21. Archivo Aurelio Acevedo (henceforth AA), Military Inspector D. Nieto to League, 16 Jul. 1936.

22. AGEPEO, Asuntos Eclesiásticos, Juquila, Public Education Departament memo, 13 Jul. 1933.

23. On the "socialist school," see Victoria Lerner, *La Educación Socialista* (Mexico City: El Colegio de México, 1979). Guadalupe Monroy Huitron, *Política Educativa de la Revolución, 1910–1940* (Mexico City: SEP, 1975); Alberto Bremauntz, *La Educación Socialista en México* (Mexico City: Rivadeneyra, 1943); José Bravo Ugarte, *La Educación en México* (Mexico City: Jus, 1966); David L. Raby, *Educación y Revolución Social en México, 1921–1940* (Mexico City: SepSetentas, 1974); *La Educación Socialista en México, 1934–1945*, ed. Gilberto Guevara Niebla (Mexico City: SEP, 1985).

24. Encyclical *Divini Illius Magistri*, cited by the Mexican episcopate in the collective pastoral in *Christus* 1, Dec. 1936.

25. Ibid., 32.

26. AGEPEO, 1935 *informe* by Governor García Toledo, 52–3.

27. Ibid., 53–4.

28. Ibid., 55.

29. In Huajuápam, only 391 out of almost 5,000 students attended class from 1935–36. Personal communication from Cayetano Reyes, 1987.

30. AGEPEO, Asuntos Eclesiásticos, Etla and Juquila districts, 1934–35: telegram, received 27 Dec. 1934, concerning the cancellation of all priests' registration (Decree 213, 11 Sep. 1934).

31. Open letter from Apostolic Delegate Ruiz y Flores to President Lázaro Cárdenas, San Antonio, Texas, 2 Feb. 1935 (author's collection). Carlos Martínez Assad, *El Laboratorio de la Revolución: El Tabasco Garridista* (Mexico City: Siglo XXI, 1979), 51.

32. Nationally, too, very few priests were able to minister. Only 333 priests were ministering throughout Mexico by February 1935, and by December that year, a nadir of 197 priests had been reached—and this in a country of more than 18 million inhabitants. By May 1936 the numbers had risen only slightly, to 293. AGEPEO, Gobierno, 1934 *informe* by Governor García Toledo, 68.

33. Ibid., 9–11.

34. Ibid., 7–8.

35. AGEPEO, Gobierno, 1935 *informe* by Governor García Toledo, 3–4.

36. Ibid.

37. AA, Oaxaca, 1932–39.

38. AA, Oaxaca, letter to Margarita Nava, dated Mexico City, 8 Apr. 1935.

39. AA, Oaxaca, David Rodríguez to Comité Especial in Toluca, 15 Apr. 1935.

40. AA, Oaxaca, M. Mayoral (Oaxaca) to National Guard Supreme Chief, 20 May 1935.

41. AA, Oaxaca, "Informe de Campaña número 1, Ejército Popular Libertador, Oaxaca"; letters, 24 Jun. 1935, 5 and 19 Aug. 1935.

42. AA, Oaxaca, 5 Sep. 1935.

43. AA, Oaxaca, D. Nieto, 14 Sep. 1935.

44. AA, Oaxaca, M.G. Sánchez to Comité Especial, Oaxaca, 16 Feb. 1936.

45. AA, Oaxaca, Justino Martínez, to Comité Especial, Tuxtepec, 4 Mar. 1936; letter (no signature) to José Vega, dated Chilapa (Guerrero), 16 Mar. 1936.

46. AA, Oaxaca, LNDLR to regional delegate in Oaxaca, "Instrucciones para el Funcionamiento de la Organización," 27 Mar. 1936.

47. AA, Oaxaca, Ejército Popular Libertador, Military Inspector D. Nieto to Gral. J.O. in Oaxaca, 30 Jun. 1936.

48. AA, Oaxaca, M. Mayoral to D. Nieto, Oaxaca, 30 Jul. 1936.

49. AA, Oaxaca, A. Morales to Mayoral, Jul. 26 1936; *informes* dated 1 Sep., 8 Oct., 22 and 28 Nov. 1936. AGEPEO, 1936 Informe de Gobierno, 4–5.

50. AA, Oaxaca, "Datos del Sub. Comité Especial de Oaxaca de diciembre de 1936 a septiembre de 1937," 20 Aug. 1937.

51. AGEPEO, 1937 Informe de Gobierno, 5.

52. AA, Oaxaca, F.G. Puerto to N. Granados, Oaxaca, 7 Jul. 1937.

53. AA, Oaxaca, F.G. Puerto to Comité Especial, 15 Nov. 1937.

54. AA, Oaxaca, letter dated Oaxaca, 22 Sep. 1938; reply dated Mexico City, 3 Jan. 1939.

55. AA, Oaxaca, Antonio García to J. Vega (Comité Especial), Oaxaca, 5 Jan. 1939.

56. AGEPEO, Revolución, Gobierno/Asuntos Eclesiásticos, Oaxaca 1926. Various pamphlets, flyers, and newspapers published by Mexican Catholic Action from 1933–37, e.g. *Cultura Cristiana, Semanal Editado por la Comisión Central de Instrucción Religiosa de la ACM*. José Miguel Romero de Solís, *El Aguijón del Espíritu: Historia de la Iglesia en México 1895–1990* (Mexico City: IMDOSOC, 1994), 371–3, 390–1, documents that the bishops "made diocesan life and the

moral regeneration of their communities their only priority, and kept generally silent in matters of conflict or of national importance, a role which was reserved for the 'Executive Episcopal Committee.'" This author's statistics for the Catechestic Office show how catechism centers doubled in number in 1936, just as pious associations emerged on all sides.

57. Lay sodalities with rotating membership that organize the religious fiestas of a particular church or chapel. Especially important in indigenous communities

58. AGEPEO, Asuntos Eclesiásticos, Villa Alta, May–Jul. 1933. File opened after the accusation made against Fr. Epigmenio Hernández.

59. AGEPEO, Asuntos Eclesiásticos, legs. 218.01 and 219.3/03. Complaint against Angel Martínez, dated Villa Alta, 10 Jun. 1934; PNR complaint against the municipal president of Comatlán ([sic], Camotlán), Mexico City, 1 Aug. 1935.

60. AGEPEO, Revolución, Asuntos Eclesiásticos. Government of Oaxaca to the municipal president of Camotlán, Villa Alta, 16 May 1935.

61. AGEPEO, Asuntos Eclesiásticos, Etla, 1935. Complaint, dated Jun. 1935. Petition signed by 1,200 women, 9 Aug. 1935. Government communication about suppression of *mayordomías*, 17 Feb. 1935.

62. AGEPEO, Asuntos Eclesiásticos, Etla, 1935. Telegram, Juquila, 5 Dec. 1935: "The priest has begun to exercise his ministry."

63. AGEPEO, Asuntos Eclesiásticos, Etla, 1935. Complaint dated Juquila, 14 Jan. 1936.

64. J.O. Núñez y Zárate, pastoral letter 13 (18 Jan. 1937), *Christus* 17 (1937): 311.

Chapter 10

"Anti-Priests" versus Catholic-Socialists in 1930s Campeche: Federal Teachers, Revolutionary Communes, and Anticlericalism

Ben Fallaw

In May 1934, congressman (and former SEP *maestro*) Fernando Enrique Angli Lara joined senator Javier Illescas and federal teachers in a cultural conference in Nunkiní, Campeche.[1] Nunkiní's restored *plaza* was inaugurated in a ceremony mixing teachers' patriotic oratory and poetry recited by children and adults. Probably the program denounced the Church. A rainstorm blew up, but the crowd was too big to shelter in the *ayuntamiento*. At this point, assembly leaders hectored officials into surrendering the keys to the church, closed under Campeche's *Ley de Cultos*.[2] Politicians and SEP teachers then launched a ritual assault on the sanctuary. Some donned clerical vestments and mounted the pulpit, delivering fiery anticlerical messages amplified by loudspeaker. To the tune of *La Internacional*, others smashed a large altar crucifix. The crowd hesitated to follow, however, and some people roused their neighbors to defend the church. What happened next? Did the population peacefully surround the building and ask the intruders to leave? Did a mob storm the church and chase out the iconoclasts? Accounts differ, but teachers felt that only General Francisco Múgica's garrison had protected them from violence.

Though Campeche was reputedly among Mexico's least "Catholic" states, this aborted SEP iconoclasm helped engineer an unlikely alliance against the national revolutionary project between *campechano* Catholics and *caciques* of the state's revolutionary—nominally anticlerical—Agrarian Socialist Party (PSA).[3] This chapter shows how federal teachers in Campeche saw "defanaticization" as the first step toward creating revolutionary communes that would be free of religious and class "prejudices" but inspired, in part, by simple Christian virtues. The chapter then shows how SEP radicals—whose political fortunes were tied to Angli Lara's electoral prospects in 1935—provoked a Catholic-Socialist coalition to counterattack successfully. That is, it shows how incoming radicalism was checked by local revolutionaries and Catholics who joined forces and supported the rival gubernatorial bid of Eduardo Mena Córdoba, a PSA candidate with links to established *caciques* and cooperative interests. In the end, SEP anticlericalism unintentionally fused localist religiosity with conservative provincialism, making local Catholicism less clerical, but no less popular.

Federal Teachers Defanaticize
Campeche, 1934–35

The Nunkiní conference occurred during a SEP defanaticization campaign to eliminate religious practices considered "superstitious" and wasteful, and to remove clerical influence from public life. The SEP probably chose Nunkiní because it lay in Campeche's north, an indigenous region considered only nominally Catholic.[4] Moreover, Nunkiní was the cradle of the nominally anticlerical PSA, and Angli Lara its midwife.[5] The 1930s SEP saw institutional and folk Catholicisms as obstacles to far-reaching modernization. Indigenous society, in particular, was seen as insular, religious, and subsistence-oriented, antithetical to market and *patria*.[6] The SEP did not oppose Christianity per se, but believed Catholicism as practised was a drain on the peasant economy and a repository of outdated beliefs. Defanaticization was therefore key to "the peasant's liberation," according to Campeche's long-serving SEP superintendent, Claudio Cortés. From 1933, Cortés implemented defanaticization as part of a major, ambitious doctrine of "socialist" education; this called on *maestros* to oversee a structural transformation approximating Marxism by organizing *ejidos*, unions, and cooperatives.[7]

A national policy, defanaticization was enacted zealously in Campeche, where the SEP enjoyed exceptional clout. Here the federalization of education started early (1922). The SEP also enjoyed strong financial support from Mexico City and ran a large cooperative network, while the state government was poor and feeble.[8] Hecelchakán's Escuela Normal Rural (ENR-H), or teacher training school, was the flagship SEP school in the Mexican southeast, and a hotbed of socialist education.[9] Cadres of radical, often communist, alumni trained teacher cohorts infused with class consciousness and anti-Catholicism. Campeche's *normal* excluded children of "*pseudo-ricos*," and attending religious services was forbidden.[10] While not exactly a statelet within the state, the SEP in Campeche enjoyed remarkable influence and authority, which emboldened federal teachers to push all parts of their agenda.

Moreover, many SEP leaders—starting with Cortés—sympathized with, or joined, the Communist Party, which considered defanaticization essential to class struggle. Cortés fired teachers who attended church, displayed icons, or married in church.[11] Tomás Cuervo, the SEP's nationally outstanding jacobin, was inspector of Campeche's fourth district in 1932.[12] Finally, federal teachers had a powerful patron—Francisco Múgica, garrison chief in Campeche city in 1934. Cárdenas's alter-ego, Múgica advocated aggressive anticlericalism since 1917.[13] Policy, personnel, and politics aside, defanaticization was driven by strong idealist strains. For some SEP leaders, Campeche was a place to transform peasant communities into communes. For one influential *maestro*, such revolutionary sites would combine Socialism with Christianity.

The SEP had no single blueprint for Campeche. Instead, teachers sampled different radical traditions: socialist education, communism, Garrido's "laboratory," masonic ideals of fraternity and equality.[14] Seemingly unique to Campeche, however, was the utopian ideology of Inspector Luis Espinosa, who tried to reconcile revolutionary anticlericalism with Christianity. Espinosa's ideas built on the four pillars of the SEP's project for Campeche: defanaticization, economic cooperativism, class and nation-based identifications, and a novel communal ideology.

First, defanaticization required breaking all contact with the Church and ending so-called "fanatical" practices, folk Catholic festivals especially. Anticlerical laws were never the long-term solution, but gave teachers space in which to change popular religious attitudes. In Bolonchenticul, Iturbide, and other villages, federal teachers used state law to halt Catholic fiestas in 1934. Cortés was particularly pleased when peasants in Dzitnup and Pocboc used "direct intervention" to expel lay catechists at Easter, and Hecelchakán anticlericals forced the cancellation of an episcopal visit. For Cortés, fiestas were "against the peasant economy," but his opposition also stemmed from a revolutionary puritanism (Reformation anticlericalism being among the SEP's historical reference points).[15] Cortés objected to fiestas because girls dressed up as boys, people danced suggestively (their movements "pervert[ing] the sexual instinct"), and delighted in reciting Yucatecan *bombas* (humorous rhyming verse) spiced with Maya and Spanish double entendres.[16]

The second pillar of transformation was the cooperative. Previously, peasants foreclosed on their crops before harvest in order to settle debts and taxes, receiving from middlemen only about a third of the value that the produce garnered in Mérida or Yucatán's henequen estates. Now, however, teachers managed exchanges between consumer/producer cooperatives in a statewide network. Producer cooperatives shared granaries (often nationalized churches) and voted when to sell maize in democratic assemblies. Tax exemptions allowed peasants to earn more for their crop. Cooperatives also pooled resources to buy cattle and pigs. Consumer cooperatives cut the price of staples; beef consumption tripled as indigenous cowboys herded cattle. Campeche's cooperatives were comparatively free of corruption and reflected peasant opinion. Some profits, for instance, went into communal funds to pay for medicine and school infrastructure.[17] This cooperative economy, the SEP hoped, would create a new consciousness. Cooperative names invoked patriotic heroes but also abstract ideals—*La Lucha, La Libertad*—suggesting how new economic realities could reconfigure social relations: cooperatives would cut client-patron ties to *mestizo* merchants, class consciousness and nationalism would supersede localism. *Mestizos* legitimized their superiority through a racialist ideology stigmatizing Maya traits and practices, but, for the SEP, ethnic inequality was just a product of the economic structure.[18]

Third, federal teachers followed national policy in rejecting bilingual education and considering the spread of Spanish as a form of nationalist modernization. Replacing indigenous languages, teaching Mexican history and geography, and spreading Western norms of housing, clothing, and recreation were also part of SEP doctrine.[19]

Fourth, SEP plans included a new sense of community knitted together by collective values and symbols. Yet revolutionary "martyrs" were not the same as saints, and replacing Catholicism as social cement proved harder than removing it. Attempting to do so, one prominent educator, Luis Espinosa, advocated the modification, not eradication, of Christianity. The SEP had no use for Catholicism's formal structure, rituals, and social policy (one inspector harangued recalcitrant Catholics on "the Ills that [religions] have caused in every epoch").[20] Espinosa too, took a dim view of religion as practised—its myths oppressed "our race," he charged, and religious traffickers extorted high fees. Others blamed alcoholism on the Church.[21] Visual propaganda matched the anticlerical rhetoric: classroom murals depicted the clergy's nefarious influence and described Catholicism as part of a "general colonial ideology."[22]

But for Espinosa, cooperatives and socialist education had strong similarities to what he termed "Primitive Christianity." Espinosa's vision enriched Christ's teachings with Marxism. "Primitive Christianity," rescued from millennia of Church distortion, would create an egalitarian, collective mindset. Espinosa interpreted the Sermon on the Mount—in which Christ told that the meek shall inherit the earth—from the perspective of historical materialism. He also looked to the Church's utopian thinkers, from Christian humanist Thomas More—who coined the term—to the Dominican, Tommaso Campanella, who ran afoul of the Inquisition for advocating empiricism and penned the utopian work, *The City of the Sun* (1602). For Espinosa, these were socialism's Christian forerunners. Historically, however, the "militant" Church—the Church of crusaders, *conquistadores*, and Inquisitors—had buried such radicalism by persecuting "heretical and secret primitive Christian organizations": these included the underground early Church, reform movements like the Cathars, and early Protestant movements like the Hussites. "Primitive Christianity" could refer, too, to the early Church martyrs, who were models for persecuted utopian Christian communities from the sixteenth-century Anabaptists in Germany to contemporary Catholic progressives. Here Espinosa's ideas paralleled those of other revolutionary anticlericals, like Francisco Múgica and Vicente Lombardo Toledano, who opposed the Church but believed Jesus was the first socialist. Campeche, Espinosa believed, would be the first place to realize his "Christian Socialism" or "utopian Socialism."[23]

Espinosa's ideas elaborated the belief, widespread in the SEP, that teachers were the secular equivalents of colonial missionary friars. From inception, the SEP often compared itself to the Franciscan order. Sixteenth-century Franciscans were inspired by a millennial vision of the Americas, believing indigenous people to be soft wax easily molded into perfect Christians.[24]

Vasconcelos's choice of the term "Cultural Missions"—to describe SEP teams charged with manufacturing ideal revolutionary citizens—thus harked back to the early missionaries who ministered to the indigenous. The friar trope was favored by teachers. Claudio Cortés spoke of "spiritually conquering" remote communities.[25] Fernando Ximello encouraged Yucatán teachers to perform "a mission similar to that undertaken by the Franciscans."[26] And of course, friars, like teachers, were not just agents of change—they believed in destroying false idols.

Espinosa's admiration for select Christian elements seems counterintuitive. After all, that epitome of revolutionary anticlericalism, Tomás Garrido Canabal, desired the extirpation of religious sentiment and a complete disenchantment of the world, so that a materialist and secular-nationalist worldview went unchallenged.[27] Religion and modernizing revolutions like Mexico's are often thought of as diametrically opposed. Yet, as anthropologist Donald Donham argues in the case of revolutionary Ethiopia, evangelical Christians could become ardent supporters of an avowedly Marxist revolution. While modernist and Christian narratives of the future can be read as diametrically opposed, they can also be reconciled at certain historical moments.[28] Espinosa's ideas, while not fully developed or systematically implemented, seemed to offer a way of doing just that.

Comparing SEP strategy with the best-known example of colonial utopianism—Vasco de Quiroga's Santa Fé hospital on the banks of Lake Pátzcuaro—sheds more light on Espinosa's Christian Socialism. Quiroga combined religious conversion and austere observance with vocational training in agriculture and crafts. Like Espinosa, he looked to More: in Santa Fé, surplus from communal herds and harvests was set aside for all, and the young were taught Christian moral doctrine; the social order provided for health, education, and subsistence.[29] This model was broadly recreated by the SEP's peasant cooperatives, which underwrote schools and public health programs. Similarly, the SEP hoped to "convert" peasants, inculcating a modern, class-conscious mentality, flattening social and ethnic inequality, and creating communal surpluses via cooperatives. The ENR-H, run as something of a commune by student-faculty government, trained pupils in agricultural methods before sending them to rural schools to form "small agricultural communities."[30] Both the SEP and Quiroga stressed work and community, then, but Santa Fé ultimately aimed to help its members reach heaven. There was no equivalent salvific transcendence for the SEP, which stressed mundane redemption. Though Espinosa's was a positive revolutionary appropriation of Christianity—we are far way from the parodic religiosity of *garridista* iconoclasm, for example—it was nonetheless fundamentally secular in that it focused on the humanistic, not the divine, aspects of colonial Christian tradition. Espinosa's Christ was a revolutionary man, not a supernatural God. If there was any room at all for spiritual consolation in Espinosa's vision, then this must occur privately, in the individual conscience, where it could not be mistaken for politically reactionary religious "fanaticism."

The problem was not just how to replace Christianity's promised salvation. As Paul Vanderwood argues, popular Catholicism also offered Mexicans codes of morality and sociability.[31] Blending Christianity and Marxism approximated a revolutionary ethics; but when it came to replacing the religious festival with its fireworks, confraternity (*gremios*), rum, *bombas*, and occasional cross-dressing, the SEP was at a disadvantage. SEP cultural programs offered mainly what Bantjes describes as the revolutionary nationalist creed: "Cultural" and "Red Sundays," propagandistic plays, political boilerplate, music, and poetry.[32] In the case of music, the new canon took. Campeche peasants learned songs—"El Himno Agrarista," "Sol Redondo y Colorado," "Bandera Roja"—taught by *normalistas*. Sports spread, but the ideological message was not always clear to players. School civic observances also provide insights into revolutionary symbolism's limits. Schools honored Mexico's patriotic heroes, and specifically Campeche's hero against the Empire, Pablo García, who was celebrated by Cortés as embodying Vasconcelos' "cosmic race": "he was not a member of any of the pure races into which skin color divides the human race."[33] Nationalistic exaltations of *mestizaje*, however, precluded a symbolic source that was potentially more meaningful to indigenous students: the Maya.

Teachers, unlike friars, eschewed mastering indigenous languages and folkways. Outsiders were often patronizing toward indigenous *campechanos*. Samuel Pérez, head of the ENR-H-based Cultural Mission in 1934, bemoaned the "infantile mentality of the Maya Indian, where psychologically the instincts of combativeness and exhibitionism dominate."[34] Native *campechanos* also had blind spots. Ramón Berzunza Pinto, the Communist Party and teaching union leader, criticized leftists for using slogans and techniques formulated nationally for "indigenous peoples in general," without adapting these to the language, social organization, and culture of specific groups.[35] SEP *indigenismo* exalted an abstract indigenous past as a font of national identity, but advocated modernization on the state's terms as indigenous people's only future. The failure to syncretize revolutionary and specifically Maya culture was a missed opportunity.

The Politics of Anticlericalism

As it was, SEP plans for a new communal ideology hinged on checking Church influence. Defanaticization was not mere iconoclasm, but the first step toward a brave new world free of *caciques* and *curas*. By mid-1934 the national political situation favored a frontal attack on the Church: after the Nunkiní debacle, local SEP leaders likewise probably believed that their future political success required a direct attack on the Church. Lázaro Cárdenas also visited the ENR-H in March, Garrido's star was still rising, and in October, garrison commander Francisco Múgica spoke to teachers and confirmed their belief: only an "open attack" on the Church would suffice. After that, resistance would crumble and society could be remade.[36] No wonder, then, that the archbishop of Yucatán compared the rural federal teacher to nothing less than an "anti-priest."[37]

Constitutionally, curbing the Church required PSA support, because only state governments could legislate on religious practice.[38] In the past, the PSA had unenthusiastically supported anticlerical measures,[39] but national authorities were now leaning on states. Under pressure, Governor Benjamín Romero Esquivel and the PSA adopted a jacobin line.[40]

Between 21 June and 21 September 1934, Romero, the legislature, and officials churned out laws, circulars, and extra-legal directives against the Church. They reduced the number of priests to five then three, and prevented bishop and clergy from practising in all but a handful of churches—meaning most of Campeche's population was denied the sacraments. Folk religious festivals, like that of the Virgen of Carmen (Palizada) were suspended to spare the population religion's "brutifying effect." On 1 August, state police fined women catechists 500 pesos for trying to enter churches to teach children. This, coupled with a September law restricting parish education, crippled religious schooling. Priests had to pay a "professional" tax; municipalities charged four to eight pesos for church wedding permits; and priests had to marry in order to minister. The state government shuttered almost all churches on 21 September. Exploiting a legal loophole, Romero refused to turn churches over to neighborhood councils as required, blocking lay access. By September, Romero could write to President Rodríguez that the laws would "liberate the working masses from religious prejudices and harms." Calculation, not conviction, lay behind his reforms. Worst of all, unlike many states—where priests dodged the law with official connivance—there was no margin for extra-legal religious practice in Campeche until anticlericalism was reigned in nationally in March 1936.[41] Carmen's only priest was expelled in December 1934, and remaining clergy soon followed. One priest who tried to return from exile in Yucatán was jailed.[42]

Catholic resistance was initially directed by a female, middle-class leadership, which used petitions, discrete lobbying, and legal avenues. To no avail: state and federal officials each said that only the other could act, and as long as Múgica and Mexico City threatened, the PSA governor would not buck national policy. Back-channel pressure on the governor, which might have led to concessions (as in Yucatán), never happened. The upper class had decamped to Mérida with Bishop Guízar and there was no *cristero* war, reflecting a lack of military options and the Church's emphasis on peaceful resistance. A petition gathered thousands of signatures and observers noted "much agitation" among some peasants; there were apparently fatal clashes in Hecelchakan and Campeche.[43] Thus Catholics would find ways to resist, but their responses were regionally distinct.

Regional Responses to Anticlericalism

Anticlericalism provoked widespread resistance. In the south, historically more churched, the SEP floundered. Here popular recalcitrance discouraged teachers, many of whom lacked the preparation and will for defanaticizing.

A saint burning (*quemasantos*) scheduled for Revolution Day 1934 was canceled because teachers and officials balked, and the population refused to turn over religious statuary.[44] That November, the south's embattled inspector, Francisco Ovalle, condemned the "adverse social environment," which meant little was achieved.[45] The SEP never grasped why resistance was so much stiffer in the southernmost municipalities of Palizada and Carmen.[46] Sweeping geographical generalizations are risky; Alan Knight argues that while regional differences are often pronounced, all political culture is essentially local.[47] Certainly, Bolonchenticul was a Catholic "island" in the indifferent northern *municipio* of Hopelchen, while the *cabecera* of Palizada was more liberal than surrounding villages.[48] Still, the pattern of a "Catholic" south and an internally divided north generally holds true.

Regional differences provide important insights into Church-state conflict. At the top of society, a similar picture emerges both north and south—it was bourgeois, lay women who led initial Catholic resistance. In Carmen, it was Josefa de la Cebada de Azcue and "well-known society *señoras* and *señoritas*."[49] Unlike the north, though, where there were descending gender, ethnic, and class divisions, all social strata in south Campeche joined a united front. Probably three factors contributed to this. First, class difference was less exacerbated by ethnic inequality (the south lacked henequen haciendas that brutalized indigenous labor).[50] Second, southern Campeche's politico-economic elites struggled bitterly against the PSA's forerunner in the early 1920s, leading revolutionaries to turn on "reactionaries" linked to the south's *chicle* economy. In 1922 in Carmen, socialists murdered José María Roura (scion of a distinguished family); in 1923, Senator Field of Palizada was killed in Mexico City.[51] Third, a community of exiles from Garrido's Tabasco arrived in Carmen by the mid-1930s.[52] Their experience of Mexico's most clerophobic regime hardened local views of SEP projects.

In the north, however, SEP campaigns gained more ground. True, the northern middle class, women, and (ironically) many teachers—again, women especially—resisted. But among the Mayan-speaking, especially male peasantry, the link between defanaticization and economic change (via cooperativism) gave the SEP a community foothold. By the time radicals assumed leadership of the SEP in Campeche in 1934, teachers had linked dozens of agricultural, milling, and ranching cooperatives in the Confederation of Revolutionary Cooperatives.[53]

Successful cooperatives enabled Communist federal teachers to connect real economic benefits to anticlericalism. The priest who charged for his sacraments was just another exploiter—like the miller who overcharged for corn-grinding, and the store-owner who speculated in grain. Religious and festive expenditure, teachers also argued, was better invested in schooling and the cooperatives.[54] SEP discourse overlaid the interlocking political, socioeconomic, and ideological bases of inequality. The same bilingual *mestizo* families owned community mills, stores, and ranches, supported the Church, patronized the seminary, and benefited from festive expenditure on alcohol. The SEP's problem, as a federal agency, was that these notables also controlled the PSA. Indeed, as local delegates the PSA usually designated the *cacique*, municipal president, or *diputado* in what one inspector called "*señoritismo*" (lordshipism).[55] The communism embraced by teachers advocated an assault on exploitation on all fronts;[56] SEP thus denounced an alliance between the provincial bourgeoisie, the Church, and "false" PSA socialists. When teachers attacked "feudalism" and the clergy's role in it, peasants understood this not as an abstract concept but a realistic description of their community, even if dislike for individual priests did not necessarily translate into repudiation of the Church.

The 1935 Gubernatorial Campaign: The Catholic-Socialist Alliance Triumphs

Given the ties between the Church and the northern elite, SEP success pivoted on breaking the PSA stranglehold on Campeche's politics. Fortunately, the 1935 gubernatorial election was contested by Angli Lara. This was still a risky strategy, as the SEP officially prohibited teachers from political involvement. However, Ramon Berzunza Pinto, a young firebrand and recent ENR-H graduate, unabashedly used the leftist Bloque de Maestros Revolucionarios to back Angli Lara.[57] And the candidate seemingly enjoyed the right connections in Mexico City: Múgica was Cárdenas's secretary of communications and public works, and Angli Lara also counted on the support of Agriculture Secretary Garrido, anticlericalism incarnate.[58]

Between Angli Lara and the governorship, however, stood the longtime arbiter of Campeche politics, a diminutive ex-tailor and federal congressman known as Campeche's *Jefe Mínimo*: Angel Castillo Lanz.[59] Castillo Lanz ordered Governor Romero to throw the PSA machine behind a rival candidate, Eduardo Mena Córdoba.[60] Castillo Lanz's control over Campeche City and the south also remained firm, hence to triumph, Angli Lara needed to win decisively in the north.[61] Unfortunately, the small-time PSA bosses who controlled elections there resented and feared federal teachers and cooperatives, so they eagerly backed Mena.

Campeche Catholics also bitterly opposed Angli because of his SEP ties and involvement in the Nunkiní incident. Mena Córdoba's wife, moreover, led Campeche's Damas Católicas union, lending credibility to her husband's back-channel appeal to Catholics.[62] The *voto morado*, or Catholic vote, provided an unlikely but potent source of support for PSA militants battling federal teachers for northern Campeche's soul.[63]

Four important local PSA leaders personified the hybrid nature of Mena's Catholic-Socialist coalition: Ignacio Reyes Ortega, Manuel J. Mex, Juan Barbosa, and José León Montero. Like most regional revolutionary parties, the PSA depended on such *caciques* in rural areas. These bosses, furthermore, were the product of a conservative political organization only nominally committed to anticlericalism. Conformity with national policy was unlikely, then, as there was no cadre of party intellectuals or a partisan press to instill radical values, as there was with regional revolutionary parties like Yucatán's Partido Socialista del Sureste.

Reyes Ortega was a confidant of the *Jefe Mínimo* and the perennial *cacique* of Calkiní, a northern *municipio* where he alternated as mayor or congressman. Reyes helped found the PSA in Calkiní as a young man in 1921, promised to build huts for migrants, and managed the fund for an electrical plant. Linked to a handful of *mestizo* families who monopolized economic and political power for decades, Reyes was barely literate in Spanish but spoke fluent Maya. He used such cultural capital advantageously to build a following among Maya-speakers. While not particularly pious, Reyes Ortega was brother-in-law of the influential priest, Lorenzo García Ortega; the federal school's location in Calkiní's ex-convent, and its decoration with nationalist and *indigenista* murals, also antagonized prominent families linked to the Church, as did the foundation of a masonic lodge, perhaps by Angli Lara. To challenge Angli Lara, Reyes Ortega assembled a network of state-controlled teachers and policemen to mobilize Catholics in places like Bacabchen and Sahcabchen, warning that federal teachers were planning another *quemasantos* should Angli win. In 1936, Reyes invaded Hecelchakán, rang the church bells, and summoned a mob to tear down the ENR-H's red flag, a symbolic and intimidating assault on this bulwark of leftist teachers.[64]

Another leader of the Socialist-Catholic force was Manuel J. Mex, a PSA apparatchik whose base was the party's charcoal and firewood cooperative. Unlike SEP cooperatives, this was run by political cronies who exploited its monopoly status for profit. Its economic leverage was considerable, because wood-gathering was one of Campeche's few growth industries. During the *Cristiada*, Mex—as PSA secretary general—telegraphed party support to Calles for "enforcing our laws that the clergy tried to trample."[65] But by the 1930s, Mex was an important lay Catholic serving on ACM's Campeche directorate, a demanding, potentially risky, position. Mex's road to Damascus experience probably resulted from the SEP's political threat and anticlerical policies. In opposing federal schools, Mex worked closely with another veteran Socialist, Bernabé "Box-To" Euán of Pomuch. A revolutionary who had fought *huertismo* in Campeche, Euán was a PSA founder in 1920, serving as Pomuch's mayor and *diputado suplente*. Euán started a boycott of Nunkiní's SEP school when the teacher demanded students—including his son—don red shirts, an anticlerical symbol of Garrido's.[66] Because of this association, red shirts symbolized atheism to most Mexican Catholics; given the SEP's invasion of Nunkiní's church, the symbolism would have been even more ominous.[67]

In Hecechakán, Mena's support was spearheaded by Juan Barbosa Barahona, a PSA *cacique* of 14-years' standing and general secretary of the state's National Revolutionary Party (PNR) branch. Barbosa's group had fought the ENR-H for years. As with Mex and Euán, his allies included Catholics and PSA powerbrokers for whom the struggle against the SEP and Angli Lara involved spiritual and material stakes. Barbosa's clique included a state congressman; a *curandero* (natural healer) whose business was ruined by the ENR-H's resident doctor; and a *cantina* owner who resented SEP prohibitionism. These old Socialists were allied with—often part of—the extended families of *mestizo* merchants and butchers that SEP-run cooperatives undercut. These clans—Ortega, Vera, Mendoza, Ortegón and Ruiz—demanded the reopening of Hecelchakán's church, a resacralization that imperiled the ENR-H existentially. Barbosa, meanwhile, raised the specter of another *quemasantos*, convincing peasant women to join local notables against federal teachers and Angli Lara.[68]

José León Montero was another old Socialist *cacique* in northern Campeche. He owned the only corn-mill in his hometown of Becal (Calkiní); his maternal kin, the Monteros, were prosperous ranchers and fervent Catholics. Becal's federal school and associated cooperative threatened an economic and political dominance dating from the Revolution. In spite of his long association with the PSA (not least as mayor, 1929–31), León was an active Catholic and quite literally the standard-bearer of his *gremio*. Not surprisingly, León led the fight against SEP teachers from 1934; during the 1935 campaign, he helped turn out the vote for Mena Córdoba by stoking Catholic resentment of federal teachers.[69]

Across northern Campeche, Socialist bosses ably played on Catholic fears (only Ricardo Marentes of Tenabo fought the SEP on purely secular grounds). They also capitalized on personal or family ties to religious organization to build strong support for Mena Córdoba.[70] The combination of clientelism and fear of cooperativism and anticlericalism was politically potent. This incorporation of Catholic groups into PSA political bases was not the kind of corporatism that the ruling party had in mind. Of course, Catholicism in northern Campeche towns was not just about spiritual matters—given the *mestizo* notables' cultural investment in the Church, to defend Catholicism was also to defend local privilege.

Catholics alone did not win the election for Mena Córdoba. The *Jefe Mínimo* and Mena himself bribed electoral observers sent from Mexico City; Mena Córdoba also cultivated the favor of Cárdenas's key political operative, Emilio Portes Gil, countering Angli Lara's national patrons. The PSA used police and civil courts to cow federal teachers, and imported voters from Yucatán by train and Tabasco by boat. Still, the religious factor should not be discounted, nor was it just a rural phenomenon. In Campeche City, Mena's promise to reopen the churches turned out Catholic voters and provided a significant share of his votes. In the end, Angli's federal teachers and cooperativists lost everywhere outside their Hecelchakán stronghold. They bombarded Mexico City with well-founded complaints of intimidation and fraud (an embittered Angli Lara denounced Campeche's "fanatics and reactionaries"),[71] and without Catholic votes it might have proved impossible to convince Mexico City to sanction Mena Córdoba's disputed victory.

In spite of the role Catholics played in his election, Mena Córdoba reneged on his promise to open churches. Like Romero before him, he blamed Mexico City for the delay, and for several months continued to expel returning priests.[72] On 4 March 1936, Cárdenas declared that the federal government would no longer make anticlericalism a priority. Five days later, Campeche's Catholics physically occupied and reopened many of the city's churches, and Cárdenas ordered no action to dislodge them. After a bloody clash in Guanajuato on 29 March, restrictions on the Church relaxed across the nation. Priests slowly returned; processions of holy images resumed.[73] Over the next few years, state and federal courts dismantled anticlerical legislation on grounds of unconstitutionality—now that the president had made his opinion clear. By 1940, 9 legal, and at least 26 extra-legal, priests practised in Campeche.[74]

In spite of Mena Córdoba's broken promise, the alliance between Socialist politicos and Catholics against federal teachers in northern Campeche persisted. Several priests endorsed Mena Córdoba's candidates over their leftist opponents in municipal elections in December 1936. Clergy reportedly preached from the pulpit that should the governor's candidates not prevail, the churches would be closed again. Plainclothed state policemen protected a Catholic demonstration against federal teachers.[75] In the elections, Catholics again played a key role in helping a rickety Socialist machine defeat leftist teachers and their peasant allies.

The Socialist machine and its Catholic allies continued to battle federal teachers and *cooperativistas* through 1937, even after Catholic services resumed. Cárdenas himself visited Campeche in July 1937 to negotiate a truce between the Mena Córdoba/PSA *camarilla* and the leftist group led by federal teachers; in return for the governor's acceptance of land reform and his concession of two seats in congress, federal teachers had to desist from attacks on Mena Córdoba.[76] Bled by the left's efforts, however, the PSA splintered fatally when Mena Córdoba and Castillo Lanz split in 1938. A cynic would conclude that the *cardenista* regime kept leftist teachers just strong enough to smash the PSA, but too weak to take power in Campeche. In any event, an outsider—dentist and alleged Communist, Hector Pérez Martínez—prevailed in the 1939 gubernatorial election, breaking the PSA at state-level forever with the help of the leftist organizations set up by federal teachers. SEP teachers now received a *cuota de poder*—their share of power— but lost their role as peasants' independent advocates. Instead they were absorbed into the consolidating national political system and expanding bureaucracy.

Caciquismo and Popular Catholicism

Socialist *caciques'* success in mobilizing against defanaticization presents an interesting paradox. Nationally, the strongest resistance to anticlericalism came in "Levitical" towns where the Church educated future elites, standardized religious practice, instilled obedience to clerical authority, and ensured that Catholicism was deeply ingrained in everyday life—in everything from bell-ringing to processions in public.[77] The history of Campeche Catholicism remains to be written, but it seems that the Socialist-Catholic alliance did nothing to make Campeche more "Levitical." In fact, it could be argued that its rise delayed, perhaps even weakened, the centralization of Church authority and the creation of Mexican Catholic Action (ACM) chapters.

To be sure, even before the *Cristiada*, Campeche was known as less than pious.[78] Yucatecans considered *campechanos* nearly agnostic.[79] As late as 1934, a conservative national paper called Campeche an "eternal bulwark of Liberalism";[80] and for Pascual Díaz it was a "diocese where for years disdain for religion has existed."[81] In fact, institutional weakness, not innate social traits, explain *campechanos*' distance from Church influence. Simply, Campeche diocese was young, small, and poor. Belatedly created in 1895 (37 years after Campeche state), it resulted not from geographical logic or grassroots demands but the efforts of Porfirian strongman Joaquín Barranda.[82] Campeche had no less than six bishops from 1895–1938; all were outsiders (non-Maya speakers) and most from the Bajío; two died after less than a year, the rest moved on as soon as something more prestigious opened up.[83] Frequent episcopal turnovers meant the diocese lacked strong leadership during periods of crisis.[84] Francisco González (1922–31), in exile during the *Cristiada*, adopted a conciliatory political attitude that reflected his personality but also diocesan weakness.[85] Luis Guízar (1932–38), another moderate, was prevented from visiting his diocese by *Maximato*-era restrictions in 1932. When he managed to visit the remote Chenes in 1933, he contracted malaria and spent much of 1934 exiled in Mérida.

A weak Mitre left the clergy loosely supervised, thus unlikely to tow the hierarchy's line. Moreover, priests were few and clustered in the largest towns: Champotón, Campeche, Carmen. In 1934, eight priests tended the entire flock; just one, Lorenzo García Ortega, covered northern Campeche (25 churches).[86] Campeche's clergy opposed revolutionary reforms almost uniformly. Friendship and kinship linked priests to *mestizo* elites threatened politically by the Angli-SEP group and economically by cooperatives.[87] Another sign of the Church's institutional weakness can be found in clerical toleration of folk Catholic rites that preserved significant pre-Conquest elements. In the Chenes, one priest used Mayan beliefs in order to teach Christianity.[88] The easy-going, numerically sparse clergy, combined with the syncretic nature of local Catholicism, produced a most un-Levitical region.[89] The clergy was also exiled during the formative period of the Catholic-Socialist alliance, so could not have been its catalyst.

Moreover, the end of normal sacramental life (1934) was, in itself, insufficient to drive Catholics into confrontation with the SEP. Rather, two other measures—banning clerical masses during village festivals, the closing of churches—were needed to push outraged Catholics into political mobilization. Mayan peasants saw priests not as unquestioned authorities, but as valued specialists in the supernatural without whom festivals were incomplete. Without access to churches—and the sacred images sheltered there—the festival lacked its umbilical connection to the sacred. No wonder that many in Hool, a central community, were distressed when a priest was barred from the annual fiesta and a schoolteacher acted to prevent the traditional pilgrimage in honor of its Virgin.[90] Indeed, Catholics objected to the seizure of churches almost as much as the barring of priests. Legally, the governor should have turned church keys over to *juntas de vecinos* (neighborhood parish administration committees) when the churches closed on 22 September 1934. Official flouting of the law was an added insult to Catholics.[91] Palizada—a center of Catholic resistance—repeatedly begged for the church keys so as to celebrate the festival of the Virgen of Carmen.[92]

Such grievances, combined with failed negotiations with the upper rungs of the PSA, pushed Catholics into Socialist *caciques'* arms. Simultaneously, clerical deportations created a vacuum that lay *mestizo* elites filled. Already *gremio* leaders, male *mestizos'* authority was built up by Bishop Guízar. In October 1934, Guízar organized all male, mainly *mestizo* committees in 22 large communities in an attempt to take possession of churches by forming *juntas de vecinos*. The Church's broader strategy was to rely on lay notables to oversee the spiritual life during postrevolutionary religious crises.[93] During Lent in 1933, Guízar oversaw "an intense religious movement" in Campeche cathedral that brought men to church, "in spite of the traditional idea . . . that religion is something only for weak-willed women."[94]

If Church strategy empowered a provincial lay elite, so did anticlericalism. Restrictions on the clergy's number, movement, and operations led the well-to-do to shelter priests in their homes, another source of social capital for *mestizo* notables. In 1931, the elite in Carmen were confident enough to open the doors while services were conducted, and to parade religious images outside.[95] The clergy needed elite laity, then, but feared laypeople's religious control during their absence. After the end of *garridismo*, the Tabasco hierarchy was dismayed by the "frightening relaxation in Church discipline." When sacramental celebrations in private homes stopped, complaints ensued: "more than a few people stubbornly want mass where they want, at the time they want."[96] Graham Greene, who attended clandestine masses in Las Casas (Chiapas), said of the housewife in whose home the service took place, "[y]ou could detect a touch of pride, of condescension, because she had sheltered God in her house. One person at least would feel regret and disappointment if the mass were ever celebrated again in the churches."[97] When *campechanos* assumed leadership over the religious life, they reaped a socio-spiritual windfall with which some parted reluctantly. Socialist *caciques'* zeal in championing the Catholic cause should also be understood, in part, as a defense of new lay religious prerogatives.

Conclusion

In the end, defanaticization went out like a lamb and the churches reopened some 20 months after Nunkiní. But the campaign had unanticipated long-term affects on Campeche Catholicism. The 1934–36 crackdown interrupted, perhaps crippled, one of the most important transformations in Mexican

Church history. The hierarchy hoped that ACM—a lay organization with separate branches for men and women recruited mainly from the middle class—would help the Church address the "social question" and spread orthodox practice among peasants.[98] In the early 1930s, the bishop and a few priests made ACM top priority,[99] yet the ban on lay catechists prevented it from reaching peasants.[100] Draconian restrictions on the clergy in 1934 further weakened the movement: subsequently, only one ACM local council was constituted, in 1938, two years after the thaw.[101] Luis Bustos, probably the key lay organizer of ACM, visited Campeche in 1941 and blamed its poor condition (young men in particular were "completely lost") on lack of clergy; priests could barely meet sacramental demands, much less the demanding organizational task of forming ACM cadres. This, Bustos speculated, left the field open to leftist ideas.[102] The end of harsh restrictions sparked an outburst of religious fervor, albeit short-lived. The number of diocesan clergy dropped from a 1939 high of 35 to only 11 in 1944. This time, the dramatic fall was due to apathy not anticlericalism. Only six other dioceses in Mexico—mostly peripheral jurisdictions in the deep south or north—had a lower ratio of priests to faithful.[103] Defanaticization provoked widespread opposition, followed by a Catholic "bounce": during this fervent period, the laity supported relatively large numbers of priests—there was probably a pent up demand for baptisms and marriages—before Campeche's religious life regressed to the mean.

Ironically, the rise of a Socialist-Catholic alliance not only frustrated the political center in terms of secular postrevolutionary politics; it also set back the ecclesiastical center's attempt to use ACM and other subordinating strategies to make the state more "Levitical." *Campechano* Catholics' unwillingness (or inability) to support many clergymen—a logical proxy for orthodox Catholicism—clearly confirms this. This does not mean Campeche was less "Catholic" per se; rather that it was unwilling to give up its regionally specific religious practices at the behest of Rome or the episcopate. *Campechanos* treasured their traditional folk-Catholic celebrations, which economically benefited rural *caciques* and seemed "superstitious" and "fanatical" to federal teachers. Their undesirability on such grounds was one of the few points of agreement shared by the SEP and the institutional, clerical Church.

Politically, the Campeche case shows not just the unpopularity of anticlericalism, but how recalcitrant Catholics could make common cause with regional revolutionaries who wanted to keep Mexico City at arm's length for different reasons. Campeche's unlikely coalition combined the casting of ballots with the casting of stones, showing how there was no single Catholic resistance strategy but many regionalized resistance repertoires. Campeche's Socialist-Catholic alliance differed significantly in ideology, tactics, and achievement compared to other regional examples, such as the *Segunda* ("Second" *Cristiada*, 1932–40) in the Bajío, the school strikes organized by Church front organizations across Mexico, and the mass Hispanicist movement of *sinarquismo*. Finally, Campeche's Catholic-Socialist alliance shows the risk of analyzing conflicts over religion only in cultural terms. Focusing exclusively on the dramatic, symbolic, and aesthetic in Catholicism (or anti-clericalism) can be just as simplistic as reducing them to superstructure.[104] Cooperatives converted peasants to SEP projects partly through economic appeal; *mestizo caciques* defended the Church for reasons not purely spiritual. Campeche's 1930s Church-state conflict stands as one example of how Catholic belief affects, and in turn is affected by, political and economic interests and social status.

Notes

1. "Puntos Concretos sobre la Persecución Religosa en el Edo. de Yucatán desde el Año de 1926 a Julio 13 de 1935," Archivo Histórico del Secretariado Social Mexicana, Conflictos Religiosos (AHSSM); Archivo General de la Nación, Dirección General de Gobierno (AGN/DGG) 2.340.24.12, Luis Guízar to Gobernación, 18 Aug. 1934; Carlos Sierra, *Dicionario Biográfico de Campeche* (Mexico City: La Muralla, 1997), 16; Alicia Gómez Montejo, *Las H. Juntas Municipales del Estado de Campeche. Una Breve Descripción* (Campeche: Congreso del Estado, 2002), 50–1. Archivo Histórico de la Secretaría de Educación Pública (AHSEP), Campeche, c. 20/exp. 70, Luis Alvarez to Ignacio García, 8 Mar. 1935. The author gratefully acknowledges a Charles A. Ryskamp/ACLS fellowship in 2002–03 that made this research possible.
2. AHSEP-Campeche, Claudio Cortés, 30 Apr. 1934, c. 21/exp. 5960.
3. Archivo Accíon Católica (AAC), exp. 2.10.1, Luis Bustos, "Informe de Visita a Dioceses de Campeche y Tabasco," 6 Apr. 1941. Moisés de la Peña, *Campeche Economico* (2 vols. Campeche: Gobierno del Estado, 1942) 1:1–42. Mario Aranda González, *El Municipio de Calkiní* (Campeche, 1981) 48, 65–6; José Alberto Abud Flores, *Campeche: Revolución y Movimiento Social (1911–1923)* (Campeche: INEHRM, 1992), 52.
4. AHSEP-Campeche, c. 1802/exp. 8, Inspector 2° zone, 2 Aug. 1933.
5. AHSSM, "Puntos concretos"; AGN/DGG 2.340.24.12, Guízar to Gobernación, 18 Aug. 1934; Sierra, *Dicionario*, 16.
6. Mary Kay Vaughan, *Cultural Politics in Revolution: Teachers, Peasants, and Schools in Mexico, 1930–1940* (Tuscon: University of Arizona Press, 1997), 46.
7. AHSEP-Misiones Culturales (MC), c. 22, Claudio Cortés to Inspectors, 24 Jan. 1933.
8. Román Piña Chán, *Enciclopedia Histórica de Campeche. Tomo IV. De la Revolución a la Epoca Moderna, 1911–1961* (Mexico City: Porrúa, 2003), 79, 87–8.
9. De la Peña, *Campeche Economico*, 1:45.
10. Andres Uc Dzib, "La Escuela Rural, una Nueva Escuela de la Epoca de Oro de la Educación en México," in *Los Maestros y la Cultura Nacional, 1920–1952*, ed. Engracia Loyo, Cecilia Greaves, and Valentina Torres (Mexico City: SEP, 1987), 5:17–25. AHSEP-Campeche, c. 20, *Informe*, Jul. 1933; AHSEP-MC, 5963/18, *Informe*, Jul. 1932; Sierra, *Diccionario*, 19.
11. Rodolfo López Sosa, *Tarjeta Presidencial* (Mérida: Guerra, 1952), 9.
12. AHSEP-Campeche, c. 47/exp. 20, Claudio Cortés, *Informe*, Jul. 1932.
13. [Luis] Amendolla, *La Revolución Comienza a los Cuarenta* (Mexico City, n.d.), 98.

14. Marío Aranda González, *Hecelchakán: Historia, Geografía, Cultura* (Campeche: CONACULTA, 2003), 134; Marío Aranda González, *Masonería en el Estado de Campeche* (Campeche, 1990), 31–4.

15. Cf. Carlos Martínez Assad, *El Laboratorio de la Revolución: El Tabasco Garridista* (Mexico City: Siglo XXI, 1979), 129–155.

16. AHSEP-Campeche, c. 21/exp. 5960, Claudio Cortés, 30 Apr. 1934.

17. AGN-Lázaro Cárdenas, 521.7.110, Governor Romero to Francisco Avalos. AHSEP-Campeche, c. 21/exp. 68, Samuel Pérez, 15 Jan. 1934; c. 1802/exp. 2, *acta*, Los Chenes; c. 1802/exp. 8, Rubén Rodríguez Lozano, 4 Jan. 1934. López, *Tarjeta Presidencial*, 10.

18. Here *mestizo* refers to a Hispanicized individual of European/indigenous descent, even though in Campeche *mestizo* refers to the Maya.

19. AHSEP-Campeche, c. 21/exp. 5960, Claudio Cortés, 30 Apr. 1934; c. 21/exp. 91, Gustavo Jarquín to Manuel Mesa, 29 Dec. 1934; c. 47/exp. 20, *Informe*, 1931–32.

20. AHSEP-Campeche, c. 1082/exp. 8, Francisco Ovalle, 9 Nov. 1934.

21. AHSEP-Campeche, c. 1802/exp. 5, Luis Espinosa, 19 Apr. 1934.

22. AHSEP-Campeche, c. 20/exp. 5, Luis Alvarez, Informe General Sintético, 10 Mar. 1935.

23. AHSEP-Campeche, c. 21/exp. 5960, Claudio Cortés, 30 Apr. 1934; c. 1802/exp. 5, Luis Espinosa Morales, 4 Feb. 1935. AGN/DGG, 2.340.24.12, Luis Guízar, 18 Aug. 1934. At Querétaro, Múgica called Christ the first democrat even as he lambasted the Church: Robert Quirk, *The Mexican Revolution and the Catholic Church, 1910–1929* (Bloomington: Indiana University Press, 1973) 90. Anna Peterson, *Seeds of the Kingdom: Utopian Communities in the Americas.* (New York: OUP, 2005), 5.

24. John Leddy Phelan, *The Millennial Kingdom of the Franciscans in the New World* (Berkeley: University of California Press, 1956).

25. AHSEP-Campeche, exp. 1, Claudio Cortés, *Informe*, 1927.

26. AHSEP-Yucatán, c. 1671, *Informes*, Fernando Ximello, 30 May 1933.

27. Adrian Bantjes, "Saints, Sinners, and State Formation," in *The Eagle and the Virgin: Nation and Cultural Revolution in Mexico, 1920–1940*, ed. Mary Kay Vaughan and Stephen Lewis (Durham: Duke University Press, 2005), 139.

28. Donald Donham, *Marxist Modern: An Ethnographic History of the Ethiopian Revolution* (Berkeley: University of California Press, 1999) 11.

29. Bernardino Verástique, *Michoacán and Eden: Vasco de Quiroga and the Evangelization of Western Mexico* (Austin: University of Texas Press, 2000), 124–40.

30. AHSEP-Campeche, c. 47/exp. 20, Claudio Cortés, *Informes*, Jul. 1932, 1931–32; AHSEP-MC, exp. s/n, Claudio Cortés, "Nueva Orientación," 18 Jan. 1933; Uc Dzib, "Escuela Rural," 5:18, 24–5; De la Peña, *Campeche Económico*, 1:45.

31. Paul Vanderwood, "Religion: Official, Popular and Otherwise," *Mexican Studies/Estudios Mexicanos* 16, no. 2 (2000): 434.

32. Bantjes, "Saints," 146.

33. AHSEP-Campeche, c. 47/exp. 20, Claudio Cortés, *Informe*, Jul. 1932.

34. AHSEP-Campeche, c. 21/exp. 68, Samuel Pérez, 15 Jan. 1934.

35. Ramón Berzunza Pinto, *Una Chispa en el Sureste* (Mexico City: La Cooperativa, 1942), 42.

36. AHSEP-Campeche, c. 21/exp. 49, Claudio Cortés, 24 Dec. 1934. AGN-Abelardo Rodríguez, 011/11, Múgica, 29 Jun. 1934; AGN/DGG 2.340.24.12, Guízar to Gobernación, 18 Aug. 1934; AHSEP-Campeche, c. 20, Claudio Cortés, 12 Dec. 1934.

37. AHSSM, "Arquiódiocesis de Yucatán. Contestación al Cuestionario No. 2," 9 Sep. 1935.

38. Peter Reich, *Mexico's Hidden Revolution: The Catholic Church in Law and Politics since 1929* (Notre Dame: University of Notre Dame Press, 1995).

39. Carlos Sierra, *Acción Gubernamental en Campeche, 1857–1960* (Mexico City: Impresión de Estampillas y Valores, 1972), 84–5.

40. *Desdeldiez* (1984), "Peninsula de Yucatán," 87–99. AHSSM, Banon Martínez, "ACONTECIMIENTOS VERIFICADOS EN QUERETARO EN EL MES DE OCTUBRE DE 1935, EN RELACION CON LA IGLESIA CATOLICA"; Records of the Department of State Relating to Internal Affairs of Mexico, 1930–39 (RDSRIAM), roll 43, Josephus Daniels, 13 Nov. 1935; Lorenzo Meyer, *Historia de la Revolucion Mexicana: Periodo 1928–1934* (Mexico City: Colmex, 1978) 178–80.

41. AGN/DGG, 2.340.25.1, Romero to Rodríguez, 23 Sep. 1934, Alfonso Castro to Cárdenas, 12 Dec. 1934 ; 2.340.24.12, Luis Guízar, 18 Aug. 1934; AGN-Abelardo Rodríguez, 514.3/3; *Ley Reglamentaria de Cultos del Estado de Campeche* (Campeche: Gobierno del Estado, 1934); Archivo Histórico del Arzobispado de México (AHAM), Pascual Díaz, c. 3/exp. 33; Murray Survey (MS), Martin Palmira to Paul Murray, 2 Jun. 1936. Thanks to Peter Reich for sharing this last document.

42. RDSRIAM, rolls 43 (Charles Taliaferro, 5 Dec. 1935) and 22 (Waldo Bailey, 30 Nov. 1934).

43. See n49, and: AGN/DGG, 2.340.24.12, Luis Guízar, 18 Aug. 1934, and Cristóbal Trapaga, 6 Oct. 1934; AGN/DGG, 2.340.25.1, Gobernación to Guízar, 3 Oct. 1934; AGN/DGG, 2.347(2).1(bis).7, Esteban García to Gobernación, 25 Sep. 1934; AGN/DGG, 2.340.25.1/25, various; AHSEP-Campeche, c. 1802/exp. 8, Francisco Ovalle, 9 Nov. 1934; AGN-Lázaro Cárdenas, 521.7/47.

44. AHSEP-Campeche, c. 1802/exp. 8, Francisco Ovalle, 9 Nov. 1934; c. 21/exp. 49, Claudio Cortés, 24 Dec. 1934; c. 20/exp. 70, Claudio Cortés, 12 Dec. 1934; Alvarez, "Informe General."

45. AHSEP-Campeche, c. 1802/exp. 8, Francisco Ovalle, 9 Nov. 1934.

46. AHSEP-Campeche, c. 21/exp. 5960, Claudio Cortés, 9 Apr. 1934.

47. Alan Knight, "Popular Culture and the Revolutionary State in Mexico, 1910–1940," *Hispanic American Historical Review* 74, no. 3 (1994): 438.

48. AHSEP-Campeche, c. 1802/exp. 8, Francisco Ovalle, 9 Nov. 1934; Mario Aranda González, *Apuntaciones Historicas y Literarias del Municipio de Hopelchen, Campeche* (Mérida: Maldonado, 1985), 188.

49. AGN/DGG, 2.340.25.1, Josefa de la Cebada to Gobernación, 14 Dec. 1934.

50. De la Peña, *Campeche Económico*, 1:18–29.

51. Archivo Plutarco Elías Calles, gav. 33/exp. 24/inv. 2115/ leg.1, Ramón Félix Flores, 12 Feb. 1923; AGN/DGG, 2.74.7. J. Certucha to Gobernación, 29 Jun., 1 Jul. 1922. Juan Bolívar, *Compendio de Historia de Ciudad de Carmen, Campeche* (Carmen: Contraste, 1989), 85–6.

52. Enrique Canudas, *Trópico Rojo: Historia Política y Social de Tabasco. Los Años Garridistas 1919/1934* (Villahermosa: Gobierno del Estado, 1982) 2:72.

53. AHSEP-Campeche, c. 20/exp. 76, Celso Flores to Banco Nacional de Crédito Agrícola, 19 Feb. 1935.
54. AHSEP-Campeche, c. 21/exp. 68, Samuel Pérez, 15 Jan. 1934.
55. AHSEP-Campeche, c. 20/exp. 75, Claudio Cortés, 12 Dec. 1934; c. 1802/ exp. 5, Luis Espinosa Morales, 19 Apr. 1934.
56. E.g. "Muera el Burgués," in *Album de Cantos Revolucionarios*, AHSEP-Campeche, c. 20/exp. 70.
57. David Raby, *Educación y Revolución Social en México (1921–1940)* (Mexico City: SepSetentas, 1974), 220.
58. AGN/DGG, 2.311.DS(2)2.138, Agente Confidencial #2 to Gobernación, 28 Jul. 1928; Sierra, *Diccionario*, 19; Amendolla, *Revolución*, 98.
59. Amendolla, *Revolución*, 87–8.
60. AGN-Lázaro Cárdenas, 544.3/3, Sen. Góngora Gala, 7 Aug. 1940; AGN/DGG, 2.311G.226, "Gran Agrupación Pro-Campeche"; 2.311G(6-3)1, *Informe*, elections 28 Jun. 1927. Primitivo Alonso Alcocer, *Cuando Quintana Roo Fue Desmembrado (1931–1935)* (Chetumal: Congreso del Estado, 1992) 187.
61. Sierra, *Diccionario*, 250; AGN-Lázaro Cárdenas, 543.11/7, Alfonso Ramírez to Cárdenas, 14 Jan. 1937.
62. AGN-Lázaro Cárdenas, LC 543.1/16, memo., 30 Jan. 1937.
63. The term is Guillermo Guzmán Flores's. "El Cardenismo y la Nueva Democracia," in *Historia de la Cuestion Agraria Mexicana, Estado de Zacatecas*, ed. Ramón Vera Salvo (Mexico City: Juan Pablos, 1992) 2:256-63.
64. AHSEP-SDER, c. 20/exp.71, Juan Pacheco to Múgica, 20/22 Feb. 1935; exp. 70, Pedro Castila, 18 Feb. 1935; AHSEP-Campeche, c. 20/exp. 70, 25 Feb. 1935; exp. 5, Luis Alvarez, 10 Mar. 1935; exps. 71 and 75, Luis Espinosa, 24 Feb./27 Apr. 1935; AGN/DGG, 2.347(2).1(bis).9, Rita Monroy to Luís Rodríguez, 12 Nov. 1936; AGN-Lázaro Cárdenas, 534.6/ 1112, Múgica to Cárdenas, 20 Jan. 1936; AHSEP-MC, 5963/18, Juan Pacheco, March 1932. Manuel Herrera, *Apuntes para la Historia de Calkiní* (Calkiní, 1966) 70, 111–91.
65. AGN/OC, 104-L-23.#3. Manuel Mex, 2 Mar. 1926.
66. Manuel Alcocer Bernes, *Historia del Ayuntamiento del Campeche, 1540–1991* (Campeche: Ayuntamiento de Campeche, 1991), 295; AHSEP-Campeche, c. 20/exp.70, Alvarez to Cárdenas, 7 Feb. 1935; ACC 2.10, Comité Diocesano 30–46, Justina Rebollado to Bustos, 17 Jan. 1939. Emilio Rodríguez Herrera, *Legislaturas Campechas: Compendio Histórico (1861–1998)* (Campeche: Congreso del Estado, 1999), 140. Euán Marío Aranda González, *Hecelchakán: Historia, Geografía, Cultura* (Campeche: Conaculta, 2003), 146.
67. AHSEP-Campeche, c. 20/exp. 70, Alvarez to García, 8 Mar. 1935.
68. AHSEP-Campeche, c. 21/exp. 53, "Informe . . . Respecto a los Sucesos de Hecelchakán," 9 Jun. 1934; c. 20/exp. 71, "Síntesis," 23 Feb. 1935. AGN/DGG, 2.340.25.1, Hecelchakán petition forwarded by Luis Guízar to Gobernación, 20 Oct. 1934; AGN-Lázaro Cárdenas, 544.4/484, Pedro Velázquez, 23 Oct. 1935; 544.2/3, Nicolas Tamayo to Cárdenas, 20 Mar. 1935.
69. AGN-Lázaro Cárdenas, 521.7/47: Herculano Farfán (24 Dec. 1934), Matilde Chí (24 Aug. 1936).
70. AHSEP-Campeche, c. 21/exp. 91, Gustavo Jarquín to Manuel Mesa, 29 Dec. 1934.

71. AGN-Lázaro Cárdenas, 544.2/3, F. Enrique Angli and Manuel Ferrer, 22/24 Mar. 1935.

72. AGN/DGG, 2.340.25.1 and 2.347(2).1(bis).8; RDSRIAM, roll 43, 5 Dec. 1935.

73. AGN/DGG, 2.340.25.1, Mena Córdoba and Tomás Hernández to Gobernación (10 Mar. 1936); RDSRIAM, roll 43: memo., 14 Mar. 1936, Josephus Daniels, 28 Mar. 1936; roll 22, Charles Taliaferro, 31 Mar. 1936, 30 Jan. 1937. AGN-Lázaro Cárdenas, 543.1/16, memo., 30 Jan. 1937.

74. In Nov. 1938, the Supreme Court issued an injunction against Campeche's *Ley de Cultos*. RDSRIAM, roll 22: William Murray, 30 May 1936; Martin Palmira, 2 Jun. 1936; Charles Taliaferro, 30 Nov. 1938; Stephen Worster, 1 Jan. 1939.

75. AGN-Lázaro Cárdenas, 2.347(2).1(bis).9, Rita Monroy to Luís Rodríguez, 12 Nov. 1936; 543.1/16, memo., 30 Jan. 1937; AGN/DGG, 2.340.24.10, Rafael Alcalá, 22 Dec. 1936.

76. Ute Schuren, "La Revolución Tardía: Reforma Agraria y Cambio Político en Campeche (1910–1940)," in *Yucatán a través de los Siglos*, ed. Ruth Gubler and Patricia Maskel (Mérida: UADY, 2001), 285–318; Raby, *Revolución*, 224–34.

77. Julio de la Cueva, "Spain: The Assault on the City of Levites," in *Culture Wars: Secular-Catholic Conflict in Nineteenth Century Europe*, ed. Christopher Clark and Wolfram Kaiser (New York: CUP, 2002), 182–3.

78. Alejandro Negrín Muñoz, *Campeche: Una Historia Compartida* (Mexico City: Gobierno del Estado de Campeche, 1991), 90.

79. RDSRIAM, roll 43, Taliaferro, 5 Dec. 1935.

80. *Hombre Libre*, 26 Sep. 1934.

81. AHAM-Pascual Díaz, c. 1/exp. 16, Díaz to Guízar, 25 Apr. 1933.

82. Román Piña Chán, *Enciclopedia Histórica de Campeche. Tomo III. Etapa independiente. Siglo XIX* (Mexico City: Porrúa, 2003), 367–8.

83. *Michoacano* Francisco Plancarte y Navarrete (1896–98, left for Cuernavaca); *guanajuatense* Rómulo Betancourt y Torres (1900–01, died); *michoacano* Francisco Mendoza y Herrera (1905–09, left for Durango); Spaniard Jaime Anesagasti y Llamas (1909–10, died); *jalisciense* Vicente Castellanos Núñez (1911–21, left for Tulancingo); *michoacano* Luis Guízar Barragan (1932–38, left for Saltillo).

84. AHAM-Pascual Díaz, c. 1/exp. 16, Guízar to Pascual Díaz, 10 Jul. 1933.

85. AHAM-Pascual Díaz, exp. Campeche, Obispado to Archbishop Mora, 20 Oct. 1927.

86. AGN/DGG, 2.340.24.8, Interim Governor to Gobernación, 21 Jan. 1930.

87. AHSEP-Campeche, c. 20/exp.71, Pacheco to Múgica, 22 Feb. 1935; AGN/DGG, 2.340.25.1, Raúl Domínguez, 2 Jan. 1936.

88. AHSEP-Campeche, c. 1802/exp. 8, Inspector 2ª zona, 2 Aug. 1933.

89. Matthew Butler, *Popular Piety and Political Identity in Mexico's Cristero Rebellion: Michoacán, 1927–29* (Oxford: British Academy/OUP, 2004), 9–10, 215, for contrasting "Levitical" (orthodox) and "folk" Catholicisms.

90. AGN/DGG, 2.340.25.1.

91. MS, Palmira to Murray, 2 Jun. 1936.

92. AGN-Abelardo Rodríguez, 514.3/3, Subrio. to Ramón Uc, 20 Jul. 1934; Manuel Andrés to Ignacio Quijano, 5 Nov. 1934.

93. AGN/DGG, 2.340.25.1, Guízar to Gobernación, 20 Oct. 1934.

94. AHAM-Pascual Díaz, c. 1/exp. 16, Guízar to Díaz, 16 Apr. 1933, and c. 3/exp. 33.

95. AGN/DGG, 2.347(2).1(bis).6, Migración, 24 Sep. 1931.

96. AHAM-Luis María Martínez, c. Comité Episcopal/exp. "T," José del Valle, 18 Feb. 1945.

97. Graham Greene, *The Lawless Roads* (London: Eyre & Spottiswoode, 1950), 221–2.

98. Kristina Boylan, "The Feminine 'Apostolate in Society' versus the Secular State: The Unión Femenina Católica Mexicana, 1929–1940," in *Right Wing Women: From Conservatives to Extremists Around the World*, ed. Paola Bachetta and Margaret Power (London: Routledge, 2002), 169–182; Boylan, "Mexican Catholic Women's Activism, 1929–1940" (PhD diss., Oxford University, 2000).

99. AHAM-Pascual Díaz, c. 1/exp. 16, Guízar to Díaz, 16 Apr. 1933.

100. AHSEP-Campeche, c. 21/exp. 5960, Claudio Cortés, 30 Apr. 1934.

101. ACC, 2.10 Comité Diocesano 30–46, Francisco Barahona (5 Jun. 1938) and Justina Rebollado (17 Jan. 1939) to Luis Bustos.

102. AAC, exp. 2.10.1, "Informe de Visita a Diócesis de Campeche y Tabasco," 6 Apr. 1941.

103. Chiapas, Tehuantepec, Huejutla, Tamaulipas, Sinaloa, Sonora. AHAM-Luis María Martínez, c. Comité Episcopal/exp. "F y G," J.M. Maya to Martínez, 16 Dec. 1944.

104. Marjorie Becker, *Setting the Virgin on Fire: Lázaro Cárdenas, Michoacán Peasants, and the Redemption of the Mexican Revolution* (Berkeley: University of California Press, 1995).

Chapter 11

"El Indio Gabriel": New Religious Perspectives among the Indigenous in Garrido Canabal's Tabasco (1927–30)*

Massimo De Giuseppe

> *It is important to control that pueblo [San Carlos] because it is the most fanatical in the state. This year they celebrated religious fiestas with ceremonies from the time of the conquest, contradicting the socialist ideas of the state government.*[1]

"Defanaticizing" the people was an important theme in Ministry of Public Education (SEP) reports from 1926–29, a time of religious crisis, church closures, and *cristero* violence. In this period, the aims of revolutionary reconstruction mixed political reforms, economic development, and sociocultural (religious, educative, pro-Indian [*indigenista*]) questions. The projects of indigenous incorporation and religious defanaticization must therefore be interpreted within a broader framework of postrevolutionary modernization, which achieved its greatest radicalism to date under President Calles (1924–28). A note written after a 1927 trip to Puebla by SEP Under-secretary Moisés Sáenz captures *callismo*'s incorporationist spirit. For Sáenz, it was necessary to "incorporate civilization into the Indian," and vice versa, so that indigenous people would assimilate "white civilization" and transform it into a true "Mexican civilization." The link between national integration and religious defanaticization was strong, and SEP missionaries were particularly concerned about "fanatical" indigenous resistance to modernization. Sáenz, too, concluded that indigenous resistance was an obstacle to "national redemption," if not militarily (as shown in the 1926 defeated Yaqui rising) then culturally.[2] This was clear in southern Mexico—in Chiapas, Yucatán, and Tabasco—where "rationalist" schools, cooperatives, and revolutionary leagues led the fight against "fanaticism."

Defanaticization climaxed in Tabasco under Tomás Garrido Canabal, who employed significantly firmer methods than the reconstructionist SEP. Garrido governed from 1922 with Obregón's support, yet the Tabascan case also sprang from a regional context characterized historically by a wide margin of political autonomy and a solid gulf coast anticlericalism. Garrido's position as governor was strengthened during the *delahuertista* revolt—which found a real bastion in Tabasco—by his loyalty to the federal government. Indeed, the unfolding of political events in 1923–24 placed Garrido in a position of unprecedented strength, as leader of the Radical Socialist Party of Tabasco (PRST) but facing—after *delahuertismo*—no effective opposition.[3] In 1924, Garrido began radical reforms that borrowed heavily from Carrillo Puerto's Yucatecan system: most significantly, Garrido founded Resistance Leagues (*Ligas de Resistencia*), which were a bureaucratic channel for corporativizing rural production and centralizing political control in Villahermosa's Central Resistance League (LCR). The Leagues gave the government effective top-down control over Tabasco, politically and socioculturally. From January 1926, *garridismo*'s "official" voice—Trinidad Malpica's newspaper, *Redención*—played an essential part in the project of forging a secular culture through literature, folklore, and education.

Garrido's fame as a political strong man fitted his landlord background (the son of southern *hacendados*), but it was the doctrines of nationalism, socialism, and "rationalist" education, charged with a puritanical anticlericalism, which proved politically fascinating. Garrido boosted Tabasco's economy nonetheless, improving its infrastructure, reviving its industry, and laying the foundations for the later petrol boom. At the same time, he supported agriculture and increased its export orientation by fortifying the production of *cacao* and sugar. His main efforts, however, were concentrated in the banana industry—the state's "green gold"—leading to Communist accusations that he was a defender of Standard Fruit interests.[4] The *garridista* machine also expanded through the foundation of 176 cooperatives. These limited the scope for agrarian reform and guaranteed Garrido's capacity to regulate social pressures once the traditional *finca* system of recruiting indebted peons was broken. Cooperatives also allowed Garrido to control production and consumption, to fix wages and prices, and to eliminate strikes.

Garrido's system was driven by a particular vision of modernization that was negatively characterized by its systematic elimination of opposition, political violence, and aggressive defanaticization. This radicalism emerged clearly in the fight against alcohol and religion, *garridismo*'s "supreme enemies." These "vices" were frequently linked in revolutionary discourse, as in the "creed" of the Tabascan farmer. This condemned "fanatical and drunken orgies" and affirmed: "we believe that modern farming methods, the selection of seeds, hygiene and thrift, are more worthy than the prayers, masses and other superstitions of the clergy. We believe firmly that false idols, fetishes, and the promise of eternal life have been thrown away forever, making a new generation of morally complete men."[5] Temperance campaigns, culminating in 1931's "Dry Law," ran from 1926; another campaign aimed to eradicate prostitution and revalorize Tabascan women.

With his Leagues and "rationalist" teachers, Garrido threw himself into an intense battle against religion. Exploiting the Tabascan Church's historic weakness—it was largely unaffected by the missionary and social militancy of *Rerum Novarum* Catholicism—Garrido passed a law limiting the number of priests to one for every 6,000 inhabitants in 1923. The crisis worsened in May 1924, when Garrido accused Bishop Pascual Díaz y Barreto of conspiring with *delahuertistas*, forcing him to flee. The campaign against rural Catholics began in 1925. Its effects were described in apocalyptic tones by "Oscar Sully"—probably the *cura* of Teapa, Carlos Hernández—who denounced government harassment of the peasantry because it reduced clerical effectiveness and increased lay superstition (a "prophet" had appeared in Macuspana). The authorities also warned the *cura* that his church must close due to a smallpox outbreak, but permitted a final Mass to celebrate New Year. On 1 January 1925, two masses were celebrated, "which the people attended with considerable fervor, since it was now known that churches were closing" in Tabasco.[6] Months later, Garrido reduced the number of priests to one for every 31,000 inhabitants, outraging *curas* in indigenous areas. Father Hernández was arrested on charges of organizing a Zoque rebellion against Garrido; the *cura* of Huimanguillo suffered the same fate.

Defanaticization and Resistance

In February 1925, news from Tabasco spread as the state responded favorably to Joaquín Pérez's schismatic "Mexican" Catholic Church (ICAM).[7] Garrido supported the schism none too subtly. Firstly, League members kidnapped a *cura*, Manuel González Púnaro, electing him "Red Bishop" in Villahermosa's Merino Theatre (an honor Púnaro refused). Another schismatic, Eduardo Coronel, petitioned for custody of "the cathedral and other churches belonging to the Nation," and offered to serve Pérez against the Roman "yoke."[8] A third priest, José Casaponsa, joined the schism in Macuspana, provoking violence in Tamulté de las Barrancas. Exiled in Mexico City, Bishop Díaz learned that the civil authorities had granted the Santa Cruz church to schismatics. Demanding guarantees, Díaz was told that the chief of military operations would facilitate his return to Tabasco. Yet this did not occur.[9]

Garrido then withdrew Villahermosa's cathedral from public cult. On 26 April, priests sent a memo to Garrido denouncing Catholics' lack of freedom.[10] The answer came in a decree (14 May) setting out impossible legal requirements for religious ministry: priests must now be Tabascan or Mexican by birth, aged over 40, educated in state schools, and married. As well as five years' residency in Tabasco, they must have no criminal record.[11] The situation was critical. Father Vicente Granados protested that outlawing clerical celibacy was "incredible and unconstitutional,"[12] and villages demanded the return of confiscated churches. In reply, Governor Ruiz—interim during Garrido's period in the Senate—converted the churches in Macuspana, Esquipulas, and Jalpa de Méndez into schools, starting an impressive "superimposition" process in Tabasco. Garrido's notoriety, meanwhile, spread in Yucatán, Campeche, and Chiapas.[13] In Villahermosa, Congress received petitions accusing Garrido of violence and murder; *Tabasco Nuevo* wrote that his actions were "characterized by endless arbitrary acts" and had "sown ill-feeling and anguish in all social classes." Whole families were abandoning the state.[14]

Defanaticization was first directed at ecclesiastical structures and personnel, and later targeted Catholicism's cultural influence. Indeed, *Redención* made a clear distinction between clergy and laity: the faithful were "an anonymous mass," the product of religious "atavism," but it was priests who crushed their "evolutionary potential" under the weight of religion.[15] The tools used to implement these programs were juridical, economic, educational, and sometimes paramilitary. The legislature issued energetic measures. In 1929, priestly numbers were reduced to one for every 100,000 inhabitants and the state's toponymy was transformed by the banning of rooftop and cemetery crucifixes and of religious names for towns, villages, and streets. "Assault groups" were recruited from the ranks of the Revolutionary Vanguard, the Revolutionary Youth Group, and (from 1931) the Young Revolutionary Block. These were the embryo for Garrido's *Camisas Rojas* (Redshirts), who followed him to the agriculture ministry in 1934 and achieved notoriety for their involvement in the violent events in Coyoacán that December. The Leagues organized "cultural Fridays" and encouraged the singing of hymns praising work and atheism. For Garrido, defanaticization was the true campaign for national "liberation": he claimed that in Tabasco "fetishes and *santos*" had disappeared as fanaticism surrendered to reason.[16] The conversion of "abandoned" churches into rationalist schools continued, and Interior Minister Tejeda received numerous secularization petitions from Tabascan municipalities or teachers' leagues. By 1929, 78 churches had been turned into schools and 16 closed; from 1927, the bishopric in Villahermosa was used as a barracks.

The most valuable defanaticizing instrument was the rationalist school. If its structure was copied from the Yucatecan model and from Luciano Kublí and José de la Luz Mena's projects, its originality derived from the autonomy Tabascan schools enjoyed from the SEP. This autonomy allowed Tabasco's League of Atheist Teachers to elaborate a state "rationalist" program, intense pedagogic activity that developed under the slogan "Only the Rationalist School educates!" *Redención* published textbooks exalting work and irreligion, such as *The Peasant Socialist's ABC*; it published antireligious plays, such as *The Lies of Religion*, and a primer (*The Tabascan's Catechism*) which contained hymns to nationalist autarky.[17] There were numeracy, cleanliness, and hygiene campaigns, and festivals substituting secular cults of fruit or the soil for religious celebrations. Coffee, yucca, and banana fairs were organized, often featuring anticlerical burlesques. Lily Taracena, president of Tabasco's Normalist Society, sloganized "Schools Not Churches, *Maestros* Not *Curas*."[18]

Garrido's education system ran 400 day and night schools, a mixed secondary school, a normal school, and an open-air school. The SEP, which ran some schools in Tabasco, was forced to adapt to *garridismo*'s cultural climate whilst furthering its objectives of modernizing peasant habits and teaching

Spanish. Tabasco's SEP director, Bolio Yenro, promised to fight "fanaticism and superstition among children and adults," whilst developing a "firm nationalist campaign."[19] SEP director Elpidio Faber asked the SEP for a school in Mecatepec because "the *pueblo*, perhaps uniquely in Tabasco, is so fanatical that it has long celebrated religious festivals." Faber had reservations about defanaticization, however, claiming Indians would only support a school that "does not attack [their] ancient customs."[20] Another *maestro*, Federico Corzo, in 1928 described the El Bayo school near San Carlos as Tabasco's "most important aboriginal nucleus" and requested the admission of two students to the Casa del Estudiante Indígena.[21] In 1929, Corzo reported that federal teachers in his area were "devoted exclusively to school activity."[22] The SEP also ran a "cultural mission," and Bolio wanted nurses to teach *maestros* how to treat malaria and typhoid: this, he said, was "more important than education."[23]

Despite SEP ambivalence, *garridismo*'s battleground was fundamentally religious. Catholic testimonies of defanaticization reach us from many sources, among them the reports sent to Bishop Díaz by Francisco Capetillo, a tobacco trader. On 27 January 1928, Capetillo wrote, "another campaign began: families were ordered to surrender the *santos* in their houses and destroy them or throw them in the river." Burning images in public *autos de fe* was part of the 1928 campaign, and represented the high point of "anti-fanatical" activity. Capetillo continued,

> In Tamulté and Atasta, disorders occurred. During the opening of the "Rationalist School" in these villages, the distinguished *señorita* María Dolores Pérez—a teacher your holiness doubtless remembers—spoke in a manner that would be the envy of Marat (if not Danton). Reading her speech and feeling an urge to empty one's bowels are one and the same thing . . . Of course, she does not direct her anger merely at Catholics but Protestants, since her objective is to destroy all vestige of religion . . . [She said that] "There will be no more sermons in vulgar Latin or barbaric Spanish, no murmuring in the confessional . . . the light of reason will illuminate a school on the pews where once the flock listened in faith to the dogma of the Mass. Now hundreds of children will be able to hear the true Mass, which deifies the only God: work."[24]

Capetillo also reconstructed the "religious pantomimes" performed by *garridistas* in Frontera:

> They came out in disguise: one was wearing the face of the Virgin of Carmen, which was hacked off the ruined image for use as a mask . . . On Sunday, they drove round in one of *licenciado* Garrido's trucks, dressed in cassocks and dousing anyone they met with whitewash; they were all armed with pistols.[25]

How did Tabascan Catholics react? Middle-class families left for nearby states or Mexico City's Colonia Roma. In the countryside, villagers signed petitions demanding the devolution of churches so that worship could be celebrated, even without priests. This happened often in ethnically mixed municipalities,

such as Huimanguillo, Cárdenas, Tecolutilla, Comalcalco, and Teapa. In the
Chol village of Tapijulapa (Tacotalpa), people demanded the "devolution of
the church" and an end to the removal of images, "because we do not wish
their continued destruction." Furious that the *profesora* had sold a wooden
flagstaff, ordered "the destruction of a baptismal font," and decreed "that an
image be removed from church, bathed in gasoline, and burned," villagers
demanded that she be refused custody of the church.[26] Complaints to the
public prosecutor led to enquiries into church-burnings in Santa Cruz and
Esquipulas.[27]

Villagers also resisted by protecting Macario Fernández Aguado, the last
cura to minister in Tabasco and, famously, Graham Greene's inspiration.[28]
Born in Michoacán, Fernández was brought to Tabasco by Bishop Castellanos
and moved to Jalpa in 1919. Despite his alcoholism, Fernández kept celebrating after Garrido expelled the clergy, conducting clandestine ministry
from his base on the Chiapanecan frontier until 1935. Then he was captured
and, despite a rescue attempt in Tamulté, deported to Guatemala.[29] The
support of Chol, Zoque, and, above all, Chontal Indians employing ancient
resistance techniques made this ministry possible. The secreting of religious
objects in caves, cornfields, grottos, and rivers, for example, preserved the
sacred from iconoclasm and initiated a process of cultural recuperation.
These strategies were common in villages whose commitment to tradition
and festive religiosity reflected the coherence of the *mayordomía* system.
Such communities practised an autonomous frontier religiosity long accus-
tomed to resisting external pressures; *garridismo* never stopped the Choles'
annual pilgrimages to the Lord of Tila, for instance.[30] New kinds of struggle
nonetheless took place as a result of defanaticization. In the part-Chontal
pueblo of Mecatepec (Huimanguillo) in 1929, for instance, the indigenous
formed a *junta* to defend images and altars, while in Cunduacán the mayor
ordered the dissolution of parish groups, the surrender of home altars, and
the exhumation of the dead from church graves, followed by burial in the
civil pantheon within eight days.[31]

A Chontal Catechist Appears

The case of Gabriel García—a Chontal catechist who led resistance to defanaticization in San Carlos (Macuspana)—is important in this context. First,
Gabriel's model of resistance was original; second, it allows us to glimpse the
heterogeneity of Mexican indigenous religiosity and to appreciate the dynamic
interrelationships joining indigenous communities, Catholicism, and wider
society. Yet the "Indian Gabriel"—as Tabasco's Apostleship of Prayer (ADO)
baptized him—or *el* maestrito—as he was known by Chontales—has attracted
little attention. During his lifetime, Gabriel's fame was localized, and his case
was posthumously ignored in official historiography and Catholic conservative writings (which preferred *cristero* martyrs). The first Catholic writings
were a 1941 article by Efraín Huerta,[32] and a pamphlet by the Jesuit Carlos
Heredia,[33] published to coincide with the ADO's first national congress. The

best-known account, however, which locates Gabriel's story in a conservative Catholic historiography, is Luis Islas García's 1957 publication of a 1937 manuscript written by Gabriel's brother, Severo.[34] This text was passed to Islas García by a Catholic lawyer and anti-*garridista* militant, Rodolfo Brito Foucher.[35]

It is important to try and lift the layers of ideological mystification from Gabriel's history because his case at first sight seems to revalidate a simple "tradition-modernity" dichotomy in a region where "de-Indianization" and modernization in fact assumed very different, apparently contradictory, forms. Indeed, if Gabriel's movement was politically and ethnically "traditional"— an agent of community resistance to defanaticization—it was *simultaneously* an agent of religious modernization. In an attempt to offer a new interpretation of the "Indio Gabriel," here I have supplemented existing sources with documents from the Tabasco State Archive, the SEP archive, and the Archdiocese of Mexico archive (which contains some of Gabriel's original texts), together with an array of oral testimonies collected in San Carlos and other *rancherías* on the Tabasco-Chiapas border.[36]

Gabriel García was a Chontal peasant from San Carlos (later Epigmenio Antonio, now Benito Juárez),[37] and author of a singular catechistic movement in the *municipio* of Macuspana from 1927–30. Born Gabriel Angel García on 18 March 1906, he was the son of Genaro García and Petrona Morales, peasant proprietors of the San Miguel *rancho*. Gabriel's primary education was fragmentary, but his family's status enabled him to learn to read and write. A 1925 SEP *informe* helps us appreciate the kind of environment in which he was raised. The *pueblos* of San Carlos, San Fernando, and Tepetitán, an inspector wrote,

> Being clearly indigenous and densely populated, each merit at least three *maestros* . . . in order to incorporate them as soon as possible into civilization. Until the ages of 12 or 13, the children—boys as well as girls—roam about completely naked; the women wear only simple cotton petticoats [*enaguas*], but neither *huipil* [smock] nor blouse, and quietly walk the streets unaware that they live in a state of backwardness.[38]

According to SEP statistics, 90 percent of the *pueblo*'s 1500 inhabitants were of "clearly Chontal ethnicity." San Carlos also lies in an area of ancient Chontal civilization,[39] and in the 1920s was the object of archaeo-anthropological explorations published in Manuel Gamio's *Ethnos* magazine.[40] Elevated by Garrido to the category of *villa* in 1923, the *pueblo*—like many in the region—as yet had no experience of *agrarismo*. The inhabitants lived mainly from agriculture, with some also engaged in cooperatives or Macuspana's cattle ranches.

From a religious perspective, San Carlos evidenced a dualism typical of many southern Mayan *pueblos*. This originated in religious differences that separated the community into "high" and "low" parts, but which do not corresponded to simple class divisions. In general, many anthropologists agree, there was a relative tolerance of external religious influences among the "low" part of the village—those who worked, for example, as *jornaleros* and engaged dynamically with the nonindigenous world—which contrasted with the religious conservatism of the "high" groupings (*altépetl*). Members of this less acculturated elite often controlled the village's symbolic capital: as occupiers of the rotating *mayordomía* system, for instance, they exercised religious tutelage and conserved social, sacred, and linguistic tradition.[41] The persistence of syncretic traits in local religiosity—in curative rites, cosmogony, and propitiatory ceremonies—reflected this traditional dualism,[42] which was partially synthesized in the *cofradía* (brotherhood) system. This system used silent resistance techniques in order to hold religious festivities, above all the celebration of the *pueblo*'s patron saint, the "Lord" of San Carlos. As in most of the frontier zone, Protestantism was unknown at this time.

Like other literate smallholders, the Garcías were distinguished by owning a small library of religious texts, such as Ripalda's catechism, a life of Loyola, Father Morrell's *Popular Theology*, and Luis de Granada's *Meditation on the Passion of Jesus Christ*. It is probable, therefore, that from childhood Gabriel experienced a tension between Chontal community membership and his exposure to fragments of an "external" religiosity inspired, in this case, by Spanish asceticism. Islas García makes much of this, yet significantly, Gabriel claimed that he began reading these texts *after* entering the apostleship ("I wanted to learn to read well, in order to read the Good Books I had").[43] The young Gabriel devoted himself to agricultural labors, moving in 1926 to Villahermosa: here he met *cura* Granados, who enrolled him in the apostleship, and Leonarda Satré de Ruiz ("*doña* Leonardita"), a catechist, ADO president, and southeastern bourgeois from Veracruz.

The apostleship—founded by French Jesuit Henri Ramière (1821–77) to spread the cult of the *Sacré Coeur*—was introduced to Mexico in 1875 by Nicolás Serra, and grew in the decades after 1900 on the back of Jesuit efforts and lay dynamism.[44] In this period, the association was essentially urban, with a minimal rural presence. The 1926 suspension of public cult, however, transformed the apostleship into a key channel for religious resistance. Boosted by the enforced privatization of worship, indeed, the association developed vivid forms of communitarian devotion among groups that met secretly in houses to pray and observe Holy Hours. Nonetheless, the apostleship generally failed to take root in indigenous regions outside the Tarahumara sierra, where Jesuit missionaries promoted it directly. Given its Christocentric character, the apostleship must also have seemed alien in rural Tabasco, where the legacy of indigenous Christianization was fragmentary, and barely sacramentalized.

It would be interesting to know if Gabriel's efforts were part of a broader rural apostleship or merely the product of his and Satre's relationship. But we know that Satré convinced Gabriel (who renounced marriage and—unusually for an Indian—considered entering a seminary) to become a militant activist on his return to San Carlos. In February 1928, Gabriel wrote to *doña* Leonardita, begging his "dearest friend" to send "three things that are most essential: Rosary cards, Apostleship of Prayer leaflets, and Catechisms," and to subscribe to the *Mensajero del Sagrado Corazón de Jesús*;[45] already, Gabriel said, "many people" had joined the apostleship (145 counting children), "and more and more are joining." Gabriel also asked for magazines and propaganda. Meanwhile, he went door-to-door, teaching the prayers he had learned in the apostleship: the Lord's Prayer, the Creed, the *Salve Regina*, and the Holy Hour. Gabriel's community quickly grew into a key local institution, which offered moral support and advice besides doctrine; this importance was reflected in the decision to buy village land and build a small *adobe* church to the Sacred Heart.

The apparent contrast between Gabriel's church (really a hermitage) and San Carlos's *parroquia* is significant. Gabriel's edifice was an original "faith school," which structured religious encounters for adults and children using a liturgical calendar that perfectly followed apostleship norms. Unlike the *parroquia*, therefore, which was used primarily as an image house for the cult of tutelary saints, Gabriel's church was strongly sacramentalized and its devotional bases—the Sacred Heart, Eucharistic adoration—were comparatively modern. This new religious site was, however, emphatically popular and accepted by the whole population. On Sundays the community congregated to recite the Rosary and prayers to the Virgin and Sacred Heart, while on first Thursdays there were nocturnal adoration vigils (*veladas*) before the Sacrament. Severo García recalls:

> [T]he people waited to hear prayers, the lesson, and meditations on the Sacred Heart; after reading these things aloud from a book, Gabriel would explain them in his own way, using the language spoken in the *pueblo* [Chontal]; he did the same with the catechism, so that anyone who did not understand Spanish understood these meditations. Afterwards there was music with choirs.[46]

Participants in these communitarian meetings came from hamlets as far away as Tepetitán, and Gabriel was soon recruiting assistants and planning secret visits to other communities where Chontal *hermandades* maintained strong festive cycles: San Fernando, Monte Largo, Palyta, Chiconal, Cerrito, Tierra Colorada, and Sábanas Grandes. José Torres, an inhabitant of the Argentina *ranchería* on the Chiapas border, describes a first meeting with the Chontal catechist:

> He was very successful. People were talking about him. He arrived with the women and his assistant because the church was closed. He took up his position, because there was no time to lose, and began to pray the Rosary. At least 15 young people congregated the first time, and I remember a catechism with a group of men after Mass, and the women singing with the girls.[47]

Gabriel thus introduced indigenous communities to unknown (or forgotten) sacramental practices: reciting the Rosary (not common in Tabasco's *tierra caliente*), listening to the Mass in silence, and participating in communitarian prayer afterward. His Christocentric attitude was also novel in a world traditionally fascinated by Mary and the saints. José Torrres's testimony, in particular, reveals the new religious mode of these fixed celebrations.

> There were beautiful ceremonies here, because he always came with four choristers: a *Marieta de los angeles*, a *Marieta de los santos*, a sister of the Cross, and her assistant. He brought four of them, and his homilies and songs were very agreeable for the whole group. The place where the ceremonies were held was always full. A house was chosen, and people congregated there.[48]

In accordance with apostleship rules, these ceremonies took place in private houses, not outdoors. Generally Gabriel brought an old gramophone so that the group could listen in silence to a Mass on disc. Afterward he led the Rosary and prayers, in Spanish. Chontal was used for catechesis, which Gabriel imparted to adults (his assistants catechized children).

This religious method opened up new paths to the faithful in a country where indigenous clergymen were taboo. In this regard, Gabriel embodied a dual condition: he was a Chontal-speaking community member who shared his interlocutors' background *and* a youthful authority bearing an "outside" message rarely heard by the Chontal. Through the power of orality, which in different ways was central to the apostleship's work and to the indigenous cosmovision, new forms of religious authority and solidarity were articulated during a period of intense secularization. Gabriel's enactment of this dual identity—this twofold belonging to the apostleship and the community—generated an original form of passive resistance that safeguarded the religious practices outlawed in Tabasco. A precise calculation is impossible, but the sources suggest that Gabriel's initiatives regularly attracted the active participation of 150–200 indigenous families, many of whom spoke little Spanish.

The congregation's indigenous character partly explains the authorities' caution when dealing with San Carlos. Indeed, the crisis between Gabriel and the authorities was provoked indirectly, by rivalry between the Garcías and Magdaleno Sánchez, a gendarme and Severo García's brother-in-law. In October 1928, Sánchez reported Gabriel's secret activity to Macuspana's mayor. The catechist's subsequent arrest provoked protests as 300 people petitioned for his release. Freed 22 days later, Gabriel resumed worship, introducing the practice of first Friday prayer. News of his arrest for "officiating with priestly character" reached President Portes Gil.[49] Gabriel did not, strictly speaking, act as a priest, but nonetheless he was summoned to Villahermosa. Garrido—surprisingly sympathetic—invited him to abandon his activity. In February 1929, Gabriel was rearrested. Two hundred people followed him to prison, ringing church bells and surrounding the barracks until Gabriel calmed their spirits. Gabriel was offered a government post in exchange for suspending his mission, more proof that the regime was reluctant to use firm methods and convert Gabriel into a symbol of Chontal rebellion.

In terms of this violence/passivity binomial, apostleship literature referred often to "soldiers of Christ"; in truth, however, pacifism was central to Gabriel's resistance, and his movement showed none of the violent messianism which, from Caneck onward, typified southern indigenous risings. Contemporary testimonies—not just propagandists' accounts—agree that Gabriel preached against violence and exalted the power of faith in his catechisms. San Carlos's surviving inhabitants state that Gabriel's Holy Hours abounded with references to docile humility. Although adapted for local audiences, such teachings echoed the *Mensajero del Sagrado Corazón* (resistance in dark times, suffering as proof of love); José Torres, too, relates that *el maestrito* taught children that it was "better not to kill."[50] Gabriel's conceptions of death and martyrdom, conversely, were indigenous, premised on obedience to supernatural power and infused with Chontal fatalism. His vision was very different to the *cristeros'* "crusader spirit" and seemed fundamentally apolitical: asked, during his second interview with Garrido, whether he was organizing a rising, Gabriel answered that he was merely instructing people in "matters of true religion."[51]

This arrest came at a delicate juncture, nonetheless. As Ausencio C. Cruz's gubernatorial period ended, Garrido sought to return and prevent the regrouping of an anti-*garridista* front that would exploit social tensions politically. Garrido, reelected in January 1930, also wanted to place himself advantageously in the National Revolutionary Party (PNR) coalition that the *Jefe Máximo* was building (he himself had presidential aspirations). In addition, Garrido faced a problem from mid-1929: how to react to the changing Church-state crisis, now that a *modus vivendi* was agreed. That the national climate had altered was clear from federal communications urging solutions to the problem of church custody. Tabasco's government was told to resolve the situation "in a general fashion, not case-by-case," in accordance with the law and "bearing in mind the Roman clergy's resumption of worship and submission to constitutional dispositions."[52] Despite mounting pressure, it was decided to proceed independently in Tabasco. This defiance explains, perhaps, why the Indio Gabriel affair turned sour after June 1929.

Events at San Carlos

In 1929, the LCR organized a yucca fair to coincide with San Carlos's patronal feast (1 September) as part of a defanaticization drive in Macuspana. The invitation promised "Enjoyment! Laughter! Amusement!" and celebrations of the fruits "of that fertile region":[53] the program comprised marching bands, cultural happenings, a talk by Antonio Ferrer, modern sports, a procession of bulls, and folk dances. The campaign reflected an LCR desire to engage with indigenous society, achieving what professor Santiago Ramírez called the Indian's "spiritual refinement" and the banishment from his soul of "factors which make him degenerate." Such events were targeted more at the young, "healthy and struggling to escape isolation," than the old, whose "customs, psychosis, and morality" were beyond modification.[54] *Redención* also published articles about Chontal wives in the hope of attracting local women—deemed "most resistant" in religion—to the fair.[55] Indeed, the majority of Gabriel's followers were women and the young.

Catholics opposed the fair, which began on 27 August, fearing it would be a pretext for image burning. Protests from men, women, and the young were drafted: according to Gabriel, these warned the LCR "to respect the *pueblo*'s voice and not to use the festival . . . to meddle with religion, which would insult the people."[56] The protests stressed that "by promoting the worship of animals instead of the true God," the fiesta insulted Christians, "because the adoration of creatures was proper only to primitive peoples." This attempt to substitute agrarian cults for spiritual tradition betrays a singular cultural misunderstanding. *Garridistas* here tried to be more "indigenous" than indigenes themselves, yet their primitivist, idealized conception of the Chontal world was based on no real knowledge of how local religion was practised or constantly reelaborated, and the result was confusion. Indian religion could be syncretic. Syncretism, however, was part of a broad religious complex, which could permit the substitution (put very crudely) of a patron saint for a divinity, a mysterious cross for an enchanted tree, or an Indian Virgin for a mother-god, because a mass of devotional meanings—concerning supernatural community tutelage, the relationships between human beings and the sacred, and life and death—was still transferred. A simple nature cult—of fruit, say—could never carry this weight of conjunctural relationships.

The Chontal Catholic José Torres says of the new secular fiestas:

> Things like the yucca fair were tremendous, but people didn't like the names. Tomás Garrido was odious to the *campesinos* because he changed the *rancherías*' names and stopped people putting crosses on their homes. Many people here, especially the religious ones, removed the *santos* to stop them being burned. I know a man who hid *santos* in the hills. And I tell you, the Holy Virgin in the parish church isn't the one we had before, because they took her to Chiapas and hid her in caves, and another Virgin came back. In those days, there was a lot of fear of power and violence. There were one or two attacks on the church here, and people defended it. In Tapijulapa, the church was closed but they [*garridistas*] were never allowed to take anything from it; and in the very old church of Oxolotán, some old men defended the church. People didn't like their patron saints being taken away.[57]

Some witnesses claim Gabriel sought to compromise with the authorities by suggesting that the *garridista* and the religious fiesta both proceed. This displeased some parishioners: according to Rosario Pascual, when the faithful heard of the agreement with Garrido, "they were angry and told Gabriel he had sold himself."[58] Nonetheless, the Chontales mobilized against the yucca fair and 300 signed a petition that was taken to the municipal president, Manuel Andrade, the local deputy José Ruiz, and professor Antonio Ferrer.

Tension mounted that afternoon. The municipal president said that Gabriel led "fanatics" against the police, forcing them to retaliate. Governor Cruz reported that at 4.45 p.m. the chief of the federal detachment "was attacked by fanatics shouting '¡*Viva Cristo Rey!*'" Three state troops and police were wounded.[59] Cruz also claimed that Gabriel, "Pascual Díaz's creature," had planned a rising and "forced" his followers to fire on the authorities.[60]

Confusion, however, surrounds the events. It is clear that the situation degen-
erated when police and troops arrived at the Sacred Heart hermitage to arrest
Gabriel. According to the municipal president, several policemen were wounded,
but indigenous victims were not counted. Catholic witnesses claim police
began shooting at the chapel and adjoining houses, where Indians armed with
machetes reacted. Overall, there were 17 Catholic victims (the count later rose
to 24, but Tresguerra's figure of 80 is unreliable[61]), and one or two police
victims: many were wounded, including Gabriel's brother Otilio, and 12 were
arrested.

According to don Manuel Antonio Gerónimo, a soldier was wounded in a
machete fight hours earlier, and this was the cause of the attack; most of the
victims died in the fire that engulfed the hermitage. Others, including Severo
García, claimed the assault was premeditated. Gabriel was able to save himself
with the help of some women, including his friend Brígida Trinidad: protected by supporters, he escaped to Chiapas, traveling day and night by
canoe. On 29 August, Gabriel wired the interior ministry to give his version
of events:

> Facing persecution in Tabasco, we came here with the aim of protesting against
> the unqualifiable assault against our *pueblo*, San Carlos, Macuspana, Tabasco,
> which claimed women and children's lives . . . Our attitude, which cannot be
> viewed as rebellious, provoked Garrido's people in Villahermosa, Jalapa, and
> Macuspana to come armed with rifles and pistols on 27 [August], just as fami-
> lies and some men were praying in the hermitage. This armed group covered the
> doorways and without reason began shooting, sowing confusion as all inside—
> their numbers cannot be ascertained—tried to flee . . . realising that the church
> and nearby houses were burning because they were torched by these armed
> strangers, some *vecinos* were obliged to arm themselves with *machetes* and guns
> and defend themselves against this unexpected attack . . . For this reason, we ask
> you to order an investigation by persons who can impartially judge the facts, just
> as we ask protection against the crimes which are committed daily in this state,
> *posting a federal detachment in San Carlos to guarantee social peace.*[62]

Despite this bloody clash, the fair continued and the LCR began destroying
images as Gabriel's congregation buried its dead. Severo García reports that
villagers were now forced into the plaza, where "impious men, dressed
wickedly as priests" encouraged children to ridicule them; these agitators
composed speeches and poems for people to recite, "in which they spoke
against God, the saints, and the clergy." People were then forced to hand
over crosses and images for burning. Well-known Catholics—"the devout
and those in the Apostleship"—were jailed.[63] In a demonstration of defanaticization's political significance, finally, the government strengthened the San
Carlos *feria* in 1930, as can be seen in intense press coverage describing the
event as "best regional *fiesta*."[64]

This political significance undoubtedly explains Catholics' negative reactions to it. As Gabriel wrote in a telegram of 31 August, the fair was "the pretext for entering our *pueblo* and committing attacks,"[65] a defensive reference

that underscores the fullness of his community membership and his desire to protect local autonomy. In it we also glimpse the importance of spiritual patronage—here caught in an ideal fusion between the old (the village *santo*) and the new (the Sacred Heart hermitage)—and its potentially antagonistic relationship to outside influences. These were deemed illegitimate in this case as they were introduced not by respected intermediaries but by armed police and radical speechmakers. Gabriel's appeal to federal authority, above all the proposal to establish a federal barracks in San Carlos, reveals a deeper trust in faraway Mexico City than in the *garridista* state.

Criticisms of Garrido did not just come from villagers. Macuspana citizens protested "the indescribable murders" ordered by Cruz and Garrido.[66] According to another critic,

> As San Carlos Indians are apparently more sensitive than the state's *ladino* population, they did not accept [defanaticization]; and because the police began pushing them aside, taking and destroying their images, beating them and imprisoning them, an accummulated hatred erupted against the regime, leaving many dead and wounded on both sides . . . Perhaps a new era of bloody revolution has begun.[67]

The revolution did not follow and a federal investigation began. Cruz defended the police, accusing Father Macario and Gabriel of inflaming Indian spirits. In hiding, Macario defended himself by sending Díaz his account of the "lamentable" events at San Carlos and Balancán (scene of more confrontations).[68] In response, Díaz sent a cautious telegram to Portes Gil on 6 September, asking the federation to concern itself in Tabasco's religious problems.

Gabriel, meanwhile, was protected in Salto de Agua until late September, when he traveled to see Díaz in Mexico City. It is not clear whether Gabriel spoke with Díaz or an assistant; his nephew, Honorato García, claimed Gabriel was not well received in the curia. Catholic conservatives—critical of Díaz's conciliatory line—fed a new myth: that Gabriel was turned away out of archiepiscopal weakness. Manifest political cautiousness is probably more accurate. In such a delicate moment, when the Church was rediscovering its institutional center and asserting control over the *cristeros*, San Carlos was unlikely to win Díaz's backing. Tabasco's situation remained uncertain, as shown in San Carlos's 1930 protests that Chontales were persecuted by "strangers" in trucks who banned religious celebrations and burned the image of San Carlos.[69] More clashes occurred in Tenosique and Vicente Guerrero. Meanwhile, Gabriel waited in Mexico City until March 1930. Back in Tabasco, he escaped capture by hiding in swamps and mountains, and located Father Macario in Chiapas. On 30 September 1930, Gabriel was betrayed in the Argentina *ranchería*. José Torres, one of the last to see him alive, remembers that his family spent days searching for the catechist's corpse, which was never found. A commonly used technique in *garridista* Tabasco was to butcher a victim and make their remains "disappear" in a river.

Conclusion

Gabriel's story is important. He embodied a series of encounters between Chontal society and modernity, both of the sociopolitical and cultural kind imposed by Garrido, and of the religious kind introduced by the apostleship. Gabriel was simultaneously a genuine community representative and an active agent in modernization. His religious "bilingualism"—his intermediate role between the community and political/ecclesial elites—emphasizes this; so does the character of his religiosity, which maintained an orthodox position in relation to apostleship teachings while showing equal capacity to conform to indigenous religious models. Gabriel's "otherness" did not undermine his community status; rather, it produced an original evangelical form that left the confines of church to reenter villagers' homes, but without abandoning its deeply communitarian character or challenging existing codes of belonging (wakes, patronal feasts). This village character explains why Gabriel's movement appealed to Chontales, but not Choles or Zoques, despite the commercial, cultural, and geographic proximity of these groups.

Even in a context in which Gabriel is increasingly mythologized, no one, significantly, talks of him in messianic tones, but only as a courageous community member renowned for his preaching ability and "powerful praying" (a phrase that translates, fittingly enough, as "speaking"—*xa'ji*—in Chontal). A different perception exists among Villahermosa's apostleship and Tabasco's Catholic *emigrés*. We turn, finally, to an emotive comment of José Torres, who describes what memories remain today of Gabriel: "Many people loved him and always remembered him, because he was very simple and taught the holy Rosary well, and with the women and the people we all learned from his stories. After his death we sang his story along with the religious songs with pride." For all its limitations, this popular memory reveals an ability to reelaborate and adapt strategies of resistance that is central to our story. If it is true, as Bonfil Batalla says, that "de-Indianization occurs when the population stops considering itself to be Indian,"[70] then Gabriel showed the Chontal a way to reimagine themselves as *modern* indigenous people, without surrendering any vital part of their identity. The "Indian Gabriel" would therefore have been that ideal "civilizing agent" which eluded both *garridista* schools and Church seminaries, neither of which opened themselves fully to the real depths of the region's autochthonous cultures.

Notes

* Translated by Matthew Butler.

1. Archivo Histórico de la Secretaría de Educación Pública (hereafter AHSEP), Depto. de Escuelas Primarias, Foráneas, y de Incorporación Indígena, Tabasco, 1925–30, c. 23/exp. 3, *informe*, 28 Nov. 1925.
2. "Informe sobre la Visita a las Escuelas Rurales Federales en la Sierra de Puebla Realizada por el C. Subsecretario de Educación, Profesor Moisés Sáenz," *Boletín de la SEP* 7, no. 7 (1927): 510.

3. Carlos Martínez Assad, *El Laboratorio de la Revolución: El Tabasco Garridista* (Mexico City: Siglo XXI, 2004); Alan Kirshner, *Tomás Garrido Canabal y el Movimiento de los Camisas Rojas* (Mexico City: SepSetentas, 1976); C. Ruiz Abreu and J. Abdo Francis, *El Hombre del Sureste: Relación Documental del Archivo Particular de Tomás Garrido Canabal* (2 vols. Villahermosa: Universidad Juárez Autónoma de Tabasco, 2003).

4. Stan Ridgeway, "Monoculture, Monopoly, and the Mexican Revolution: Tomás Garrido Canabal and the Standard Fruit Company in Tabasco (1920–1935)," *Mexican Studies/Estudios Mexicanos* 17 (2001): 143–69.

5. "El Credo del Agricultor Tabasqueño," *Redención*, 20 Jun. 1931.

6. Archivo Histórico de la Arquiodiócesis de México, Fondo Pascual Díaz, Tabasco (henceforth AHAM), c. 3/exp. 37, O. Sully, "Apuntes para la Historia Eclesiástica de la Diócesis de Tabasco, 1925."

7. Jean Meyer, *La Cristiada* (3 vols. Mexico City: Siglo XXI, 1973–4), 2:148–66.

8. Archivo Histórico-Fotográfico de Tabasco (henceforth AHFT), Gobernación, rollo 11/exp. 26, telegram, 9 Mar. 1925.

9. See *Plutarco Elías Calles: Correspondencia Personal (1919–1945)*, ed. Ricardo Macías (Mexico City: FCE, 1993), 187.

10. "Los Presbíteros Romanos Se Dirigen al Gobierno del Estado", *Redención*, 19 May 1925.

11. AHAM, c. 3/exp. 83.

12. AHAM, c. 3/exp. 62.

13. AHAM, c. 5/exp. 32, "¿Quién Es Tomás Garrido Canabal? El Tirano Más Bárbaro y Cruel Conocido hasta Hoy en Toda Latinoamérica."

14. *Tabasco Nuevo*, 22 Oct. 1925.

15. *Redención*, 19 May 1925.

16. *Informe Presentado por el Lic. Tomás Garrido C., Gobernador Constitucional de Tabasco ante la Legislatura Local* (Mexico City: Imprenta Mundial, 1933).

17. *Labor de Cultura del Departamento de la Liga Central de Resistencia de Propaganda Nacionalista para Ideologizar el Niño Campesino* (Villahermosa, 1929). *Redención*, 19 May 1925.

18. "¡Escuelas y No Templos! ¡Maestros y No Curas!" *Redención*, 11 Jul. 1931.

19. AHSEP, c. 23/exp. 15, *informe*, 22 Feb. 1930.

20. AHSEP, c. 20, *informe*, 8 Mar. 1927.

21. AHSEP, c. 23/exp. 23, *informe*, 28 May 1928. *La Casa del Estudiante Indígena: Dieciseis Meses de Labor. Una Experimentación Psicológico-Colectiva con los Indios, Febrero 1926–Junio 1927* (Mexico City: SEP, 1927). Engracia Loyo, "La Empresa Redentora: La Casa del Estudiante Indígena," *Historia Mexicana* 46, no. 1 (1996): 99–131. Massimo De Giuseppe, "Costruire la Nazione nel Messico Post-Rivoluzionario. Il Ruolo dell'Educazione Indigena e Campesina," *Contemporanea* 2 (2005): 233–66.

22. AHSEP, c. 25, *informe*, 8 Feb. 1929.

23. *Redención*, 31 Mar. 1933.

24. AHAM, c. O, Capetillo to Díaz, 3 Feb. 1928.

25. AHAM, c. O, Capetillo to Díaz, 28 Jan. 1928.

26. AHFT, Gobernación, rollo 13/exp. 1020; petition signed by Víctor Martínez, 3 Oct. 1928.

27. The film was *La Cruz y el Mauser*. AHFT, Gobernación, rollo 11/exp. 110.

28. Graham Greene, *The Power and the Glory* (London: Hanheim, 1940).
29. Archivo Aurelio Acevedo (AA), c. 38/exp. 64, "Datos Biográficos del Pbro. Macario Fernández Aguado."
30. M.A. Rubio, *La Morada de los Santos: Expresiones del Culto Religioso en el Sur de Veracruz y en Tabasco* (Mexico City: INI, 1994). J. Pérez Chacón, *Los Choles de Tila y su Mundo* (Mexico City: INI, 1994).
31. Carlos Martínez Assad, *Breve Historia de Tabasco* (Mexico City: FCE, 1996), 161.
32. E. Huerta, "La Huella de Sangre," *Así*, 10 May 1941. Also C. Tresguerras, "Tomás Garrido Canabal, el Coloradote," *La Prensa*, 19 May 1939.
33. AA, c. 38/exp. 64, C.M. Heredia, "Retrato del Protomártir Mexicano Gabriel Angel García" (ms., n. d.). In "Apuntes y Datos Biográficos Recopilados por el Padre Carlos Heredia, Sacerdote Jesuita, Relativos a la Persecución Religiosa en Tabasco," Heredia wrote: "I had the opportunity of talking with many of those who knew Gabriel; among them his brother Severo García, who in a *ranchero* style gave me invaluable information about the death of the tireless propagandist of the Apostleship of Prayer in his home region."
34. The 1937 ms., "Apuntes sobre la Persecución Religiosa en Todo el Municipio de Macuspana y Muy Particularmente en el Pueblo de San Carlos," was published as Severo García, *El Indio Gabriel (La Matanza de San Carlos)* (Mexico City: Jus, 1957). This work has recently been reprinted (2003) by the parish of San Carlos with unpublished documents, including Gabriel García's "Diario de Mi Vida."
35. For anti-*garridismo*, Salvador Abascal, *La Reconquista Espiritual de Tabasco en 1938* (Mexico City: Tradición, 1972).
36. For support with the fieldwork, I would like to thank don Enrico Lazzaroni, Abelino and María Isabel de la Cruz López, and Marcos Domínguez Avalos, *cura* of San Carlos.
37. Founded in 1766 by Pedro Maldonado, who brought in Chontal migrants from Nacajuca, San Carlos Olcuatitlán was renamed Epigmenio Antonio during the campaign to "defanaticize" toponyms.
38. AHSEP, c. 23/exp. 3, *informe*, 28 Nov. 1925.
39. F.J. Santamaría, *Documentos Históricos de Tabasco* and *Antología Folklórica y Musical de Tabasco* (Villahermosa: Gobierno del Estado de Tabasco, 1950/52 respectively).
40. J.D. Ramírez Garrido, "Tabasco Histórico Antiguo," *Ethnos* 2 (1920).
41. Henri Favre, *Cambio y Continuidad entre los Mayas de México: Contribución al Estudio de la Situación Colonial en América Latina* (Mexico City: INI, 1984).
42. C. Inchaustegui, *Las Márgenes del Tabasco Chontal* (Villahermosa: Gobierno del Estado de Tabasco, 1987), 259–303. S. Cadena Kima-Chang and S. Suárez Paniagua, *Los Chontales ante una Nueva Expectativa de Cambio: El Petróleo* (Mexico City: INI, 1988).
43. Cited in Heredia, "Retrato."
44. Leonor Correa Etchegaray, "El Rescate de una Devoción Jesuítica: El Sagrado Corazón de Jesús en la Primera Mitad del Siglo XIX," in *Historia de la Iglesia en el Siglo XIX*, ed. Manuel Ramos Medina (Mexico City: Condumex, 1998), 369–80.
45. AHAM, c. 4/exp. 54, Gabriel García to Leonarda Satré de Ruiz, Macuspana, 22 Feb. 1928.

46. García, "Apuntes."
47. Interview with José Torres, Graciano Sánchez, Tacotalpa, 27 Jul. 2005.
48. Ibid.
49. AHFT, Gobernación, rollo 13, telegram, 27 Dec. 1928.
50. Interview with José Torres, Graciano Sánchez, Tacotalpa, 27 Jul. 2005.
51. García, "Apuntes."
52. AHFT, Gobernación, rollo 13/exp. 1135, f. 2, 1929.
53. Flyer, 31 Aug. 1929, AHFT, Gobernación, rollo 13/exp. 1301.
54. S. Ramírez, "Cultura Indígena. El Pulimento Espiritual del Indio," *Redención*, 1 Jul. 1931.
55. *Redención*, 30 Aug. 1931.
56. García, *Indio Gabriel*, 44.
57. Interview with José Torres, Graciano Sánchez, Tacotalpa, 27 Jul. 2005.
58. Rosario Pascual, personal communication.
59. AHFT, Gobernación, rollo 13/exp. 1280.
60. AHFT, Gobernación, rollo 13/exp. 1283.
61. *La Prensa*, 19 May 1939.
62. AHFT, Fondo Emilio Portes Gil, rollo 1/exp. 1293–95 (my emphasis).
63. García, *Indio Gabriel*, 51.
64. "Es Desbordante el Entusiasmo que Reina en Epigmenio Antonio, Mac. La Fiesta de la Yuca Es la Mejor Fiesta Regional," *Redención*, 26 Aug. 1931.
65. AHFT, Gobernación, rollo 13/exp. 1300.
66. AHFT, Gobernación, rollo 13/exp. 1288.
67. Martínez, *El Laboratorio*, 170.
68. AHFT, Gobernación, rollo 13/exp. 1304, "Los Penosísimos Sucesos Acaecidos en Balancán y San Carlos."
69. AHFT, Gobernación, rollo 13/exp. 1330, letter from E. de la Cruz, 5 Sep. 1930.
70. Guillermo Bonfil Batalla, *México Profundo: Una Civilización Negada* (Mexico City: CONACULTA, 2001), 73.

Chapter 12

A Revolution in Local Catholicism?
Oaxaca, 1928–34

Edward Wright-Rios

Antes de llegar a las grutas hay una cruz en donde se hace penitencia; sin esto no es posible ver nada . . . Al llegar frente a la gruta se ve desde luego que de una orilla destila agua y la entrada es toda de piedra. Desde luego no se ve absolutamente nada, pero si todos rezan con devoción, aparece instantáneamente la Virgen Maria y un Ángel, aquella echa la bendición y desaparece. En seguida las piedras se transforman en una especia de pantalla y desfilan por ella las imágenes de la Virgen del Carmen, la Soledad, y la de Juquila.[1]

[Before arriving at the caves there is a cross where penitences are performed; without doing that, it is not possible to see anything . . . On arriving at the cave, it is seen at once that water runs down one side and that the entrance is made of stone. Of course, absolutely nothing is seen, but if everyone prays with devotion, the Virgin Mary and an Angel appear instantly, the Virgin giving a blessing and then disappearing. Right away, the stones are transformed into a kind of screen across which pass the images of the Virgins of Carmen, La Soledad, and Juquila.]

In the 1930s Father Ausencio Canseco described himself as a diligent spiritual soldier, serving Oaxaca's coastal mountains *"doctrinando, predicando, y sacramentando."*[2] As model seminarian and young priest in the 1890s, Canseco caught Archbishop Eulogio Gillow's eye, and thus found himself assigned an important and notoriously difficult parish in 1902—Santa Catalina Juquila, home to the region's most popular Marian devotion. The community was a rural nerve center as a shrine site, regional head parish, district seat, and municipality. Juquila was also a hub of coffee production and a magnet of unrest. Chatino Indians crying "Death to those wearing pants!" sacked the town in 1896 before authorities crushed the rebellion and decreed that Chatinos don trousers. From 1913 until the late 1920s, armed bands representing various local factions and revolutionary affiliations fought over Juquila and took turns plundering its church, homes, and businesses. Canseco, nonetheless, managed to remain in post and serve the parish's far-flung villages, despite violence and what he considered the insidious efforts of new civil authorities to gain control of the Virgin's festival and pilgrim donations. Archdiocesan authorities even asked Canseco to resolve problems in neighboring parishes, sending him to mediate conflict along the coast and investigate a colleague's schismatic dalliances.

Beleaguered, Canseco weathered these challenges assuming that the Virgin was testing him.[3] Events in the summer and fall of 1928, however, caught the resourceful priest off guard and divided the faithful. In one of his parish's poorest villages, San Francisco Ixpantepec, a young Chatina girl called Nicha claimed to see and speak to the Virgin Mary in a mountain cave. Moreover, her visions and warnings of divine chastisement coincided with a series of earthquakes. Soon throngs of pilgrims choked the trails to the village and its alpine grotto, and Nicha gained an evocative soubriquet as the "Second Juan Diego." Aside from Nicha's persistent revelations, many sojourners began to report extravagant visions. Canseco was at a loss to explain what was going on. Initially he led rituals at the apparition site, but after several weeks began to distance himself from the movement coalescing around the seer. His reports detailed a cautious investigation of the matter. Many faithful proved less inhibited. According to Canseco's assistant, Hilario Cortés, many locals and pilgrims concluded that eighteenth-century prophecies foretelling the Church's return to preeminence in Mexico after disasters and bloody social upheaval were coming true. The Catholic school principal, one of Canseco's most trusted allies, became the Chatina visionary's local champion. This woman, Matilde Narváez (also known as *doña* Matildita), organized rituals at the apparition site and served as a docent for visiting pilgrims, explaining that the Virgin had taken up residence in the cave above Ixpantepec. Moreover, she wrote her own reports to the archdiocese and even undertook a four-day trek to Oaxaca City to present the girl's case before ecclesiastical authorities. From 1928 into the early 1930s, Juquila and Ixpantepec Catholics sparred over Nicha's revelations and pilgrims' reported visions. Were they divine, demonic, or deviant? In short, amidst political unrest, natural disasters, economic turmoil, and threats to Juquila's shrine, Canseco found himself face to face with a mutiny in local Catholicism.

Thus far in Mexican studies we tend to conceive of the revolutionary period as a time when the Church and local Catholics faced various levels of persecution. We underscore the importance of a patchwork religious resurgence during the 1890s and 1910s when Catholics bolstered institutional structures, expanded the Church's grassroots presence, and longed for open political participation. We sketch the emergence of stronger Catholic sociopolitical networks and broad gains in the proverbial heart-and-minds struggle in cities and the countryside. In some regions, particularly the center-west, these developments forged the foundations of Catholic resistance to the revolutionary state. Yet we have spent less energy examining the lived experience of these years and tensions within the flock, especially outside the *cristero* heartland. Oaxaca experienced a Catholic resurgence of considerable proportions during the episcopacy of Euologio Gillow (1887–1922).

Although the impact of this process was more urban than rural, Gillow and his cohorts significantly expanded the Church's presence in the countryside.[4] In addition, despite the fact that it did not become a center of rebellion from 1926–29, Oaxaca evinced considerable *cristero* sympathy, particularly in the Juquila region.

I argue that the combination of factors between 1910 and the fall of 1928 in Juquila and Ixpantepec exposed complex fault lines in local Catholicism, particularly regarding gender, and strained the long-standing personal relationships that form the backbone of parish life. Our primary sources on the visions and the conflict they catalyzed come from three close collaborators and dedicated Catholics: Canseco, the diligent curate; Narváez, the Catholic lay intellectual and local organizer; and Hilario Cortés, Canseco's protégé. Oral history adds crucial information. If we listen to these sources we can perceive a deep concern that the faith and flock confronted grave dangers during this period. These anxieties inspired dissension among Church stalwarts when individuals, particularly women led by Narváez, concluded that Nicha's visions were divine, whereas Canseco claimed that Satan was responsible, and Oaxaca City journalists suspected fraud.[5] Cortés documented his agreement with the latter several decades after the fact. An additional contention simmered in Ixpantepec: Nicha and her mother apparently sought to retain control over the emerging devotion to the Virgin of Ixpantepec, and thus excluded their village's authorities, all men, from the new cult's organization and management.

Canseco's and Narvaez's relationship resides at the crux of this history. Elsewhere I have scrutinized *doña* Matildita's actions and her remarkable decision to support Nicha's visions in 1928.[6] The focus of the present chapter is Canseco's testimony. This priest's effort to describe and discredit visionary fervor in his parish provides a unique portrait of a local crisis within the Church and popular religious thinking during the revolutionary period.

Born in Oaxaca City in 1870, Ausencio Canseco entered the seminary in 1887, the inaugural year of Gillow's campaign to revamp clerical education and churn out fervent, disciplined priests steeped in ultramontane revivalism. In many ways Canseco emerged from a nexus of Mexico's oft-cited Catholic resurgence. When scholars seek examples of the pre-revolutionary surge in Church institution-building and "social" Catholicism, they find them in Gillow-era Oaxaca. At the seminary the young clerical aspirant enjoyed a sterling reputation.[7] Gillow ordained Canseco in 1896, and he ministered effectively in two parishes before gaining a transfer to Juquila in 1902.[8] He served admirably for 31 years, although he allegedly fathered a child in town.[9] Like many of his counterparts, he sustained a ministry on horseback, visiting communities separated by large distances and rugged terrain. Canseco worked hard, often administering neighboring parishes in addition to Juquila, and literally died on the job. On 24 August 1933, Canseco fell off his horse and drowned in the Sola River as he hurried between *pueblos*.[10]

When Canseco confronted news of Nicha's apparitions he was coping with local manifestations of the 1920s Church-state conflict. Juquila struggled through a period of turmoil that does not correspond to conventional periodizations—the Revolution arrived late, and lingered. Rival groups professing allegiance to Zapata and Carranza traded the plaza several times into the late 1910s, troops supporting Oaxaca's ill-fated sovereignty movement attacked in 1915, and revolutionaries still roamed in the late 1920s.[11] Canseco's letters demonstrate his triage-like approach to ministry, seeking above all to sustain the faith in the parish seat while preserving its Marian festival and safeguarding the shrine. Like many priests, he ceded his church to a local junta in 1926. Attesting to his skills, Canseco succeeded in shaping the make-up of this body with the exception of a few individuals with ties to the municipal president. He maintained that these individuals represented a cabal bent on plundering the church. He worried, however, that his allies would be easily duped due to their humble indigenous nature.[12]

The struggles Canseco faced were part of a broader transformation.[13] After centuries on the periphery of regional economics and politics, Oaxaca's coast had become a destination of entrepreneurial Central Valley *mestizos*. In the mountains Chatino municipalities still controlled land, but faced pressure to grant coffee lands to newcomers. Over time Juquila became a center of non-Chatino population and state power. One remarkable aspect of this process was its intimate mechanics. Often entrepreneurial individuals took up residence in Indian communities to gain access to land, using marriage or informal union to inaugurate these ventures. Priests even took part; a Juquila curate in the 1890s started a coffee plantation and raised a family with a local woman.[14] In the 1930s, Canseco arranged for his nephew to acquire coffee lands, too. The present-day municipal president is this individual's grandson.[15]

We cannot, however, characterize this process as a simple imposition of commercial capitalism. Many Chatinos and bicultural locals took part. The pace of change, as well as social violence, became more intense after 1930 when coffee production, land privatization, and social differentiation surged simultaneously within communities. In the 1920s Juquila's Hispanic/*mestizo* population was in the process of replacing the community's historically Chatino officials. Regional Church-state issues insinuated themselves into this dynamic, and muddled what we might otherwise interpret as an ethno-cultural and economic struggle. Juquila's Chatinos tended to side with conservative Catholic Hispanics, like Canseco and Narváez, in opposition to the new municipal president who proclaimed allegiance to the anticlerical federal government.[16]

Canseco claimed that this official disrupted religious practice, but his correspondence suggests that the real apple of discord was economic. Factions in Juquila believed they sat atop a gold mine, and angled for access to the Virgin's wealth.[17] According to the curate, his opponents argued about how to allocate church funds, with different groups lobbying for their use in legal disputes, public education, musical-instrument purchases, salaries, or loans. Canseco apparently outmaneuvered them, placing most of the Virgin's funds out of reach while they bickered. He spirited 3,000 pesos to the archdiocese, and hid considerable sums with trusted locals, such as *doña* Matildita. He also coached his supporters, tapped the Church hierarchy's political connections, and arranged for allies to receive preferential treatment. Thus a pesky tax collector found himself transferred, and the archdiocese waived impediments to a helpful lieutenant's marriage plans.[18]

If Canseco was a product of Mexico's Catholic resurgence, so was Narváez. In fact, the Church's revival owed much to legions of women who embraced calls to action and service. Particularly after the sundering of Church-state ties, and perhaps more importantly, the weakening of parish-municipality cooperation, priests leaned heavily upon activist women. Traditional sodalities within the indigenous *cargo* system remained prominent throughout Oaxaca. Although women played crucial roles in festive work, men dominated *mayordomías*. The Church's revitalization, however, provided new opportunities for religious women, particularly by emphasizing religious education and establishing a new kind of lay institution, the canonically approved association. Devout women embraced teaching and religious indoctrination, finding productive outlets for their intellectual and social energies at a time when secular options remained slim. New religious associations attracted women in droves, where they often outnumbered men.[19]

Although the nineteenth century proved difficult for the Church, the population remained devout. Mexico's Catholic resurgence, however, was less a reconversion of apostates or a rekindling of the tepidly faithful than a harnessing of lay energies. Oaxacans remained fond of the *mayordomía*-based fiesta cycle, but the newly militant Church and its associations pushed for the more disciplined fervor of individually focused, sacrament-centered practice. Unsurprisingly, priests and activist women were at the center of these endeavors, and their efforts impacted dramatically on urban religiosity. The results were mixed among indigenous communities. Village priests frequently commented that the small core of parishioners embracing modern orthodoxy were female association members. In short, women proved to be trusty foot soldiers and the primary respondents to ecclesiastical efforts to transform local piety. Oaxaca's archdiocesan organ instructed priests to engage communities through women, incorporating them in the Church's revival as teachers, catechists, and association members, and deploying them as models of reformed piety and Catholic sociopolitical opinion.[20] The Church often spoke of women as the "pious sex," lauded their tender preservation of the faith, and suggested that men could be returned to the fold through their wives and daughters. In other words, clergymen viewed women as the worker bees of Catholic revitalization. They did not, however, value them as interpreters of doctrine or leaders of men.

Matilde Narváez, an elderly spinster in 1928, epitomizes the devout Catholic women who were crucial assets of the Church. A long-time resident of Juquila from a well-off *mestizo* family, she was the right-hand woman of Juquila's curates since the 1890s, widely recognized for her loyalty to the Church. Canseco noted that he and his predecessor had such confidence in her that they entrusted her with Juquila's Catholic school. Older residents still recall her as the tireless leader of local women and the elderly schoolmarm.[21]

That she administered the parochial school and taught classes for many years attests that she possessed a relatively high degree of education, and inspired respect. She also donated land for a building to house visiting pilgrims.

In 1928 Ixpantepec was a poor village connected only by a mule trail to the municipal seat of Juquila 22 kilometers away. The *pueblo* enjoyed a pro-clerical reputation prior to the apparitions. When Canseco fled from *carrancistas* in 1919, he chose this hamlet as his refuge.[22] At some 2,000 meters above sea level, it has a relatively cold, extreme climate. An 1883 statistical survey of Oaxaca listed 194 inhabitants.[23] Hilario Cortés referred to the town as "*miserable*," suggesting abject poverty and hopelessness. He described the community as a monolingual Indian backwater, whose residents "have not Castilianized themselves and live without evolving."[24] The village depended upon low-yield, subsistence corn farming, maguey cultivation, and fruit collection. Due to its cooler temperatures and low rainfall, Ixpantepec failed to attract the coffee entrepreneurs who increasingly Hispanized the region.

Nicha left us without her testimony when she died in 1999. But if her version of events and feelings about her visionary role remain a mystery, we can glimpse her short-lived fame through Narváez and local oral history. Although sometime in late July or early August 1928 news of Nicha's visions reached Juquila, none of our sources recorded the exact date when Nicha began to consult the Virgin. The apparitions, however, had been occurring in Ixpantepec for at least several weeks. In fact, as nonindigenous (*ladino*) outsiders, our sources may have been ignorant of the devotion's indigenous origins prior to Ixpantepec's civil authorities' decision to alert their curate. Something enabled this local happening to breach cultural barriers and emerge as a regional phenomenon and cross-cultural/class movement. Some spark initiated the Chatina Virgin's miscegenation (*mestizaje*). Canseco had investigated rumored schism earlier in the year, and this troubled the devout. The local economy had not recovered from the revolution and simmering regional conflicts. In addition, if the state's newspapers are accurate, Juquila's parishioners found themselves at the center of *cristero* action in Oaxaca in 1928.[25]

This combination of concerns, conditions, and violent events added to local unease when Nicha's visions came to light, but a series of powerful earthquakes—and the girl's uncanny ability to predict them—probably catalyzed the broadcasting of her miraculous claims. According to the skeptical Hilario Cortés, when Nicha initially reported her visions, many people refused to believe her, prompting her to prophesy cataclysmic punishments. Cortés argued that it was the synergy of threats and earthquakes in the summer of 1928 that turned the tide of belief; he underscored a popular notion that the apparitions and earthquakes announced the impending, apocalyptic fulfillment of the prophecies of *La Madre Matiana*, a late-colonial seer.[26]

Doña Matildita provided the earliest concrete date concerning Nicha's visions—16 June 1928—and underscored the link to seismic activity. After a minor earthquake on that date, Nicha returned from a trip to the cave above her village and told people that the Virgin recommended that they come to her on their knees and beseech Christ for forgiveness, worship the Blessed Sacrament in her temple (the cave), and redouble their devotion to the Virgin of Juquila. Narváez alluded to popular skepticism by invoking the Guadalupe narrative, noting that the Virgin led Nicha into a supernatural rose garden within the mountain, telling her, "If I give you these roses and you take them as a sign, it will bring about another result."[27] Aside from these pronouncements, the event that most likely nudged locals from doubt to devotion was a devastating *temblor* on 4 August that reduced towns along Oaxaca's coast to rubble. Heavy rains and aftershocks followed, and villages became muddy ruins.[28] According to present-day oral testimony, Nicha even predicted the great *temblor* that destroyed much of Oaxaca City and Juquila's shrine on 14 January 1931.[29] Thus a combination of Nicha's dire prophecies and the August earthquake probably inspired Ixpantepec's civil authorities to call on Canseco.

Canseco set out for Ixpantepec at once, with Narváez not far behind, leading a group of Juquila women. In her report (written in 1932), Narváez depicted a heady early period when many people, including Canseco, were convinced of the apparitions' legitimacy and keen to follow Nicha's indications. First, Canseco said a rogation Mass and led a large group to the grotto. This included Ixpantepec's civil authorities, village residents, and probably Narváez, her female companions, and Cortés. Upon arrival, Nicha entered the grotto and emerged telling Canseco that the Virgin was present. The priest proceeded to bless the site and pray the Rosary with those present. Nicha also communicated frightening news. An angel accompanying the Virgin told Nicha that her efforts on the Virgin's behalf had enraged the devil, and he planned to accost her in horrible fashion. Narváez asserted that this indeed happened. But the angel also told Nicha that if she and her family confessed, the demonic apparitions would retire. Nicha, apparently, had not yet received confession and communion. According to Narváez, Canseco immediately ordered a woman to begin preparing Nicha for confession. Nicha, however, refused, saying the angel had prepared her. Canseco, Narváez maintained, discovered this was true when he confessed the girl.[30]

Narváez crafted her narrative to convince archdiocesan authorities of the veracity of Nicha's visions and the girl's inherent sanctity. She sought to establish Nicha's credentials as an authentic seer, stressing Satan's necessary opposition to Nicha's fulfillment of the Virgin's will (her *servicio*), the girl's natural piety, and her miraculously precocious religious knowledge. Oral testimony adds complexity to Nicha's supernatural encounters. A present-day Ixpantepec resident recalls that her grandfather told her about the frenetic excitement surrounding Nicha's visions and a short-lived economic boom as Ixpantepec became a magnet for pilgrims. He concurred that civil authorities sent for Canseco, but maintained that no villager beyond Nicha witnessed any miracles. Our informant's grandfather claimed to have administered curing rites to Nicha after her visions. Apparently she returned from the grotto in a dazed hysteria, babbling fearfully about a beast in the church that threatened

to consume the village. This man exorcized this uncontrollable panic by praying over her and performing rituals.[31]

While oral history does not contradict Narváez, it reveals that she did not
witness all the rituals inspired by Nicha's apparitions, or chose to omit them
from her report. Regardless of these unknowns, clearly more than one religious tradition was in play. It is likely that people such as Narváez, the
Chatino folk healer (*curandero*), and Canseco perceived this overlap of religious practice as routine, even if they disapproved. Common sense suggests
that Narváez would have muted any hint of heterodoxy, but Canseco did not
mention them either. It is also possible that indigenous rites took place
before outsiders knew about the visions, or during rituals from which residents deliberately excluded them.

Doña Matildita reported that increasing numbers of pilgrims visited the
grotto as the fall progressed and that they shared a fervent desire to see the
Virgin. Nicha assured visitors that the Virgin intended to reveal herself, and
many queries addressed to Nicha asked when, and under what conditions,
this would take place. On All Saints Day 1928, visitors learned that if they
came together to form "a single heart," the Virgin would appear in a sensational manner for New Year. This issue of having a "single heart" (*un solo
corazón*) comes up repeatedly in image-centered devotionalism in the region.
In ethnographic studies of indigenous Catholics and Oaxacan apparition
movements, a single heart denotes honest faith and intentions.[32] The idea
often emerges in the contentious environments surrounding unofficial
apparitions in which devotees sense that some visitors come with "two
hearts"; that is, to discredit the devotion.

According to Narváez, on 4 November Nicha informed those gathered at
the site that the Virgin wanted a small altar placed beneath a cross inside the
grotto. Narváez instructed devotees to pray the Rosary there early next
morning so the Virgin could bless her children, and added that if Canseco celebrated Mass at the grotto then all "who were graced" would see her.[33] By this
time, Canseco was distancing himself from the visions. Probably he was
increasingly uncomfortable with heterodox elements of the emergent devotion, and its growth was also beginning to undercut Juquila's Marian devotion. Indeed, rumors circulated that the Virgin of Juquila had relocated to
Ixpantepec.[34] With Juquila's annual pilgrimage fiesta (8 December) approach-
ing, it is not surprising Canseco avoided the grotto. The faithful beseeched
the Virgin to appear before them all, and organized a novena culminating on
the same day as Juquila's feast. Nicha repeated that the Virgin wanted a priest
to bring the Sacrament and celebrate Mass, but Canseco refused.[35] The
Virgin never showed herself to the crowds before the grotto.

A particularly salient aspect of Nicha's visions and the Ixpantepec devotion
was the amount of anxiety focused on gaining Father Canseco's participation. No one within the movement emerged as a popularly ordained specialist even when it became clear that Canseco sought to suppress the devotion,
nor did Narváez mention efforts to find another priest to officiate. Possibly
the movement's epistolary voice exaggerated devotees' orthodoxy, or was

simply expressing her personal concerns. But even if Narváez overstated interest in priest-led ritual, the repeated gestures and visions aimed at securing Canseco's mediating/sanctifying ritual presence underscore tensions within the fold, particularly between the curate and the one-time Catholic school principal and Church stalwart.

Since *doña* Matildita had been Canseco's close spiritual and political collaborator, their falling out was rancorous. As with most rifts, events predating actual conflict stressed the once solid alliance. The revolution and its aftermath lay at the root of these tensions. Indeed, the key individuals in this story experienced considerable personal upheaval during the period. We have seen that Juquila's sociopolitical transformation in the 1920s tested Canseco. The new authorities also closed Narváez's school. Cortés, the curate's protégé, abandoned the Oaxaca City seminary after the government expropriated its buildings. Political upheaval also set the stage for a financial dispute between Narváez and the curate. Apparently, Canseco entrusted 1,900 pesos of shrine capital to the trusted spinster, to protect them from marauding soldiers and greedy officials. When he sought to recover these funds in 1926, however, Narváez informed him that she had spent the money. This dispute festered until the apparitions and remained a thorny issue while the formidable woman and the priest were at variance over Nicha's visions. Canseco pressured Narváez to repay him for five years before bringing up the issue with the archdiocese in 1931.[36] Canseco did not, however, link the debt question to Narváez's support for Nicha's visions. In the 1930s he denied her the sacraments and convinced the archdiocese to pursue the case with her family, but he never employed the easiest means of discrediting his nemesis: accusing Narváez of fraud.[37] Perhaps accusing the respected spinster of alms profiteering was simply not credible in Juquila. Nonetheless, while this dispute took its course behind the scenes, Narváez threw her energy and prestige behind the effort to gain ecclesiastical recognition of the visions.

Canseco's early indecision and final analysis of the apparitions show him grappling with the conundrum of Catholicism in a modernizing society. Dogma dictated that miracles indeed occurred, and Marian apparitionism was especially important among Catholics who felt their faith to be under rationalist assault during the period. Yet Canseco must also have known that stories of visions in an infamously rebellious indigenous region during the *Cristiada* would spark suspicion. In addition, it would be difficult to convince his superiors that the Ixpantepec visions *were* divine. An archdiocesan investigation posed significant risks—arising from his earlier participation in grotto rituals—for the padre. Moreover, official validation would have occasioned the Church many problems, from interpreting the miracles' meaning and controlling devotional practices, to explaining them to modern urbanites and managing the political fallout.

These problems must have been on his mind in late 1928 and early 1929, because Canseco truly believed that supernatural visions were taking place. He also had to explain the apparitions in his own parish among people whose worldview was less encumbered by modern rationalism. This was crucial, since Narváez backed the visions. Nonetheless, it took Canseco several months to document his opinion. Perhaps he waited, in the vain hope that the apparition movement would subside. In January 1929, he finally wrote to his superiors, maintaining, "The fact of the apparitions of the divine images is true, very true, but not everyone sees them. Hence, it is necessary to determine if the cause of these apparitions is good or bad; either it is God through the ministry of his angels, or it is the devil planning some evil outcome."[38] Had he uncovered fraud, the priest could have simply ignored the visions or denounced the perpetrators, but allegations of real supernatural visions necessitated detailed descriptions.[39] In his reports Canseco assumed the voice of expert observer. Describing a crescendo of visionary claims and pilgrimages from early November 1928, the curate emphasized the experiences of male visitors while relegating Nicha to secondary status and sowing doubt about her character. In fact, he minimized women's role in general. His overarching goal was to convince his superiors of the great number and extraordinary nature of the experiences reported, and to highlight the disturbing characteristics and doctrinal errors that indicated darker forces were afoot.

In his first letter, Canseco described three distinct types of grotto experience at Ixpantepec. One set of visitors saw nothing out of the ordinary. They arrived on their knees, praying, singing, and doing penance, yet perceived nothing. A second group observed images in the patterns produced by the combination of water seeping across the stones inside the grotto and the multitude of burning candles crowding the entrance. A third group described three-dimensional moving visions that abruptly appeared and disappeared, and were often seen best from a distance. Canseco recounted that visionaries most often claimed to see advocations of Mary. Some told of entire processions: the Virgin of Solitude leading a group of saints, the Blessed Sacrament heading a glowing parade, glimpses of the Crucifixion. Still others described seeing the Virgin of Solitude bless them, making the sign of the cross like a priest at Mass, although the Virgin apparently signed the cross from right to left, instead of left to right.[40]

Canseco also listed several troubling visions. For example, echoing classic rural depictions of the devil, one man allegedly saw a dapper individual seated on an altar inside the cave surrounded by flowers. The supernatural dandy wore mostly black, with a long white-collared shirt, dashing sideburns, and a stylish cowboy's hat with iridescent points shimmering around its rim. Other visionaries maintained they had seen hell and purgatory, and one described a wheel turning inside the grotto with demons and souls dangling from its perimeter. Another, perhaps inspired by contemporary sociopolitical turmoil, described a princely archangel in insurgent garb. This figure appeared wearing ammunition belts around his shoulders and waist, and was backed by many armed followers.[41] The variety and number of visions astounded Juquila's curate. In exasperation he listed some incomprehensible apparitions such as a loosely saddled, riderless, and bellowing horse; a woman with a tall ghost on her head; and flying flowers, before giving up and writing "etc, etc . . ." Canseco also stressed laughable inconsistencies. In one instance, two men praying together saw a figure emerging from a cave; one reported seeing the Virgin of Juquila, the other a chicken.

In the report's second half, Canseco turned to Nicha. The priest described her as an uncivilized, taciturn, eight- or nine-year-old native, and suspected that the girl's hovering mother controlled her actions. Since the beginning, he reported, Nicha maintained that she met with the Virgin and one or two angels in the small cave, and allegedly told him that the Virgin seldom spoke but relied on an angel to transmit her dispositions. The curate then sketched the typical pilgrim-Nicha-Angel-Virgin interactions. Visitors would congregate before the cave and Nicha would ascend to the grotto with supplicants' petitions for the Virgin's blessing, responses to various questions, and/or cures. Some pilgrims apparently required a translator to communicate with Nicha.[42] Then the girl would enter the small opening in the stone while the anxious pilgrims awaited her on a flat patch of land in front of the cave. In many cases Nicha returned suggesting that they drink the water that emerged from the cave, or apply it to afflicted areas of the body. Some witnesses observed miraculous transformations in Nicha's attire while she conferenced with the angel and the Virgin. Instead of her usual impoverished aspect she appeared brilliantly clad in white stockings, good shoes, and a rich dress. Canseco asserted that many individuals left unsatisfied, but others professed a blind faith in the Chatina seer.

The cures became a key component of Canseco's argument against Nicha's revelations. The careful padre chose a symbolic range of ailing individuals: a man with a stroke-induced speech impediment and crippled arm and leg, another with a mental disorder, and a blind woman. Canseco stressed that all journeyed to Ixpantepec devoutly, but Nicha proclaimed that none was worthy of cure. She rebuffed them, stating enigmatically that the first two should remember the cause of their illness. The suspicious curate also emphasized other troubling characteristics of Nicha's testimony and comportment. He was particularly critical of statements and actions that Nicha attributed to the Virgin, deeming these worthy of transcription. She occasionally denied pilgrim entreaties saying, "The Virgin is not here—she will return later," or "She is too busy." She even asked supplicants to wait, claiming, "The Holy Virgin went to take a bath, but she will bathe quickly." Perhaps most damning in the cleric's eyes, Nicha allegedly proclaimed, "The Holy Virgin says that the girl should be in charge of all the alms collected at the grotto."[43]

Toward the end of his 12 January letter, Canseco offered his opinion that grave doctrinal errors had emerged from Ixpantepec. Many visitors, including "educated people," believed that within the cave the Virgin Mary resided in body and soul, "as if she lived there." Some claimed that the celestial court also dwelt there. Nicha, he asserted, instructed believers that the Virgin would soon depart for heaven and leave behind her likeness, hence many devotees began to refer to the grotto and surrounding stone as the Virgin's sanctuary or temple. Canseco identified the key propagator of these ideas as a pious Juquila woman (clearly Narváez), who had taken it upon herself to attend pilgrims arriving at the site. She provided visitors with information about the apparitions, he reported, inculcating the notion that the Virgin inhabited the very stones and that within the mountain the Mother of God maintained a magnificent, invisible shrine.[44]

The oral testimony of Juquila resident Justina Vásquez reveals that others found Nicha's statements, comportment, and visions troubling. Vásquez— born after the apparitions—learned of them from family members who rushed to Ixpantepec when the news reached Juquila. Revealing the rift that these apparitions caused among Juquila's Catholics, Vásquez reported that Matilde Narváez was her mother's godmother and a blood relative. In addition, Vásquez's mother taught under *doña* Matildita in Juquila's Catholic school. The two women were close confidants who labored in support of the Church, and Vásquez's mother was probably among those Narváez led to Ixpantepec. The Vásquez family went reverently but became apprehensive of Nicha when she announced that the Virgin was unavailable because she was visiting other nations. Suspicion turned to alarm when pilgrims reported visions of faceless sacred images. Vásquez maintains that Nicha's statements inspired great concern and respect, especially when she accurately predicted another powerful earthquake on 14 January 1931. Nonetheless, falling in line with Canseco, Vásquez cautioned that the devil also knows what the future holds.[45]

Canseco's 12 January report is missing its concluding page, or pages, but the last extant page lists "other strange details." Nicha, he claimed, went back and forth from her supposed celestial consultations without demonstrating any change in emotional state. She remained cold and indifferent after her alleged meetings with the Virgin. He also mentioned that another girl occasionally fulfilled Nicha's role as the Holy Mother's intermediary.[46] Canseco also noted that rumors of new apparitions had emerged in different nearby communities.[47] According to Vásquez, Canseco performed a test to expose the supernatural force behind the visions, reciting incantations and sprinkling holy water on a boulder in front of the grotto. This split the stone in half, apparently indicating to the priest that the enemy (*el enemigo*) was at work in Ixpantepec.[48] Canseco never mentioned this experiment to his superiors.

Lamentably, descriptions of apparitions and grotto activity dwindle after January 1929. Canseco sent another letter on 16 January reconstructing the visions of a respected, pious man from Miahuatlán that portrayed the high clergy as an obstacle to the Virgin's mission among the faithful.[49] This same visionary's testimony appeared in Oaxaca newspapers in February, and *El Mercurio* called for state action to end religious fraud.[50] By then, Canseco's and Narváez's differences had become irreconcilable, and in the 1930s the issue of shrine funds appears in their letters. In previous reports, Canseco refrained from naming Narváez. But in May 1930 the curate attacked his one-time ally with passion. Demonstrating that there is no dispute so bitter as a challenge within the fold, Canseco maligned Narváez's character and apparitionist crusade. He referred to her as the "fomenter and soul of the disturbances at Ixpantepec's cave," and asserted that she subverted others by teaching that "those diabolical visions" were divine apparitions. Worse, Narváez openly challenged his religious authority, claiming that as Catholics believed in the sanctity of Mass, so they should accept the Virgin's presence in Ixpantepec. Hoping to outmaneuver Canseco, *doña* Matildita undertook the four-day trek to Oaxaca City in April 1930, although we have no record of what happened when she appeared at the archdiocesan offices.[51] Two years later, the persistent Narváez sent her own report to the archdiocese detailing Nicha's visions.

By the mid-1930s, the struggle was over. Canseco had drowned and *doña* Matildita had given up. On 8 February 1934, the apparitions' defender wrote a final letter to the archbishop.[52] She no longer hoped for the apparitions' official recognition, but revealed profound angst regarding her standing in the Church and an enduring faith in Nicha's visionary calling. She pleaded for permission to take communion and revisit the apparition site so that she could go with Nicha to ask the Virgin for advice and succor.[53] Two weeks later, the vicar general outlined the archdiocese's policy in a terse letter to Canseco's successor.[54] He appended a typed copy of Narváez's 1932 report, noting that she had been instructed to address all further inquiries to her new curate. Regarding the Ixpantepec Virgin and Nicha, the vicar general said that Narváez knew of the ruling against the visions. Moreover, she was forbidden to visit the apparition site. After this letter, news of Nicha, *doña* Matildita, and other visionaries ceases. Nicha stayed in her village and raised a family, and many of her neighbors claim no knowledge of her apparitionist past. As for Narváez, although her campaign to legitimize the apparitions collapsed, her faith did not. She died impoverished and disgraced in the 1940s, convinced of the sacrality of Nicha's revelations.[55]

At the outset of this chapter I argued that Father Canseco faced a local religious mutiny in the aftermath of the Mexican Revolution, and amidst waxing anticlericalism, socioeconomic turmoil, and natural disaster. But why did the apparition movement flounder? As with most episodes of visionary fervor, the answer resides in the interwoven realms of social norms, evolving conditions, religious lore, practice and belief, and individual agency. Although certainty is impossible, Nicha's supporters probably lost the struggle to bring a lasting devotion into being in two critical arenas of gendered contention: Ixpantepec's local indigenous community, and regional Catholic society.

Nicha's visions evolved within a Chatino environment, and thus were subject to deeply Mesoamerican interpretations and apparitionist traditions, most of which remain beyond the reach of historical inquiry. Much of what we know about the apparitions can be interpreted as thoroughly indigenous if analyzed in light of present-day ethnographic studies. But a fascinating aspect of these events was their multi-vocality: they proved deeply meaningful to indigenous and Hispanic residents of the region. Nonetheless, considering that it took weeks, or even months, for news of the visions to reach Juquila, initially they were a local Chatino issue. It seems likely that Nicha's early visions were leading toward her emergence as a classic Mesoamerican religious specialist, an intermediary between the social group and the sacred.

Only later did spreading news transform the visions into a broader devotional movement. Due to the absence of archival documentation in Ixpantepec and the sketchy nature of oral testimony, making firm conclusions about exactly what occurred in the girl-seer's community is risky. Nonetheless, clues suggest that the apparition supporters erred in their exclusion of local Chatino men from the movement's leadership, and in their failure to institutionalize their upstart devotion.

Although rarely well-documented, Oaxaca boasts other episodes of indigenous apparitionism that evolved into lasting devotions through institutionalization and incorporation into specific communities' fiesta cycles.[56] In short, apparitionist movements can graft new practices within local variants of the Mesoamerican *cargo* system. The key involves including prominent political actors and acquiring the trappings of traditional image-centered devotion. Ixpantepec, like other villages in the region, had its hierarchy of male-dominated *mayordomías* controlling public ritual culture.[57] Nicha and her mother, perhaps inspired by the pilgrim crush of 1928 and Narváez's energetic backing, seemingly focused on official recognition. Moving to control the flow of alms, they failed to create a new *mayordomía* and produce a physical image of the Virgin that could sustain and focus devotion in the face of clerical opposition. In addition, the market around the apparition site was destroyed after Canseco pronounced the visions demonic. Hilario Cortés hinted that this was done at the curate's behest.[58] Given Canseco's discordant relations with municipal officeholders, the likely agents were the men that had summoned the curate to investigate the visions in the first place—Ixpantepec's Chatino officials.

Facing local opposition, the "Second Juan Diego" floundered regionally when Narváez attempted to go over her parish priest in hope that the archdiocese would back the cause. Although gaps remain, we know more about this level of contention thanks to ecclesiastical documentation. Still the question remains as to why scores of people beyond Ixpantepec decided to support the Chatina girl's visions. I believe the answer lies in the conjunction of three pairs of factors relating to local conditions—political upheaval and festering social violence; religious doubts/fears and rising anticlericalism; economic turmoil and natural disasters—and the prophecies of *Madre Matiana*.[59] According to Hilario Cortés, the basis of broad belief in Nicha's visions in 1928 was the synergy of social unease, rooted in prevailing conditions, and popular interpretations of these millenarian prognostications. The Matiana prophecies, allegedly derived from the visions of a colonial convent servant, proved powerful for two reasons: first, they speak directly to the concurrence of anticlericalism, political violence, religious turmoil, and natural disaster; and second, they are phrased in the militant, gendered religious discourse that proved attractive to activist women such as Narváez. In brief, a superheated apocalyptic feminism suffuses these Mexican prophecies. They clearly frame doctrinal error as male and defense of the faith as female, predicting the Church's ultimate revitalization thanks to a female-led crusade of expiatory fervor that would end in a year ending in the number eight.

Moreover, official Church publications during the period, including Oaxaca's official archdiocesan organ, admonished the faithful to take the prophecies seriously.[60]

Cortés failed to mention Narváez by name, but probably had her in mind when he explained the foundations of credence in the Chatina seer's revelations. It is this conjunction of Matiana's and Nicha's prophecies, and *doña* Matildita's role as Juquila's chief female Catholic activist/intellectual, that makes her decision to break with the clergy understandable. A Matiana-tinged interpretation of the Ixpantepec visions would have allowed Narváez to perceive a new role for herself in Catholicism's Mexican struggle at what seemed like a dire moment for religious Mexicans. In essence, the intertwining of these Marian narratives transformed the Catholic school principal, shrine benefactress, and curate's right-hand woman into one of the Virgin's chosen agents of miraculous renewal. This would explain *doña* Matildita's willingness to challenge Father Canseco's religious and patriarchal authority. Perceiving a far more powerful spiritual superior, she took up the banner of Nicha's devotional insurgency and assumed her place in the pious female phalanx taking shape at Ixpantepec's grotto.

Canseco felt that Nicha's visions sparked an uprising in the fold that merited careful suppression, lest pernicious heterodoxies take hold in his parish. His depiction of the apparition site suggests a religious and social world turned upside-down, and a state of apparitionist chaos. His letters smear Nicha, her mother, and Narváez as insubordinate, untrustworthy women, without carefully examining their religious beliefs or experiences. For this priest, the very assertiveness of these women was proof of error and disorder. Instead, he focuses on the testimony of male pilgrim visionaries. For the usually circumspect, steady curate, the insidious and bewildering complexity of their visions implied that Satan was the motor of unrest among the faithful. It would have been easier simply to accuse Narváez of fraud, but this probably would not have been convincing in Juquila. Canseco had to explain why this well-regarded Church stalwart would support the Indian girl's visions and openly challenge him. Oral history suggests that even Narváez's relatives ultimately accepted that the devil tricked *doña* Matildita. Conversely, Nicha's supporters may have perceived a supernatural hand in Canseco's untimely death, but in the end, without broader local foundations to sustain the struggle, they lost in the face of ecclesiastical stonewalling and the Church's ability to let time erode popular fervor and defeat Ixpantepec's revolution in local Catholicism.

Notes

1. "En las grutas de Ixpantepec, Juquila, los Creyentes Ingenuos Ven Aparecer Raras Visiones," *El Mercurio*, 7 Feb. 1929.
2. This translates to "Teaching, preaching, and giving the sacraments." Canseco to Secretary Augustín Espinoza, Archivo Histórico de la Arquidiócesis de Oaxaca (hereafter AHAO), Diocesano, Gobierno, Correspondencia (hereafter DGC), 7 Jul. 1931.

3. Canseco to Espinoza, AHAO DGC 1926, 31 Aug., 6 and 16 Oct., and 28 (illegible month).

4. The limited clericalization of Oaxacan Catholicism proved to be a strong point during the *Cristiada*. Communities generally organized ritual with only sporadic contact with the clergy, and thus were well prepared for anticlerical efforts to limit the priesthood's presence in the countryside; see Meyer in this volume.

5. *El Mercurio*, 7 Feb. 1929.

6. Edward Wright-Rios, "Visions of Women: Revelation, Gender, and Catholic Resurgence," in *Religious Culture in Modern Mexico*, ed. Martin Austin Nesvig (Lanham: Rowman and Littlefield Press, 2007).

7. Canseco's ordination file, AHAO, Diocesano, Gobierno, Seminario (hereafter DGS) 1893–94; Fondo Luis Castañeda Guzmán (hereafter FLCG), Eulogio Gillow, Libros de Visitas Pastorales del Señor Eulogio Gillow, vol. 7.

8. FLCG, Gillow, vol. 7.

9. James Greenberg, *Blood Ties* (Tucson: University of Arizona Press, 1989). This book is especially useful since the chief informant was raised by his god-father, Ausencio Canseco.

10. Cornelio Bourget to Espinoza, AHAO DGC, 3 Sep. 1933.

11. Greenberg, *Blood Ties*, 59–60.

12. Canseco to Espinoza, AHAO DGC 1926, 31 Aug., 6 and 16 Oct., and 28 (illegible month).

13. Greenberg, *Blood Ties;* Miguel Bartolomé and Alicia Barabas, *Tierra de Palabra* (Oaxaca: UABJO, 1996); Jorge Hernández-Díaz, *El Café Amargo* (Oaxaca: UABJO, 1987); Gonzalo Piñon Jiménez and Jorge Hernández-Díaz, *El Café* (Oaxaca: UABJO, 1998).

14. FLCG, Eulogio Gillow, vol. 5; AHAO DGC, Manuel Ramírez to Gillow, 16 Jan. and 31 Aug. 1897; AHAO DGC, Canseco to Espinoza, 25 Jan. 1926; AHAO DGC, Canseco to Espinoza, 4 Feb. and 10 Dec. 1930, 13 Nov. 1931.

15. Interview with Rafael León, 13 Feb. 2002.

16. Greenberg, *Blood Ties.*

17. Interview with Luis Castañeda Guzmán, 23 Jan. 2002. This issue remains contentious in Juquila; Cesar Morales Niño, "La Iglesia y los Políticos de Juquila Pelean por las Jugosas Limosnas de los Peregrinos de la Virgen," *Noticias*, 1 Jan. 2006.

18. Canseco to Espinoza, AHAO DGC 1926, 31 Aug., 6 and 16 Oct., and 28 (illegible month).

19. AHAO *Boletín Oficial y Revista Eclesiástica de Antequera* (heretofore *Boletín*), 1 Aug. 1901.

20. *Boletín*, "Sobre Todo Orar y Hacer Orar," 15 Jul. 1902.

21. Interviews with Rafael León (13 Feb. 2002); Teresa Narváez (10 Mar. 2002); Justina Vásquez (11 Mar. 2002); Guillermo Rojas (26 Jan. 2002).

22. Interview with Rafael León, 13 Feb. 2002.

23. Manuel Martínez Gracida, *Colección de Cuadros Sinópticos de los Pueblos Haciendas y Ranchos del Estado Libre y Soberano de Oaxaca* (Oaxaca, 1883), 292.

24. Hilario Cortés, unpublished ms.

25. *El Mercurio*, 12 and 28 Sep.; 6 and 27 Oct.; 6 Nov.; 23 Dec. 1928: 11 Jan.; 7, 18, and 26 July; 3, 8, and 14 Aug. 1929.

26. María Josefa de la Pasión de Jesús, *Profecías de Matiana* (Mexico: Imprenta de la calle del Cuadrante de Santa Catarina, 1861).

27. Matilde Narváez, "Algunos Datos Proporcionados por la Señorita Matilde Narváez," AHAO Diocesano, Gobierno, Parroquias (hereafter DGP) 1930–43, 5 Apr. 1932.

28. *El Mercurio*, 8 Aug., 8 and 23 Sept. 1928; 3 Mar. and 10 Apr. 1929.

29. Interview with Justina Vásquez, 11 Mar. 2002. Tomás D. Barrera, *El Temblor del 14 de 1931* (Mexico City: UNAM, 1931).

30. Narváez, "Algunos Datos."

31. Interviews, Ixpantepec, 14 Feb. 2002. Informants' anonymity requested.

32. Alicia M. Barabas, "El Aparicionismo en América Latina: Religión, Territorio e Identidad," in *La Identidad*, ed. Ana Bella Pérez Casto (Mexico City: UNAM, 1995); and Barabas, "La Aparición de la Virgen en Oaxaca, México," *Thule* 2, no. 3 (1997). Also Enrique Marroquín, *La Cruz Mesiánica* (Mexico City: Palabra Ediciones, 1999).

33. Narváez, "Algunos datos."

34. Cortés, unpublished ms.

35. Narváez, "Algunos datos."

36. Canseco to Francisco Campos, AHAO DGC, 14 and 29 May 1931. Canseco to Espinoza, AHAO DGC, 12 Aug., 28 Sept., and 13 Nov. 1931. Narváez to Campos, AHAO DGC, 17, 26 May 1931.

37. Francisco Campos to Samuel and Efrén Narváez, Tututepec, AHAO DGC, 21 May 1931; Narváez to Archbishop Núñez, AHAO DGC, 8 Feb. 1934.

38. Canseco to Gracida, AHAO DGC, 12 Jan. 1929.

39. Ibid.; Canseco to Rafael Torres, AHAO DGC, 16 Jan. 1929.

40. Canseco to Gracida, AHAO DGC, 12 Jan. 1929.

41. Ibid.

42. Narváez, "Algunos datos."

43. Canseco to Gracida, AHAO DGC, 12 Jan. 1929.

44. Ibid.

45. Interview with Justina Vásquez, 11 Mar. 2002.

46. Canseco to Gracida, AHAO DGC, 12 Jan. 1929. The possibility of a second girl seer appears in other sources—see *El Mercurio*, 7 Feb. 1929. One informant reported that two girls spoke to the Virgin and the angel; Ixpantepec interviews, 14 Feb. 2002.

47. Canseco did not name the places, but Cortés's ms. notes that they were Temaxcaltepec and Nopala.

48. Interview with Justina Vásquez, 11 Mar. 2002.

49. Canseco to Torres, AHAO DGC, 16 Jan. 1929.

50. *El Mercurio*, 7 Feb. 1929.

51. Canseco to Espinoza, AHAO DGC, 27 May 1930.

52. Narváez to Núñez, AHAO DGC, 8 Feb. 1934.

53. Ibid.

54. Carlos Gracida to Frías, AHAO DGP, 23 Feb. 1934.

55. Interview with Justina Vásquez, 11 Mar. 2002.

56. John Monaghan, *The Covenants with the Earth and Rain* (Norman: University of Oklahoma Press, 1995); Edward Wright-Rios, *Piety and Progress* (Ph.D. diss., University of California, San Diego, 2004); Wright-Rios, "Envisioning Mexico's Catholic Resurgence: The Virgin of Solitude and the

Talking Christ of Tlacoxcalco, 1908–1924," *Past and Present* 195 (May 2007).

57. James Greenberg, *Santiago's Sword* (Berkeley: University of California Press, 1981); Bartolomé and Barabas, *Tierra*.
58. Cortés, ms.
59. De la Pasion de Jesus, "Profecías."
60. Luis G. Duarte and Antonio Martínez del Cañizo, *Profecías de Matiana acerca del Triunfo de la Iglesia* (Mexico City: Imprenta del Círculo Católico, 1889); "Las profecías de Matiana," *Boletín*, 1 Apr. 1910.

Chapter 13

"The Priest's Party": Local Catholicism and *Panismo* in Huajuapam de León

Benjamin Smith

On 8 September 1947, the people of Huajuapam de León assembled to celebrate the centennial of the death of Antonio de León, the independence leader who died fighting American forces at Molino del Rey and whose name had been adopted by his home town. The commemoration was designed to heal two decades of bitter division in Huajuapam under the umbrella of national unity. The Mexican flag was to be raised and a tree planted with the soil of each Mixtec municipality.[1] Furthermore, supporters of both the Partido Acción Nacional (PAN) and the Partido Revolucionario Institucional (PRI) took part in the organizing committee. At the same time, Oaxaca's *priísta* governor, Eduardo Vasconcelos, and the PAN's lay and clerical leaders agreed to preside over the event.[2] However, during the speeches and festivities, it became clear that both sides were celebrating different ideas of patriotic accord. While the local PRI chief's speech was restrained and secular, those of PAN supporters were steeped in religious imagery:[3] Miguel López y López reminded the crowd that de León's banner was the flag of Iguala, "with its three symbols, union, independence, and religion," before breaking into a song celebrating de León's attachment to La Guadalupe, Huajuapam's churches, and God himself.[4] Another *panista* claimed that the "Angel of Mexico" was celebrating the Immaculate Conception the day de León died, and thus neglected to care for one of her "chosen sons."[5] However, despite the tonal disjunctions between the speeches, the event passed off quietly until the reenactment of the royalist siege of Huajuapam in 1812. Despite protestations by PRI and PAN representatives, the reenactment turned violent as PAN ranchers from surrounding villages turned on PRI supporters, beating them with wooden swords until they fled to the municipal palace.[6] This centennial exposes sustained divisions within Mexican society in the period after the revolutionary state had retreated from the anticlerical extremes of the 1920s–1930s. Furthermore, it reveals how these rifts translated into the political and cultural atmosphere of succeeding decades.

Following this example, this chapter recounts how discord over postrevolutionary culture and the Church's place in local and national society translated into the political ruptures of the 1940s–1950s, and thus suggests an alternative sociology and teleology of the PAN.

Histories of postrevolutionary Mexico point to a gradual compromise between religious conservatives and the state after 1936. Indeed, historians argue that in the late 1930s leaders of both the Catholic Church and revolutionary state put an end to the conflicts of preceding decades.[7] According to Roberto Blancarte, this tentative convergence established a *modus vivendi* that was cemented during Avila Camacho's *sexenio* (1940–46). Not only did Avila Camacho promote an ideology of national unity, publicly avow his Catholicism, and dismantle article 3 of the Constitution, but the country's bishops pulled rebels into line by absorbing them into Mexican Catholic Action (ACM).[8] Political scientists have built upon this perceived appeasement to describe the growth of the organized opposition to the revolutionary government, the PAN. National studies have focused on the PAN's intellectual foundations, elite leadership, relationship with business interests, and role in the "legitimization of the one-party system."[9] Although previous scholars such as Donald Mabry and Franz von Sauer attempted to locate the PAN in the context of the cultural divisions of the 1930s, their investigations hinged on the ideology of the party's national leaders, rather than its scattered, provincial supporters.[10] In fact, political scientists have generally avoided discussing the links between the national party and its provincial adherents, leaving scholarship of Catholic radicalism from the late 1930s to historians of the *sinarquistas*, echoing Carlos Velasco Gil's view that while "the PAN [was] the brain, cold, calculating and proud; [*sinarquismo* was] the heart, burning, blind, fanatical, and willing to shed its blood to the very last drop."[11]

Local affairs rarely parallel national politics, however, and radical antistate Catholicism and *panismo* both developed according to regional circumstances. Scholars have thus turned to local studies to bridge the gap between the conflicts of the 1930s and the apparent banality of biparty politics in later decades. Pablo Serrano Alvarez situates the emergence of *sinarquismo* in the Bajío's regional politics and culture,[12] and Daniel Newcomer has argued that religious differences fuelled the León massacre of 1946.[13] Moreover, anthropologists have started to examine the PAN's local trajectories. In particular, Rossana Almada has analyzed the party's birth in Zamora among ambitious but disenfranchised merchants.[14] In Huajuapam, I will argue, the PAN's roots lay in the nineteenth-century formation of a distinctively local Catholic culture drawing together both ethnic groups (particularly Mixtec Indians) and social classes. The strength of this localized religious culture ensured that resistance to revolutionary anticlericalism was intense, and that divisions opened up by the state's anticlerical campaigns would linger on past mid-century. Opposition to the regime's political, cultural, and economic interference, articulated during the 1930s, framed the political discourse and conflicts of the 1940s and 1950s as a reinvigorated Church and its followers across the social spectrum continued to oppose the government through Catholic Action and, latterly, the PAN.

Land, Power, Culture: The Creation of the Diocese of Huajuapam (1880–1930)

The roots of the PRI-PAN divisions that dominated the second half of the twentieth century in Huajuapam lay in the ethnic, agrarian, political, and religious conflicts of the late nineteenth century. During this period, Huajuapam developed a distinct local Catholic culture through which the Church attempted to attract indigenous Mixtecs. First, the Church and indigenous communities defended communal property in unison by creating what were known as agricultural societies; second, the relationship between politics, religion, and ethnicity was mediated well into the late nineteenth century by resilient Indian caciques, cementing the Church's appeal to indigenous groups at a time of unpopular and disruptive Spanish immigration; and third, the diocese of Huajuapam de León—established in 1903—maintained a proto-*indigenista* program of accepting—even encouraging—syncretic Mixtec religious practices.

The 1850s Reform Laws forbade communal property ownership by indigenous *pueblos* or the Church. During the Porfiriato, politicians and speculators attempted to implement these laws throughout Mexico: in Oaxaca alone there were over 30 edicts decreeing the division of communal lands.[15] However, as historians are discovering, many *pueblos* managed to negotiate or avoid the laws' implementation. The effects of the *reparto* in the Mixteca have elicited a bewildering array of opinions: some stress the retention of indigenous communal land, others its division into smallholdings, and a few the acquisition of large estates.[16] In part, the debate rests on a misunderstanding of the actual nature of Mixtec landholding and on a stereotyping of indigenous attitudes to land. In the first place, many communal lands *were* privatized, but remained in indigenous villagers' hands;[17] in the district capital of Huajuapam, for example, communal lands were divided among 2,000 families, and dissolution did not lead automatically to speculation and despoilment. Second, although some Spanish families took advantage of privatization to amass large estates (*latifundios*), these remained exceptional.[18] Third, the Reform threw up a novel form of landownership blending private and public property: the agricultural society. This was a localized institution built on the extinct holdings of *caciques* who in the eighteenth century rented land to Mixtec farmers for pasture or growing the maguey cacti that attracted cochineal-giving insects. With the nineteenth-century collapse of the cochineal trade, successive ethnic revolts, and the push for municipal independence, however, *caciques* sold up to indigenous peasant-farmers.[19] These formed agricultural societies within which land could only be sold to other society members; land surrounding individuals' private grazing and woodland plots remained effectively communal.[20] By 1910, many Huajuapam villages—Tequixtepec, Mariscala, Dinicuiti, Chazumba, Huastepec, Huajolotitlan, Silacayoapilla, Chilixtlahuaca, Yucuna,

Ayuquila, Cuiloto, Suchitepec, Cuyotepeji, Atoyac, Estancia—had purchased as agricultural societies lands that they formally rented.[21]

Catholics priests were instrumental in this shift to indigenous-*ranchero* landholding in two ways. First, priests acted as middlemen between economically ailing *caciques* and indigenous clients, encouraging the peaceful settlement of land disputes through village purchases of rented lands. In 1875, the *cura* of Huajuapam lent the Santa Caterina Estancia agricultural society 1,500 pesos to acquire land.[22] Others took a more active role; the priest of Tonala and the indigenous population together bought the lands of Suchicalco.[23] Second, priests safeguarded *cofradías* by creating "Catholic Agricultural Societies" linked to the secular versions. In 1914, Jicotlán's priest persuaded villagers to form a Catholic agricultural society to take over *cofradía* lands. Huajuapam's first bishop, Rafael Amador y Hernández (1903–23), "brought about the arrangement, so that the possessors recognized the rights of the Church."[24]

The bond between the Church and Huajuapam's Mixtecs was strengthened by the ethnic configuration of political power. As John Monaghan has demonstrated, indigenous *caciques* survived long after the colonial period in the Mixteca Baja,[25] and families such as the Guzmán, Villagómez, Bautista, Mendoza, Velasco, Aja, and Pimentel clans controlled lands until the late nineteenth century.[26] On the one hand, these indigenous *caciques* freed the Church from ethnic conflict by acting as vital cultural intermediaries; not only did some agree to sell their entailments to agricultural societies, they also aided in the construction of churches and schools, and the payment of religious festivals. From the late nineteenth century, moreover, many reinforced these attachments by joining the Church. In 1904, for example, Andres Villagómez's sons funded the rebuilding of Suchitepec's Church, paid for a "magnificent fiesta" of inauguration that the bishop attended, and opened three schools.[27] Furthermore, as the *cacique*'s lands were divided up in the 1880s–90s, many of his sons joined or became closely connected with the Church. Two of Villagómez's grandsons went to Puebla's Palafox seminary, joining the diocese of Huajuapam as priests in 1909; another became an important schoolteacher in the diocese, and a third married Bishop Amador's sister.[28]

The Church was not merely linked to indigenous leaders, however, but found itself in opposition to the region's Spanish community. Indeed, the arrival of a cabal of Spanish families and the creation of Hispanic *cacicazgos* in the late nineteenth century destabilized the political process, bred community divisions, and forced the Church to take sides. Spanish landowners and merchants radically altered the region's economic and political profile. First, they started to dominate Mixteca Baja commerce. From their base in Huajuapam, their commercial networks carried products from the coast and Mixteca to Tehuacán (Puebla). Most importantly, the Gómez and Solana families controlled the commerce of livestock slaughtered each spring in their ranches outside Huajuapam. Other Spanish merchants monopolized textiles, comestibles, and seafood.[29] Second, Spaniards started to monopolize political posts. During the last decade of the Porfiriato, Spanish rancher Félix Solana Alonso was "in league with the *jefes políticos* of the region":[30] Solana, his sons, and a group of Spanish allies dominated the municipal government of Huajuapam and surrounding villages where they owned properties. At the outbreak of the revolution, Spanish *caciques* and the *jefe político* defended the Porfirian regime against the *maderista* insurgency, which took hold in outlying towns and villages. With Madero's assassination, predictably the *caciques* supported Huerta, after whose exile they eschewed the chief revolutionary groups and formed *Los Fieles*, an armed force of Hispanic merchants and *hacendados*, and *mestizo* and indigenous servants and peons. For five years, *Los Fieles* defended Huajuapam against *carrancistas* and *zapatistas* before making peace with Obregón in 1920.[31] In the postrevolutionary decades, the group cemented its hold over local government and dominated political posts.

The Porfirian Church had seemingly attempted to bridge the divide between traditional society and the Spanish interlopers: Catholic agricultural societies were established in agreement with the *jefe político*, and Spanish newcomers donated generously to the Church.[32] However, the revolution obliged the Church to take sides. While local Spaniards backed Díaz and Huerta, the *maderista* and *zapatista* revolts united *mestizos* from the region's other merchant centers—jealous of the commercial and political power of Huajuapam's Spanish leaders—and Mixtec Indians impoverished by the *caciques'* commercial activities.[33] Although some priests from outside the region allied with *Los Fieles* and holed up in the district capital, most remained in their parishes among the revolutionaries and even preached on their behalf. For Bishop Amador, the revolution—at least at first—offered the opportunity to harness Catholic Social teachings to political power; Amador was thus instrumental in creating a branch of the National Catholic Party (PCN) in 1912.[34] Other priests took a more radical line. The priest of Ayuquililla, Mauricio Ramírez, supported the *zapatista* rebellion of the surrounding villages.[35] The animosity between the Church and Huajuapam's Spanish leaders grew to the extent that Amador was forced to leave the district capital and base himself at the shrine of the Virgin of Ixpantepec Nieves for the revolution's duration.[36] When peace returned to the Mixteca in the early 1920s, revolutionary divisions remained. These were expressed at the annual Independence celebrations when revolutionary *"chirundos"* ("those without clothes") threw rocks through the windows of the houses of conservative *"cientificos."*[37] In 1923, tensions came to a head when Spanish *caciques* led by Rodolfo Solana Carrión attempted to remove pro-*chirundo* priests from the diocese. In league with a handful of Spanish priests, the *caciques* removed Mixtec Catholic art from Huajuapam cathedral and forced indigenous priests including José Cantú Córro, Odilón Vásquez, Juan Ramírez, and Eugenio Martínez to flee.[38] This move was counterproductive. Utilizing the discourse of Catholic nationalism and disparaging "foreign" priests, Cantú Corro persuaded the archbishop of Mexico to eject Spanish priests and allow the natives to return.[39] The conflict ended any lingering alliance between Spanish *caciques* and the diocesan Church. Over the next three decades, men like Carrión Solana and García Peral widened the divide by leading the National Revolutionary Party (PNR), suppressing the *cristero* revolt, and implementing anticlerical policies.[40]

Finally, during the 1890s–1900s, syncretic aspects of indigenous religious practice became gradually accepted in Huajuapam. Amador y Hernández— then Huajuapam's *vicario general*—lobbied persistently for the creation of a diocese in the Mixteca Baja, and in 1903 a papal bull created the diocese of the Mixtecas (renamed Huajuapam de León in 1904).[41] Under Amador's stewardship, the political and economic links between the Church and its Mixtec parishioners were overlaid with a particularly indigenous Catholic culture. Language was the key to this process of cultural miscegenation. In 1899, the Colegio Pío de Artes y Oficias in Puebla reprinted a 1755 Jesuit translation into Mixtec of Ripalda's catechism designed for priests heading off to "sow the Catholic faith in these remote, barbarous, and uncultured regions."[42] The 1899 catechism, however, was pointedly retranslated by "a Mixtec:" in the preface, an anonymous author—probably the priest of Teposcolula—claimed that the previous translation by "European Catholics" included a succession of errors including the misspelling of the Mixtec word for "priest" and the misapplication of accents.[43] Furthermore, this author added a new chapter on emergency lay baptisms, indicating that the catechism was for Huajuapam's inhabitants not priests and that the lines between ecclesiastical and lay sacred duties had been somewhat redrawn.[44] Bishop Amador also emphasized the importance of indigenous culture by introducing courses in Mixtec in the diocesan seminary and Carmelite nunnery, and by celebrating the local cult of Ixpantepec Nieves.[45] This local Catholicism, which sought to bring indigenous worshippers into the Church, was best expressed by Cantú Corro's speech at Huajuapam's Fiesta de la Raza on 12 October 1919. Cantú Corro claimed that the descendants of the Spaniards and the Indians (whom he rather confusingly called Creoles), "with the blood of Cuauhtémoc and El Cid in their hearts," held the future of the world in their hands. This "great family," by fusing the burning passion of the Iberians and the melancholic imagination and aspiration for freedom of the Indians, had produced painters, poets, pugilists, and philosophers to rival any of the Old World. Cantú Corro laid his vision of racial superiority within a religious framework whose center was the Virgin of Guadalupe, "the Creole Virgin."[46] This creation of an alternative culture that linked ethnicity and religion to localism and patriotism would provide the Catholic Church, its parishioners, and the PAN with the fundamental framework for future resistance during the succeeding decades.

The Radicalization of the Diocese of Huajuapam de León (1930–40)

Although the diocesan structure introduced by Bishop Amador was partly constructed in response to post-Reform liberal policies, during the first decades of the twentieth century there were few conflicts with the state or federal governments. Furthermore, though Calles's anticlericalism inspired some violent responses in the diocese in the 1920s, it was not until the educational reforms of 1934 that the Church and its lay supporters started to offer a radical alternative to state policies. During this period, the state government's anticlericalism—in particular its efforts to eradicate Church involvement in the region's educational establishments—encouraged prelate, priests, and parishioners to place themselves in firm opposition to the postrevolutionary state.[47] The divisions created during this decade overflowed into the next half century when they were formalized with the creation of the local branch of the PAN.

In 1934, federal pressure on Oaxaca's state government to amplify its anticlericalism increased. In September 1934, the new governor, Anastasio García Toledo, reduced the number of priests in Oaxaca to 18, leaving only 3 for the diocese of Huajuapam.[48] Six months later private schools were banned, "socialist education" introduced by the state's rural teachers, and prelates of Oaxaca's dioceses forcibly exiled to Mexico City.[49] Huajuapam's new bishop, Jenaro Méndez del Río (1933–52), and his priests organized resistance to the campaign of state anticlericalism and socialist education. During the period, over 60 priests remained in the diocese, using the pulpit, the local plaza, and municipal palace walls to urge parents to keep their children out of official schools, and threatening excommunication for noncompliance. The campaign was well received by the diocese's Mixtec parishioners. In July 1936 Bishop Méndez proudly claimed that "public cult, with exception of the parish of Tezoatlán, is sustained in Oaxaca and Puebla." Parents' organizations wrote petitions, marched, fought, and foot-dragged against state schools. As a result, these remained the lonely preserve of teachers' children and state officials.

The emergence of ACM in the late 1930s was molded by this culture of radical resistance to the state. In February 1936, President Cárdenas announced that it was not his government's—or federal education's—intention to "combat religious beliefs." Over the next two years, churches were unlocked and priests allowed to return to their parishes.[50] Oaxaca's new governor, Constantino Chapital, permitted Bishop Méndez to return to his see.[51] Despite the apparent reconciliation, however, the divisions opened up by the preceding period of anticlericalism/resistance did not disappear. In fact, as the government shied away from direct confrontation with Oaxaca's clerical Catholics, the Church and its supporters reorganized. The Church in Huajuapam undertook a sustained social and religious campaign, further estranging the region's parishioners from the state government. Central to this program was the creation of the ACM. This was first founded in Mexico in 1929 and was designed to impose a strict episcopal structure on Catholic efforts to aid the clergy's social and religious duties. According to Pius XI, Catholic Action would stimulate the "participation of laypeople in the apostolic hierarchy, for the defence of religious and moral principles [and] the development of a sane and beneficial social action": but this would be placed "under the ecclesiastical hierarchy, outside and above all political party, [so as] to restore the Catholic life in family and in society."[52] The organization "became the principal auxiliary of the parishes in their efforts to develop vigorous catechetical centres, schools, charitable foundations, public dining halls, medical dispensaries, and homes for the wayward."[53] The ACM was composed of four branches: the Union of Mexican Catholics (UCM), the Mexican Catholic Female Union (UFCM), the Catholic Association of Mexican Youth (ACJM), and the Mexican Catholic Female Youth (JCFM). These subdivisions were organized by parish, and each was subject to an ecclesiastical assistant. As a result, traditional appreciations of the ACM have stressed how the Church employed the organization to assert control over the errant and violent forces of the *cristero* revolt.[54] However, the ACM soon transformed itself according to divergent local political, social, and religious contexts. In Huajuapam, the movement formed the basis of political opposition to the state government for the next two decades. Despite ecclesiastical edicts to the contrary, Huajuapam's ACM was a distinctly political organization, which eventually elided with the newly formed PAN party.

The ACM arrived late to the diocese. Although the female branch was founded in 1930 and Bishop Méndez expressed admiration for the group— advising the establishment of parish cells as bulwarks against socialist education—in reality the bishopric lacked any formal ACM framework until a series of meetings between Church and laity in 1938.[55] After general assemblies held by the ACM's four composite organizations in Mexico City, Huajuapam delegates arranged the "Primera Jornada de Acción Católica" with the idea of invigorating the organization. According to the local clerical advisor, representatives attended from all the surrounding parishes. Members were encouraged to become "secular apostles," to remove impiety from their homes, and generally to lead moral lives. Although the ACM's national representative encouraged a "greater understanding with the representatives of the state," however, many Huajuapam Catholics used their speeches to attack the continuing government attachment to socialist education. Thus Pascal Villa emphasized parents' role in "educating children within Catholic norms," rather than "selling this right for a plate of lentils." In what Manuel Cubas Solano—the ACM's clerical leader in Huajuapam—described as the most popular speech, José Arrellano gave a puritanical emphasis to Bishop Amador's idea of an integrated local Catholic-Mixtec culture, in order to delineate the decline in Catholic education and morals. Arrellano argued that the Mixteca's customs were becoming "sacrilegious," "filled with dancing and drunkenness and all sorts of acts against morality" because of parental and school failures to impose "the norms of Catholicism" and repress the "detestable habits of adolescence."[56] During the next two decades, Acción Católica grew throughout the diocese. Cubas invited Dr. Angel Mora— brother of Tezoatlán priest Avelino de la T. Mora—to set up his dental surgery in his house in Huajuapam. In return, Mora propagandized vigorously on behalf of the ACJM and UCM. A former student of the diocesan Carmelite school for girls, Soledad Paz, traversed diocesan parishes on behalf of female organizations.[57] By 1939, according to Cubas, the efforts of clergy and ACM members had "led to a great increase in pious spirit of the community" and a "marked enthusiasm to join the Acción Catolica."[58]

The Church's strong links to indigenous parishioners led to the failure of the state's anticlerical project during the 1930s. Though the federal and state governments retreated from the extremes of Jacobin radicalism, however, diocesan Catholicism was radicalized by the campaign. Furthermore, the creation of the ACM in Huajuapam formalized diocesan parishioners' opposition to the state by assembling them into organized groups. Although nationally this institutionalization was designed to increase the hierarchy's control over the faithful and to minimize conflict with the government, parishioners' continuing resistance to state intrusions and Cubas Solano's ambivalence toward any form of reconciliation led to the formation of strong antigovernment caucuses within Huajuapam's villages.

The Emergence of the
PAN, 1940–52

The ACM groups formed in the late 1930s were the basis of the emergence of the PAN in the next decade. In Oaxaca, the PAN was formed by Manuel Aguilar y Sálazar, a rich lawyer and businessman from Silacayoapam. At first, membership of the central organization based in Oaxaca City was limited to the clerical Catholic elites of the Central Valleys.[59] In Huajuapam, however, the organization soon spread beyond the devout clerisy to become the focus for all popular opposition to the Party of the Mexican Revolution (PRM). Aguilar y Sálazar appointed a fellow graduate of Oaxaca's Instituto de Ciencias y Artes, Miguel Niño de Rivera, as regional representative and on 25 May 1939 formed the PAN's regional committee. Niño de Rivera took advantage of his work on village boundary disputes to persuade municipalities such as San Vicente Nuñu and Ayuquillila to support the new party.[60] The local ACM branch also offered its support, despite the pope's admonition to keep the organization out of politics. Niño de Rivera—in 1940 head of the male branch of the ACM as well as the PAN—argued that men with a "Christian civic spirit" should involve themselves in the struggle for power. In fact, the lack of a "civic spirit" among Mexican men had itself "caused many misfortunes in our country."[61] Angel Mora recounts how "by the elections of 1940, the ACM and the PAN were as one. We would travel around the villages and give out the propaganda of the PAN at the meetings of the UCM."[62] The ACM was not only a PAN propagandist; it offered the party an organizational structure. Priests such as Cubas Solano and seminary students such as Zenón Martínez Rodríguez spoke at ACM meetings in support of the PAN; prominent Catholic Action members such as Procopio Martínez Vásquez and Angel Mora became party foot soldiers. The network of priests, parents groups, and the ACM—strengthened by the state's anticlerical campaign—shaped the party's expansionist framework. By 1940 there were PAN municipal committees in Huajuapam, San Vicente Nuñu, and Tezoatlán, and support from groups in Silacayoapam, Tamazulapam, and Juxtlahuaca.[63]

The 1940 presidential election was the first test for this new political organization. According to the public transcript, Manuel Avila Camacho's electoral victory in Oaxaca was easy. Arriving in Oaxaca in June 1939, Avila Camacho was greeted by "thousands of *campesinos*, Zapotecs and Mixtecs, from the coast, the mountains, and the Valley region."[64] Over the next year, the state government's official newspaper—run by the head of the Pro-Avila Camacho State Committee, Artemio Velasco—declared the Oaxacan masses' unfailing support for the PRM aspirant.[65] Under headlines such as "Avila Camacho is the savior of the country" and "Avila Camacho is a friend of the working class," journalists opined that "Oaxacans, with their traditional patriotism, have raised the only flag of the Revolution, the flag of *avilacamachismo*."[66] When Juan Andrew Almazán visited Oaxaca, the paper lauded popular indifference to the opposition contender and scorned the pitiful demonstrations of support whipped up by a vengeful mercantile elite and fanatical clergy.[67] According to Arellanes Meixueiro, Avila Camacho won Oaxaca with a landslide, acquiring a greater percentage of the vote than in any other state.[68]

In the Mixteca Baja, however, ACM strength and the PAN's corresponding popularity led to an increasingly fractious, bitter election campaign. Almazán's Revolutionary Party of National Unity (PRUN) already had some local support among Almazán's former *zapatista* contacts and workers on the Acatlán-Huajuapam-Nochixtlán stretch of the Pan-American Highway, for which Almazán was a contractor.[69] As the PAN did not have its own nominee, it threw its organization behind the PRUN's presidential candidate if not its gubernatorial contender, Federico Cervantes, who unwisely professed an admiration for the liberalism of Juárez.[70] When Almazán visited Oaxaca in December 1939, he traversed centers of PAN support, visiting Huajuapam, Tamazulapam, Tejupán, Nochixtlán, Tlaxiaco, and Oaxaca City. According to a confidential government report, he was accompanied by Niño de Rivera and a host of "fanatics brought by the clergy." In Huajuapam, seminary students rang the bells of the church of Guadalupe and the cathedral.[71] Over the next six months, support for Almazán, especially among groups formed to obstruct socialist education, increased. In Zapotitlán Lagunas (Silacayoapam), the priest, José María Cañongo, interspersed his preaching against the socialist school with the claim that "Almazán was a saint and Camacho the devil."[72] The election was highly contentious. According to the PRUN, voting booths were placed in the houses of PRM authorities or socialist schools and *almazanistas* were intimidated and beaten up.[73] As a result, between the July election and the December transfer of power, reports of an "*almazanista* rebellion" were rife.[74] In August, there were rumors that relatives of PAN leader Aguilar y Sálazar were handing out munitions to bitter *almazanistas* in Silacayoapam.[75]

The electoral conflict in the Mixteca Baja was an important development in state politics. Resistance to socialist education and state anticlericalism was now formalized in organized PAN groups throughout the diocese. During the 1940s, the party grew as the new ACM head, Angel Mora, continued to link the religious life of the diocese to the embryonic party. This process of political organization can be seen clearly in the emerging political divisions of the village of Tequixtepec. During the 1930s the priest, Vicente Arroyo, persuaded parishioners to shut down the school and run various socialist teachers out of the village. When the state eventually managed to impose a school on the village in 1940, the priest again rallied support against the federal representatives. On Sunday, 28 June 1941, Mora reportedly started his sermon with a sustained attack on the socialist school and threatened to excommunicate parents who sent their children there. In an afternoon festival organized in honor of the village's mothers, children of the Catholic school finished with a song entitled "Free us Lord, Free us Lord, from the Impious Socialist School." Despite the reform of article 3 in 1946, this opposition continued and became formalized when the new priest, Pedro Gómez Ayala, created the ACM and PAN organizations in 1947. In Sunday masses and on religious holidays, Gómez Ayala used the pulpit to read PAN pamphlets, organize resistance to the school, and arrange electoral campaigns against the municipal authorities. In 1948, the *cura* organized a PAN demonstration against "the school of the devil" and fraudulent elections for local deputy. The handful of local liberals was disgusted at this intermingling of religion and politics: "The PAN is formed of Catholic Action groups, predominantly ill-educated and ignorant indigenous women. They march from the church to the municipal place, insult and threaten the supporters of the PRI . . . [PAN] is the party of the priest."[76]

Despite some government repression, this political organization made the PAN an electoral force in Huajuapam by the mid-1940s. In 1943 Mora and Niño de Rivera "organized the AJCM and Catholic Action again," and Niño de Rivera was put forward as PAN candidate for federal deputy, one of only 21 PAN candidates in Mexico.[77] There were demonstrations of support throughout the diocese and a mass rally at the Las Peñitas ranch outside Tezoatlán.[78] However, according to *La Nación*, the PRI removed voting booths, assaulted voters, and miscounted votes in areas of PAN strength such as the parishes of Huajuapam, Tequixtepec, Chazumba, and Miltepec.[79] Although Niño de Rivera went to plead his case in Mexico City to the electoral college, his impassioned speech was overshadowed by another failed candidate's public suicide next day.[80] In the 1947 elections, Manuel Aguilar y Sálazar, the head of Oaxaca's PAN and a former inhabitant of Huajuapam, ran for local deputy in the district of Huajuapam. Although the electoral *junta* and state governor were forced to accept his victory by the threat of revolt, the federal PRI refused to permit the defeat, sent troops to the region, and ordered the state legislature to nullify the election.[81] However, there were notable PAN victories. In 1950 national PAN representatives visited the region, declared it "a *panista* bastion," and formalized 20 working committees in the diocese's major towns.[82] For the first time, the national party put funds into fighting elections, allowing local leaders such as Mora, Vásquez Martínez, and Moisés Sánchez to devote themselves to electioneering.[83] As they traversed the region, they were helped by priests such as León Flores,

Isaías Durán, Silvestre Andrade, and Rutilio Flores Ayala, who recommended the party to their flocks.[84] For example, during Tamazola's 1950 *Cristo Rey* festival, the priest assembled the parish's Adoración Nocturna groups in the *casa cural* where they heard Niño de Rivera announce the foundation of a PAN committee in the village.[85]

Despite increasing levels of repression and the constant threat of electoral fraud, organization brought results. In 1952, the PAN's *planilla* ran in the municipal elections of Huajuapam under the name "Voto Libre Huajuapeño." Their manifesto began with demands for "complete liberty of religion" and the furnishing of "all the temples necessary" for worship. In the December 1952 elections, Voto Libre Huajuapeño won with 1804 votes against the PRI's 152, though the state governor, Manuel Cabrera Carrasquedo, soon announced that the PRI had triumphed despite "attempts at electoral fraud." The PAN refused to back down and within a week, the former municipal president was sending worried telegrams to the governor claiming that the "Catholics" were going to take over the municipal palace at the change of powers on 1 January 1953. Although the governor attempted to take a middle course by imposing a Junta of Civil Administration, Voto Libre Huajuapeño members were dissatisfied. On 23 January, they established a separate municipal council in a private residence and the majority of the population refused to pay taxes. Three days later, the governor conceded and appointed another council staffed by members of the PAN.[86] Outside the district capital, the PAN achieved other notable victories. In Camotlán, the PRI claimed victory by disallowing the votes of women and known members of Catholic Action. However, by April 1953 the village was "ungovernable" and the judicial authorities had to grant victory to the PAN.[87] Similarly, in Suchitepec, the government was forced to allow the electoral success of a group "directed by the priest Matías Pacheco and a group of women of Acción Catolica."[88] Finally, in Tequixtepec, seminary student Miguel Castillo "organized a campaign with members of the female sex and, by making the most of the religious organizations, said that this *pueblo* should not keep following the PRI." Despite the jailing of its leader and the intimidation of its members, the *planilla*, called the "Frente Zapatista," won.[89]

Conclusion

This study of the PAN's emergence in Huajuapam suggests a reinterpretation of Catholic relationships among certain indigenous groups. The Catholicisms of the indigenous south/southeast have always been held to be a heady and unorthodox mix of overliteral, often chiliastic, doctrinal interpretations and quasi-pagan practices.[90] However, the Church in Huajuapam managed to create a regional clerical stronghold by making astute land transactions and political alliances, and by creating a Mixtec Catholic culture. Moreover, the narrative of the PAN's origins, formation, and growth in Huajuapam offers some corrections to traditional representations of national *panismo*. Although at national level the PAN was distinctly elitist and composed predominantly of merchants and bankers, at the local level in Huajuapam it emerged from popular resistance to state anticlericalism and, as a result, became the party of popular opposition to the PRI. If, as Alan Knight argues,[91] a close map of postrevolutionary Mexico shows thousands of dots representing community responses to *agrarismo*, anticlericalism, organized labor, and education—some red, some white, some pink—then by the 1940s an intimate study of Mexico also reveals splashes of blue, azure, and aquamarine. Local religious culture and the conflicts of the 1930s, at least in the Mixteca Baja, produced many PANs, just as the *agrarismo, caciquismo*, and labor reforms of other regions produced many PRIs. Furthermore, the development of the PAN in Huajuapam, its links to the ACM, and its continuing obsession with issues of education and religious liberty point to the religious conflict's continuation beyond the supposed watershed of 1940. For the region's priests and parishioners, the federal school was still "the school of the devil," and people who sent their children there risked excommunication. The ACM, which the ecclesiastical hierarchy hoped would bring to an end *Cristiada* excesses, simply fed into a new political conflict between the PRI and the PAN as priests and group leaders lent support to the new political party.

Finally, this investigation also demonstrates the importance of looking at political conflict within a broadly cultural context and over the *longue durée*. As such, the particularly indigenous response to the liberal project that fed into the Mixteca Baja's twentieth-century political conflicts warrants comparison with the fierce political independence of the Zapotecs of Juchitán. As numerous researchers have argued, Juchitán's Coalition of Workers, Peasants, and Students of the Isthmus (COCEI), had its roots in nineteenth-century resistance to Oaxaca City's overweening liberalism.[92] The COCEI emerged in the 1970s after almost 50 years in which an indigenous *cacique*, Heliodoro Charis Castro, checked autonomist urges by acting as middleman between the federal government and his Zapotec followers. In contrast, the revolution in Huajuapam de León split the church from its Spanish supporters and provided space for a politicized, indigenous Catholicism, which confronted the elite supporters of the state and eventually morphed into the PAN, which was often more radical, and certainly more democratic, than the official party.

Notes

1. *La Voz de Oaxaca*, 7 Sep. 1947.
2. Archivo de la Diócesis de Huajuapam de León (henceforth ADHL), Bishop Méndez to Manuel Cubas, 27 May 1947; *La Voz de Oaxaca*, 19 Jun. 1947.
3. *La Voz de Oaxaca*, 10 Sep. 1947.
4. ADHL, speech, Manuel López y López, 8 Sep. 1947.
5. ADHL, speech, Rodolfo Solana Cruz, 8 Sep. 1947.
6. Interview with Procopio Martínez Vásquez, Aug. 2003; Procopio Martínez Vásquez, *Relatos y Vivencias de Huajuapam* (Mexico City, 2000), 116.
7. E.g., Lyle C. Brown, "Mexican Church-State Relations, 1933–1940," *A Journal of Church and State* 6, no. 2 (1964): 202–22; Soledad Loaeza, "La Iglesia y la Democracia en México," *Revista Mexicana de Sociología* XLVII,

no. 1 (2005): 161–8; Martaelena Negrete, *Relaciones entre la Iglesia y el Estado en México, 1930–1940* (Mexico City: El Colegio de México, 1988); Peter Lester Reich, *Mexico's Hidden Revolution: The Catholic Church in Law and Politics since 1929* (Notre Dame: University of Notre Dame Press, 1995).

8. Roberto Blancarte, *Historia de la Iglesia Católica en México* (Mexico: FCE 1992), 63–92.

9. Carlos Arriola, *Ensayos sobre el PAN* (Mexico City: Porrúa, 1994); Frank R. Brandenburg, *The Making of Modern Mexico* (Englewood Cliffs: Prentice Hall, 1964); Soledad Loaeza, "El Partido Acción Nacional: La Oposicion Leal en Mexico," *Foro Internacional* 14, no. 3 (1974): 352–74; Juan José Rodríguez Prats, *La Congruencia Histórica del Partido Acción Nacional* (Mexico City: EPESSA, 1997); David A. Shirk, *Mexico's New Politics, The PAN and Democratic Change* (Boulder, Col.: Lynne Rienner, 2005).

10. Donald J. Mabry, *Mexico's Acción Nacional: A Catholic Alternative to Revolution* (New York: Syracuse University Press, 1973); Franz A. Von Sauer, *The Alienated "Loyal" Opposition: Mexico's Partido Acción Nacional* (Albuquerque: University of New Mexico Press, 1974).

11. Carlos Velasco Gil, *Sinarquismo, su Origen, su Esencia, su Misión* (Mexico City: Editorial Olin, 1962), 360; Hector Hernández, *The Sinarquista Movement, With Special Reference to the Period 1934–1944* (London: Minerva, 1999); Jean Meyer, *El Sinarquismo, el Cardenismo, y la Iglesia (1937–1947)* (Mexico City: Tusquets, 2003).

12. Pablo Serrano Alvarez, *La Batalla del Espíritu: El Movimiento Sinarquista en el Bajío (1932–1951)* (2 vols. Mexico City: Conaculta, 1992).

13. Daniel Newcomer, *Reconciling Modernity: Urban State Formation in 1940s León, Mexico* (Lincoln: University of Nebraska Press, 2004).

14. Tania Hernández Vicencio, *De la Oposición al Poder: El PAN en Baja California, 1986–2000* (Tijuana: El Colegio de la Frontera del Norte, 2001); Rossana Almada, *El Vestido Azul De La Sultana, La Construcción del PAN en Zamora, 1940–1995* (Zamora: Colmich, 2001).

15. Francie Chassen-López, *From Liberal to Revolutionary Oaxaca: The View from the South, Mexico 1867–1911* (University Park: Pennsylvania State University Press, 2004).

16. Manuel Esparza, "Los Proyectos de los Liberales en Oaxaca (1856–1910)," *Historia de la Cuestión Agraria Mexicana, Estado de Oaxaca, Prehispánico -1924*, ed. Leticia Reina (Oaxaca: Juan Pablos Editor, 1988), 1:269–330; Ma. Cristina Steffen Riedemannm, *Los Commerciantes de Huajuapan de León, Oaxaca, 1920–1980* (Mexico City: UAM-Iztapalapa, 2001); M.T. De la Peña, *Oaxaca Económico* (Mexico City, 1950), 36; Rodolfo Pastor, *Campesinos y Reformas: La Mixteca, 1700–1856* (Mexico City: El Colegio de México, 1987), 442–7.

17. Archivo General del Poder Ejecutivo de Oaxaca (henceforth AGPEO), Asuntos Agrarios, 12.2, Huajuapam land sales list.

18. See Constantino Esteva, *Nociones Elementales de Geografía Histórica del Estado de Oaxaca con una Reseña del Movimiento Revolucionario en Cada Distrito desde 1911 hasta 1913* (Oaxaca, 1913), and AGPEO, Junta de Conciliación y Arbitraje, Fomento 1912, 6.2.

19. Brian Hamnett, *Politics and Trade in Southern Mexico, 1750–1821* (Cambridge: Cambridge University Press, 1971), 134–54; Marcello Carmagnani, *El Regreso de los Dioses, El Proceso de Reconstitución de la Identidad Etnica en Oaxaca, Siglos XVII y XVIII* (Mexico City: FCE, 1988), 230–8; John Hart, "The

1840s Southwestern Mexico Peasants' War: Conflict in a Transitional Society," *Riot, Rebellion, and Revolution: Rural Social Conflict in Mexico,* ed. Friedrich Katz (Princeton: Princeton University Press, 1988), 249–68; Leticia Reina, *Las Rebeliones Campesinas en México, 1819–1906* (Mexico City: Siglo XXI, 1980), 233–9; Francisco Abardia and Leticia Reina, "Cien Años de Rebelión," in *Lecturas Históricas del Estado de Oaxaca, III, Siglo XIX,* ed. Ma. de los Angeles and Romero Frizzi (Mexico City: INAH, 1988), 435–92; Karen D. Caplan, "The Legal Revolution in Town Politics: Oaxaca and Yucatán, 1812–1825," *Hispanic American Historical Review* 83, no. 2 (2003): 255–93; Antonio Annino, *Historia de las Elecciones en Iberoamerica: Siglo XIX* (Buenos Aires: FCE, 1995).

20. John Monaghan, "Mixtec Caciques in the Nineteenth and Twentieth Centuries," in *Codices, Caciques y Comunidades,* ed. Maarten Jansen and Luis Reyes García (Amsterdam: Asociación de Historiadores Latinoamericanistas Europeos, 1997), 275; AGPEO, Gobernación, Porfiriato, 42.16.

21. Archivo Judicial de Estado de Oaxaca (henceforth AJEO), Huajuapam, Ramo Civil, 1850–1910.

22. AJEO, Huajuapam, Civil, Isabel Navarrete, 1882.

23. AJEO, Huajuapam, Civil, Eduardo Calixto de la Palma, 10 Jan. 1855.

24. ADH, Concepcion Buenavista, Sociedad Católica to Bishop Amador, 24 Sep. 1914.

25. John Monaghan, Arthur Joyce, and Ronald Spores, "Transformations of the Indigenous *Cacicazgo* in the Nineteenth Century," *Ethnohistory* 50, no. 1 (2003); Monaghan, "Mixtec Caciques," 265–81; Monaghan, "El PAN y las Comunidades de la Mixteca Baja," paper presented at the American Anthropological Meeting, Oaxaca, 2002.

26. AJEO, Huajuapam, Silacayoapam, Teposcolula, Juxtlahuaca, Ramo Civil, 1850–90.

27. ADH, Informe de Suchitepec, Oct. 1905.

28. AGPEO, Ricardo D. Sánchez to governor, 30 Jan. 1936.

29. Riedemann, *Los Comerciantes,* 30–52.

30. Condumex, Venustiano Carranza Archive, leg. 11063, carpeta 9, Samuel Soriano to Carranza, 16 Dec. 1916.

31. Genaro Legaria Corro, *Huajuapan Recondito* (Huajuapan, n. d.); Alvaro Acevedo Martinez, *Apuntes Histórico-Geográficos de la Ciudad de Oaxaca* (Huajuapam, 1945); AGPEO, municipal presidency documents, Huajuapan, 1917.

32. ADH, Adelita Carrion to Bishop Amador, 23 Oct. 1906.

33. Francisco J. Ruiz Cervantes, "El Movimiento de la Soberanía en Oaxaca (1915–1920)," in *La Revolución en Oaxaca, 1900–1930,* ed. Víctor Raúl Martinez (Mexico City: Conaculta 1993), 244–5.

34. Jean Meyer, "El Conflicto Religioso en Oaxaca: ¿Un Caso Excepcional?": paper presented at "God's Revolution? Faith and Impiety in Revolutionary Mexico, 1910–1940," conference held at Queens University Belfast, UK, Oct. 2005.

35. ADH, Concepción Barragán to Manual Cubas, 23 Jan. 1919.

36. Interview with Angel T. Mora, Jan. 2004.

37. Luis de Guadalupe Martínez, *La Lucha Electoral del PAN en Oaxaca, Tomo I (1939–1971)* (Mexico City: ROM, 2002), 10; interview with Angel T. Mora, Jan. 2004.

38. AGPEO, Periodo Revolucionario, 140.4, men of Huajuapam to Governor Vigil, 25 Jun. 1923. These clergymen were genuine Spanish immigrants who probably arrived in Huajuapam in the late 1890s. Interview with Luis Martínez, Sep. 2003; Riedemann, *Los Comerciantes*, 33–56.

39. AHAM, Cantú Corro to Archbishop of Mexico, 1 Jul. 1923.

40. AGPEO, Gobernación, Secretario General de Despacho, Asuntos Relacionados con el Ayuntamiento de Huajuapam de León, 1929; Riedemann, *Los Comerciantes*, 45.

41. Interview with Luis Martínez, Sep. 2003. ADH, Circulars 1 (18 Sep. 1903) and 2 (23 Oct. 1903). Eulogio Gillow, *Reminiscencias del D. Eulogio Gillow y Zavala, Arzobispo de Antequera, (Oaxaca)* (Los Angeles, 1920), 194; Alfredo Galindo Mendoza, *Apuntes Geográficos y Estadísticos de la Iglesia Católica en México* (Mexico City: Revista "La Cruz," 1945), 63–4.

42. *Catechismo de la Doctrina Cristiana Compuesta por P. Geronymo de Ripalda de la Sagrada Compañía de Jesús* (Oaxaca, 1755).

43. Frederick Starr, *In Indian Mexico: A Narrative of Travel and Labour* (Chicago: Forbes, 1908).

44. *Catechismo de la Doctrina Cristiana Compuesta por P. Geronymo de Ripalda de la Sagrada Compañia de Jesús, Traducido por un Mixteco* (Puebla, 1899).

45. ADH, Circular 12, 13 Sep. 1905; ADH, Bishop Amador to Cantú Córro, 9 Aug. 1921.

46. Jose Cantú Corro, *Patria y Raza* (Mexico City, 1924).

47. See Benjamin Smith, "Anticlericalism and Resistance in the Diocese of Huajuapam de León, 1930–1940," *Journal of Latin American Studies* 37, no. 3 (2005): 469–505.

48. Archivo General de la Nación (AGN), Dirección General de Gobierno, 2.340/65/27908.

49. Archivo del Arzobispado de Oaxaca (AAO), Diócesis, Gobernación, Autoridades Civiles; AGPEO, Asuntos Católicos, 1934; *Periódico Oficial*, 11 Sep. and 27 Oct. 1934. *El Oaxaqueño*, 6, 10, and 16 Dec. 1934, 7 Feb. 1935; *El Informador*, 6 and 20 Jan. 1935; AHSEP, 173.28.

50. Reich, *Mexico's Hidden Revolution*, 57.

51. AGPEO, Gobernación, Chapital to Núñez y Zárate, 4 May 1937; ADH, Bishop Méndez to Cubas Solano, 8 Apr. 1937.

52. Negrete, Relaciones, 242–3.

53. Maria Kelly, "A Chapter in Mexican Church-State Relations: Socialist Education, 1934–1940" (PhD diss., Georgetown University, 1977), 223–37.

54. Negrete, *Relaciones*, 242–3; Blancarte, *Historia*, 33.

55. AHD, Biografía de Sr. Luis Altamirano Bulnes; ADH, Bishop Méndez to Huajuapam clergy, 30 Nov. 1930; Archivo de Acción Católica Mexicana (AACM), 2.10 Huajuapan, Bishop Méndez to Luis Bustos, 4 Dec. 1936.

56. AACM, *informe*, Daniel Moya and Manuel Cubas, 28 Nov. 1938.

57. Interview with Angel Mora, Jan. 2004.

58. AACM, *informe*, Daniel Moya and Manuel Cubas, 8 July 1939.

59. Archivo del Partido Acción Nacional, Oaxaca, Statement of Foundation, 1939.

60. AGPEO, Gobernacion, Justicia, Miguel Niño de Rivera to men of San Vicente Nuñu, 4 Apr. 1942.

61. AACM, *informe*, Miguel Niño de Rivera, 26 Feb. 1940.

62. Interview with Angel J. Mora, Jan. 2004.

63. Martínez, *La Lucha Electoral.*
64. *Oaxaca Nuevo*, 25 Jun. 1939.
65. Martínez, *La Lucha Electoral*, 43–4; *Oaxaca Nuevo*, 29 May 1940.
66. *Oaxaca Nuevo*, 31 May 1939, 1 and 5 Jul. 1940.
67. *Oaxaca Nuevo*, 5, 9, 10, 11 Dec. 1939, 29 Jan. 1940.
68. Anselmo Arellanes Meixueiro, *Oaxaca, Reparto de la Tierra, Alcances, Limitaciones y Respuestas* (Oaxaca: Universidad Autónoma Benito Juárez, 1994), 231.
69. AGPEO, Gobernación 1939; Rodolfo Solana Carrión to Governor Chapital, 30 Dec. 1939; AGN, Ramo Lázaro Cárdenas, 544.2/19, Confidential Report, Jun. 1940.
70. Interview with Procopio Martínez Vásquez, Oct. 2003; Martínez, *La Lucha Electoral*, 41–9; Federico Cervantes, *Candidato Para Gobernador del Estado de Oaxaca* (Oaxaca, 1940).
71. AGPEO, Gobernación 1939, confidential report to Governor Chapital, 23 Dec. 1939.
72. ADH, Parish records, Zapotitlán Lagunas, Simeón Hernández to Bishop Méndez, 5 Mar. 1940.
73. AGN, Dirección General de Gobierno, 2.311.17.1, c. 12, PRUN state committee to Gobierno, 8 Jun. 1940.
74. AGPEO, Gobernación 1940, Zapotitlán Lagunas municipal president to secretario del despacho, 10 Sep. 1940.
75. AGN, Ramo Lázaro Cárdenas, 544/34–19, Apolinar Ramírez to Cárdenas, 18 Sep. 1940; Vicente Lombardo Toledano to Cárdenas, 13 Sep. 1940.
76. AGPEO, Gobernacion y Justicia, 1/082 (7)/2816, Aniceto Ruiz Muñóz to Governor Vasconcelos, 18 Mar. 1949; 1.0821 (7) 931, Unión Pro-Tequixtepec to Vasconcelos, 3 Mar. 1948; 2.0827 (7), municipal president of Tequixsitlan to Vasconcelos, 24 Feb. 1948.
77. Interview with Angel Mora, Jan. 2004.
78. AGPEO, Gobernación, Rodolfo Carrión Solana to Governor González Fernández, 5 May 1943.
79. *La Nación*, 5 Aug. 1943.
80. Benjamin Smith, "El Suicidio de un Diputado: La Inestabilidad del Régimen Posrevolucionario," *Agenda Política, Periodismo de Investigación y Análisis* 1, no. 2 (2004).
81. AGPEO, Gobernación, Miguel Peral to Vasconcelos, 16 Aug. 1947.
82. Martínez, *La Lucha Electoral*, 86–7.
83. Interview with Angel Mora, Jan., 2004.
84. Martínez, *La Lucha Electoral*, 88–98.
85. ADHL, Miguel Niño de Rivera to archdiocese, 30 Oct. 1950.
86. AGPEO, Elecciones Municipales, Huajuapam, 1952–53.
87. AGPEO, Elecciones Municipales, Camotlán, 1952–53.
88. AGPEO, Elecciones Municipales, Suchitepec, 1952–53.
89. AGPEO, Elecciones Municipales, Tequixtepec, 1952–53.
90. Terry Rugeley, *Of Wonders and Wise Men: Religion and Popular Cultures in Southeast Mexico, 1800–1876* (Austin: University of Texas Press, 2001); Jan Rus, "Whose Caste War? Indians, Ladinos, and Mexico's Chiapas 'Caste War' of 1869," in *On Earth as it Is in Heaven: Religion in Modern Latin America*, ed. Virginia Garrard-Burnett (Wilmington: Scholarly Resources, 2000), 24–59.

91. Alan Knight, "Popular Culture and the Revolutionary State in Mexico, 1910–1940," *Hispanic American Historical Review* 74, no. 3 (1994): 393–444.

92. Jeffrey W. Rubin, *Decentering the Regime: Ethnicity, Radicalism and Democracy in Juchitán, Mexico* (Durham: Duke University Press, 1997); Howard Campbell, *Zapotec Renaissance, Ethnic Politics, and Cultural Revivalism in Southern Mexico* (Albuquerque: University of New Mexico Press, 1994).

Contributors

Adrian A. Bantjes is Associate Professor of Latin American History at the University of Wyoming, United States. He is the author of *As If Jesus Walked on Earth: Cardenismo, Sonora, and the Mexican Revolution* (1998), and has published a series of articles on the political, cultural, and religious history of the Mexican Revolution, including, most recently, "Religion and the Mexican Revolution: Towards a New Historiography," in *Religious Culture in Modern Mexico*, ed. Martin Austin Nesvig (2007). He is currently completing a book tentatively titled *So Far from God: Popular Religion and the Mexican Revolution*.

Jean-Pierre Bastian is Professor of the Sociology of Religion at Strasburg Marc Bloch University and Research Director at the Institute for Higher Study of Latin America (IHEAL), Paris III University. Among his publications: *Los Disidentes: Sociedades Protestantes y Revolución en México, 1872–1911* (Mexico City: FCE, 1989); *Le Protestantisme en Amérique Latine. Une Approche Socio-Historique* (Geneva: Labor et Fides, 1994); *La Mutación Religiosa de América Latina* (Mexico City: FCE, 1997); and, as editor, *La Modernité Religieuse en Perspective Comparée: Europe Latine-Amérique Latine* (Paris: Karthala, 2001).

Kristina A. Boylan received her PhD from the University of Oxford and is an assistant professor of history and interdisciplinary studies at the State University of New York Institute of Technology in Utica, NY. She has published several book chapters and articles in the *Encyclopedia of Christian Politics* concerning Catholic activism in revolutionary Mexico. Her current book project examines Catholic women's mobilizations in the 1930s and explores the intersections of gender, spirituality, and civic engagement in revolutionary Mexico.

Claire Brewster is a part-time lecturer in American History at Newcastle University, UK. Her research interests are on twentieth-century Mexico. Recent publications include a monograph discussing the social and political work of Mexican intellectuals (1968–95).

Keith Brewster is Senior Lecturer in Latin American History at the University of Newcastle, UK. His research interests are varied but focus primarily on the political and cultural history of postrevolutionary Mexico. His publications include a monograph and several articles on military *caciquismo*, and his contribution to this book is a natural extension of these studies.

Matthew Butler is Lecturer in Latin American Studies at Queen's University Belfast, Northern Ireland. He is the author of *Popular Piety and Political Identity in Mexico's Cristero Rebellion: Michoacán, 1927–1929* (Oxford, 2004) and of various articles exploring the *Cristiada*'s social origins and Catholic religious experiences under persecution. At present he is writing up a project on the *callista* schismatic Church and researching a history of popular religious practice and parish life in revolutionary Mexico.

Fernando Cervantes is Senior Lecturer in History at the University of Bristol, UK. He is the author of *The Devil in the New World: The Impact of Diabolism in New Spain* (1994) and coeditor, with N. W. Griffiths, of *Spiritual Encounters* (1999).

Robert Curley has received degrees from Grinnell College (BA), the University of Illinois-Chicago (MA), and the University of Chicago (PhD). This chapter draws on research conducted for his doctoral dissertation, "Slouching towards Bethlehem: Catholics and the Political Sphere in Revolutionary Mexico" (2001). He teaches and continues his studies into public Catholicism at the Universidad de Guadalajara, Mexico.

Massimo De Giuseppe teaches modern history in Milan's IULM University and at the University of Bologna, Italy. He is the author of the books *Messico 1900–1930. Stato, Chiesa, e Popoli Indigeni* (Brescia, 2007) and *Giorgio La Pira. Un Sindaco e le Vie della Pace* (Milan, 2001), and has recently edited *Oscar Romero. Storia, Memoria, Attualità* (Bologna, 2006). He has written numerous essays, among them "I Gesuiti in Messico. Lettere dalla Missione Tarahumara" and "Costruire la Nazione nel Messico Post-Rivoluzionario." He also contributes to the journals *Contemporanea, Ricerche di Storia Politica,* and *Revista de Estudios Religiosos.*

Ben Fallaw received his doctorate at the University of Chicago in 1995. He teaches history and Latin American Studies at Colby College in Waterville, Maine, United States. Duke University Press published his first book—*Cárdenas Compromised: The Failure of Reform in Postrevolutionary Yucatán*—in 2001. He recently coedited *Heroes and Hero Cults in Latin America* (Texas, 2006), and is currently working on a larger project on Church-state conflicts in the 1930s.

Alan Knight is the Professor of Latin American History at Oxford University. He is the author of *The Mexican Revolution* (2 vols., 1986), and of two volumes of a general history of Mexico—*From The Beginning to the Spanish Conquest* and *The Colonial Era* (2002)—as well as numerous articles on Mexican and Latin American history. He is currently working on volume three of the general history and a more detailed study of Mexico in the 1930s.

Jean Meyer was born in southern France in 1942 of Alsatian parents fleeing from the Nazi invasion. He lived until 1959 in Aix-en-Provence and studied history at the Sorbonne before going to Mexico in 1965 to study an episode of the Mexican Revolution: *La Cristiada*. He has taught and researched at the Colegio de México, the Sorbonne, the University of Perpignan, and the Colegio de Michoacán. Since 1993, he has worked at the Centro de Investigación y Docencia Económicas (CIDE), in 2000 founding the Division of History and the quarterly journal, *ISTOR*. Until 1987, he published exclusively on Mexico and Latin America. Since 1988, he has also written about the history of Russia and the Soviet Union. His work has been published in Mexico by Siglo XXI, Colegio de México, Vuelta, Jus, CEMCA, Fondo de Cultura Económica, and Tusquets; in France by Gallimard, Payot, and Desclée; and in England by Cambridge University Press. Since 1988 he has written weekly articles for the press in Mexico City (*UnomásUno, La Jornada, El Universal*) on national and international affairs. Of Franco-Mexican nationality since 1979, he is married to the historian Beatriz Rojas. They have five children and several grandchildren.

Benjamin Smith is an assistant professor at Michigan State University. He received his PhD at the University of Cambridge in 2006. He studies nineteenth- and twentieth-century Mexican politics and has published articles in *Journal of Latin American Studies*, *Mexican Studies/Estudios Mexicanos*, and various edited volumes.

Edward Wright-Rios is assistant professor of Latin American history at Vanderbilt University. He has published on the convergence of religion and Indian-centered nationalism in nineteenth-century Mexican literature, "Indian Saints and Nation States," *Mexican Studies/Estudios Mexicanos* 20, no. 1(winter 2004). In addition, he has penned forthcoming essays on topics such as the gender issues related to popular apparitionism, and local religious institutional innovation. His manuscript, *Revolutions in Mexican Catholicism: Vision, Shrine, and Society in Oaxaca, 1887–1934*, is now under contract and forthcoming with Duke University Press.

Index